THE
ENCYCLOPEDIA
OF FURNITURE

by

JOSEPH ARONSON

AUTHOR OF THE BOOK OF FURNITURE AND DECORATION:
PERIOD AND MODERN

———

*ILLUSTRATED WITH 1,115 PHOTOGRAPHS
AND MANY LINE CUTS*

———

CROWN PUBLISHERS :: NEW YORK

FOREWORD

It has long seemed to me that the art and industry of furniture sorely needed a convenient encyclopedia. Everyone who buys or uses furniture, who makes, designs or sells it, collectors, architects, decorators and students must feel frequently the singular lack of a handy reference work for the checking of details, the verification of periods, the inspiration of designs, the nature of materials, etc. etc.

In preparing this work I have kept that need before me. Of course, a balanced condensation of the vast body of furniture history and technique could not be achieved without the sacrifice of an infinity of detail, all interesting and pertinent to the critic and the specialist. That sacrifice seemed justified in the cause of compactness. If accuracy, accessibility and thoroughness could compensate for brevity and limited details, it seemed that a handy one-volume encyclopedia could prove useful and valuable for most needs. I have sought therefore to provide dependable *initial* information. The seeker after more detailed knowledge has available a vast library from which the bibliography (page 201) is selected as having been of most assistance to the writer.

One picture, say the Chinese, is worth ten thousand words. This numerical ratio based on the quantity of photographs offered in this volume would probably satisfy the writer and the reader in their joint temptation to delve into the endlessly fascinating details of furniture lore. The major part of this book consists of monographs of the important items of furniture knowledge, supplemented by some 2500 separate definitions and descriptions. The larger subjects or classifications—America, Chairs, Construction, France, Gothic, Modern, Woods, etc. are treated at some length and are related to the arrangements of pictures. More than half of the book is devoted to photographs, in the hope of effecting the economies suggested by the aforementioned Chinese proverb. Thus Number 150, a Gothic cupboard of Flamboyant style, is grouped with *Cabinets and Cupboards* but is also listed by number under *Gothic* and *Flamboyant*. The sequence of types pictured in these groups is roughly based on the chronological development from the basis or prototype; it also seeks to demonstrate the flow of influences over national boundaries, and the bridge of time as well as locale in these developments.

That omissions of more or less importance exist is a foregone conclusion, their importance depending on the point of view. The accuracy of material presented is often a matter of choosing between conflicting sources; for more palpable errors, I beg the reader's indulgence in advance. In this connection it is interesting to observe that actual furniture relics of older days are sometimes less dependable as sources of knowledge than are the old documents, engravings and paintings.

But for the careful, gracious and untiring co-operation of many persons this work could scarcely have possessed whatever merit it has; to them, I am deeply indebted. The Metropolitan Museum of Art has been most generous with photographs and data. The photograph collections of the American Art Association—Anderson Galleries have been invaluable. For the assistance of the editors of the *Architectural Forum,* thanks are hereby extended; so also to the Pennsylvania Museum of Art and the Boston Museum of Fine Arts for permission to publish photographs of objects in their collections. To the many individuals and organizations whose photograph collections, data and advice contribute so largely to this work I am permanently grateful. Among these I am privileged to list: Arthur S. Vernay, French and Company, Ginsburg and Levy, Mr. Henry Weil, A. Olivotti and Co., Symons Galleries, Inc., Charles of London, Mr. Angelo Romano, Stair and Company, Stefano Cavallo, Mr. Charles Henders, Cassard Romano, Lavezzo Inc., Mr. Don Ruseau, The St. James Galleries, Bruce Buttfield, Inc., Colchester Galleries, Ltd., The Swedish News Agency. And finally to Mr. W. Richmond Bradshaw for the small sketches.

JOSEPH ARONSON

New York, N. Y.
October 10, 1938

NOTE

The photograph illustrations are grouped as follows and each group is placed approximately adjacent to the article on the subject.

American Furniture	Lowboys
Beds	Mirrors
Bookcases	Modern Furniture
Cabinets and Cupboards	Rest Beds
Chairs	Screens
Chests and Commodes	Settes and Sofas
Desks and Secretaries	Sideboards
English Furniture	Spanish Furniture
French Furniture	Stools and Benches
Germanic Countries	Swedish Furniture
Gothic Furniture	Tables
Highboys	Victorian Furniture
Italian Furniture	Woods

THE
ENCYCLOPEDIA OF FURNITURE

ABACUS. The topmost member of the capital of a column. See *Orders*.

ACACIA. A group of trees similar to the locust. Some varieties from Australia and the Sandwich Islands yield beautiful veneers ranging in color from yellow-brown to red and green. In England the name is given to the American Locust, the wood of which is tough and durable and similar in texture to oak.

ACAJOU. French word for mahogany.

ACANTHUS. Conventionalized leaf of a plant growing in Asia Minor. It is found as the basis of all foliage ornament in classic Greek and Roman decoration. Romanesque and Byzantine acanthus were stiff and spiny. The Renaissance revived its use in graceful designs for every purpose. Every succeeding style has used the acanthus in exuberant or restrained manner, according to its type. See *Ornament*.

GREEK ACANTHUS

ACORN. Turned ornament resembling an acorn; common in Jacobean furniture as finials on chair- and bed-posts, as pendants, and as the profile of leg turnings in Jacobean tables. See *Turnings*.

ACROTERIUM. Originally an ornament on the roof corners of Greek Temples. In classical furniture, similar ornaments applied to the top corners of Secretaries, Bookcases, Highboys and other important furniture.

ACANTHUS SCROLL

ADAM, The Brothers. Robert, 1728-1792; James, 1730-1794. Robert, elder son of a Scotch architect, began practising his art in London in 1758 after four years in Italy. There he had been fascinated with the excavations at Herculaneum to such an extent that it became his, and through his influence, England's basis of decoration for half a century. This classical influence displaced the Rococo forms exploited by Chippendale and his school, and led to an excessively refined, ofttime inappropriate delicacy of structure and ornament.

The Adams practised as architects, employing cabinet makers, painters, sculptors, etc., to execute their designs. Thus we find a mixture of names around some designs, such as Hepplewhite, Angelica Kauffmann, Pergolesi, Flaxman and others, presumably in the association of designer and craftsman. They believed that every detail of the house and its furnishing must grow from the same mind and carried this out

ACROTERIUM

in all the minutiae of decoration; witness their designs for carpets, lighting fixtures, sedan chairs, table service, snuff-boxes, and what not. The fundamentals of all this they state in their book, "The Works in Architecture of Robert and James Adam" (1773). "We have been able to make use of . . . the beautiful spirit of antiquity, and to transfuse it with novelty and variety. . . ." While there exists in their work the delicate splendor of the style of Louis XVI, it derives not from the French but directly from the Roman remains. This classicism is in the earlier work imposed upon the accepted forms and proportions of Georgian furniture; later it demanded lighter lines, in style and delicacy far removed from the mid-Georgian solidity.

The Adams fostered the transition from the Age of Mahogany to the Age of Satinwood. Their choice of woods covers just this span; beginning with the accepted mahogany, they later employed whole surfaces of satinwood, harewood (sycamore dyed gray) and much painted decoration. Sycamore or satinwood had delicate designs painted over in outline, or with plaques and medallions; whole pieces were likewise painted and exquisitely decorated by or in the manner of Angelica Kauffmann and her followers. Gilding over a base of white or green paint was extensively employed, particularly for mirrors, consoles, etc.

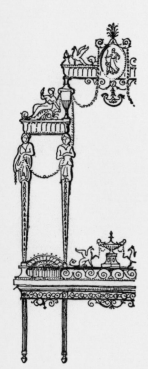

The architectural picture being of first importance, Adam rooms possessed a unity of design previously found only in the French palaces. Most of the furniture was designed for special places. Consoles, mirrors, couches, buffets, etc., were as integral a part of the room designs as the mantels and doors. Ceilings were exquisitely ornamented with classical plaques and rinceaux; walls, generally painted light gray or jasper, were a foil for the gilt, painted, or light wood furniture. Their decoration was after the antique model of Pompeii and Herculaneum; rich ornamentation of great delicacy was painted or executed in raised plaster (composition), with medallions of classical figures, architectural motives as pilasters, arches, niches, etc., generously distributed. Floors were patterned to reflect the ceiling design, either in carpet or stone.

Their distinguishing details are: a preference for straight lines or square outlines; swags, festoons, rinceaux, in fact all ornaments freely drawn but exceedingly fine in scale and painstakingly executed; mythological figures, rams' heads, lions' heads and claws, centaurs, griffins, sphinxes, caryatids, etc., with plant forms and vases on most surfaces in paint, low relief carving, composition, and inlay.

The style has great charm and beauty, and an academic spirit of architectural correctness. Yet its very perfection brought it the criticism, in its own day as now, of being excessively polite, lacking in human warmth and the quality of livability. 133, 338, 561 et seq., 893. See *England*.

ADELPHI, THE. Signature or trade name of the Brothers Adam.

AGE OF OAK, WALNUT, MAHOGANY, SATINWOOD. Easy division of the prime English periods by the woods employed in Furniture, as defined by Macquoid. Though the use of the woods may overlap, the general separations are:

> Age of Oak 1500-1660.
> "   " Walnut 1660-1720.
> "   " Mahogany 1720-1765.
> "   " Satinwood 1765-1800.

ALCOVE. Recessed part of a room. Bed alcoves exist in Pompeiian ruins, and this placing of the sleeping quarters was common in Northern Europe thru the Middle Ages and later. In the 18th century special beds were designed for such recesses. (105) Alcoves are also used for bookcases and cabinets, dining groups, etc.

ALMERY, ALMONRY. See *Ambry*.

ALPINE. The mountainous sections between Germany and Italy were meeting places of the Northern and Southern styles. In lands like Switzerland and the Tyrol mixed styles developed, too individual to be associated definitely with either source. 95, 685.

AMARANTH. Purplish wood used for veneering since the 18th century; also called *Violetwood* and *Purpleheart*.

AMBOYNA. An East Indian wood, used as veneer and inlay. The burls are light reddish brown, highly mottled and curled. Known and used in furniture since Roman times.

AMBRY. In medieval churches a recess for the storage of goods. The addition of doors gave it the cupboard form. The English equivalent became a large cupboard with doors; the interiors were fitted with shelves for storage. See also *Armoire*.

AMBULANTES (French). Small portable tables, used for serving tea, etc. Period Louis XV and after.

AMERICAN. The furniture of Early America, far from being a single consistent style, is the furniture of many lands, periods and castes. Each colony imported its furniture or its way of making furniture. Englishmen, Swedes, Hollanders and Frenchmen, Spaniards and Germans brought to their isolated seaboard settlements the crafts of their homelands. There was virtually no intercommunication that might have amalgamated their various talents; most communication was with the home country, from which the changing styles slowly came. Consequently the basic theme of Colonial American furniture is a laggard echo of the simpler European styles of the day.

The English colonies were predominant. Two distinct strains appear: the Puritan colonies in New England, and the royal-grant plantations in the South. The Dutch colonized the Hudson Valley, but yielded to the British merchant class. Swedes brought to the Delaware Valley their own arts, and later German colonists established their culture in the Pennsylvania forests. The French and Spanish colonies, less permanent, bore little fruit.

EARLY COLONIAL PERIOD—17TH CENTURY

The New England colonists were provincial middle class. Possessed by the religious zeal which later precipitated the Civil War in England, they left their homes shortly after Elizabeth's death. Inevitably the homes they built in the New World were direct reminiscences of the late Gothic-Tudor tradition. Novelty of a decorative nature was excluded for reasons of religious principle, economy, and possibly a lack of skill. New England furniture of the period 1620-1720 is largely distinguished by its directness and the persistence of English Jacobean characteristics. Pictures 2 and 3, 202, 221, 223 show chairs of clear Gothic lineage. The 18th Century cabinet in Picture 16 has fluted panels recalling the linen-fold decorations of two centuries earlier. Chests and cupboards bore the distinctive rectangular panelled construction, as illustrated in pictures 1, 6, 7, 16, 153, 162, 377, 379, 380, 387, 438. Tables of trestle type were supplemented by box styles and simple drop-leaf types as 4, 5, 17. Desk boxes, Bible boxes, forms or stools, a few crude beds, probably complete the meager inventory of the period. The materials were usually those closest at hand and for expediency, those most easily worked. Pine was available in tremendous widths; oak, birch, and maple were largely used also. The wood was generally left raw, acquiring color and depth and polish through simple friction and natural darkening.

Virginia and most Southern colonies were settled by a wealthier, more secular group. Their earliest furniture probably comprised the more elaborate Jacobean efforts and it is likely that they actually imported more English furniture than did the New Englanders.

Medieval European furniture also appears in the Pennsylvania settlements of Germans and Swiss, the Swedish colonies in the Delaware Valley after 1636, and the Dutch communities on the Hudson. Straightforward peasant workmanship and inspiration appears in the typical chests and cupboards, tables and chairs. A naive type of painting embellishes much of this work and indicates its descent from the Germanic peasant decoration. Compare the cradle 24, with the Tyrolean bedstead, 685, or the table 19, with table 967 as evidence of the resistance to change of these deep influences.

The older influences followed the pioneers, and pushed away from the coast to the frontiers, while the coastal settlements advanced closer to the current European model. By 1680 there was a well established merchant class on the seaboard. Wealth and fine houses begat fine furniture. Europe was in a fine rash of commercial development and the process of style exchanging and communication was immeasurably accelerated. French and Flemish versions of the Italian Baroque style were rapidly translated in England into the styles of the Restoration and William and Mary. There were modifying influences through Spain and Holland, and the Chinese urge was never altogether absent after the formation of the various trading companies.

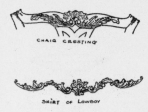

CHAIR CRESTING

SKIRT OF LOWBOY

This later 17th century phase is identified in American furniture by the use of walnut, by turnings of bold trumpet or inverted-cup shapes, spiral turnings, elementary forms of cabriole legs, carved shells and pendants, and the appearance of highboys, lowboys, chests, upholstered chairs, etc.; in fact, the roots of the entire furniture program of the 18th century.

With the 18th century came mahogany, the development of separate style centers in various cities, the Rococo influence and the wealth and culture to employ them. The Queen Anne style is a generalization for the use of cabriole legs with shell carvings, pad or animal feet, and a consistent refinement of style and finish. The Georgian styles were sometimes executed in walnut, but mahogany ultimately came to the fore. By 1750 there were distinct styles of cabinetmaking in Boston, Newport, New York, and Philadelphia. Goddard in Newport, Savery, Randolph, Gostelowe and Gillingham in Philadelphia produced furniture comparable to the better English work. Their styles were individual, employing architectural details, intricate Rococo curves, claw feet and in fact most of the ornament vocabulary current in England.

CHEST ON FRAME

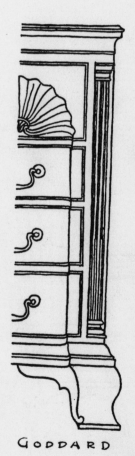

GODDARD

The country or village styles of colonial American furniture developed many utilitarian types absent or scarce in city life. Chief of these is the Windsor chair, with its innumerable local variations (236-252). Stools, chairs, benches, chests, cabinets, etc., of unique type made in pine, maple, hickory, oak, apple or cherry wood exhibit the tremendous vitality of a people dependent on their own resources. Beds with short posts, ladderback chairs, wagon seats, rocking chairs, writing chairs, etc., are uniquely American. By far the greatest independence of design and technique is found in these robust folk arts that declined only with the machine age.

FEDERAL PERIOD

The colonial period may be considered ended by the Revolution. When the war was over there was enough resentment of English things to promote the French influence; however, since English style of the period was strongly classical it is difficult to isolate the direct Italian influence through Thomas Jefferson, the French imports or the English classicism of Adam, Hepplewhite, Shearer and Sheraton. Of the latter

there remain excellent interpretations by the Salem carver, Samuel McIntire, by Charles Bulfinch and by Robert Wellford of Philadelphia. The pinnacle of American classicism was attained by Duncan Phyfe with his superb designs after Sheraton and the French Directoire manner. 76-80.

The houses into which this furniture found its way had by this time established their own idiom, differing from the European sources and from each other according to climate. In the South the rich plantations supported great Italian villa forms more naturally than either Italy or England. More compact houses of stone and brick developed with local variations in all seaboard cities. New England produced a superb type of wooden house, beautifully adapted to the climate and the materials. Sound craftsmanship flourished. A discreet classicism embellished architecture and furniture alike. Exterior corner boards became pilasters, flat cornice boards were moulded into classically dentilled friezes, gables became pediments. Interior parts affected the same architectural costuming: fireplaces, doors and windows, dados and cornices were fine-scaled after Palladio and Vignola. The furniture of the period 1780-1810, whether imported from France or England or of domestic manufacture was notably free of architectural excesses.

EMPIRE

The French Empire style was not long in arriving. It added to furniture a forced architectural heaviness that symbolizes the decline of pure line. Even Phyfe's work after 1825 took on a thick graceless quality that earned the title "Butcher's Furniture." Closely following the Regency mannerisms in England, the Pompeiian-Roman delicacy yielded to a Greek-Egyptian solidity. A mistaken archeology interpreted the solid stone work of the latter into wood furniture of massive plainness. Curved brackets, legs, etc. were thick and heavily ornamented. Sleigh beds, massive bureaus, scroll sofas, heavy pedestal tables, etc. were decorated with coarse carving sometimes gilded, suggested by the bronze appliqués used in France. 350, 904.

In this period of Empire influence the application of power to woodworking developed a few distinctive designs. Spool turning could be made by the mile at low cost and the familiar spool bed and its variations, with applications of the turning to other articles, are still evident everywhere in the land. Lambert Hitchcock's Yankee ingenuity produced a type of Sheraton "fancy chair" by mass production methods. Jig-saw scroll work accompanied a Gothic revival. Victorianism after the Civil War implied an over-elaborated system of curves remotely Louis XV but in coarse scale, done in black walnut and horsehair.

Changing styles since then have followed too many fads, revivals, and deliberate promotions to be judged consistently. Eastlake, Morris,

Art Nouveau, Empire, Mission, the Louis', Italian Renaissance, Spanish, Colonial, French Provincial, etc. ad infinitum, have had their day. Only the perspective of future years will permit judgment on the value of the interpretations. 1098 et seq.

AMORINI (Italian). Cupids, painted or carved in decoration. Sometimes only the winged head is used. Profuse in Baroque work, especially under direct Italian influence. (761)

ANCIENT FURNITURE. Our knowledge of the furniture of the ancient civilizations is gleaned from two sources: (a) actual remains, or remaining models, and (b) pictorial, sculptural, or written descriptions.

Thanks to the Egyptian custom of providing the dead with objects of daily use, we find in their tombs a key to the earliest furniture forms. Of the furniture of Assyria and nearer Asia there remains only the record of stone sculptures. Greece and Rome likewise left picture records in carving and vase ornaments and wall paintings, plus some relics in stone and metal. These point to a highly developed art of woodworking in keeping with the architectural superiority of these peoples, but actual forms and styles are conjectural. 188, 189, 985.

AMORINI

Egypt may be regarded as the source of most ancient furniture ideas, some vestiges of such development being attributed to the era prior to 1800 B. C. In this remote time, tables and chairs, couches, stools, and chests of recognizable form were in use, indicating skill in turning, carving, joining, inlay and painting. These talents and their products were exported to the then-known world—Crete, Assyria, Babylonia, Phoenicia, later Persia and Greece. More or less similar motives were reworked to the local taste and materials, and descended to the present day. 919 et seq. 1029.

See *Egypt, Greek, Roman, Antique, Pompeiian.*

ANGEL-BED. Bedstead with a canopy, but with no pillars in front. The curtains are drawn back at the sides next to the head of the bed. Usually the canopy extends over only a part of the bed, while the counterpane goes right down over the foot. Chiefly French, 18th century. See *Beds.* 104.

ANGEL BED

ANIMAL-COUCHANT FOOT. Furniture leg ending in the form of a reclining animal. See *Feet.* 463.

ANTHEMION. The Greek honeysuckle pattern conventionalized to radiating cluster.

ANTIMACASSAR. 19th century doily or cloth used to protect chair backs from soiling by hair which at that time was dressed with macassar oil. 1101.

ANTIQUE, THE. Reference to the Classic Greek and Roman styles.

ANTHEMION

ANTIQUES. In current use the description "Antique Furniture" implies something more than "Old Furniture." The something more is a relative thing depending on local attitudes and values, particularly as to age and cultural worth.

Antique furniture is prized for age, rarity, unique beauty, association or documentary interest or personal sentiment. Though the U. S. Customs rules that antiques must be "before 1830," age alone is too relative and includes too much. In the young West a piece of Civil War date might earn reverence as an antique, which would be regarded as mere junk in three-century old New England. In the South the same piece might evoke a nostalgia for a departed and glorious past, the sentiment overcoming possible aesthetic deficiencies. Original worth or style is of prime importance, yet many crude or rough styles are valued. The market for antiques is therefore one of specialties.

The cult of antique collectors comprises a complete industry, with values and standards and ethics. The genuineness of antiques is almost as relative as age. Excluding deliberate counterfeiting or outright deception, the dealer has rarely more than his judgment to offer as evidence of age or authenticity. Thus there is a premium on reliability. This in turn must invite a degree of reticence on the part of reliable dealers. The signs by which authenticity is recognized are too precarious for the average collector.

Antique furniture may be described as repaired, restored, or copied. The last frankly admits to being newly made, but more or less painstakingly after an old model, often employing old wood and old processes. Restorations are a pitfall, since the restored sections may represent the greater bulk; an old table top mounted on a new base, no matter how well studied and matched, should not be represented as an antique, although such representations are occasionally detected. Repairs are often necessary for the continued existence of the piece. The extent of these and the care with which they are effected will be the determining factors in the valuation of the piece. See *Antiquing, Replica, Fakes, Reproductions.*

ANTIQUING. Process of treating wood or finish on furniture to make it look old. Wood may be simply worn off at the edges and corners; it is sometimes scratched, gouged, planed, etc. Even fine bird shot and nails are used to simulate worm holes and other ravages of time. Wood is also subjected to various acid treatments to suggest age. Paint finishes are glazed with washes of dirt colors to reduce the brilliance and provide an uneven surface.

APPLE. The wood of the apple tree is very hard, of a brown-pink color, polishes well, and can be used for small parts in furniture. It is ideal for turning, and as such is found in many American 18th century pieces. Like all fruit woods it has been extensively used in provincial furniture throughout Europe.

APPLIQUÉ. Applied ornament. See *Ornament.* 649.

APRON. A structural part of furniture. In tables, the piece connecting the legs, just under the top; in chairs, beneath the seat; in cabinets, etc., along the base. Also called SKIRT. See *Construction*.

ARABESQUE. Painted, inlaid, or flat carved designs, composed of floral and geometrical scrolls, human or animal and mythological forms, etc. Usually framed within a simple shape as a rectangle. 919.

ARCA. Chest for storing treasures, chiefly Middle Ages and Early Renaissance in Spain and Italy.

ARCADE. In furniture, a carved decoration representing a series of arches; also, a chair back in this form. 110, 456.

ARCADED BACK

ARCADED BACK. Typical French turned side chair, late 18th century, having spindle shaped and fluted shafts with hat shaped top, or pediment. Usually straw seated.

ARCADED PANEL. Typical English Renaissance panel decoration consisting of two stubby columns with arch in low relief. 155.

ARCHED STRETCHER. Arched or hoop-shaped stretcher in chairs, tables, and cabinets of the English Restoration Period. 270.

ARCHED STRETCHER

ARCHITECT'S FURNITURE. Specifically, English furniture of the 18th century, designed by architects and exhibiting architectural features, as arches, columns, etc.

ARCHITECT'S TABLE. Desk with drawing board in a drawer or otherwise attached, with other drawers for supplies. Made in England in the late 18th century for the then fashionable interest in architecture. 1013.

ARCHITRAVE. Lowest member of a cornice. Also a door moulding. See *Orders*.

ARKWRIGHT. Early English cabinetmaker. From ARK, the old name for cabinet, and WRIGHT, mechanic or maker. ARKWRIGHT furniture refers to late Gothic types in England in which the construction resembles carpentry rather than cabinetwork.

ARCHITECT'S TABLE

ARM CHAIR. See *Chair*.

ARMOIRE. A tall cupboard or wardrobe, with doors. The Gothic types are massive and are decorated chiefly with elaborate iron hinges and locks. The earliest armoires were probably painted and used for the storage of arms and armor. Later they were carved with elaborate pictorial panels or simple linenfold patterns. In France the Renaissance influence endowed the armoire with a wealth of columns, pilasters, canopied niches and panels carved with mythological pictures. 178.

ARM PAD. The upholstered part of a chair arm. 308.

ARM PAD

ARM STUMP. The front vertical support of the arm of a chair. See *Construction, Chair*.

ARRAS. Tapestry, particularly as used to drape beds and walls after the 14th century. Derives from the city, ARRAS, where the weaving of tapestries was a major industry in the Middle Ages.

ARRIS. Sharp or salient edge formed by the meeting of two surfaces. Particularly the ridge between the channels of a Doric column. See *Orders*.

ARROW. Decorative theme used in revivals of classic styles; Renaissance and later, especially Directoire, Empire and Biedermeier. 177, 351.

ARROW SPINDLE. Flattened spindle with one end resembling an arrow. Found on some Sheraton chairs, and on derivative forms in American chairs of the Federal Period. 876.

ART MODERNE. French term for the various schools of contemporary design, affectedly used in America during the 1920's to label the earliest modern work. See *Modern*.

ART NOUVEAU. A revived interest in the decorative arts flowed over Europe about 1875 giving rise to a concerted rebellion against the stale eclecticism of the time. A conscious effort to create along new lines inspired this "New Art." It drew on various motives—Gothic and Japanese principally—and established an ornamental vocabulary based on natural growing forms. The typical line is long and slightly curved, ending abruptly in a whip-like sharp curve.

Henri Van de Velde is the outstanding name of the style. His exhibitions in Brussels and Paris in 1894 and 1895 demonstrated his personal style. The copyists were numerous but less successful. His manner particularly influenced French design for about a decade, while the Arts and Crafts movement in England was a contemporary expression, as were developments like the Jugendstil and Secession in Germany and Austria.

Generally, the results of these rebellions were more successful in the minor arts as silver and jewelry than in furniture or architecture. Most vital is the impetus toward a clearer, more rational expression. See *Modern*.

ARTS AND CRAFTS MOVEMENT. A revival of interest in decorative art in England began about 1875. By 1884 it grew to a definite revolt against tasteless overmechanization, and inspired groups like the Art-Workers Guild to seek to re-establish the individual quality in the crafts. The ideal was the personal craftsmanship of the Middle Ages. Neo-Gothic architects such as the Pugins, Henry Shaw and Philip Webb, and the Pre-Raphaelite group of painters led by Dante Gabriel Rossetti and Edward Burne-Jones, and such strong personalities as William Morris and John Ruskin all contributed to this ideal. Their efforts created new interest and new expression in furniture and architecture, pottery, jewelry, textile and book design. A deliberately amateur quality, glorifying handwork, was too violently in opposition to all but the most intellectual trends, and the movement failed to elicit a popular response. In America it materialized in a parallel movement; Elbert

1

AMERICAN FURNITURE OF THE EARLY COLONIAL PERIOD

Furniture made in the English settlements in the 17th century evidences the survival of Tudor forms after their disappearance in England.

3

1. **OAK CHEST, C. 1650.** Motifs of Gothic and Earliest Renaissance Types.

2. **TABLE CHAIR,** New England.

3. **CARVER CHAIR,** New Jersey (ash).

4. **BOX TABLE** with Lid, Maple and Oak; 1660-1680.

5. **OAK TABLE** with Jacobean Turnings; New England, C. 1670.

6. **COURT CUPBOARD;** Oak, New England 1660-1670.

7. **COURT CUPBOARD.** Oak and Pine, C. 1670.

5

7

17. BUTTERFLY TABLE, Massachusetts. Late 17th Century.

16. CUPBOARD FROM MASSACHUSETTS, Early 18th Century Fluted Decoration Reminiscent of Linenfold Panelling.
Anderson Galleries

15. HIGH CHEST, William-and-Mary Style. About 1700.
Metropolitan Museum

PROVINCIAL TYPES OF AMERICAN FURNITURE

show the persistence of European forms beyond the Colonial Period and into the 19th Century. German, Swiss, Dutch, Swedish and other Continental forms remain in the domestic furniture of the Colonists from those countries.

14. SLAT BACK.

13. DUCK FOOT TABLE.

8-9. COURTING MIRRORS. XVIII Century.

10. WILLIAM AND MARY TABLE. *Weil*

11. FIRESIDE SETTLE. XVIII Century.
Metropolitan Museum

12. BANISTER BACK. *Weil*

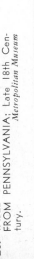

18. PENNSYLVANIA WINDSOR SETTEE. About 1760.

19-20. TABLE AND HANGING CUPBOARD FROM PENNSYLVANIA; Late 18th Century.

Metropolitan Museum

21. SIX-SLAT LADDER BACK. **22.** PENNSYLVANIA WINDSOR.

Anderson Galleries   *Ginsburg & Levy*

23. PAINTED CORNER CUPBOARD, Late 18th Century.

24. PAINTED WALNUT CRADLE. Pennsylvania German. About 1780.

25. PAINTED WEDDING CHEST. Pennsylvania German. About 1760.

Anderson Galleries

26. PENNSYLVANIA Table. About 1725.

27. CURLY MAPLE LOWBOY. Early 18th Century.

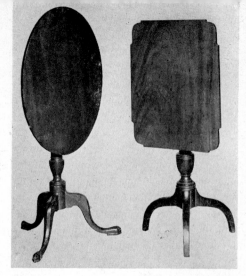

28-29. MAHOGANY TIP-TOP TABLES. *Weil*

32. ROCOCO M
About 1770

30. DESK, SHELL MOTIVE.
Anderson Galleries

31. NEW ENGLAND HIGHBOY, 1725-1750. Dutch Pad Feet. Painted with Chinese designs in imitation of oriental lacquer.
Metropolitan Museum of Art

AMERICAN COLONIAL, EARLY 18th CENTURY

Most furniture made in the American Colonies followed in even simpler fashion the simpler early Georgian designs.

35. FULLY DEVELOPED QUEEN ANNE STYLE.
Weil

36. NEW JERSEY DUTCH VERSION OF QUEEN ANNE TYPE. *Weil*

33. SLAT BACK.

34. EARLY QUEEN ANNE.

37. COMB BACK WI
Anderson

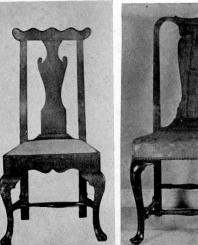

APLE TABLE, SPOON FOOT. About 1760.
Anderson Galleries

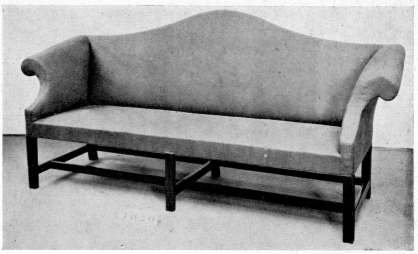

46. EARLY CHIPPENDALE TYPE SOFA. *Weil*

ALNUT SLANT-TOP SCRUTOIRE ON FRAME.
out 1725. *Anderson Galleries*

44. WING CHAIR. *Anderson*

42. CHINA CABINET. Early Chippendale style. About 1750. Mahogany.

OUNDABOUT CHAIR. een Anne style. *Weil*

39. WINDSOR TYPE. *Weil*

40. RHODE ISLAND WING CHAIR. *Weil*

41. ARMCHAIR.

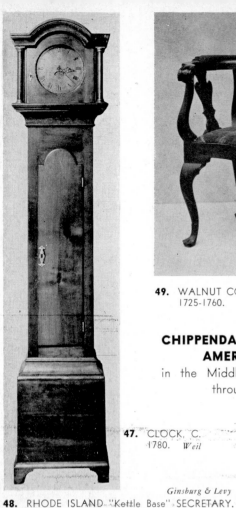

49. WALNUT CORNER CHAIR. Philadelphia, 1725-1760.   *Metropolitan Museum*

50. SETTEE. By Joseph Cox, New York. About 1760.   *Metropolit.*

CHIPPENDALE'S STYLE DOMINATED AMERICAN FURNITURE
in the Middle Eighteenth Century and through the Revolution.

47. CLOCK, C. 1780.   *Weil*

Ginsburg & Levy
48. RHODE ISLAND "Kettle Base" SECRETARY.

52. SERPENTINE FRONT DESK. Mahogany. 1765-1780.
Metropolit.

51. TILT-TABLE. Mahogany.

53. Philadelphia, 1765-1775.
Metropolitan Museum

54. CHIPPENDALE LADDER-BACK.   *Weil*

55. CHIPPEN GOTHIC.

290

64. FOLDING TOP CARD TABLE, inlaid mahogany.   *Weil*

OW POSTER BED. Maple. Late 18th Century.

62. CLOCK.
Metropolitan Museum

61. BLOCK FRONT
CHEST-ON
CHEST. Rhode
Island, Mid-18th
Century, Mahog-
any.

AHOGANY LOWBOY, Philadelphia, 1770.
aborate style of William Savery.
Metropolitan Museum

58. SHERATON AND HEP-
59. PLEWHITE INFLUENCE.
Metropolitan Museum

EPPLEWHITE STYLE.   **57.** CHAIR.   *Anderson Galleries*
Metropolitan Museum

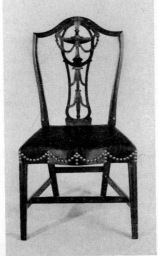

THE FEDERAL PERIOD

English forms, predominant even after the Revolution, gave way to the French influence toward classic forms.

66. SIDE TABLE OF SHERATON STYLE, early 19th Century.
Metropolitan Museum

65.

68. TAMBOUR DESK of mahogany with inlay. Sheraton style, 1780-1810.
Metropolitan Museum

71. *Anderson G*

72.

67. MAHOGANY CLOCK made by Joakim Hill of Flemington, N. J., 1790-1800.
Metropolitan Museum of Art

69.

70. MAHOGANY SOFA by Duncan Phyfe (early style). *Metropolitan Museum*

DUNCAN PHYFE

was the leader in the use of exquisite classic forms, developing the graceful Directoire and Sheraton styles.

73. CURLY MAPLE SEWING TABLE. Sheraton style. Abou 1800. *Anderson Gallerie*

GILT MIRROR.
MAHOGANY TABLE, About 810. *Anderson Galleries*

Anderson Galleries

76. SERVING CHEST of Mahogany. By Duncan Phyfe.
Ginsburg & Levy

80. GILT MIRROR of French or Italian inspiration. About 1810.
Weil

78. PHYFE SOFA.

Anderson Galleries

79. SEWING TABLE.
Ginsburg & Lev

EARLY 19th CENTURY

styles were inspired chiefly by the French Empire in varying degrees of provincialism.

93. WORK TABLE PRESENTED TO GENL. LAFAYETTE.
Ginsburg & Levy

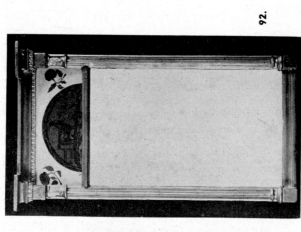

91. WORK TABLE BY DUNCAN PHYFE, 1825.
Ginsburg & Levy

90. CLOCK BY SAWIN & DYER, Boston, 1810.
Weil

89. *Weil*

92. *Weil*

87. "FANCY" CHAIR, C. 1830.

88. WAGON SEAT, C. 1830.

Weil

Anderson Galleries

86. MAHOGANY TABLE from Baltimore. About 1815.
Anderson Galleries

82. BRACKET CLOCK.

83. DROP LEAF TABLE.

84-85. DIRECTOIRE TYPE CHAIRS.

RTH GERMAN, RENAISSANCE—1568. Corner of Room, Enclosed
Wood Canopy and Curtains.
JTH GERMAN, LATE RENAISSANCE. About 1600.

95. LATE GOTHIC ALPINE—German. About 1500. Detached, Box-like
Enclosure.

97. ENGLAND, 1593. SEPARATE BED FRAME with Wood Canopy Carried
on Columns.

98. THE GREAT STATE BED OF THE 17th CENTURY: From Rushbrooke Hall, Suffolk, England, C. 1685. This example illustrates the great size and costly decoration of beds of the Restoration Period in England and of the era of Louis XIV in France.

...NISH BED WITH WROUGHT IRON POSTS AND HEAD-DECORA-
...N.
Courtesy Anderson Galleries

100. IRISH, LATE 18th CENTURY, SHERATON STYLE.

Anderson Galleries

EIGHTEENTH CENTURY BEDS WERE LIGHTER AND SMALLER

The development of smaller, more intimate rooms eliminated the enclosure feature of the bed. The canopy and curtains are almost entirely decorative, and the posts are ornamental.

102. AMERICAN BED-POSTS.

103. ENGLISH, STYLE OF CHIPPENDALE, with Carved Wooden Cornice. About 1770.

...MERICAN, LATE 18th CENTURY. *Courtesy Ginsburg & Levy*

104. FRANCE, PERIOD OF LOUIS XVI. The canopy is fixed on the wall.

105. BED IN ALCOVE, PERIOD OF LOUIS XVI. From Hotel De Gaulin, Dijon, 1772.

Now in the Metropolitan Museum of

106. FLEMISH, CA. 1625. Free-standing Bed without Canopy.

Courtesy Ginsburg & Levy

107. COLONIAL AMERICAN, 1725. The Partial Canopy Curtains are purely decorative. *Metropolitan M*

108. ITALY, POLYCHROMED BEDSTEAD. 16th Century.

IN SOUTHERN COUNTRIES THE BED ENCLOSURES DISAPPEARED EARLY: POSTS REMAIN AS DECORATION

SPAIN. 17th Century.

110. ITALY. 17th Century.

111. ITALY. Late 18th Century. Polychrome & Gold, Upholstered Headboard. *French & Co.*

18th CENTURY FRENCH STYLES WERE FREELY ADAPTED IN ITALY

112. ITALY. Early 18th Century. *Olivotti*

113. ITALY. Late 18th Century.

114. ITALIAN BAROQUE.

A. Olivotti & Co.

ITALIAN BEDS WERE ELABORATELY PAINTED AND CARVED

ITALIAN ROCOCO. Style of Louis XV. *Olivotti*

116. ITALIAN. Middle 18th Century. *Olivotti*

118. FRENCH. Style of the Regency.

117. ITALIAN. WALNUT. Early 17th Century. *Cavallo*

119. ENGLISH. OAK. CA. 1660. *Stair & Co.*

LOW SIMPLE BEDFRAMES

were a development of the 18th Century, largely replacing the heavily draped and architectural styles of the preceding century.

120. FRENCH. Period of Louis XVI. PAINTED FRAME with UPHOLSTERED HEADBOARD. *Cassard-Romano*

121. FRENCH. Louis XVI. CANE PANELS. *Cassard-Romano*

122. AMERICAN, 18th Century, Maple.

123. AMERICAN, Late 18th Century.   *Weil*

124. FRENCH, DIRECTOIRE, C. 1800.

125. AMERICAN, MAHOGANY, French influence. Made by Honoré Lannuier, New York, 1810-15.   *Ginsburg & Levy*
127. FRENCH, DIRECTOIRE, C. 1800.   *Cassard-Romano*

SWEDISH, EMPIRE STYLE, C. 1815.

128.

BEDS OF THE EMPIRE STYLE IN FRANCE AND ELSEWHERE WERE
LOW, HEAVY AND ORNAMENTED WITH METAL APPLIQUE

129.

Hubbard and his Roycroft crystallizing the ideal, while various degrees of success attended the efforts of commercial manufacturers who accepted the outward forms for machine-made products. The Mission style is one of the offshoots. The furniture forms of the Arts and Crafts movement are essentially simple and crude; in their joinery concepts, rudimentary. They consciously lack grace, lightness and charm. The value of the intellectual movement cannot be overestimated. It clearly set a track for later thought. Schools of design and individuals were moved to examine the forces at work and the result is only now materializing.

ASH. A family of trees, the woods of many of which are used for furniture. The European ash belongs to a group which includes also olive, lilac, privet and jasmine. The olive ash burls of both England and France are exquisitely figured and capable of beautiful veneer matching. The color varies from a light honey color to a medium brown. The American ashes are used principally as lumber where great strength is required, as in upholstery frames. The wood is a very light creamy color, heavy and dense, with a prominent grain resembling oak. It was used for some turnings and bent work in very early Windsor chairs.

ASIATIC. See *Oriental*.

ASPEN. Species of poplar; the wood is light in weight and color, satiny in texture. Poor structurally, but decorative as veneer.

ASSYRIAN. Assyrian decoration art was approximately contemporaneous with the Egyptian. Ornamental motives were borrowed, the lotus and other natural forms being adapted. Animal forms were more distinctive, featuring the winged bull, lion and eagle. Bronze, ivory, and gold ornaments remain; the wood has disappeared, so that the forms of Assyrian furniture are conjectural.

ASTER CARVING. On Connecticut chests, three flowers on a central panel; also sunflower carving. See *Connecticut Chest*. 379.

ASTRAGAL. Small half round or convex bead moulding; moulding on overlapping doors. 165.

ATHENIENNE. Round tripod table or stand, adapted in Louis XVI and Empire period to washstands, etc. 631.

ATLANTES. Supporting columns in the shape of male figures. See *Caryatids*. 945.

ATLANTES

AUBUSSON. Fine hand woven tapestries or carpets originating in the French village of that name.

AUSTRIA. Austrian furniture is essentially German, following the Gothic phase with the Renaissance influences of Italian origins. Proximity to Italy brought the Italian manners but the German character is basic. The Alpine variants of these styles are found in Austrian furniture of the 16th and 17th centuries; oak, pine and fir in panelling, chests and beds recall the Swiss types. Cabinets are in the South German manner. Occasionally, there were periods when the High Renaissance Italian types dominated, but Austria must be considered aesthetically a German province. There are no distinct types or schools; the local variations while highly characteristic and individual may be considered uniformly German in character. 659.

AVODIRE. African wood of medium density and strength, light yellow color and satin-smooth texture. Extensively used in decorative veneering in modern cabinetwork.

AYOUS. Light-colored wood similar in color and markings to Prima Vera, but softer in texture.

BAG TABLE

BACKGAMMON BOARDS & TABLES. The game goes back to the Middle Ages, and furniture for its play appeared as soon as specialized tables came in the 17th century. Fine examples occur in French and English work. 1054.

BACK STOOL. Early form of chair without arms, as the Sgabelli of Italy and similar forms in Alpine countries. 258.

BAG TABLE. Small work or serving table, with one or two drawers, the lower having a cloth bag attached. Common in 18th and early 19th century, England and America. See *Tables.* 571.

BAGUETTE. Small bead moulding, smaller than an astragal. See *Mouldings.* 155.

BAHUT (French). In the Middle Ages, a portable coffer or chest used for personal luggage. It usually had a rounded top, leather covered and studded with nails. It developed into a chest permanently mounted on feet, used for storing household goods. The current form in France is a decorative high cabinet.

BAIL. Metal loop or ring forming a handle. See *Hardware.*

BAKELITE. Synthetic plastic material used in modern table tops, etc. See *Plastics.*

BALDACHIN. A free standing canopy supported on columns.

BALL-AND-CLAW. See *Claw-and-Ball.*

BALL-AND-RING. A turning of a ball and narrow member, found in 17th century work. 271.

BALL FOOT. Round turning used as foot on chests, etc. Chiefly in 17th century furniture. Same as Bun foot in England. 453.

BALLOON-BACK. Chair back style developed by Hepplewhite. 330.

BALUSTER. Small column, turned, square or flat, supporting a rail: also, forming chair backs in architectural forms. 597.

BAMBINO. Representation of the infant Jesus, used as a decorative feature in Early Italian Renaissance work and subsequently. 464.

BALL FEET

BAMBOO. The wood of the Bamboo tree is used for furniture in the East, and came to the Occident with the various waves of Chinese influences. In the 18th century this was so important that the characteristic appearance of the bamboo was simulated in wood turnings in England and America, and the type is known as the BAMBOO TURNING. 242.

BANDEROLE. Painted or carved ribbon decoration, often with an inscription or other device.

BANDING. A narrow edging or border of veneer around the fronts of drawers; a contrasting band of inlay. 389.

BANDY LEG. Cabriole leg.

BANISTER. Baluster.

BANISTER BACK. Chair back with spindles, or similar upright members. Common in 17th century English and American work, as split turnings. 12.

BANJO CLOCK. 19th century American wall clock in the form of a banjo.

BANK. A long seat of the Middle Ages. (England).

BANQUETTE (French). An upholstered Bench. 931.

BANTAM WORK. Type of lacquering in late 17th century Dutch and English work, derived from Bantam in Dutch Java. Design usually incised in black ground.

BAROMETER CASE. Barometers, with other scientific instruments were objects of great interest in the 18th century. Handsome cases were designed for them, particularly in England, France and Italy in the various Rococo and classical styles.

BAROQUE. The whole tendency of European design in the 17th century was toward exaggeration, overemphasized brilliance. The movement was a natural sequence of the increasingly ornamental Renaissance style; its extremes resulted from the Jesuit Counter-Reformation, the effort of the militant Catholic order to recapture the imagination of the masses through over-awing splendor. Italian art had exhausted the simpler vocabulary by 1550. The need for new types opened a path for unrestrained virtuosity. The spreading Renaissance carried this free manner everywhere and for two centuries most European art was Baroque.

Motion is the essence of the Baroque, as distinguished from the repose of the classic ideal. Large curves, fantastic and irregular, are explosively interpreted, reversed, ornamented. Twisted columns, distorted and broken pediments, oversized mouldings, sacrificed the structural sense to a tremendous theatrical effect. Scale and proportion had new meaning, everything being calculated to strike the eye, to excite rather than to suggest quiet and harmony.

In furniture the earlier Baroque tendencies were merely exaggera-

BANJO CLOCK

BAROMETER
(LOUIS XVI)

BAROQUE PEDIMENT

tion of scale. Fantastically overloaded ornament was added later; the earlier work was actually freer of plastic decoration than the preceding late Renaissance types. Cabinets whose midsections were simply, if insistently, panelled, were carried on excessively carved bases and bore great pediments, usually broken and capped with towering finials. Chairs were elaborately scrolled and carved. Tables had bases of rich sculpture, fancifully shaped stretchers; others had twisted columns or complex scrolls as legs. Beds, particularly in France and England, were colossal structures of draped textiles.

Surface treatment became more splendid after 1650. Earlier solid wood surfaces were then painted, gilded, polychromed; inlays and marquetry reached their ultimate heights in the work of Boulle and the imitative scrollwork of seaweed marquetry. Marble and imitation stone, vivid textiles, cane and metals all contributed to this unrestrained decorative orgy.

LATE ITALIAN BAROQUE

The Baroque is withal a masculine style, virile and blustering and bold. Its feminine counterpart, the Rococo, came in the 18th century, substituting prettiness and charm for Baroque magnificence. 114, 263 et seq., 469, 475, 476, 597 et seq., 659 662, 735, 739, 993, 1045, 1046.

BARREL CHAIR. A chair, usually upholstered, shaped like a half barrel cut vertically.

BASE. The lowest member of a piece of furniture or of a column. As "Basses" the word designated the lower part of 17th century English Beds.

BASIN STAND. Washstand; light table on which basins were set. Common in 18th cent. English work, sometimes spelled BASON-STAND. 574.

BAS RELIEF. Sculpture in which the carving projects only slightly from the background. 459.

BASSET TABLE. Card table, Queen Anne Period.

BASSINET. Bed for a baby. Originally basket shaped, and made of wicker.

BASIN STAND

BASSWOOD. American wood of light color and weight, soft texture, slight figure and medium strength. Works well and does not warp or check readily. Used for inexpensive painted flat work, but chiefly valuable as core-stock for plywood panels.

BATIK. Figured fabric produced with wax resist and successive dyeings or paintings, after an ancient Javanese process.

BATTEN. Strips of wood used as a brace or cleat across one or more boards.

BAYWOOD. Honduras mahogany.

BEAD. Half round moulding, usually small. See *Mouldings*.

BEAD AND REEL. Bead mould in which is carved alternate round and oval forms. Same as Pencil & Pearl. See *Mouldings*.

BEARING RAIL. Member in table or cabinet work which carries the drawer. See *Construction*.

BEAU BRUMMEL. Late 18th century English dressing table with complex arrangements of adjustable mirrors, candle brackets, shelves and drawers. Designed for men's use, they became increasingly complicated after Early Georgian types, as male dandyism spread. The name was acquired during the George IV period. 1014, 1017.

BEAUFAIT, BEAUFATT, BEAUFET. Early spellings of Buffet.

BED BOLT. Covered bolt and sunken nut used in some styles of bed to fasten the rail to the head- and foot-boards. Decorative brass cover plates occur in Federal American beds. See *Hardware*.

BED MOULDING. Small mould under the corona or large moulding of a cornice.

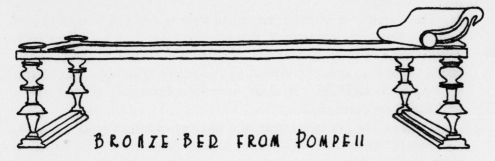

BRONZE BED FROM POMPEII

BEDS. Ancient drawings portray well developed bed types in Egypt, Assyria, Persia, Greece and Rome. Over basic structures of stone, wood, or metal were thrown animal skins and textile for softness and warmth. The framework was often well designed and adorned with inlays or appliques of metal, ivory, etc.

Egyptian tomb remains show typical couches, wood frames with lacing of hide or rope, often made to fold. Turned or animal shaped legs of good design are common. Bedding consisted of manifold layers of linen sheets. The pillow was a wooden stand curved to fit the head and more comfortable than it looks; it was cool in the hot summer nights and prevented the elaborate headdress from becoming disarranged.

Greek sculptures show high frames, with turned legs, probably of wood. Roman beds were even higher, with a raised head section and inlays of gold and ivory in fine woods. Bronze and even silver were also used. The fabric parts were elaborate and costly. Some Pompeiian houses had curtained alcoves for beds.

The first beds in Northern Europe were piles of leaves upon the floor covered with skins, followed at an early date by a shallow box or chest filled with leaves and moss. Mattresses stuffed with feathers, wool or hair were invented early in the Middle Ages. These were piled upon benches against the wall or into the low boxlike structures which persisted in provincial sections through the 18th century. Such a bed of Swedish origin appears in picture 943. Probably the Crusades yielded the idea of the canopy or curtain, for after the 12th century, beds are always pictured with draperies which could enclose the bed. These grew in elegance and size; in the north the addition of wood panels made a complete room-within-a-room. After the 14th century fabrics were richer and thicker. One type of free-standing bed had suspended tester or canopy and several layers of draperies; this form grew in importance through the 17th century when it attained tremendous size and splendor and extremes of costliness. In Northern Europe the wooden enclosure idea was favored, utilizing the two walls of a corner. Picture 94 shows a North German example with curtains forming the enclosure. The step in the foreground is a chest for bedding, etc. In the Northern French provinces a similar type lasted through the early 19th century, often with sliding wood panels in place of curtains. Pictures 95, 96, 97 and 685 show free-standing structures of wood embodying the same idea, smaller in scale and freer for ventilation. In the English example No. 97, it is significant that the bed stock is a separate frame, while No. 106 suggests a trimmed-off version of No. 96.

The wooden superstructure and enclosure reached its zenith in England in Elizabeth's reign. By that date the Continental tendency toward multiplication of fabric parts had spread to England. The period saw the bed grow, like the dinosaur, to the exaggeration that predicted its doom. In France the state bed was a composition of over thirty textile parts, with yardage of embroidered satin and bullion fringe and cloth of gold enough to run the cost into fair fortunes. No wood was visible. There was a multiplicity of fabric members,—pentes, basses, cantonniers and bonnegraces covering everything, and topped off by clusters of plumes or swags. In England too the bed remained a colossal symbol of wealth and position up to the reign of Queen Anne. Measuring 7 by 8 feet and 11 feet high, the cost often ran up to many thousand pounds.

The 18th century scaled down rooms and furniture. Beds became lighter and simpler in woodwork and drapery. In France many variations appeared: the small separate bed frame in an alcove, draperies covering the open front (105); the baldaquin bed, or crown bed, (104) the angel bed, with suspended canopy and curtains looped back; the duchess bed, and others. In England the general type was a simpler four-poster bearing canopy and draw curtains. Beds by Chippendale, Hepplewhite, the Adams, and Sheraton, were important and highly decorative structures but the draperies are less voluminous and the whole scale finer. The "field bed" appeared as a smaller canopy type which became popular in America. Beds of the Empire period were low, chunky blocks, usually undraped; sometimes set on a dais, often with the typical heavy scroll. In America this was known as the "Sleigh" bed.

Most significant about all 19th century beds is the low, solid quality. American four-posters with abnormally heavy posts, richly carved, are still common. The current styles of beds are chiefly based on these designs, scaled still smaller, and ornamented with period forms, rather than copied literally from the larger prototypes.

The perfection of modern springs and mattresses has removed the necessity for the heavy wood framing which was required by the laced-rope floor of 19th century beds. The minimum framing, just enough to raise the bedding from the floor, with a panel for the head, is favored in much contemporary designing.

Metal frames, usually iron or brass tubing, came forward after 1850, and have held more or less favor since. Cheaply produced, durable and hygienic, they are too purely functional or too tastelessly designed to be accepted in any decorative way.

BED STEPS. Low steps made for climbing into high beds; 18th century English & American work.

BED STOCK. In Elizabethan and some continental types the posts of the bed often stood clear of the bed proper. In this type the bedstock was the framework that actually supported the bedding. 97.

BEECH. Northern hardwood, Europe and America; dense texture and light color. Used chiefly in middle-quality work, country style in England, etc., since the 17th century; found in good French provincial furniture. Adapted to turning, polishes well to light brown color.

BELL FLOWER. Ornamental detail, carved or painted resembling bell-shaped flowers arranged vertically. Also Husk ornament. 57.

BELL SEAT. Round seat, Queen Anne period. 269.

BELTER, JOHN H. American cabinetmaker; had a shop in New York after 1840. Made rosewood, walnut, and oak furniture in the style of the Second or late Empire, generally referred to as Victorian. Highly carved sinuous framework lines with heavy roll mouldings and fine naturalistic flower carving; upholstery in brocades and damasks. The craftsmanship was excellent, and much of his work survives. An exhibition of Belter furniture was held in the Metropolitan Museum in New York in 1935. 1099.

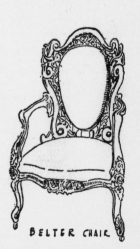

BELTER CHAIR

BENCH. Seat without a back, usually a long oval or oblong. In England sometimes refers to seat with a back or ends, or a settee. 919 et seq.

BENCH—Workmans, joiners, etc. Heavy work table, usually fitted with vise, tool racks, etc. "Bench-made" implies hand work, as distinguished from machine or quantity-assembled work.

BENEMAN, GUILLAUME. Outstanding cabinetmaker-designer of the earlier Empire style in France; noted for monumental mahogany cupboards and commodes of architectural character.

BENT-WOOD. Process of moulding wood after softening with steam into continuous structural shapes. Such are the bow backs and arms of Windsor chairs. The process came into use in Austria in the late 19th century and was extensively used for chairs, being inexpensive and strong. Modern designers as Aalto in Finland are again encouraging its use. 797, 798.

BÉRAIN. French family of designers and craftsmen. Jean, 1638-1711, published books which spread style of Louis XVI; designed arabesques, etc., for Boulle. Claude, Brother of Jean; Jean (the younger), 1678-1726. See *France.*

BERGÈRE. Upholstered armchair with closed upholstered sides. Specifically, chairs of French style, copied in England and Germany. Also spelled BIRJAIR, BARJAIR. 306 et seq.

BEVEL. A sloping edge, of various angles, applied to any material—wood, glass, metal, etc. Similar to CHAMFER.

BIBLE BOX. Small slant-top table or desk, used to hold the Bible. 437, 655.

BIBLIOTHÈQUE. French term for large architectural bookcase.

BIDET. Small bedroom stand.

BIEDERMEIER. German style, first half 19th century, chiefly based on French Empire forms. It is essentially a style of the lesser nobility and the bourgeoisie, imitating the Paris Empire "Meubles de Luxe" of the grander houses. These adaptations, the products of local materials and skill, are odd mixtures in varying degrees of sophisticated motives with naïve proportions and techniques. Architectural themes and classic ornaments are given homely interpretation. Carved details are represented in paint, black or gold; the classic flora are sometimes rendered as more familiar vegetable forms. Simplified surfaces and details recall Empire outlines. The woods are largely local—pear and other fruitwoods, walnut, maple, birch, beech—but much mahogany furniture remains.

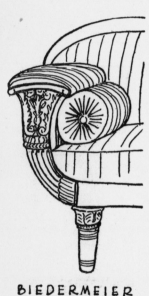

BIEDERMEIER

The name derives from a comic-paper character, Papa Biedermeier, symbol of homely substantial comfort and well being—*gemütlichkeit.* It later came also to connote old fashioned, stodgy.

In either case the style, imitative and awkward as it may be, is an interesting example of the process of copying and adapting a foreign style in toto. 668, 670, 794, 879. See *Germany.*

BILBOA. Mirror with frame of marble or of marble and wood. Popular late 18th century, named after the usual port of origin. Also spelt BILBAO.

BIRCH. Wood family of many varieties found in temperate zones. White and sap birches are soft; red, black and yellow are hard. Used everywhere for furniture, usually inexpensive. Harder varieties have great strength, work well and polish well, often as imitations of mahogany and walnut. Most extensively used for structural work, next to gumwood.

BIRDCAGE. Openwork box of wire, wood, wicker, etc., used for caging birds. Occurs decoratively in most styles, and often forms an important feature in the decoration of rooms.

BIRDCAGE CLOCK. English brass clock with open pendulum and weights, chiefly late 17th century.

BIRDS BEAK. Rounded V-cut on moulded corners: English & Early American.

BIRDSEYE. Small figure in wood grain resembling bird's eye. Principally in maple but occasionally in other woods. It is produced by cutting tangentially through the indentations which sometimes appear in the annual rings. 1108.

BLACKAMOOR

BISELLIUM. Roman seat for two persons.

BLACKAMOOR. Negro figure used as table base in Baroque Continental furniture, early 18th century and again in Victorian work, 1850-1870, England and America. 1098.

BLACK WALNUT. See *Walnut*.

BLANKET CHEST. Any chest for the storage of blankets. Now, particularly, chests with a hinged top section with drawer in or near the base. 380.

BLEACHED FINISHES. A recent vogue for light or blond woods has produced methods of chemical bleaching, most successful on medium dark, open textured wood like mahogany. It tends to lose the brilliance of the wood and its permanence is somewhat doubtful.

BLISTER. Figure in some woods, as maple, mahogany, cedar, poplar and pine.

BLOCK FOOT. Square end of an untapered leg, as in Chippendale work. 1078.

BLOCK FRONT. Front of chest, desk, etc. divided vertically into three panels, the center concave, the end panels convex. The best types are mainly flat, curving only near the panel edges. The tops end in flat arches or better with a carved shell. The type seems to be peculiarly American, a Baroque expression dating from the period 1760-1780 and associated with the work of John Goddard and the Newport School. 410, 478.

BLOCK FRONT by GODDARD

BLONDE WOODS, FINISHES. A vogue for light wood tones has brought forward many of the lighter woods as holly, prima vera, avodire, aspen, birch and maple. In poorer work these are given a cloudy whitish finish, tending to obscure the irregularities of grain and color. Other devices include bleaching, successful to a degree in mahogany and walnut; pigmentation in which the open grain is filled with light opaque fillers; pickling, using plaster on soft woods.

BOARD. Table, prior to the XVI century. Early dining tables were loose boards borne on trestles. Later, refers to sideboard.

BOAT BED. Low heavy bed of Empire period, chiefly American, like the gondola or sleigh bed.

BOBBIN-TURNED. The bulging or swelled part of the turned stretchers of Windsor chairs.

BODYING-IN. The operation of filling the grain of a coarse wood in the process of finishing.

BOISERIE. French term for woodwork; used specifically for 18th century carved panels.

BOLECTION. Important projecting moulding, used to frame a fireplace, large panel, etc. Generally with outward roll and ogee shape in section.

BOMBÉ COMMODE
(GERMAN)

BOMBÉ. Swelling or convex surface; bulging fronts and sides, as found in furniture of period of Louis XV, late 18th century Italian and other Baroque work. 400, 476.

BONHEUR du JOUR. French desk consisting of a flat cabinet with fall front, carried on legs. Developed for the use of ladies in the era of letter and diary, period of Louis XVI and after. 625.

BONNETIÈRE. French cabinet, tall and narrow, and deep enough to accommodate the elaborate bonnets peculiar to Normandy and Brittany in the 18th century. 177.

BONNET TOP. An unbroken pediment or top section of a high-boy, secretary and the like; also Hooded top. Typical late 17th, early 18th century English design.

BOOK BOX. Same as Bible Box.

BOOKCASES. The earliest bound books were stored in shelved closets, and the architectural bookcase was the only type known until the 17th century. About the middle of that century detached cases appeared, retaining their architectural relationship to the room. About 1700 smaller cases were known in France.

The architectural character remained throughout the 18th century, in which the bookcase form developed. The three-part break-front form was most popular in France and England. The best examples, from the point of contemporary usage, were made in England. These were usually conceived as the permanent decorative features of a given wall, in which respect they developed from the architectural idea. (Cf. 130 with 132). Chippendale, the Adams, Hepplewhite, etc., valued the bookcase as a wall feature, and their bookcases are among the best of their designs.

The small bookcase (book-stand, 1089) seems to have originated in France, but its superior development took place in England toward the close of the 18th century. The Regency period shows the best of this size, with numerous variations, as alcove and recess cabinets, smaller stands, combinations with work tables, shelves for display of bibelot, curios. 130 et seq.

BOOKREST. Slanting framework, sometimes adjustable, on which to rest a book.

BOOKSTAND. See *Bookcases; Standing shelves.* 1089.

BOOTJACK. Hinged or solid board with V-cut to fit the heel, used to help pull off boots; in Early American work, a V cut in the end board of a chest, for the same purpose.

BORAX. Colloquial for cheap, showy furniture, particularly intended for the installment trade. Its style is generally a haphazard combination of many motives grotesquely adapted, featuring sheer weight and bulk, flashy combinations of many materials, aimless ornamentation and shiny finishes. Construction is poor, employing constructional features in the letter if not in the spirit, which are used as sales arguments. Tricky nomenclature as well as specious constructive features permit high sounding descriptions which trap the unfortunate egoist possessed of a dangerous little knowledge as readily as the gullible ignoramus capable only of signing an "easy terms" agreement. The caricaturing of good style and good construction is only part of the implication of the word; the essential balance is the method of advertising, describing and selling.

The origin of the word is speculative. One guess places it in the premiums formerly given with a well known cleaning compound of borax; others identify it as corrupted foreign-language slang.

BORNE. French type of sofa, oval or round, with a pillar in the center.

BOSS. Round or oval ornament after Gothic sources common in 17th century English and American work, particularly on chests. Usually half turning painted black. 379.

BOSTON ROCKER. Rocking chair, American 19th century, with wood seat curved upwards, wide scrolled top rail and delicate spindles. Usually painted with fine ornamental detail.

BOSTON ROCKER

BOTTLE TURNING. William and Mary leg turning reminiscent of the shape of a bottle. Originally Dutch.

BOULLE, ANDRE CHARLES, 1642-1732, French cabinetmaker under the patronage of Louis XIV. He designed and executed the mirrored walls, "wood mosaic" floors, inlaid panelling and pieces of marquetry of the Palace of Versailles. He advanced the art of marquetry and introduced the practice of inlaying brass into wood or tortoise-shell. This distinctive style has come to be known by his name, often spelt *"Boull"* or *"Buhl"* work. 446, 598.

BOW BACK. Windsor chair back in which the bow or hoop is continuous either down to the arms or the seat. 244 et seq.

BOW FRONT. Convex shaped front of a chest, buffet, etc., characteristic of 18th century work. 898.

BOW TOP. Continuously curved top rail of a chair.

BOX 22 BRITISH COLONIAL

CLOCK BRACKET

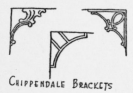

CHIPPENDALE BRACKETS

BOX. One of the most primitive pieces of furniture, boxes are used as receptacles for every conceivable object. They lend themselves to the widest variety of decoration, and so are more easily described by their special uses. See *Coffer, Chest.*

BOX BED. Early beds of Northern Europe were more or less box-like enclosures, an open side having wood panels (in France) or curtains. Later a folding type, common in Scotland.

BOX SETTLE. Low chest used as a seat with back formed by a hinged lid. Early development from coffer. 4, 847.

BOX STOOL. Stool with hinged lid over box section; chiefly early Renaissance. 923.

BOXWOOD. Dense, light yellow wood of genus BUXUS. Its uniform close grain is excellent for carving and small articles, as turned parts, handles, rules, inlays, etc.

BRACED BACK. See Fiddle-Brace. 240.

BRACKET. A small ornamental shelf. Also any wall lighting fixture. Also, in furniture, a supporting member between the leg and seat of a chair or table, or the leg and body of a case. Pierced brackets of many designs are characteristic of Chippendale work.

BRACKET CLOCK. English clock intended to stand on a bracket or shelf. 82.

BRACKET CORNICE. Cornice supported by brackets or modillions at regular intervals. 473.

BRACKET FOOT. Simple base on chests and case furniture of the 18th century. The foot runs two ways from the corner, in more or less simple shapes. The type was highly ornamented by Chippendale in England, by Goddard and others in America. 451.

BRASSES. Handles.

BREAK. Marked projection on a cabinet.

BREAK-FRONT. Front formed on two or more planes. Specifically, the word is now used to describe a bookcase or cabinet in which a center section projects forward from the two end sections. 135, 1093.

BRETON. French provincial style of Brittany.

BREWSTER CHAIR. Early New England type either originated by the Pilgrims, or brought over by them. It has heavy turned posts, many turned spindles, and a wood seat. Provincial Jacobean in type, its general characteristics are common in earlier chairs from the Continent. 223.

BRIDAL CHEST. Same as Dower chest or Hope chest. A decorated box for the accumulation of household and personal goods. The romantic implications led to its becoming the object of considerable decoration, particularly in New England, Germany, and Sweden. 25. See *Connecticut Chest.*

BRITISH COLONIAL. Style in architecture and furniture developed by British settlers and officials in colonies as the West Indies

BREWSTER CHAIR

(Bahamas, Bermuda, etc.) South Africa, India, etc. in late 18th and early 19th centuries. Consistently simple and reminiscent of late Georgian work, it exhibits local influences in appropriate planning and materials.

BROCADE. Textile woven with a pattern of raised figures resembling embroidery. Originally in gold or silver, in later use any fabric richly wrought or flowered with a raised pattern. An important upholstery and drapery fabric originating in India and extensively used in the Renaissance and other ornate styles.

BROCATELLE. Heavy fabric, chiefly silk, woven usually in large patterns which appear to be embossed.

BROKEN ARCH. Elliptical, segmental or round arch whose curves are interrupted at the apex, as in a pediment, for the introduction of a decorative feature as a finial. 470.

BROKEN-FRONT. Breakfront.

BROKEN PEDIMENT. Pediment, straight, swan neck or goose neck, the side lines or scrolls of which do not meet at the apex. 470.

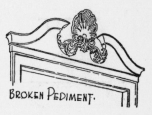

BROKEN PEDIMENT.

BRONZE. Extensively used for furniture in the ancient world, its strength permitted an extreme lightness of design which is accepted as typically Greco-Roman and was so copied in the classic revivals of the 18th cent. 985. ORMOLU, process of gilding bronze, became very popular in 18th century France. Louis XV and subsequent work is noted for its superb bronze chasing and modelling. 413.

BUBINGA. African hardwood of even stripe with mottle figure, medium red-brown. Very hard and durable and polishes well.

BUFFET. Sideboard; dining room dresser of almost any description used as a receptable for articles not immediately wanted at the table. Originally Italian, the buffet was highly developed in France and in England in the Stuart period, and later in many forms thruout the Georgian era. See *Sideboard; Court Cupboard; Tables (Side)*. 881 et seq.

BUHL. Spelling used in England for BOULLE work.

BUILT-IN FURNITURE. Chests, cabinets, corner cupboards, bookcases, etc., treated as integral parts of the structure have been known since the earliest times. In the Far East, particularly Japan, the practice is universal in the case of receptacle furniture. In Europe the upper classes in the Middle Ages lived a nomadic existence necessitating portable chests, etc., but the lower classes developed built-in beds and benches, chests and cupboards. Recent styles have favored such built-in equipment as cupboards, closets and bookcases. The contemporary functional style utilizes the economy and efficiency of built-in furniture, including even seatings to an unprecedented degree.

BULBOUS. Turning resembling a bulb, common to most European styles from the Renaissance on. The Dutch passed it on to the

B U N
F E E T

English, who made it an outstanding characteristic of their furniture in the 16th and 17th centuries. 152 et seq.

BULL'S EYE MIRROR. Round ornamental mirror, often with convex or concave glass. 766. See *Girandole.*

BUN FOOT. English term for Ball foot, usually somewhat flattened. 389.

BUREAU. Originally a cloth cover for a table, used when writing. In France a desk derived from a chest set upon a table, and pushed back to afford the writer an arm rest (Louis XIII).

Sheraton defined the bureau as a "common desk with drawers," and this was the name given in England to the entire family of desk and drawer combinations known in America as "Secretary." In America the word came to refer to a chest of drawers, generally for the bedroom, and was highly developed during the early 19th century.

BUREAU BOOKCASE. Chippendale's term for a piece of furniture the lower part of which was a desk, the upper a bookcase. 136.

BUREAU TABLE. Goddard's name for his knee-hole table. 1016.

BURJAR. Chippendale's name for a large upholstered chair, like the French Bergere.

BURL. Excrescences or abnormal or diseased growths appearing on trees, often from an injury to the bark. When sliced into fine cross sections for veneer they produce beautifully figured mottled or speckled patterns. These are used for the most decorative veneering. As the usable portions are often small, they are matched into symmetrical panels. Walnut, Maple, Ash are the commonest American Burls, but many fine Burls occur all over the world. 460.

BURR. Burl.

BUTT. The stump end of the log. The root spreads away from the trunk so that sections through the juncture possess a unique grain, desirable for decorative veneering.

BUTTER CUPBOARD. Ventilated cabinet used in England for the storage of bread.

BUTTERFLY TABLE. Small drop leaf table whose leaves are supported by a swinging bracket resembling a butterfly wing or rudder. Chiefly American, after 1700, the earliest examples are of maple. 17, 977.

BUTTERFLY WEDGE. Butterfly-shaped cleat inserted into adjoining boards to hold them together.

BUTTERNUT. Hardwood similar to black walnut. Importance increases with demand for black walnut. Also known as white walnut. Figure similar to black walnut but color is lighter, texture softer.

BUTT HINGE. Common type of hinge for hanging doors. See *Hardware.*

BUTT JOINT. Joining either of solid wood or veneer, at the ends of the grains. See *Construction*.

BYZANTINE. Roman Empire of the East, centering in Constantinople 476-1200; furniture, entirely royal or ecclesiastical, was debased Roman with profuse ornamentation in Near Eastern style. Rich carving, inlays of gold, glass, stones, in motives of ritual significance. Interlacing bands, stiff animal forms, sharply-cut foliage, etc., remain in later Russian and South European as well as Italian work.

BYZANTINE. Specifically, a three cornered chair believed to have originated in Scandinavia and then popularized in England in the Middle Ages. 221.

BYZANTINE

CABINETMAKER. The general term for case-furniture maker. The original classification separated cabinetmakers, chairmakers, etc., but now all furniture craftsmen working chiefly in wood are so grouped.

CABINETS. Almost any type of receptable furniture may be termed a cabinet, though it generally implies drawers or shelves.

The cabinet or cupboard form has a mixed ancestry in the coffer or chest, and the closet-like armoire (636) or ambry (634). It is primarily a receptacle; as such its variety must be infinite. It was early realized in Italy and France that the top of a coffer could be used as a seat or table; this suggested the front opening instead of the top, the first stage in the cabinet. The form was complete when the cabinet was mounted on legs high enough to eliminate stooping to see the interior (150). This type is the sideboard-credence type. The parallel type, the boxlike cupboard, whatever its source, came to resemble the chest-on-legs as soon as it was found expedient in the latter to make use of the lower section by closing in the open space. The convergence of these elementary types is shown in the evolution of French cabinets from the simple Gothic box (165, 168) to the Burgundian cabinet (167) with vertical emphasis, or from the the horizontal cabinet of Earliest Renaissance style (151) to the mature style of Louis XIII (170). In this period, the early 17th century, the cabinet was the dominant article of furniture, embellished by every decorative resource. Carving and painting, inlaying, marquetry, and encrustation with stones of beauty and value, with mirrors (735), or metals, panelling, and mouldings were lavished on the monumental cabinets of Italy and France. Their height and physical importance made them focal points in the room, and their association with articles of value and beauty justified the lavish decoration. The cabinetmaker was therefore the head of the wood-working craftsmen, and the name persisted.

Another structural point caused this name to stand out. Earliest coffers were solid wood planks. Sometime in the Middle Ages the carpenters who specialized on furniture hit on the framed panel (a thin panel fixed in grooves in a stout frame). For lightness and strength this was far superior to the solid board. It also reduced the risk from cracking and warping from shrinkage. The panelling itself provided some decorative character. The guild of *huchiers-menuisiers* broke away from the guild of simple *charpentiers*. Ever since the *huchier*—hutch-maker, cabinet-maker—has isolated his craft from that of the mere carpenter.

The ornate cabinet passed its zenith in France but did not deteriorate in the provinces for two centuries. The bold pointed panels of this style are characteristic (593, 637); these passed to England and characterize Jacobean work. German cabinets favored twisted turnings, applied at corners (658). The Augsburg style was famous. Another development was the desk-cabinet. Since money and papers had been stored in coffers, the specialized cabinet providing many small compartments and drawers persisted (910, 458, 463).

Charles II brought back to England the craze for cabinets. Styles are largely exemplified by cabinets after that; William and Mary highboys with their turned bases and marquetry top-sections; the Chinese lacquered cabinets of Queen Anne and Georgian times; the richly carved and gilded bases of late 17th century cabinets, and the important cabinets of Chippendale and the Georgian designers testify to their vitality.

Specialization in the 18th century led to so many types that they can scarcely be listed; the use is part of the name, as jewel-cabinet, sewing cabinet, etc. Cabinets were less imposing as they became smaller, so that today the usual implication is a box or case for a particular use. Many cabinets are built in, or so designed as to form part of the plan of the room, such as corner cupboards, recess cupboards, etc.

Small cabinet-stands appeared in the 18th century as accents in architectural decoration, and for the housing and display of collections of objets d'art, and curios. See *Buffet; Hutch; Chest; Desk; Highboy.*

CABINET STANDS. Decorative stands for cabinets, chests, etc., appeared as soon as life in Europe ceased to be nomadic. The handsome chests and later Oriental cabinets were mounted on elaborately carved and gilt frames. Planned for use against a wall, only the fronts were ornamented. There was often a rim to hold the cabinet in place. The shape either evolved into a side table form, or combined with the cabinet to form the highboy and the tall cabinet. 656.

CABINET WORK. The finer classification of interior woodwork and furniture, as distinguished from carpentry.

CABLE. Rope moulding.

CABLE FLUTING. Fluting whose lower ends are filled in with a convex moulding.

CABOCHON. Carved ornament resembling a gem or polished stone, common in French Rococo work and English derivatives.

130. WHITE AND GOLD PAINTED BOOKCASE FROM THE HOTEL DE GAULIN, DIJON, 1772. Style of Louis XVI. Now in the Metropolitan Museum of Art, New York.

While this Bookcase is not wholly detached from the wall panelling, its shape is essentially that of the Breakfront Type Bookcase which developed during this time.

131. ENGLISH BOOKCASE OF MAHOGANY. Middle 18th Century style of Chippendale.

Vernay

132. ENGLISH MID-18th CEN-
TURY PINE BOOKCASE.
Probably originally painted.
Gothic tracery.

Vernay

...GLISH, CA. 1780. Adam style, pine stained to imitate
...ogany.
Metropolitan Museum

134. ENGLISH, MIDDLE GEORGIAN. Mahogany.

Vernay

137. SHERATON STYLE. Satinwood, end of 18th Century.

136. STYLE OF CHIPPENDALE MAHOGANY BOOKCASE.

138. ENGLISH, HEPPLEWHITE STYLE.   *Vernay*

139. ENGLISH, CA. 1800.   *Colchester*

140. ENGLISH, STYLE OF HEPPLEWHITE.   *Vernay*

141. ENGLISH REGENCY, CA. 1824. Rosewood.   *Col*

2. ETAGERE, ENGLISH, Late 18th Century. *Vernay*

NGLISH, HEPPLEWHITE STYLE. *Vernay*

No. 688

146. FRENCH, ETAGERE, CA. 1790. Style of Louis XVI. Acajou, brass gallery.

143. ENGLISH REGENCY. *Vernay*
144. (Center) "RECESS CABINET." *Colchester*
145. ENGLISH, Late 18th Century. *Vernay*

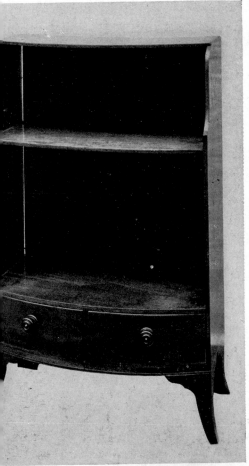

148. ITALIAN, EARLY 19th CENTURY. Glazed doors. *Lavezzo*

149. FRENCH, LATE LOUIS XVI OR DIRECTOIRE. Open Front Bookcase with excellent Ormolu inlays and mounts. *Symons*

150. GOTHIC, ENGLISH OR FLEMISH, about 1550. This type clearly indicates its origin in the chest set upon legs. *Charles of London*

151. OAK CABINET showing Renaissance details imposed upon the Gothic form. The medallion heads are called Romayne work. French or Flemish, Period of Francois I, 1515-1547. *Courtesy Anderson Galleries*

CABINETS AND CUPBOARDS

The Portable Chest form developed into every type of case for storage by the substitution for the lid of doors or drawers in a box-like case. No precise definition of classes is possible. Other types of cases, of similar ancestry are pictured in the sections called "Chests," "Highboys," "Lowboys" and "Sideboards."

COURT CUPBOARDS

One of the most important early developments of the chest was the Court Cupboard, a chest-serving table for dining accessories. Its highest form appeared in England, but parallel types appeared as the Credenza in Italy, the Credence in France, and other variations over Europe.

52. ELIZABETHAN OAK COURT CUPBOARD, CA. 1600. Inlaid with holly and yew, splay front; strapwork, gadrooning and bulbous supports are of the height of the style.
Charles of London

153. AMERICAN, OAK, MIDDLE 17th CENTURY. A simpler version of the Elizabethan type.
Metropolitan Museum

154. OAK SIDEBOARD, ENGLISH TUDOR, CA. 1600. This typ oped from the Court Cupboard rather than from the table omission of the enclosed section above. *Charles of*

The "Hutch" type of Cabinet evolved out of the early Credence or Court Cupboards. These examples illustrate the development of the completely enclosed Cabinet from the chest on legs.

155. AMERICAN COURT CUPBOARD, OAK, CA. 1650. Connecticut Valley, after English Lancashire types.
Metropolitan Museum

OAK COURT CUPBOARD, NEW ENGLAND, CA. 1660. Jacobean influence.
Metropolitan Museum

157. LATE ELIZABETHAN CABINET, canted sides and enclosed lower cupboard. The conventionalized carving of Tudor Rose.
Charles of London

158. (Left) ENGLISH OAK CUPBOARD. Da
1692. The simplified panelling and overhang
cornice show a later date than the preced
examples. The corner pendants are proba
vestiges of the corner columns formerly
ployed. *Stair &*

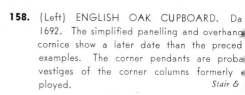

159. (Lower Left) TUDOR CABINET, Italian
fluence in inlay and guilloche carving.
Charles of Lon

160. (Below) LARGE JACOBEAN CABINET. Ca
ing shows French influence. *Charles of Lon*

161. ENGLISH OAK CABINET, very late 17th Century. Scratch carving and degenerate balusters indicate country origin. *Vernay*

162. NEW ENGLAND CUPBOARD, 1660-1680. Diamond point panel moldings and arches recall styles of Continental Europe as transmitted through England. See below. *Metropolitan Museum*

163. NEW ENGLAND CABINET, end of 17th Century. General form of English example above. *Metropolitan Museum*

164. LATE JACOBEAN CABINET. Strong influence of France and Italy appears in the strong geometric panel shapes and the arched perspective. *Charles of London*

165. GOTHIC OAK CABINET, LATE XV CENTURY FRENCH. Post-and-panel construction, with linenfold panel decoration. The carved astragal and wrought-iron lock and hinges are superior features.

Metropolitan Museum of Art

NSYLVANIA DUTCH PAINTED PINE CUPBOARD
s), end of 18th Century.

THIC DOLE CUPBOARD, 1510, French or Flemish,
nted red.   *Anderson Galleries*

167. FRENCH, 16th Century (Burgundian), from the Castle of
Ancy-Le-Franc.   *French & Co.*

169. DUTCH, 17th Century, Baroque. Rosewood and ebony.
Metropolitan Museum

170. FRENCH, PERIOD OF LOUIS XIII (1610-1643). Carved ebony, ivory, gilt bronze.
Metropolitan Museum

171. FRENCH, ABOUT 1650. Walnut, inlaid.   S:

173. ARMOIRE, FRENCH XVI CENTURY (Burgundian). School Hugues Sambin. Walnut.   *Metropolitan Mus*

172. FRENCH, ABOUT 1600.   *Ginsburg & Levy*

MERICAN, WALNUT, ABOUT 1745.
Metropolitan Museum

NGLISH, BLACK LACQUER WITH
HINESE DECORATION, 1725-1730.
Metropolitan Museum

176. CONNECTICUT, PINE, MID-18th CENTURY. *Metropolitan Museum*

CORNER CUPBOARDS

179. ROCOCO ITALIAN CABINET, MIDDLE 18th CENTURY. Gilt and painted.
French & Co.

178. FRENCH, EARLY 18th CENTURY (Regence). Armoire of oak. Carving typical of the transition period from Louis XIV to Louis XV.
Metropolitan Museum

177. BONNETIERE, FRANCE, END OF 18th CENTURY. Normandy type of traditional Louis XV design but with revolutionary symbols.
French & Co.

182. ENGLISH, ABOUT 1800. Satinwood. *Vernay*

181. MIDDLE 18th CENTURY ITALIAN ROCOCO CABINET, gilt and painted. *French & Co.*

180. ENGLISH, LATE 18th CENTURY, in the French manner. Satinwood, inlaid. *Symons*

183. PROVINCIAL FRENCH. Beech. *Ruseau*

ENCOIGNURES
SMALL CORNER CABINETS,
CHIEFLY 18th CENTURY.

184. AMERICAN, ABOUT 1790. S⸺
Sheraton. Mahogany.

186. PAINTED ITALIAN ROCOCO. *Lavezzo*

185. ITALIAN EMPIRE STYLE EARLY
19th CENTURY. *Lavezzo*

187. ENGLISH, MAHOGANY.

CABRIOLE. Furniture leg shaped in a double curve, the upper part swelling out, the curve swinging in toward the foot which again flares out. Its use in European furniture began late in the 17th century with the many efforts at varying the familiar turned and square legs. Baroque virtuosity sought new complexities for this member, having exhausted all manner of decorated and spiral turnings. First it added scroll forms to the feet; then double and reversed scrolls. In time the sharp break was smoothed out and the whole leg made into a sinuous line. Elaboration appeared at the knee, the top out-curve, and at the foot, while in the method of articulating the vertical leg to the horizontal apron came the development of flowing lines that distinguish the Rococo style.

The foregoing development is particularly exemplified in the Dutch, Flemish and English schools of the late 17th century, but illustrates only one phase of the general trend toward curvilinear forms. In France the transition from Baroque Louis XIV to Rococo Louis XV through the Regence is illustrated in the growing importance of the curved leg. Here the type evolved through the fancy of the animal foot —*pied-de-biche*—being carved from the square block in a slight curve ending in a carved animal's foot—doe, goat, ram, horse, etc. In time the curve became richer, the shoulder or knee (upper part) being more continuously joined to the curve of the horizontal structure. In later Rococo work the animal resemblance was abandoned and became an abstract sinuous line ending in a scroll.

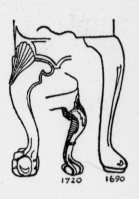

Another source of the cabriole form may be in the Far East, whence the Dutch navigators brought the dragon foot, clasping the jewel. This general form is heavily echoed in some work of the middle 17th century.

The name springs from the root "capra"—goat—through the Spanish "Cabriole," suggesting its resemblance to the bent leg of animals.

CABRIOLE DEVELOPMENT

In all styles in which it appears the excellence of the cabriole leg is an index of the quality of the whole design. A good flowing line which nevertheless retains an unbroken center line in conformance with the grain of the wood is more pleasing to the eye than an excessive curve which cuts the vertical quality. 49-53, 60, 234, 269 et seq., 398, 441, 519, 607 et seq., 697.

CACQUETEUSE. French chair with high narrow back and curved arms. Late 16th century. 205.

CAFFIERI, JACQUES (1678-1755), PHILIPPE (1714-1774). French bronze workers; made important metal decorations for furniture, period of Louis XV.

CAMBER. Hollowed or slightly convex surface, to correct the illusion of sagging in unsupported horizontal lines.

CAMEL BACK. Double curved chair back, shield shaped; characteristic Hepplewhite type.

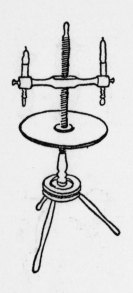

CAMEO. Raised carving, usually delicate, on stone or imitations of stone. Used as furniture ornaments by Sheraton, the Adams, and in the Empire style. 580.

CANAPE. Sofa or couch, originally curtained. 615, 623.

CANDLE BOARD. Small sliding shelf beneath a table top, used to hold a candlestick. Principally English 18th century. 474.

CANDLE SLIDE. Sliding shelf just over the desk section of secretaries, on which candlesticks were placed. 474.

CANDLE STAND. Small table, usually tripod, pedestal or with four legs, for candlestick or small objects. 1081 et seq.

CANE. Flexible rattan woven in open patterns for chair seats, backs, etc. First occurring in English furniture about the time of the Restoration, it was favored by furniture makers of the periods of Charles II, William and Mary, and Queen Anne; again during the revivals of the Chinese Taste in the late 18th century, and in the classic work of the Adams; also French furniture of the corresponding periods, particularly the Louis XV and Louis XVI styles. 121, 608.

CANNELLATED. Fluted. 149.

CANOPY. Covering or hood over bed or throne, suspended from wall or ceiling or carried on posts. Architecturally, an ornamental projection. See also *Tester*. 99-105.

CANT. Bevel or chamfer, as on an edge. 157.

CANTEEN. Small box or case, partitioned for cutlery or bottles.

CANTERBURY. In current use, a magazine rack; originally a portable stand with partitions for sheet music, etc., also used to carry supper tray, cutlery and plates. Named for the Bishop who first ordered such a piece.

CAPITAL. The head of a column or pilaster. The various orders of architecture are easily distinguished by their capitals. All types are used in furniture ornament. See *Orders*.

CAPPING. A turned or square ornament.

CAQUETEUSE, CAQUETOIRE. See *Cacqueteuse*.

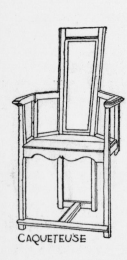

CAQUETEUSE

CARCASE, CARCASS. Body or framework of a piece of cabinet furniture.

CARD CUT. Lattice work ornament in low relief (not pierced) in the Chinese manner. Favored by Chippendale.

CARD TABLES. Appearing in the later 17th century, card tables reached their zenith in 18th century England. From Queen Anne through the Regency every style has fine examples. Leisure and a passion for gambling universal among the upper classes, made the card table an outstanding necessity. Card Tables were almost always made to fold. Earlier types featured scooped-out guinea holes. Finely ornamented cabriole legs are typical. The style spread to the continent, and fine types are found in late Italian work, especially in the Directoire style.

The fixed type or permanent Bridge table and the completely collapsible utilitarian table are the chief types today. 538, 581, 804, 1054 et seq.

CARLTON TABLE

CARLTON TABLE. English writing table, end of the 18th and early 19th century. In Sheraton's Drawing Book it appears as a "Lady's Drawing and Writing Table," with a bank of small drawers and compartments placed upon a table. The central part of the table top pulls out or is adjustable to an angle, and beneath this leaf are wide drawers for drawing paper. Usually mahogany or satinwood, with brass gallery. 1009, 1010.

CAROLEAN. Referring to the period of Charles II, King of England 1660-1685. See *England, Restoration*. 98, 264, 267.

CARTON-PIERRE. Composition substitute used to simulate wood carving, introduced by Robert Adam.

CARTONNIER (French). Ornamented box for holding papers.

CARTOUCHE. Ornamental feature in the form of an unrolled scroll or oval tablet with the edges curled or rolled over; originally a card partly unrolled or turned over at the corners, often emblazoned with arms, initials, etc., as a central decoration in architecture and furniture. Derived from Italian Renaissance architectural forms, it occurs extensively in Italian furniture after the 15th century, and similarly in French work from Francis I on. Chippendale employed cartouches extensively as the central motive on high cabinets.

17ᵀᴴ CENT. FRENCH
CARTOUCHE

CARVER CHAIR. Early American chair of turned wood parts, named after a chair owned by Governor Carver of Plymouth. Earlier models are ash, later of maple, usually with rush seats. 3, 223.

CARVING. Carving applied to furniture includes every type of relief from simple scratching, gouging and chipping, using conventional patterns largely in one plane, to full relief in plastic or sculptural form. Semi-savage decoration includes the carving of geometric spaces in flat relief. Relics of the most ancient civilizations show the application of this decorative technique to articles of everyday utility like stools, boxes, etc. Egyptian furniture was carved with religious symbols and representations of animals done with meticulous craftsmanship. There is every reason to believe that the Greeks, Assyrians, Romans and other ancients used plastic forms in wood furniture as well as in stone. Byzantine and Romanesque carving of the early Middle Ages show classic vestiges, together with the Near Eastern or Mohammedan influences which include sharp geometric forms in low relief. During this era the Far East enjoyed the labors of superlative craftsmen using highly conventionalized motives and methods. China, Japan and India exploited carving beyond most other arts; these were largely in wood and partake of the wood quality.

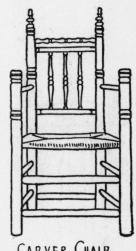

CARVER CHAIR

European Gothic wood carving is in the greatest tradition. Its style was perfected in oak and superbly adapted to the hard, brittle, coarse texture. Renaissance carving, largely in walnut, is finer and subtler, in the classic contrast of thin detail against smooth surface, but the drawing and architectural outline is uniformly firm. As the Renaissance waxed carving grew more bold, approaching the great plastic compositions with much free standing relief, by which Baroque art is distinguished. This robust high relief also typifies the Late Renaissance in France. In particular the Burgundian school of Hugues Sambin spread carving over everything, to the obliteration of architectural outlines.

In the north countries, the early Gothic tradition clung; indeed, Romanesque-Celtic influence in the form of complex convolutions persisted in cruder work while the Gothic and earlier Renaissance styles dominated the upper classes. Scandinavian, German, Celtic and even English carving of the 15th and early 16th centuries show such qualities. On them and their Gothic mixtures was imposed the classical Renaissance formula. England carved in oak for another century before accepting the walnut prevalent on the continent. The Renaissance forms of fruit and flowers, angels and instruments, carved throughout Europe, inspired Grinling Gibbons and a great art in England.

Eighteenth century carving throughout Europe follows the trend from free naturalism to stiff classic decoration. In England the Grinling Gibbons school, full formed and robust, persisted through the period of Chippendale influence, and some authorities establish 18th century chronology by types of carving; lion-mask, satyr-mask, etc. In continental carving the Baroque was lush, large and full. The Rococo tended toward lightness and grace, replacing mythological figures and large scale classic motives with rocks and shells, flowers, swags and ribbons in unclassical asymmetry, graceful and rambling. Much plastic or modelled decoration of this style was executed in bronze, cast and chased and overlaid upon fine wood veneers.

The classic revivals of the later 18th century miminized carved ornamentation. The Adams and the Louis XVI styles used the thin classical carvings of Herculaneum; scrolls and mythological figures, always attenuated, as were acanthus and water leaves and other formal band moldings. Paterae, medallions, swags, vases, etc., were contained within severe outlines, differing from the loosely composed Rococo compositions. The Empire style used carving more sparingly than any other, but later 19th century developments employed coarsened classic forms. Modern styles have almost completely eliminated carving on furniture. See *Ornament*. 95, 150, 173, 191, 401, 437, 927.

CARYATID

CARYATIDS. Greek architectural ornament in the form of female figures used as supporting columns. Male figures of the same character are called Atlantes. Adapted to form legs of tables, chairs, stands of cabinets, etc., and as pilasters for beds, cabinets, mantels, panelling, etc., they are found in the classic revivals and in all the more decorative architectural styles of furniture, as the later Italian Renaissance, Jacobean, Francis I, Louis XIV, Empire, etc. 652.

CASE. General term for any receptacle, cabinet or box, used for holding things. In cabinetwork *case* refers to the boxlike structure which forms the shell of a chest of drawers, cabinet, etc.

CASKET. Small box or chest, often of value and beauty, made of precious woods and metals; inlaid, carved, or painted, they were used to hold money, jewels, papers and other valuables. See *Chest, Coffer.*

CASSAPANCA. Italian settee formed by adding arms and back to a chest—literally "Cassone" plus "Banca." Chiefly middle Renaissance Florentine; prototype of English Box Settle, etc. 844.

CASSONE. Italian chest or box with painted, carved, or inlaid decoration. 370.

CASTELLATED. Architecturally, a regularly pierced cornice, from the parapets of fortified castles. The motive was copied in some Gothic furniture. 95.

CASTERS. Small rollers attached to the feet or base of a piece of furniture, for ease in moving around without lifting. Caster making was a distinct trade in England by the end of the 17th century. Early casters were of wood; later superseded by leather and brass, they are now principally made of rubber and synthetic materials. At the height of their use in the 18th and 19th centuries they were used as a definite part of the design. This commendable practice died in the 19th century, and even now for the most part casters are merely applied after the piece is completed, with the result that they often mar a good design. 1041.

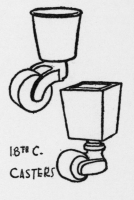

18TH C. CASTERS

CATHEDRAL SHAPE. Pointed arch in bookcase tracery, late 18th and 19th century Gothic revivals in England and America; also on the backs of some Sheraton chairs, and the shaping of the bases of some simple chests of drawers. 132.

CAUSEUSE. Upholstered armchair with open sides.

CAVETTO. Concave moulding usually found as the important member of a cornice. In English walnut furniture this was often veneered crosswise.

CAVETTO

CEDAR. The *Juniperus Virginiana* of N. America, and the *Cedrela odorata* of the West Indies are the fragrant red cedar familiarly used for protection against moths. It first appears in 18th century English furniture for drawer linings, boxes and travelling chests, which use is still current.

CEDAR CHESTS. The current American household chest for storage of woolens, etc., for protection against moths.

CELLARET. Deep drawer for bottles in a sideboard. Also a separate cabinet for liquors, glasses, etc. See *Wine Cooler.*

CELLULOID. Synthetic material used in furniture as a substitute for ivory in inlays, handles, etc.

CENTER DRAWER GUIDE. Wooden track under the center of a drawer as a guide for its operation when drawn. See *Construction.*

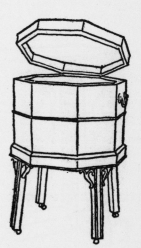

18TH CENT. ENGLISH CELLARETTE

CENTER TABLE. Round, oblong, oval, square, or any other shaped table finished on all sides so that it may be used in the center of a room for any purpose. 985 et seq.

CERTOSINA. Style of inlay employing bone or ivory on a dark wood ground. Usually small geometric patterns—stars, triangles, crescents, etc., suggesting Mohammedan origin. Appears in Venetian work in the 14th century; also in Spanish work of Moorish type, and subsequent derivations. 253, 457.

CHAIR. The chair, a single movable seat, is most ancient. Most familiar types were known in ancient Egypt, Greece and Rome; significantly the names for special types are ancient.

Egyptian remains indicate the use of chairs of wood as well as of ivory and metal. The folding or X-type is found in tombs; it was often carved with animal forms and covered with whole skins. Fixed four-legged chairs were significantly carved and painted, animal feet, as of the bull and lion, being common. Greek chairs, evidenced by sculptured reliefs were of gracefully curved form; the grand type was called *Thronos*. From Rome there are relics of light turned chairs of metal, wood and ivory elaborately wrought and cushioned with silk pillows. The X-chair had in Rome some significance of caste; it seems to have been reserved for magistrates and nobles on public occasions. The *Cathedra* was a chair with a back, used by women.

The early Middle Ages left little evidence of a common use of chairs; the curule type, developed as a folding form, persisted for the use of dignitaries. Later medieval chairs were entirely a prerogative of high estate; they travelled about with the lord and when set up were mounted on a dais and capped with a tester or canopy. A more permanent type of chair evolved in late Gothic times by the addition of a seat to the wall panelling—the wainscot chair which with a solid panel back is found as late as the 17th century in New England. Elsewhere the panel became posts, the whole structure lighter and more comfortably proportioned; but the connotation of caste remained.

In Italy the Renaissance brought forward (besides the development of the curule chair into Dantesca and Savanarola types) the simple chair structure of four posts with arms, less architectural than the wainscot or panelled chair, though scarcely more comfortable. Comfort came with the addition of upholstery, at first loose cushions, later attached pads with fine fabric or leather covering. The development of ornamentally carved members as slats and stretchers was rapid and significant. Lesser chairs were usually a narrow board or frame as back, added to a stool (sgabelle type); early domestic types of turned frameworks with rush seats were known. Spanish chairs followed the Italian in most respects; the rustic types of crude workmanship probably became common in the 17th century.

France produced the earliest comfortable chairs and the widest variety. The *chaire* always has had special significance. Under Francis I it begot scaled-down versions with modifications, always toward lightness, producing a simple armchair type at first called *chaires à femmes,* finally a simple portable framework dubbed *caquetoire:* gossip chairs. The *chaises à vertugadin,* like the farthingale chairs of England were made necessary by the women's extravagant skirts. Later the *fauteuil* developed, a comfortable chair with arms, utilizing the newly-invented upholstered seat. Louis XIV saw the development of magnificent, luxurious chairs, scaled from thrones to simple styles—and by 1700 most of the familiar forms had appeared: fauteuils, bergères, wing chairs, confessionals. During the Régence the lines became flowing, curved; stretchers disappeared. Chairs of the Louis XV period are delicate, exceedingly graceful, masterpieces of fluid line. About this time springs were invented, changing the upholstery principle.

In England the same progress followed the French example with local variations. Jacobean chairs were still basically Gothic and the Renaissance appeared slowly adding details from Italy, Spain, Flanders. Heavy oak was universal in square box construction through the Commonwealth, with little but sausage turnings to modify the angularity. With the Restoration came Baroque details, spiral turnings, boisterously carved stretchers and crestings; imposing but rarely comfortable. The X-chair fairly disappeared at this time, but the elementary overstuffed chair came soon after. The Dutch William and Mary established the cabriole leg and Queen Anne's style shows a wholly new type, Baroque in its wholesale curvature, yet distinctly English. Seat plan, back posts and front legs, splats and cresting were all curved yet the curvature was entirely different from the contemporary French chair. For some years the development of the English chair followed this decorated Queen Anne style. Chippendale developed pierced slats, new top-rail shapes and finally the square front-foot after Chinese lines in place of the ubiquitous claw-and-ball cabriole leg. Chippendale chairs are notably wider, lower, more comfortable.

The French influence again became dominant after 1750. Hepplewhite and others literally reproduced the exquisite Rococo shapes. Even the Classic Revival accepted the whole proportion and silhouette, substituting for the sinuous lines a set of sharply rectilinear shapes that we identify as Adam, Louis XVI, etc. This angularity invited new forms, and Sheraton and the other late 18th-century designers produced them without limit, borrowing, adapting, distorting every motive from classical times. Early 19th century chairs show clearly in their extreme variety the frenzied search for novelty. Probably the most significant type was the graceful chair form associated with Duncan Phyfe in Federal American work.

Of course chair forms were multiplied everywhere in Europe. The Sgabelle type appears in all provincial work, most ornate and uncomfortable in the excessively carved Swiss and German forms. The northern versions of Regence and Rococo bergères, etc. are almost new types in themselves. The old chairs of turned parts persisted in outlying districts into the 19th century, even the triangular type. The ladderback developed both into a crude rush-seated affair and into beautifully proportioned slat-backs, best of all in America. The exquisite straw-seated chairs of France also grew out of these turned post forms.

The Windsor chair, utilizing turnings and bent parts, developed in America into a triumph of lightness, comfort, strength and economy.

Nineteenth century chairs produced little except novelty of line, usually worse rather than better. The Morris chair was a contribution toward comfort, but alone was unable to bring popularity to that school.

Contemporary essays in chair design are groping toward new principles expressed in new materials. The bent-tubing chair of Marcel Breuer, probably the most radical step forward, is almost the only change in fundamental furniture forms. Aalto has utilized the same theme in bent plywood. It is probable that the question of seating will bring forth a typically 20th century collaboration of artist and engineer. 188-366.

CHAIR BED. 18th century English chair which could be extended to form a bed.

CHAIR TABLE. Chair with a hinged back which forms a table top when tipped up. 2.

CHAISE-LONGUE. A long chair; a form of sofa or day bed with upholstered back, for reclining. French 18th century types were often made in two or three parts; the two-part type consisting of a deep bergere and a large stool; the three-part style had two armchairs and a stool between. See *Restbeds, Daybeds*. 816 et seq.

CHAMBERS, SIR WILLIAM (1726-1796). English architect. After travelling in China he published in 1757 his "Designs of Chinese Buildings, Furniture, etc." strongly influential in developing the fad for Chinoiserie.

CHAMFER. Canted, splayed or beveled-off corner of a post or a moulding. 405.

CHANNEL. Groove or fluting cut into the surface as decorative accent; sometimes filled with reed shaped convex mould.

CHARLES I. King of England, 1625-1649. Furniture style classified as Early Jacobean. See *England*.

CHARLES II. King of England, 1660-1685. Furniture style referred to as Carolean, Restoration, Late Jacobean, Late Stuart. See *England, Carolean*.

CHASING. Ornamentation of metal by etching, engraving or incising. 149.

CHAUFFEUSE. Small French fireside chair with low seat. 590.

CHECKER, CHEQUER. Decorative use of alternately colored squares, as in a checkerboard. 373.

CHEESE BOX SEAT. Chair seat, usually rush, and round or bell shaped with thin rim of wood bent around the edge. American, early 19th Century. 347.

CHENILLE. A kind of velvety cord with short thread ends standing out, used in trimming and banding upholstered furniture. It is also used in rug weaving, and in fabrics for upholstery and drapery fabrics.

CHERRY. American wild cherry wood is a hard compact fine grained, red-brown wood, usually light. It is highly suitable for cabinet making, is beautiful and strong both for structural and decorative uses; it resists warping and takes a fine polish. It was favored by the colonists wherever it was found, and much old American furniture of cherry remains from the entire period of colonization as well as from the 19th century. The European cherry is similar but lighter in color; it appears in much country furniture and extensively in Biedermeier and similar 19th century styles.

CHERUB. Winged child figures used in decoration from the Renaissance and after, also called *Amorini*. In Italian and French work the whole figure is usual, but after Charles II the English carvers, as Grinling Gibbons, often used the winged head alone. 761.

CHERUB

CHESS BOARDS, TABLES. See *Game Tables*. 1057.

CHESTERFIELD. Overstuffed sofa or couch with upholstered ends.

CHESTNUT. Moderately soft grayish-brown wood with coarse open grain resembling oak, but lacking the large rays. Rather weak structurally, its principal use now is for veneer cores.

CHEST OF DRAWERS. Case fitted with drawers, for storage, usually of clothing.

The drawer chest or commode completely superseded the coffer-chest, by reason of its greater convenience, by the end of the 17th century. France and England led in the development of the drawer chest. Once the type was established it remained to the present as the favorite storage furniture; various styles have only changed the detail and ornamental aspects.

"Highboys," "tall-boys," "chest-on-chests" are one chest on top of another, or on a table-like base. Other chests are used as desks, dressing-tables, etc., by slight changes in profile or drawer-arrangements. 382 et seq.

CHEST-ON-CHEST. Chests of drawers in two sections, one placed upon the other. Surmounted by elaborate cornices or pediments they were often imposing pieces of furniture. They are chiefly English and American, 18th and 19th centuries. 512. 703-6.

CHESTS. Originally a large box with hinged lid, the *coffer* or chest is the primary form of all receptacle-furniture. In ancient Egypt and Rome they assumed artistic form, and developed variations for special purposes. In the Middle Ages, the instability of life made the portable chest the most vital piece of furniture. As conditions settled and life became more sedentary, chests became larger and produced the deviations recognized as chests of drawers, credences, cabinets, buffets and sideboards, bureaux, and all receptacle types; also traceable to it are bed forms, from the retainers' habit of sleeping on the chest; as well as several seating forms.

Early chests everywhere were small and sturdily constructed, often with iron bands (682). Gothic chests generally were larger and more ornately carved and painted (947, 367, 678). Renaissance chests were made with a clear architectural profile and classic ornament (909, 370, 713). In the same century the French Gothic chest began its evolution into *credence* (Cf 368 with 151 *archebanc-couchette* (588) etc. In the 16th century the Italian chest had begun to yield to the variety of credenza, sideboards, etc.; the influence in England produced court cupboards, and modification of the chest by means of drawers and door compartments, which gradually raised the total height and produced, finally, the chest of drawers (379-389). For special purposes the chest with hinged lid has survived, as the marriage or dower chest in Germanic communities, including the Pennsylvania Dutch (25); the blanket chest and ceremonial or decorative types (959).

CHEVAL GLASS. Large mirror, usually full figure length swinging from vertical posts mounted on trestles. Best examples occur in French and English work of the second half of the 18th century. A small form, often with a drawer between the posts is made to be placed upon chests or tables. 738 et seq.

CHEVAL SCREEN. Fire screen mounted upon two feet. 842, 843. See *Screens*.

CHEVRON. V-shaped design for inlay and other decoration.

CHIFFONIER (French). A tall narrow bureau or chest of drawers.

CHILDREN'S FURNITURE. Small scaled furniture for children, such as tables and chairs, are found in every style. Cradles and beds have always been made as distinct designs, rather than merely smaller models. This tendency is observed today in the design of most articles for children: that is, the child's needs are not merely those of a physically small adult, but are highly specialized. Modern Children's furniture comprising beds and cribs, tables, bookcases, chairs and chests are planned to facilitate learning, self-help, etc., and colors and decoration are less quaint, less fancifully pictorial or fairy tale than formerly.

CHIMAERA, CHIMERA. Mythical fire-breathing monster, used as a motive in ornament.

CHIMERA

CHIMNEY FURNITURE. The accessories of a fireplace: Andirons, Chimney Boards, Coal Bin or Scuttle, Fenders, Bellows, Fire Backs, Forks and Shovels, Hobgrates, Cranes, Trivets, Potbooks, and other utensils.

CHINA CABINET, CHINA CLOSET. Important cabinet, often with glass front and sides, for the storage and display of fine china. 42.

18TH CENT CHINESE

CHINESE. Chinese furniture, other than for ceremonial use, is rare, due to the scant requirements of Chinese living habits. Slight attention is paid to outline or plastic form; surface decoration is highly developed in the form of lacquering and decorative painting. Coffers and chest are perfectly simple in outline, often standing on low bases of bracket form and ornamented with intricate metal mounts. Tables and stands are low, and usually have turned-in scroll-like feet. Chairs are very rare; ceremonial types are square in plan and silhouette, with elaborate inlay or carving on flat surfaces. Beds are box-like enclosures. While some highly-polished teak and other wood is used, most Chinese furniture is lacquered and extensively decorated. Dragons, flowers, landscapes with figures, etc. are used with geometric borders. Some lacquer is carved.

Chinese furniture is interesting chiefly for its effect on Baroque and Rococo European styles.

CHINESE TABLE

CHINESE CHIPPENDALE. 18th century adaptation of Chinese motives to English furniture, chiefly after Chambers' drawings. Chippendale used these suggestions freely and the typically amalgamated style is now associated with his name. The simple rectilinear outlines have suggested their use in some phases of modern design. 286.

CHINESE FOOT. Bracket foot.

CHEST

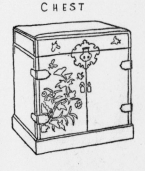

CHINESE TASTE. Europe became fantastically aware of the Far East in the 17th century, a result of the commercial exploitation following exploration and colonization. Dutch, English and French trading companies brought over silks and lacquers, paintings and utilitarian objects and their curious decoration stirred a mad craze for "Chinoiserie." In varying degree this lasted for almost two centuries. Rarely analysed or understood, it embraced designs from Persia, China, India, Japan without discrimination, mixing pagodas, monkeys, foliage, landscapes, mandarins and abstract designs with the greatest freedom. The result is often quite charming. It undoubtedly inspired a large part of Rococo design, although in the earlier Louis XIV work it had had great popularity. The English styles after William and Mary had constant recourse to the Chinese, and after the publication of Chambers' drawings the Chinese manner of Chippendale formed a definite style. The tendency toward the Chinese taste disappeared with the classic revivals. 31, 175, 664.

CHINESE CHIPPENDALE

CHINOISERIE (French). Referring to things Chinese; the Chinese taste or manner. 286, 462.

CHINTZ. Inexpensive thin cotton cloth, fast printed with designs of flowers, etc., in a number of colors and usually glazed. It is useful for minor draping and slip covers.

CHIP CARVING. Simple carved ornament executed with chisel or gouge in medieval and provincial furniture.

CHIPPENDALE, THOMAS (1718-1779). Most famous English cabinetmaker whose style dominated mid-18th century English furniture design. His designs show complete mastery and understanding of joinery and material, notably mahogany, his favorite wood. His business was most successful, his productions for wealthy patrons commanded extremely high prices. Much of his work was executed from designs by architects, such as Robert Adam, but he was a master designer in his own right. Indeed most of the style called Chippendale derives from his printed work rather than from the few authenticated pieces of furniture.

Chippendale published his book "The Gentleman and Cabinet-Maker's Director" in 1754. Other editions followed in 1759 and 1762. Europe had seen publications on design for two hundred years but never before one so specialized on furniture, so thorough a catalogue of the prevailing types and styles. Its influence spread everywhere; the continent and the colonies used it as a guide to style, design and construction. Hence the freedom with which so much furniture of this school is labelled Chippendale. Chippendale himself executed few of these designs. Most were in the late Baroque-Rococo manner, adaptations of Louis XV and Georgian shapes with bits of Chinese and Gothic detail.

As a designer Chippendale was open to every changing whim or influence. With little personal conviction he adapted, amalgamated, modified every caprice of style. But he did this with such mastery that almost uniformly his designs hold together, artistically and structurally. He added style and distinction to whatever he borrowed. His furniture is solid yet graceful; it looks and is firm, at no sacrifice of grace or refinement.

Chippendale's early work shows a refinement of the solid Georgian style, richly decorated and rather heavy, using a rich claw-and-ball foot, complex Rococo scrolls with the typical natural forms. He later borrowed freely from Chambers' Chinese designs and also took over literally the prevailing French shapes. Chairs of Chippendale design are most characteristic, particularly the types in which the solid splat is made lighter by being pierced into graceful openwork convolutions of ribbons and scrolls. Bookcases and cabinets are remarkably well-proportioned; sideboards and chests, cabinets, tables show the same mastery. 282 et seq., 406, 541 et seq.

Chippendale died in 1779. His son succeeded to the partnership with Thomas Haig which lasted until 1822. See *England*.

CHOP INLAY. Primitive form of inlaying by fitting pieces into the surface of solid boards.

CHURN MOULDING. Zigzag moulding occurring in Norman architecture.

CHURRIGUERESQUE. Spanish Baroque style, 17th century, so-called after the architect Churriguera. See *Spain*.

CINQUECENTO. Italian period 1500-1600. The High Renaissance. See *Italy*. 716 et seq.

CINQUEFOIL. Gothic foliated ornament of five points, used in some furniture of the Gothic revivals.

CIPRIANI, GIOVANNI, 1727-1785. Florentine artist who worked in England, painting the decoration of many houses and public buildings. His style inspired much of the painted decoration of furniture of the period.

CIRCASSIAN WALNUT. Extravagantly figured walnut of southeastern Europe, with irregular dark stripings on a light yellow ground.

CISELEUR (French). Engraver or maker of metal ornaments.

CLASSIC. The ancient styles of Greece and Rome, called Classic or Classic antiquity, were the inspiration of the Renaissance. The Middle Ages had descended so low in the scale of culture that the early Humanists, looking backward over twenty centuries saw in ancient history a Golden Age of art, literature, philosophy and government. The antique, often confused and misunderstood, inspired all the arts; Classicism alone was beautiful. The Romanesque and Gothic of the past six centuries were regarded as crude, barbaric. The ancient ruins were excavated and studied for the secrets of classic beauty. Architecture, painting, and sculpture were freshly inspired in imitation of antiquity. Furniture followed; the shapes and ornaments were taken directly from ancient architecture since no furniture remained from of old. This mistaken use of architectural details identifies Renaissance furniture, and all subsequent styles in which architectural sources are so used are called *classic revivals*. Such are the great periods of the late 18th and early 19th centuries. The classic style of Louis XVI was principally derived from the archeological studies of Herculaneum and Pompeii. This inspired the style of the Brothers Adam in England, and it became the fashionable gentleman's duty to extend the researches into antiquity. Italy and the Mediterranean islands, Northern Africa and Greece were dug over for ruins. These inspired the publication of splendid folios, which in turn became source books for furniture designers. After the Adam and the Louis XVI styles came Hepplewhite, Sheraton and the Directory, animated by the Greco-Roman discoveries. About the turn of the 19th century the research into antiquity was extended to Egypt and Greece. These inspired the Empire style and its many offshoots—Regency, Biedermeier and the local Empire versions of Italy, Spain, Sweden, Russia, and America. See *Adam, England, France, Italy; Orders; Ornament*.

CLASSICISM

CLAVICHORD. Early keyboard musical instrument, the forerunner of the modern piano.

CLAW-AND-BALL. Foot carved in the form of a bird's foot gripping a ball. Its earliest form in Chinese bronzes shows a dragon claw holding a jewel; the cabriole leg terminating in the ball and claw was a favorite motive in Chippendale's earlier work, but it ceased to be fashionable after 1765. 277, 701, 978.

CLEAT. Strip of wood fastened to a flat surface to brace or strengthen, or to prevent warping.

CLOCKS, CLOCK CASES. Wood cases appeared late in the 17th century, earlier clocks being encased in brass or metal. The tall clock, now called 'grandfather's' was a development of the Louis XIV style where it attained great magnificence. Carolean English oak cases remain from about 1680; walnut soon took the lead and in the Queen Anne style the Chinoiserie lacquered cabinet is common. Clock cases in England tended toward narrowness and smaller size; on the Continent clocks in Rococo style had bombé cases, often monumental in size and heavily ornamented. 515, 518, 539, 606. Decoratively carved and painted clock cases are found in most peasant styles, German, French, and Swiss styles being most familiar. 667.

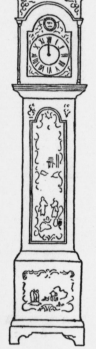

Wooden clock cases flourished in America. Fine mahogany tall cases were made in Boston about 1725 by Bagnell. The Willards helped New England maintain leadership in clock production for most of the 18th century. About 1800 Simon Willard designed the banjo clock. Shelf clocks of Sheraton character were made by Eli Terry. These types were developed by Seth Thomas and other New Englanders to the extent that clock-making was a major industry with many makers known for decorative cases. 47, 67, 82, 90.

CLOTHES PRESS. Wardrobe: cabinet for storing clothes, with or without drawers.

CLOTH-OF-ESTATE. Medieval decorative cloth draped over the throne or chair of persons of exalted rank.

CLOVEN FOOT. Table- or chair-leg ending in the form of an animal's cleft foot, English and Continental work, chiefly 18th century.

CLUB FOOT. Stubby foot of a furniture leg resembling the head of a club, the leg swelling out to a knot with a thick flat base; 18th century.

CLUSTERED COLUMNS. Three or more small wooden columns clustered together to form a single support used as bedposts, table legs, chair legs, etc., in 18th century work, particularly by Chippendale and Ince in their work showing Gothic influence. 288.

COASTER. English tray fitted with small rollers, used for circulating food and bottles on a dining table, 18th century. They took many fanciful forms, such as cannon or kegs, but the later ones were simple cylindrical shapes handsomely chased or engraved.

CLUSTERED

CLOVEN FOOT

COCKBEAD, COCKED BEADING. Small half-round projecting moulding applied to the edges of drawers. First appears in English work after 1730, and American work somewhat later. Sheraton and many French designers sometimes used strips of brass for this purpose. 412.

COCKLE SHELL. See *Shell Motive*.

COCK'S HEAD HINGE. Hinges with the leaves cut to resemble the shape of a cock's head. They occur in wide variety in English cabinets of the 16th, 17th and 18th centuries, in both brass and iron. See *Hardware*.

COCOBOLO. Dark purple-brown wood from Bengal and Burma, very dense and heavy.

COFFEE TABLE. Low, wide table now used before a sofa or couch. There is no historical precedent, but the shape permits the adaptation of low tables or bench forms of every style.

COFFER. Chest which served as seat, table, trunk or for storage of valuables; one of the earliest forms of furniture in Europe, when the unsettled conditions made it imperative that furniture and contents be readily transported together. 368, 492, 503, 588, 909.

COFFERED PANEL. Deeply sunk panel.

COIN. 18th century English corner cupboard. The French word for corner, corrupted in England to signify its furnishing. See *Encoignure*.

COLLAR. Horizontal moulding on a leg.

COLLARED TOE. Foot with a wide band.

COLONIAL. American period from the earliest settlements to the Revolution. Improperly applied to most American furniture up to 1850. See *America*.

Other Colonial types developed from current styles in the mother countries wherever explorers and colonists extended the spheres of England, France, Spain, Germany, Holland and Scandinavia. For example, South Africa has a distinct English style; the Spanish roots in South and Central America produced a brilliant provincial Churrigueresque.

COLONNETTE. Miniature columns used ornamentally on furniture. 170.

COLUMN. In architecture, a pillar or post, usually round and associated with pedestal, base, capital and entablature to form an 'order' or conventional style. (See *Orders*.) Its use in furniture consists of the ornamental treatment to simulate an accepted style of a pedestal or supporting member, or as a purely ornamental feature applied to a case or similar structure to suggest support.

COMB BACK. Windsor chair back in which several spindles extend above the main back, resembling an old fashioned high comb. American, 18th century. 236 et seq.

COMB-BACK

COMMODE. The commode is a loosely defined type of chest or cabinet, usually low and used against a wall as a receptacle, bureau, chest, console, etc. It may have doors or drawers, on the Continent the word applying generally to the English chest or chest of drawers. It evolved out of the earliest coffers or chests, mounted on legs, but the name only appears about 1708, connected with a Régence type by Bérain. The development was rapid in the early 18th century, becoming a favorite ornament for drawing rooms. Some references mention them as "Tables with deep drawers," but the more common type, the *"commode en tombeau"* describes Boulle's sarcophagus-like idea. The English borrowed the idea; early Georgian commodes, especially by Kent, were lavishly decorated but lacked the unity of the French designs. Chippendale produced many fine designs and probably was the first to plan the commode for the bedroom and clothing storage. Bombé and other shapes were common; Chinese motives were favored and no resource of cabinetmaking and decoration was overlooked. German console-commodes were elaborately carved and metal-trimmed.

The Classic revival brought to the commode a consistent architectural form, pilasters or colonnettes forming the corners. In the Empire style this was exaggerated, the actual casework being subordinated to the architectural frame. 398 et seq., 554, 607, 614, 621, 638, 668, 949.

COMMODE, BEDROOM. Enclosed "chamber boxes" or "close stools" of the 17th and 18th centuries were developed into decorative pieces of furniture, later being combined with wash stands. The term "night stand" was applied to them after Chippendale.

COMMONWEALTH. Puritan or Cromwellian Period in English History, 1649-1660. Severe austere forms replaced the ornate Stuart styles. See *Cromwellian, England*.

COMPO, COMPOSITION (Carton-Pierre). Moulded substitute for wood carving. Whiting, resin, and size are kneaded and moulded in carved shapes, which are then attached to wood furniture for decoration. 953.

COMPOSITE. Architectural order of columns combining the Corinthian and Ionic Capitals. See *Orders*.

CONCERTINA MOVEMENT. Type of folding mechanism used for card tables, in which the back half of the frame (under the extended top leaf) is hinged to fold in upon itself.

CONFESSIONAL. Large, high, upholstered easy chair with wings. French, 18th century.

CONFIDENTE. Sofa or settee with separate seats at each end.

CONFIDENTE

CONNECTICUT CHEST. New England chest, 17th or 18th centuries, ornamented by three carved panels and split spindles. They were extensively used throughout the northern colonies as dower chests and for storage generally, and many fine examples remain. Sunflower

188.

190.

191.

192.

CHAIRS

The furniture outlines of classical antiquity reappear in spontaneous revivals, such as the Renaissance and the Empire style of the early Nineteenth Century.

188. (Top, Center) GREEK TOMBSTONE, showing Chair, 5th Century B.C.

189. (Top, Left) EGYPTIAN, 2nd Century B.C.

190. (Top, Right) EGYPTIAN, 2nd Century B.C.

191. (Left) ROMAN, STONE, 1st Century A.D.

192. (Right) ROMAN, STONE, 2nd Century A.D.

Lower Row, Left to Right:

193. FRENCH EMPIRE, 1815.   *Ruseau*

194. ITALIAN EMPIRE, C. 1820.

        Metropolitan Museum

195. ITALIAN EMPIRE, C. 1830.   *Lavezzo*

194.

195.

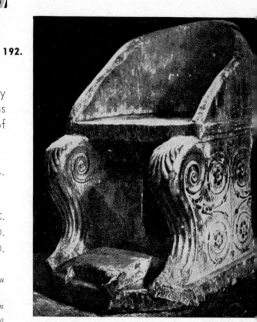

196. ENGLISH, C. 1550. Wall Cupboard with seat and arms attached.
Charles of London

197. ITALIAN, C. 1550. Walnut Choir Stall showing typical box form.
French & Co.

Lower Row, Left to Right:

198. SPANISH GOTHIC, C. 1470. Church Stall. *French & Co.*

199. ENGLISH, STUART. Late 17th Century but still shows solid back panel. *Vernay*

200. ENGLISH JACOBEAN, C. 1620. Inlaid oak, mixture of Gothic, Italian and French motives. *Stair & Co.*

201. FRENCH, HENRI II, WALNUT (1547-1559). Complete simplification of framework. *French & Co.*

Upper Left:

202. AMERICAN WAINSCOT CHAIR, C. 1650. The Jacobean style, a mixture of many Continental details, came to New England with the Puritans. *Metropolitan Museum*

SOME TYPES OF CHAIRS GREW OUT OF WALL PANELLING AND BECAME KNOWN AS WAINSCOT CHAIRS

OMANESQUE FORM, NORWAY,
owing origin in box form. Typical
edieval Scandinavian carving.

204. ITALIAN GOTHIC, 1450-1500. Piedmont,
Church of San Orso, Val D'Aosta.
Metropolitan Museum

205. (Right) FRENCH 16th CENTURY "CAQUE-
TEUSE." *French & Co.*

Lower Row; Left to Right:
206. ITALIAN, LATE 16th CENTURY. Venice or Brescia. *Metropolitan Museum*

207. ENGLISH, 17th CENTURY. Compare with 199 and 206. *French & Co.*

208. ENGLISH. C. 1630. Yorkshire Oak Side Chairs, showing influence of Italian
209. and Flemish motives on established Tudor shapes. *Stair & Co.*

THE SIMPLIFICATION OF THE EARLIER
BOX-LIKE STRUCTURE PRODUCED A
VARIETY OF LIGHTER SIDE CHAIRS

210. SICILIAN, 16th CENTURY. Embossed gold or red velvet. *Olivotti*

LOWER ROW:

211. ITALIAN, 16th CENTURY, high-back armchair gilt finials. Red velvet.

212. ITALIAN, 16th CENTURY, carved walnut Red velvet with gold embroidery.

213. ITALIAN, 16th CENTURY. Walnut. Leather with rows of brass-headed nails.

214. SPANISH, EARLY 17th CENTURY. Walnut, tooled leather back. Seat merely a leather strip nailed at sides.

All Photographs from French & Co.

DEVELOPMENT OF THE UPHOLSTERED CHAIR

The simplified framework was made more comfortable with attached cushions, after a period of using loose cushions on the hard seats. Fabrics, leather and needlework replaced carving as embellishment.

211.   **212.**   **213.**   **214.**

EMISH, 17th CENTURY. Oak.

French & Co.

216. FRENCH, 16th CENTURY. Walnut. Leather with brass nails. Compare with 213.

French & Co.

17th CENTURY CHAIRS WERE NO LONGER THRONES. SIMPLER,
LIGHTER, MORE COMFORTABLE, THEY LOST THEIR LORDLY SYMBOLISM.

ALIAN, LATE 17th CEN-
RY. Walnut.
Metropolitan Museum

218. FLEMISH, 17th CENTURY.
Early Baroque spiral turnings.

219. FRENCH, HENRY II. Walnut, needlework cover. *French & Co.*

220. SPANISH, 17th CENTURY.
Walnut and red velvet.
French & Co.

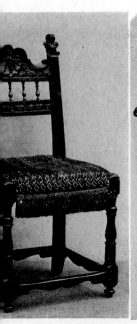

CHAIRS MADE OF TURNED PARTS

Turning or throwing was known from ancient times. Common types of chair
assembled from turned members and known examples date from the 13th C

221. AMERICAN, JACOBEAN INSPIRATION, C. 1630. Such Chairs were made in
Europe in the 13th Century. *Metropolitan*

222. GERMANY. Probably 14th Century.

223. AMERICAN, 17th Century. SPL
SEAT.

224. SWEDISH. Early 18th Century

225. ENGLISH, COUNTRY TYPE. C.
RUSH SEAT. Eccentric turning
forms cabriole type leg.

226. (Lower Left)—ENGLISH. CROMWELLIAN STYLE. *French & Co.*

227. (Center Left)—AMERICAN, C. 1730. Highly-developed style with turned baluster
halved to form smooth back. *Wei*

TS REPLACING TURNED PARTS FORM LADDERBACKS

These were more comfortable and less monotonous in design.

228. FRENCH, Late 18th Century. Provincial type with some Louis XVI characteristics, although stretcher is survival from 17th Century.
Ruseau

229. SPAIN, 18th Century. Late Baroque, painted.

230. FRANCE, NORMANDY, 17th Century, Flemish influence.

MERICAN, RUSH SEAT, C. 1700. acobean turning.
Weil

232. SLAT BACK COURTING CHAIR, DEERFIELD, MASS. Maple, Early 18th Century.
Anderson Galleries

(Lower Right) ENGLISH LADDERBACK, COUNTRY STYLE, end of 18th Century.
Stair & Co.

(Center Right) AMERICAN, NORTHERN NEW ENGLAND, Early 18th Century. Late Stuart form in slats.
Metropolitan Museum

Top Row, Left to Right:
236. CHILD'S COMB-
BACK, 1750-1790.
Ash, Oak and Pine.
Metropolitan
237. ROCKER, Bamboo
Turnings. C. 1800.
Weil

238. WRITING - ARM
AND DRAWER UN-
DER SEAT. C. 1775.
Weil

239. ENGLISH (
BACK, C.
Cabriole Le
Seat.

WINDSOR CHAIRS

Developed from the chair made of turned parts, co
mon throughout Europe. The continuous back post ga
way to a bow or similarly framed section; great
development in America.

235. COMB-BACK, Prop-
erty of Yale College.
Weil

Lower Row, Left to Right:
240. BRACED-BACK,
Pennsylvania. *Weil*

241. YOKE CREST, New
England.
Anderson Galleries

242. BAMBOO TURN-
ING, C. 1800.
Weil

243. ENGLISH, C. 181
Stair & C

244.
245. ENGLISH WINDSORS, C. 1790. *Stair & Co.*

246. ELABORATE ENGLISH WINDSOR, end of 18th Century, Gothic detail.

247. (Top, Right) CONTINUOUS BACK AND ARMS, NEW ENGLAND, C. 1770. *Weil*

248. (Right) EXCELLENT AMERICAN WINDSOR. *Ginsburg & Levy*

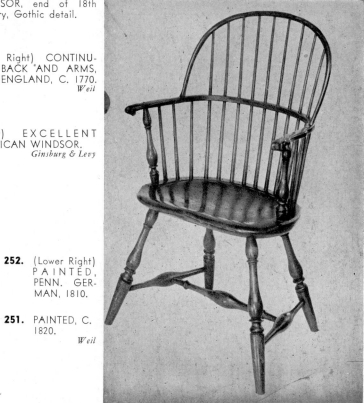

The Bow Back of Bent Ash, Maple or Hickory Is the Feature of the Most Distinctive Windsor Type

252. (Lower Right) PAINTED, PENN. GERMAN, 1810.

251. PAINTED, C. 1820. *Weil*

...TING WINDSOR. This may ...have had a tall back. *Weil*

250. STRETCHER UNUSUAL IN AMERICAN CHAIRS. *Weil*

255. DANTE CHAIR, ITALY, 16th Century.   *Olivotti*

254. FRENCH, 16th Century, DANTE
CHAIR, walnut.
          French & Co.

253. (Top) SAVONAROLA CHAIR,
CERTOSINA INLAY, LOMBARDY,
late 15th Century.
          Metropolitan Museum

FOLDING CHAIRS

Date from ancient times. They were extensively used in the Renaissance Period
throughout Europe.

257. ENGLISH, C. 1600. GL
BURY FOLDING CHAIR.
          Metropolitan

258. ITALIAN, 1490. Wal-
nut. Strozzi Pal. Flor-
ence.

259. ITALIAN, 16th Century,
hinged box seat.

260. ENGLISH, C. 1790. Mahogany.
          Stair

261-262.
17th CENTURY
FRENCH CHAIRS.
          Symons

256. (Top) ITALIAN, 15th
BEECH FOLDING CHAIR.
          Fren

LEMISH, 17th Century.   *Symons*

264. ENGLAND, Restoration, C. 1685.
Charles of London

265. AMERICAN, C. 1700. Spanish Foot.   *Weil*

BAROQUE EXAGGERATION INFLUENCED ALL DESIGN OF THE LATTER 17th CENTURY

ENCH OR FLEMISH, C. 1680.
alnut.   *Symons*

267. ENGLISH, C. 1680. Beechwood.
Metropolitan Museum

268. AMERICAN, Flemish Influence. C. 1700.
Sycamore.   *Weil*

270. ENGLISH, C. 1700. Figured walnut, arched stretcher .
Symons

271. AMERICAN, C. 1710. Maple feet, solid splat and curved cr
Metropolitan

LATER BAROQUE INFLUENCE

was extravagant in shape and ornamentation and became the familiar style most commonly identified as "Queen Anne.

269. (Left) AMERICAN, C. 1710. Walnut cabriole leg with Spanish foot. Shell knee and cresting.
Weil

272. ENGLISH, CANED BACK.
Symons

273. ROUNDABOUT CHAIR, ELM, QUEEN ANNE, C. 1700.
Vernay

274. NEW ENGLAND, C. 1725. Walnut.
Metropolitan Museum

275. ENGLISH, C. 1710. Compare with 269.

RENCH, PERIOD OF LOUIS XV. Beech
de Chair by Jacques-Marin Courtois.
Metropolitan Museum

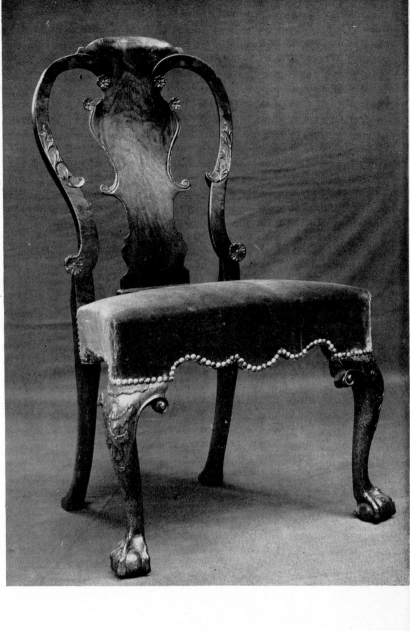

277. ENGLISH, C. 1715 (Early George I).
Burl walnut, hoop back, claw-and-ball foot.
Apron was probably exposed originally.
Vernay

ALIAN TYPE, Mid-18th Cen-
y.   *Ruseau*

279. SWEDISH, DUTCH INFLUENCE.
Early 18th Century.

280. ITALIAN, PAINTED, STYLE OF
LOUIS XV.   *Olivotti*

281. GERMAN, 1725-1750. Walnut, Rococo.
Metropolitan Museum

THE SCHOOL OF CHIPPE

The culmination of the Baroque
England.

Top Row, Left to Right:

282. AMERICAN, GOTHIC MANNER,

283. ENGLISH, GOTHIC, C. 1755.

284. ITALIAN, LATE 18th CENTURY.

285. AMERICAN, LADDERBACK, C. 1

Center:

286. ENGLISH, CHINESE TASTE, G1
1765.   *Metropolit*

287. ENGLISH, ELABORATE RIBBONB/
of Manwaring.

Lower Row, Left to Right:

288. ENGLISH, CHINESE TASTE, CL
LEG, 1750-1770.   *Metropolit*

289. AMERICAN, GOTHIC TASTE.

290. ENGLISH, WOOD SEAT.

291. ENGLISH, PIERCED LADDERB/
1770.

dale was influenced
in turn influenced the
tyles of many lands.

Left to Right (Claw and
:

LADELPHIA, DUTCH UN-
RBRACING, Gothic splat,
1760.   *Weil*

LADELPHIA, HEIGHT OF
'LE, 1770-1780.
              Metropolitan Museum

ORNER CHAIR, C. 1780.
                          Weil

eft to Right:
    Both Metropolitan Museum

LADELPHIA, 1770-80.

W YORK, 1770.

w:

ERICAN, MAPLE, 1760-75.
ple bracket.   *Weil*

ERICAN, PIERCED
RETCHER, RIBBON BACK.
                          Weil

GLISH, COUNTRY TYPE.
                    Symons

GLISH, GOTHIC MAN-
R, C. 1755.   *Vernay*

Left:

302. FRENCH, LATE LOUIS XIV. Walnut frame, tap
try cover.   *Metropolitan Museum of*

Below, Left to Right:

303. ENGLISH, CHARLES II, C. 1675. Walnut.
                    Metropolitan Muse

304. FLEMISH OR ENGLISH, C. 1670.   *Syme*

305. ENGLISH, CHIPPENDALE STYLE, C. 1750. M
hogany.   *Vern*

GLISH, C. 1740. Chippendale's French manner.   *Vernay*

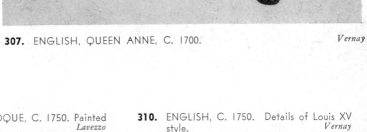

307. ENGLISH, QUEEN ANNE, C. 1700.   *Vernay*

THE BERGÈRE TYPE
developed along lower and deeper lines.

8. FRENCH, LOUIS XV, C. 1750. Carved and gilded frame.   *Metropolitan Museum*

309. VENETIAN, BAROQUE, C. 1750. Painted frame.   *Lavezzo*

310. ENGLISH, C. 1750. Details of Louis XV style.   *Vernay*

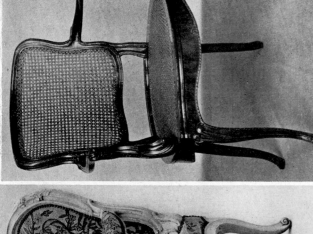

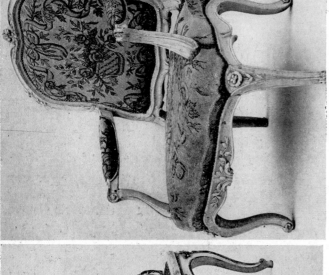

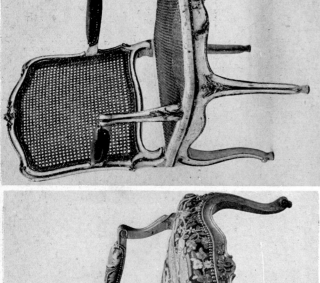

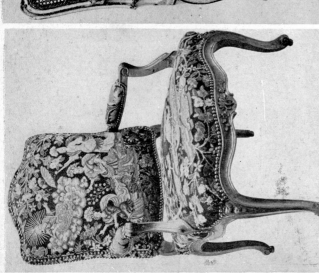

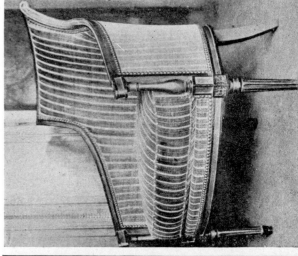

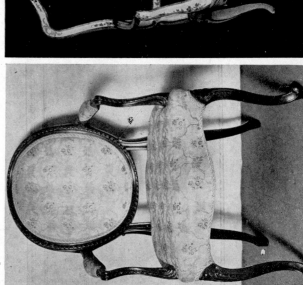

311. ENGLISH, CHAIR OF PURE LOUIS XV OUTLINES, C. 1775. *Vernay*

312. FRENCH, MADE BY CLAUDE SENE (Period of Louis XV). *Metropolitan Museum*

313. FRENCH, LOUIS XV. Made by Nicolas Heurtant. *Metropolitan Museum*

314. ENGLISH, SCHOOL OF HEPPLEWHITE, French influence. *Vernay*

THE ELEGANCE OF EUROPEAN LIFE IN THE LATER 18th CENTURY

LIGHT, GRACEFUL, COMFORTABLE CHAIRS EXPRESS THE

315. ENGLISH, LATE LOUIS XV INFLUENCE ON HEPPLEWHITE STYLE. *Vernay*

316. ITALIAN, MANNER OF LOUIS XV. *Lavezzo*

317. FRENCH BERGERE, END 18th CENTURY. *Ruseau*

318. ITALIAN, ADAPTATION OF LOUIS XVI FORM. *Lavezzo*

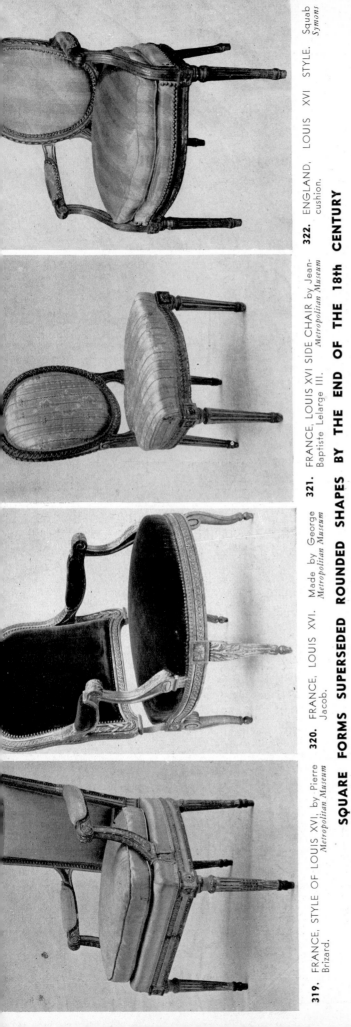

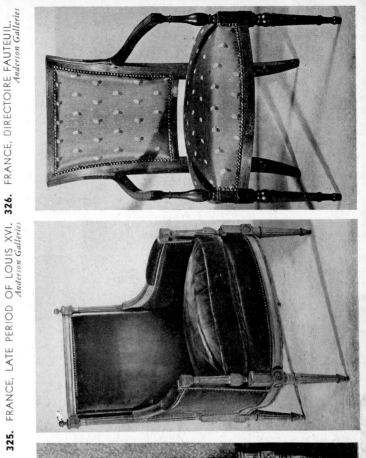

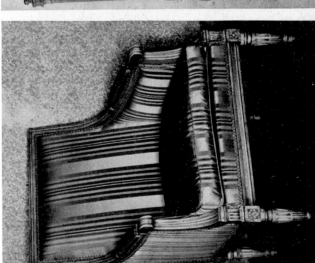

319. FRANCE, STYLE OF LOUIS XVI, by Pierre Brizard. *Metropolitan Museum*

320. FRANCE, LOUIS XVI. Made by George Jacob. *Metropolitan Museum*

321. FRANCE, LOUIS XVI SIDE CHAIR by Jean-Baptiste Lelarge III. *Metropolitan Museum*

322. ENGLAND, LOUIS XVI STYLE. Squab cushion. *Symons*

SQUARE FORMS SUPERSEDED ROUNDED SHAPES BY THE END OF THE 18th CENTURY

323. FRANCE, MARQUISE, PAINTED FRAME DIRECTOIRE. *Anderson Galleries*

324. ITALY, BERGÈRE OF LOUIS XVI STYLE. *Cavallo*

325. FRANCE, LATE PERIOD OF LOUIS XVI. *Anderson Galleries*

326. FRANCE, DIRECTOIRE FAUTEUIL. *Anderson Galleries*

328. ENGLISH, C. 1780. *Colchester*

329. AMERICAN, ROUNDABOUT CHA
C. 1785. *Metropolitan Muse*

327. ENGLISH, C. 1785. Shield back of Good
type. *Vernay*

HEPPLEWHITE

HEPPLEWHITE, SHERATON, SHEARER, ADAM, ETC., WORKED TOWARD
THE LIGHTER, MORE ELEGANT FORMS REPRESENTING THE ULTIMATE
REFINEMENT OF THE STYLE OF LOUIS XVI: IN THESE STYLES THE
BAROQUE-ROCOCO CHARACTERISTICS ARE GRADUALLY SUPER-
SEDED BY THE STRAIGHT LINES OF THE REVIVED CLASSICISM.

330. ENGLISH, BALLOON BACK. *Vernay*

331. ENGLISH, HOOP BACK. Early modification of Chippendale type. *Colchester*

332. EARLY TYPE OF DIVIDED SPLAT.

ERICAN, INFLUENCE OF
ERATON. *Weil*

334. ENGLISH, PAINTED CHAIR OF
LATE SHERATON TYPE.
Metropolitan Museum

SHERATON

AMPLES OF SHERATON'S DESIGNS ARE NOT
SCRIBED WITH CERTAINTY. THEY ARE CALLED
HERATON'S STYLE BECAUSE OF SIMILARITY TO
SIGNS IN HIS BOOKS OR TO PIECES OF
KNOWN AUTHORSHIP.

335. ENGLISH, C. 1795. Sheraton style with Louis
XVI detail. *Metropolitan Museum of Art*

GLISH, details of feather ornament
stretcher are of Hepplewhite types,
whole form is Sheraton. *Vernay*

337. AMERICAN, SHERATON INFLU-
ENCE, C. 1810. *Metropolitan Museum*

338. CLASSICAL DETAIL OF ADAMS STYLE.
Vernay

EARLY NINETEENTH CENTURY

Infinite variety of form and detail characterized the increasing use of furniture. The original classic influence was modified and adapted so freely as to be unrecognizable.

339. (Top Left) ENGLISH, C. 1800. Painted Gothic Revival back.
Anderson Galleries

340. (Top Right) ENGLISH, C. 1810. Late influence of Sheraton

341. ENGLISH, SHERATON. *Vernay*

342. ENGLISH, SHERATON, PAINTED, 1810.

343. ITALIAN. *Cavallo*

344. ITALIAN, DIRECTOIRE.

345. ENGLISH, 1818. *Colchester*

346. AMERICAN, SHERATON INFLUENCE. *Weil*

347. AMERICAN, 1825, SHERATON INFLUENCE.

348. AMERICAN, C. 18 *Ginsbur*

CLASSIC AND ECLECTIC

The classic sources inspired fine work of the first years of the 19th Century. These were exhausted early and designers then borrowed details from all schools. The essential structural feeling of the chair remains fairly uniform and characteristic.

349. (Top Left) DUNCAN PHYFE, C. 1810. Excellent example of lyre back and animal foot.
Metropolitan Museum

350. (Top Right) AMERICAN EM-PIRE, C. 1820. Horn-of-Plenty back. *Ginsburg & Levy*

NGLISH, SHERATON. *Anderson*

352. ITALIAN, EMPIRE. *Buttfield*

353. ITALIAN, DIRECTOIRE. *Lavezzo*

354. ITALIAN, EARLY 19th Century. *Angelo Romano*

ENCH, PROVINCIAL RECTOIRE.

356. ITALIAN, DIRECTOIRE. *Cavallo*

357. FRENCH, EMPIRE, C. 1815. *French & Co.*

358. MODERN SWEDISH, by Carl Malmsten. *Metropolitan Museum*

UPHOLSTERED CHAIRS

of the 19th Century show great inventiveness in modifying the classic sources into comfortable shapes.

359. HEPPLEWHITE TUB CHAIR, C. 1790. *Vernay*

362. ENGLISH, C. 1830.

360. ENGLISH, C. 1790.

363. ITALIAN, EMPIRE.

361. ENGLISH, C. 1830.

364. SPANISH, LATE 18th CENTURY. *Olivotti*

365. ITALIAN, EMPIRE. *Lavezzo*

366. AMERICAN, VICTORIAN, C

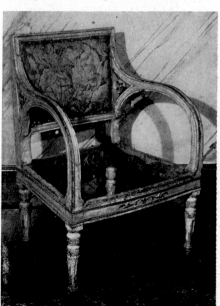

CHESTS

der various forms and names the Chest
 the all important article of furniture in
 Middle Ages. Its versatility in use
y have suggested many other types of
niture: Benches, Cabinets, Chests, Buf-
, Sideboards, etc., which evolved when
 became less nomadic.

367. FRENCH GOTHIC OAK.

Anderson Galleries

LISH OAK COFFER,
 years of Henry VIII.
ayne Medallions show
aissance influence.
ction Sir George
ldson, Bart. Hove,
x. *Anderson Galleries*

369. SWEDISH, 18th Century. Pine with wrought iron fittings.

ITALIAN CASSONE OR
MARRIAGE CHEST. Early
Renaissance, from the
Strozzi Palace, Florence.
Metropolitan Museum of Art

371. ITALIAN (Florence), 16th Century.   *Metropolitan Museum*

372. ITALIAN (Venice), 16th Century.   *Metropolitan*

373. ENGLISH, late 16th Century.   *Charles of London*

374. ENGLISH, OAK, 16th Century.   *Charles of*

375. AMERICAN, 17th Century. Pine, scratch carving.
Metropolitan Museum

376. FRENCH, WALNUT, INLAID. Mid-16th Century.

377. AMERICAN, OAK, 17th Century.   *Metropolitan Museum*

378. SWISS, INLAID, 17th Century.   *Metropolitan*

379. CONNECTICUT TYPE, late 17th Century. Oak and pine.

Metropolitan Museum of Art

ESTS OF THE 17th CENTURY WERE PREDOMINANTLY COFFERS ON FEET, THE DRAWERS BEING INCIDENTAL

AMERICAN, 17th or early 18th Century. Oak and pine.
Metropolitan Museum

381. ITALIAN, UMBRIAN, early 17th Century. Carved panels, lid top and drawers typical.

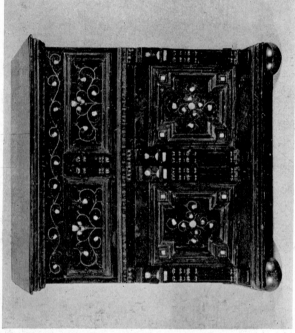

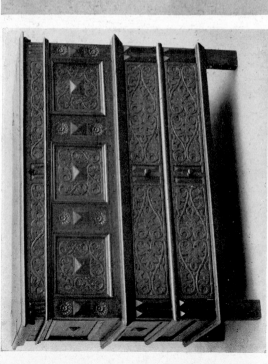

384. AMERICAN, late 17th Century. *Metropolitan Museum*

383. ENGLISH, CROMWELLIAN, C. 1660. Lid, drawers and doors. Oak, mother of pearl inlay; Italian influence. *Anderson Galleries*

BY THE END OF THE 17th CENTURY THE DRAWERS WERE THE REASON FOR THE CHEST

387. AMERICAN, 1675-1700. True chest form. *Metropolitan Museum*

386. ENGLISH, C. 1680. Oak. *Vernay*

382. CARVED OAK CHEST FROM MADISON, CONNECTICUT, C. 1700. Lid top. *Metropolitan Museum*

385. AMERICAN, 1675-1700. Oak and pine. A true chest of drawers, retaining appearance of coffer chest. *Metropolitan Museum*

390. ITALIAN, DRAWER CABINET,
C. 1620. Carved and inlaid.
Olivotti

391. (Upper, Center) ITALIAN (Florentine), credence 16th Century.
Metropolitan Museum of Art

388. ITALIAN (Florentine), 16th Century Walnut Cupboard.

389. ENGLISH. C. 1685. Oystered top, ornate marquetry.
Anderson Galleries

392. (Above) ENGLISH, WALNUT, C. 1710.
Anderson Galleries

393. (Upper Left) PENNSYLVANIA WALNUT, early 18th Century.

394. (Left) SWEDISH BUREAU, about 1700.

BAROQUE MANNER — 18th CENTURY

Lower Row: *Photos Courtesy Charles H. Henders*

395. SOUTH GERMAN, style of Louis XIV.

396. ALSATIAN, middle 18th Century.

397. SOUTH GERMAN (Wurzburg), style of Louis XV.

ow, Left to Right:

ITALIAN, ROCOCO. Painted, late 18th Century. *Olivotti*

HOLLAND, C. 1750. Baroque Commode. *Henders*

ITALIAN BAROQUE. *Olivotti*

(Center) SOUTH GERMAN ROCO-CO. Designed by Francois de Cuvillis; executed by Joachim Dietrich. Mid-18th Century. *Metropolitan Museum*

Row, Left to Right: *Photos from Lavezzo*

ITALIAN, late 18th Century.

ITALIAN, BOMBÉ.

405. AMERICAN, PHILADELPHIA CHIPPENDALE SCHOOL. Made by Jonathan Gostelowe, C. 1790. *Pennsylvania Museum of Art, Philadelphia*

404. (Upper Left) ENGLISH, mahogany bracket base. *Vernay*

406. (Left) ENGLISH, serpentine front, fretwork corners. *Anderson Galleries*

BAROQUE TENDENCIES, SIMPLIFIED IN THE STYLE OF CHIPPENDALE, INSPIRED ENGLISH AND AMERICAN DESIGN OF THE ENTIRE EIGHTEENTH CENTURY

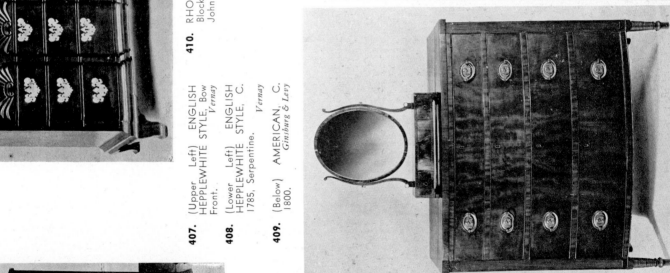

411. AMERICAN, MAHOGANY AND SATIN-WOOD, C. 1800.
Metropolitan Museum

412. (Below) ENGLISH, HEPPLEWHITE MANNER.
Yellow lacquer, Chinese decoration, C. 1780.
Anderson Galleries

410. RHODE ISLAND, CHIPPENDALE.
Block front with shell top, style of John Goddard, C. 1775.
Metropolitan Museum

407. (Upper Left) ENGLISH HEPPLEWHITE STYLE, Bow Front.
Vernay

408. (Lower Left) ENGLISH HEPPLEWHITE STYLE, C. 1785, Serpentine.
Vernay

409. (Below) AMERICAN, C. 1800.
Ginsburg & Levy

413. FRENCH, LOUIS XVI. Painted
made by Riesener, Bronze Mo
Pierre Gouthiere.

Metropolitan

FRENCH CHES

of the 18th Century were hig
decorated in the Rococo sp

Below: *Photos from Anderson C*

414. (Left) ACAJOU, LOUIS XV. PFU
COLLECTION.

415. (Right) Louis XVI, ROSEWOO

416. (Left, Lower) LOUIS XVI (E
ACAJOU. By Louis Aubry.

417. (Right, Lower) LOUIS XV, AC.
Made by Francois Antoine M

FRENCH COMMODE, style of Louis XV. Tulipwood, inlaid, C. 1750. *Symons*

(Left) FRENCH, early Louis XVI. Tulipwood, rosewood. *Anderson Galleries*

(Right) ENGLISH, 1765-1770. Satinwood, inlaid. Style of Louis XV. *Metropolitan Museum*

(Lower Left) LOUIS XVI COMMODE signed OEBEN. Collection of Viscount Gormaston. *Symons*

(Lower Right) ENGLISH, Chippendale style. Yew-wood and palisander. *Anderson Galleries*

424. FRENCH, PROVINCIAL, LATE 18th CENTURY.

423. PROVINCIAL FRENCH, ROCOCO STYLE.

Ruseau

THE STYLE OF LOUIS XV PERSISTED IN PROVINCIAL FRANCE THROUGHOUT THE EIGHTEENTH CENTURY

TALIAN (Siena), 17th Century. Walnut with painted decoration.

426. FRANCE, LOUIS XIV. Boule Cabinet, marble top.

COMMODES

E CHEST WITH DOORS DEVELOPED SIMULTANEOUSLY WITH THE DRAWER CHEST. THE NAME COMMODE IS
T DEFINITIVE. ACCORDING TO USE, SIZE AND LOCALE THE SAME TYPE MAY BE CALLED CHEST, CABINET, SIDEBOARD, ETC.

427. FRANCE, LATE 18th CENTURY, LOUIS XVI. Important Commode with burl panels and
Ormolu Mounts.   *Metropolitan Museum*

428. ITALIAN, EARLY 19th CENTURY. Inlaid Commode of Directoire Style. *Anderson Galleries*

429. FRENCH, DIRECTOIRE STYLE. Mahogany, brass gallery and mountings. Fluted posts. Rectangular handles and sunken drawer panels are typical. *Anderson Galleries*

430. F R E N C H, Walnut, Provincial Type, Louis XVI style. *Ruseau*

SEVERE RECTANGULAR LINES CHARACTERIZE CHESTS OF THE LOUIS XVI STYLE OF THE END OF THE EIGHTEENTH CENTURY

RENCH, MAHOGANY. Pierced Brass Gallery.   *Ruseau*

432. FRENCH, ACAJOU AND BRONZE. C. 1790. Filled Flutings.   *Symons*

433. GERMAN, C. 1800. Directoire Style, the basis of Biedermeier.

434. FRENCH, C. 1815. Empire Style, Mahogany. Sphinxes, lion handles, shield keyplates.

EARLY NINETEENTH CENTURY

435. GERMAN EMPIRE, C. 1810. Mahogany, bronze mounts.

chests, oak chests with various decorative motives, survive to illustrate the artistic abilities of the colonists. 379.

CONSOLE. Architectural term for a bracket of any kind used to support cornices or shelves. The bracket is usually of scroll form. The word console is also applied, rather incorrectly, to tables fixed to the wall and supported only at the front by legs, a carved eagle, or other figure. Currently, almost any type of wall table. 75, 502, 535, 597, 612, 741, 998 et seq.

CONSTITUTION MIRROR. American mirror of about the period of the adoption of the Constitution, 1791 or after. The head or cornice of the frame usually has a series of balls as decoration. 785.

CONSTRUCTION. Furniture making is still largely a handicraft. Its strength and excellence depend finally on the assembling of parts, a hand process. The machine has improved furniture to the extent of more precise preparation of the wood, of the exact cutting and shaping of the various parts, of better techniques of glueing and drying. Yet the skill of the workman, the joiner, is still the critical factor. To this extent there is today no such thing as completely machine-made furniture, nor on the other hand scarcely any hand-made furniture. Good furniture—good material, scientifically prepared and cut, intelligently and skillfully put together—has never been so much the rule as it is today.

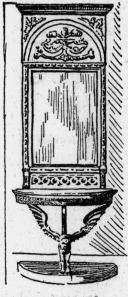

CONSOLE

The steps in making furniture are:

1. FULL SIZE DETAIL or pattern. The paper drawing is usually transferred to wood, a full sized section called the *Rod*. From this is taken the *stock list,* or list of parts and dimensions.

2. PREPARATION OF WOOD. The dried selected wood is cut into required sizes; panel sections are veneered, etc. The individual pieces are then turned, carved, moulded, rabbeted or grooved, bored or otherwise machined preparatory to joining; large surfaces are smoothly sanded. This is the machine's greatest part in furniture making: in modern plants almost every part of this work is performed by highly specialized machines.

3. ASSEMBLY. The hand part, called bench work. This is the part which today most affects the price and quality of the work. The various pieces are assembled by the cabinetmaker, the joints are dowelled, glued and clamped together until they are firmly set. Afterward, drawers and loose or moving parts are fitted. The whole is then finished off, the joints sandpapered, carved parts touched up where they meet at joints, the whole surface cleaned.

4. FINISHING. The process of protecting or embellishing the wood surface with paint, varnish, lacquer, shellac, wax, etc. according to the result desired. Here again a certain amount of machine work is possible by spraying and rubbing; the greater part of fine work is still chiefly hand work.

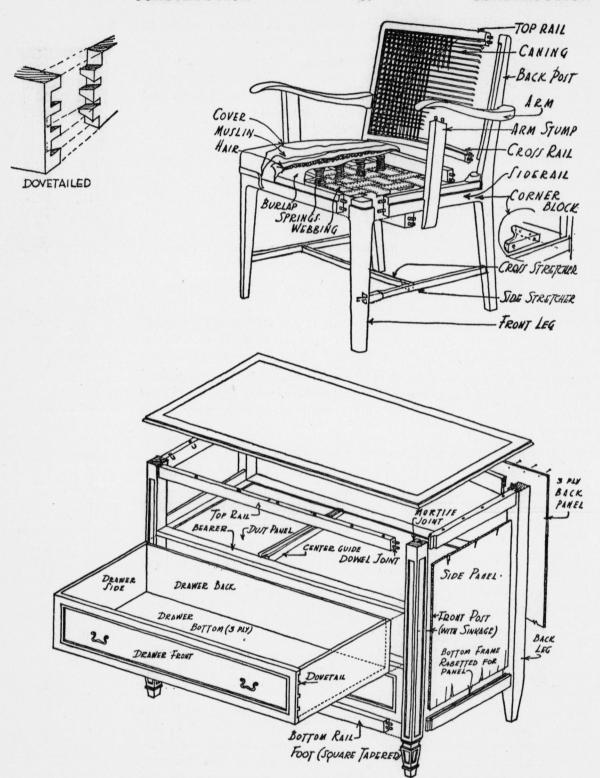

DOVETAILED

COVER
MUSLIN
HAIR

TOP RAIL
CANING
BACK POST
ARM
ARM STUMP
CROSS RAIL
SIDE RAIL
CORNER BLOCK
CROSS STRETCHER
SIDE STRETCHER
FRONT LEG

BURLAP
SPRINGS.
WEBBING

TOP RAIL
BEARER
DUST PANEL
CENTER GUIDE
DOWEL JOINT

MORTISE JOINT

3 PLY BACK PANEL

DRAWER SIDE
DRAWER BACK

SIDE PANEL

DRAWER BOTTOM (3 PLY)

FRONT POST
(WITH SINKAGE)

DRAWER FRONT

BACK LEG

BOTTOM FRAME
RABETTED FOR
PANEL

DOVETAIL

BOTTOM RAIL
FOOT (SQUARE TAPERED)

5. UPHOLSTERING, application of fabric, glass, metal, synthetic or other parts is done after the woodwork is completed.

JOINERY, better known as cabinetmaking, differs from carpentry in that it requires a greater precision, a different understanding of strains and materials. Carpentry is concerned with weight and strains and their balance by the form and position of structural parts: joinery is concerned with the strength of joints. There are a number of primary joints:

1. PLAIN BUTT
2. REBATED
3. DOWELLED
4. MORTISE-AND-TENONED
5. SPLINED
6. DOVETAILED

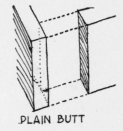

PLAIN BUTT

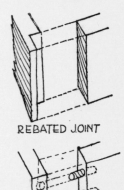

REBATED JOINT

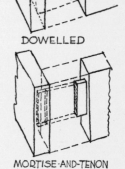

DOWELLED

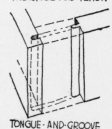

MORTISE-AND-TENON

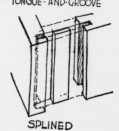

TONGUE-AND-GROOVE

SPLINED

There are infinite variations of these joints, developed for special purposes or through the joiner's ingenuity.

Rebated or rabbeted joints are known as dadoed, housed, grooved, with many combinations. Dowelled joints, the most generally used today, are in effect a secured butt joint. Splined joints are known as tongue-and-grooved when the edges of the boards are shaped to go together, instead of a strip being inserted in identical meeting grooves. Dovetailing, now used to join drawer sides, occurs in older casework at the meeting of sides and top.

All rules for joinery are qualified by position and material.

Virtually all joints require glue, or would be improved by it. Glueing is an art and science in itself. See *Glue*.

Nails are rarely used except for temporary setting until glue takes hold. Screws or clip fasteners are often used to allow movement of the wood in some planes.

Frameworks, as chairs, tables, etc. depend for rigidity on the strength of the joint, plus scientific cross bracing. Dowelled joints are most commonly used, with braces arranged to distribute the strains into other planes. Such are stretchers which being visible may not be used in some styles, corner blocks universally used in the concealed structure of upholstered chairs and under the tops of tables.

Casework, as chests and cabinets, is based on the box idea. The oldest types were boards joined together. Excessive weight and the perpetual danger of warpage and cracking in wide boards condemned this method as soon as the panel idea appeared about the 15th century. True cabinetmaking dates from this time. A heavy framework frames a thin panel set into grooves on the inner edges; this forms a rigid, light panel, the warping of the individual parts reduced to a minimum by their narrowness. Modern casework uses the corner posts as vertical framing, even the leg being part of the same piece. Best practice in modern casework uses framed panels between each drawer, providing bracing for the whole case and dustproofing for each drawer.

Modern plywood has changed much case construction. Warping, cracking, etc., being eliminated, flat panels are used for sides. The joints with the top are often mitered where a completely flush effect is required, as in contemporary design. Doors in cabinets may be made flat in the same way; best practice in large doors uses a framed core. Drawers are generally dovetailed and are often in commercial work equipped with center guides or tracks, mechanically accurate enough to dispense with much of the slow hand-fitting.

CONSULATE. Napoleon's term as First Consul, 1799-1804. The Style continued the Directoire manner up to the development of the Empire. See *France*.

CONTRE-PARTIE. Boulle work in which the brass predominates.

CONVERSATION CHAIRS. Loose term for comfortable chairs, not quite so low or so deep as lounge chairs, but more comfortable than straight chairs.

CONVOLUTE. In the form of a scroll.

COPIES. Reproductions, replicas. Furniture copies are usually made of old pieces having historic or antiquarian interest, with more or less fidelity. The patina of old pieces with their wear marks is sometimes so skillfully duplicated that they are carelessly or intentionally sold as originals. See *Antique*.

COQUILLAGE. Shell motive in ornamental design for frames and other carved surfaces, after the French Coquille, a shellfish. It is Rococo and occurs in French work of the early 18th century and in the French-influenced English work. Chippendale's school used it extensively as the central ornament surrounding a cabochon on seat rails of chairs.

CORBEL. Bracket or brace to carry some weight, deriving from the architectural "to corbel out," in which one or more bricks or stones project to carry a weight. Common decorative theme in 17th and 18th century furniture.

CORDOVA LEATHER. Leather working in Europe derived most of its inspiration from the technique of decorating leather evolved in Cordova in Spain during the Middle Ages. By the time the Renaissance spread over Europe all leather work came to be known as Cordova leather. Flanders inherited the method from the conquerors of the Lowlands whence it was popularized in French and English decoration. Much of the leather was stamped with ornate, rather Oriental designs, gilt and polished. 508.

CORE. Internal part of plywood, usually poplar, chestnut or similar porous woods, upon which the crossed layers of veneer are applied. See *Plywood*.

CORINTHIAN. Architectural order of column, ornate with scrolls growing out of acanthus leaves. The most ornate Greek form, it was adapted and highly developed by the Romans. See *Orders*.

CORNER ARMCHAIR. Armchair with the back on two sides based on 3 legs, the fourth leg being in the middle of the front. Also Roundabout chair. 536.

CORNER BLOCK. Triangular blocks set in the corners of chair frames, etc., as reinforcement. See *Construction*.

CORNER CUPBOARD. China cupboard designed to fit a corner, the front being diagonal or curved. Smaller ones were made to hang; very important ones were built integral with the room. Panelling lines often carry through in the architectural forms. They were common throughout the 18th century in England and America, and in France as ENCOIGNURES. 23, 174-6, 183-7.

CORNICE (Cornish). Horizontal top or finish moulding or group of mouldings of a piece of furniture or architectural unit. Detached boxes or frames from which curtains hung were also so called in the 18th century. See *Orders, Mouldings*.

CORNUCOPIA. The horn of plenty, overflowing with fruits and flowers. A motive in decoration of many styles from the Renaissance to the present. 350.

CORNUCOPIA SOFA. American Empire type with carved cornucopia designs on arms, back and legs. 675.

COROMANDEL. Bombay ebony from the Coromandel coast; blackish rosewood in texture, with light stripes. 614, 829.

COTTONWOOD. Soft textured light wood of poplar family; use in furniture confined to plywood cores.

COUCH. Sofa which has a half-back and head-end only. See *Sofa, Restbed*.

COUNTER-BOULLE. Brass groundwork with tortoise-shell inlay. *Contre-partie*.

COUNTERS. Originally tables or chests whose top surface are marked off for either measuring or counting, originating in Flanders in the 15th century.

COUNTERSINK. Conical boring in wood to receive a screw head so that the surface of the screw is lower than the wood surface.

COURT CUPBOARD. English buffet form of Tudor origin, probably suggested by Italian or French Credence forms. Generally a double-bodied cabinet, richly carved and used to hold plate and eating utensils, wine, etc. Highest development in early Jacobean times. Similar forms appear in American work. 6, 7, 155-164, 495, 501.

COURTING CHAIR. Two-chair-back settee or sofa. 232.

COURTING MIRROR. Small wood-framed mirror, usually pine with a picture over the glass, a conventional courting gift. American, 18th century. 8, 9.

CORINTHIAN CAPITAL

VELVET COVERED CRADLE G 1610

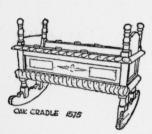

OAK CRADLE 1575

HEPPLEWHITE

CRESTING

CRICKET

COVE. Large concave or hollow moulding.

COVED CUPBOARD. Early American cupboard whose top is swept forward like a hood.

COX, JOSEPH. Upholsterer and cabinetmaker, had a shop in Dock Street, New York, in middle 18th century. Settee with his label now in the Metropolitan Museum of Art. 50.

CRADLE. Child's bed of ancient type, mounted on rockers or some swinging arrangement. Every style has produced a variety of types from simple boxes to the great draped state cradles of 18th century France. Renaissance forms are unbridled imaginative designs; similar complex forms appear in Sheraton's drawings and a notably elaborate cradle is that of Napoleon's son, in the Empire style. Peasant styles bear much painted and carved ornament, especially in rural Germany, Switzerland and France. The cradle is now almost obsolete in favor of the more functional crib. 24.

CREDENCE. Important side table of Gothic style, usually oak. Origin probably religious, suggested by name from "credere," to believe. Later used as sideboard for carving meat, displaying plate, etc. Prevalent in Northern Europe, it evolved into the buffet-sideboard type. 391, 681.

CREDENZA. Credence, Italian form. An important production of the 15th and 16th centuries. See *Italy.*

CRESCENT STRETCHER. Bowed stretcher on Windsor chair, American, 18th century. 250.

CRESSENT, CHARLES—1685-1768. French furniture maker and *ciseleur,* pupil of Boulle and leading figure in Régence and Rococo design. 605.

CRESTING. Carved decoration on top rail of chairs, daybeds, mirrors, etc. 227.

CREWEL WORK. Embroidery of fine worsted on linen, English, 16th and 17th centuries. 818.

CRIB. Child's bed with enclosed sides.

CRICKET. Old English wooden foot stool, usually low. Also simple versions in American work.

CRICKET TABLE. Small Jacobean three-legged table, generally round.

CRINOLINE STRETCHER. Stretcher on Windsor chairs, the two front legs joined by a semi-circular curve, with short stretchers to the back legs. See *Crescent Stretcher.* 250.

CRISS-CROSSED WORK. Lattice work. 286.

CROCKET. Gothic architectural ornament consisting of mouldings terminating in a curve or roll. Used on medieval woodwork, and again in work of the 18th century.

CROMWELLIAN. The brief period 1649-1660 of Puritan domination in England is named after its central figure, Oliver Crom-

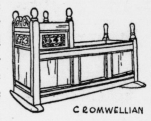

CROMWELLIAN

well. The furniture of this time is a severe undecorated version of the Jacobean out of which it grew. These Puritan influences were naturally those carried across the sea by the Puritan settlers of the New England colonies; consequently the early gateleg tables, Welsh dressers, square-backed chairs and other furniture of the colonies exhibit the same qualities. The wood was chiefly oak; turnings of simple ball profiles are the chief ornament. See *England.* 505, 508.

CROSS BANDING. Border bands of veneer in which the grain runs across the band. Treatment is characteristic of walnut furniture after Charles II, and follows throughout the 18th century in England and on the continent. 428.

CROSS FIRE. Regular mottled figure across the grain of wood, yielding a brilliant transparency, particularly in some mahogany, walnut, satinwood, and other tropical woods.

CROSS RAIL. Horizontal bar or rail in a chair back.

CROSS STRETCHER. Intersecting X-stretcher, straight or curved, on tables, lowboys, and chairs. Baroque Italian inspiration developed by the French Renaissance designers and employed in England in the William and Mary productions and later. 318.

CROTCH. The wood from the intersection of a branch with the trunk of the tree has an unusual V-shaped figure when cut into veneers. The matching of these veneers produces striking patterns much favored by cabinet makers. 1093.

CRUSHED BALL FOOT. Furniture foot similar to club foot. 687.

CROWN. Motive in decoration. In carving it is found in Italian, French, Flemish and English work after Charles II. It occurs also as painting, as in medieval wall decorations. Its use as a motif in weaving dates from the early Saracenic textiles and the Sicilian weavers of the 12th century. 517.

CROWN CRESTING

C-SCROLL. Carved C-shaped design found in much late 16th and 17th century French and Flemish work and later in England.

CUP-AND-COVER TURNING. Turned ornament consisting of a bulb, topped by a lid or cover. Jacobean and later.

CUPBOARD. Cabinet or box with doors for storage. The special types and names are numerous, springing from special uses and locations. Sometimes a cupboard is considered an architectural feature only, the free-standing equivalent being a cabinet. See *Cabinet, Corner Cupboard, Court Cupboard.*

CUPID'S BOW. Double ogee curve, bow shaped, such as favored by Chippendale for top rails of chairs. 291.

CUP-TURNING. Cup-shaped bulge in turned legs.

CURLED FIGURE. Feathered appearance in the grain of some woods when cut across the grain. Maple, birch, walnut and others show distinct cross grain markings in some parts of some logs. This figure is prized for special veneerings, inlays, etc. 480, 1109.

CURLED HAIR. Upholstery filling made principally from the mane and tail hair of horses, valued for its resiliency and long staple. Less valuable is the curled hair of cattle and hogs.

CURRICULE CHAIR. Sheraton's term for a classical type having semi-circular back and elongated seat. See *Curule Chair*.

CURULE CHAIR. X-shaped chair, the *sella curules* of the Romans, 253 et seq., 711, 921, 936.

CUSPS. Gothic ornamental knob or point projecting from the intersections of two curves.

CUTWORK. Fretwork.

CUVILLIES, FRANÇOIS DE. Bavarian architect to Frederick I of Prussia. Worked in Rococo style. 401.

CYLINDER FRONT. Quarter round fall front of a desk. Also the name of the desks having such roll tops, made during the late 18th century in France and England. 482, 483.

CYMA. From the Greek for wave—a simple double curve.

CYMA RECTA. The ogee moulding.

CYMA REVERSA. The cyma recta reversed.

CYPRESS (Cupressus Semperoneus). Dark reddish wood of very hard texture valued for its durability. Cypress chests were made as early as the 14th century. Cypress crotch is known as "FAUX SATINE."

DAIS (Dias). Raised platform at one end of medieval rooms, upon which was the table for the master while the retainers sat below. Also occurs in Empire Styles for beds.

DAMASK. Silk figured fabric used for draperies and upholstery, named after Damascus, where it appears to have been made before the 12th century. The manufacture of damask began in Italy very early, and until the end of the 17th century Venice and Genoa supplied most of Europe. The French weavers took over the process with the Renaissance, while Dutch and Flemish weavers carried it to England about 1570.

DANTE CHAIR (Dantesca). X-Chair of the Italian Renaissance, having four heavy legs curving up to arms with leather or fabric seat. Spanish type rather top heavy: French, English and Teutonic versions more ornate. 255.

DARBY AND JOAN SETTEE. Two-chair-back settee.

DARLY, MATTHIAS. 18th century English designer and engraver. Published books on design.

DAVENPORT. Small writing desk. In current American use, an upholstered sofa.

DAVENPORT BED. Couch which may be unfolded to form a bed.

DAVENPORT TABLE. Long narrow table used behind a sofa when placed in the center of a room.

DAVID (David Roentgen). French designer and cabinetmaker, 1743-1807. See *Roentgen*. 667, 668.

DAYBEDS. Rest beds, chaise-longues and other elongated seating forms may be called daybeds; these usually have a raised pillow-like end. They are pictured in ancient Greek and Roman remains and occur in France after the Louis XIV era. They appear in England with the Restoration. The commoner reference in America is to a true bed form with both ends the same height and placed lengthwise to the wall. This form grew from the alcove bed of 18th century France which evolved through the Louis XVI and Empire styles into the familiar shape of the current style. See *Rest Beds, Chaise Longues*. 815 et seq.

DEAL. English term for pine, particularly the Scotch pine. Sheraton explains the name as the Dutch term for "a part," signifying the division of boards when used as the core for veneering.

DECALCOMANIA. Picture applied in reverse to paper, then transferred to furniture by sticking and removing the paper. As a substitute for painted decoration it appeared in the late 18th century, but became popular only in early 1800's, chiefly in America. Hitchcock and similar chairs were sometimes decorated with such transfer patterns.

DECANTER STANDS. See *Coasters*.

DECORATED QUEEN ANNE. English style approximately 1710-1730; Early Georgian. Essential details of Queen Anne style as cabriole legs, round back chairs with fiddle splats, claw-and-ball feet, and generally curved forms were enriched in scale and heavily adorned with carving.

DECORATED QUEEN ANNE

DEMI-DOME. Half dome, as the shell-top niche in a cupboard. 176.

DEMI-LUNE. Half round in plan, as in a console or commode.

DEMOISELLE. Early French pedestal table fitted with the form of a woman's head, and used to hold head-dresses. Also wig-stand.

DENTILS. Equally spaced rectangular blocks in a cornice moulding, resembling teeth.

DERBYSHIRE CHAIR. English country chair, Jacobean period.

DESK. The original desk was a writing box, a small chest with sloping lid. Inside were kept writing materials and valuables. This form was known in ancient China and Egypt; it is the monastic *scriptorium* of the Middle Ages. These Gothic forms, growing larger, came to be mounted on stands and presently the hinging of the lid was reversed so that the inner side formed a writing surface when opened. (45.) Hence the slant front and fall front types which are known today. The desk box survived into the 18th century. (43.) From the French practice of covering it with a woolen cloth (French *Bure*) comes the word BUREAU, later signifying any desk compartment and corrupted in America to mean chest of drawers.

The filling in of the desk-frame with drawers to the floor came in the late 17th century with the appearance of the chest of drawers. In England and later in America this type became a leading article of furniture. The addition of the bookcase top made the tall secretary. The name is derived from scrutoire or scriptoire (523). Italy, Austria and Germany produced elaborate secretaries in all Baroque complexity. The late 18th century types of England and America are superb architectural compositions. In the Empire period the slant front almost disappeared and the straight fall front cabinet, in one front plane, was a rectangular mass of superimposed architectural motives. 580, 649, 674, 750.

Biedermeier secretaries carried this even further; tall compositions sometimes of three architectural facades, complete with columns and cornices and pediments were made in light woods. American desks of the same period favored a debased Sheraton form with slightly slanted fold-over leaf and turned legs. In the Victorian era the tall slant front came back, very large with softened contours.

Smaller desks, the type known as "ladies' desks," appeared about 1680 in England. An epidemic of letter-writing and memoirs raged in France during Louis XV's reign and with its counterpart in England made desks essential in every room. These were dainty, table-like affairs with small enclosed top sections, closing with lids, doors, tambours or cylinders which rolled back. From the cylinder type came many important variations; through the Empire they were popular (667) and begot the 19th century roll top, the "Carlton desk" and numerous other table forms flourishing in England.

Table desks developed naturally from the simple writing table; banks of drawers were added below and often a small block of drawers sat loosely on the top. A form of kneehole arrangement occurs frequently, often identical with dressing table forms. (602, 664, 1005, 1015, 1024.) In American work a practical work desk, sometimes called George Washington, set precedent for modern utilitarian pieces. These types are called Library Tables in England.

DESK-BOX. Portable box, for writing materials and valuable papers; usually with hinged slant top for writing. In earliest furniture history they were small; as they grew larger they were equipped with stands, to which they finally became attached and so were the ancestor of the modern Desk. See *Desk*.

DIAMOND-MATCHED VENEER. Straight-grained woods cut diagonally and put together in quarters so as to produce a diamond pattern. 621.

DIAMOND-POINT. Lozenge; geometric shaped panel in casework, typical of early 17th century work in France, Flanders and England. 162, 593.

DIAPER. Design in regular repeats, usually small, spaced to form diagonal pattern. Probably first woven in Ypres in the 16th century, it took its name from d'Ypre. Also a basic pattern in conventional wall painting, wallpapers, inlays, etc.

DINING TABLES. See *Tables.* 973 et seq.

DIRECTOIRE. French period of the Revolution, 1799-1804, in which classic Greco-Roman motives were favored, developed on Louis XVI themes. See *France.* 625 et seq.

DISC FOOT. Flat, rounded foot in Queen Anne work. 274.

DISHED. Hollowed out. 51.

DISHED CORNER. In card tables, a hollowed out space in each corner for holding money. 538.

DIVAN. Upholstered couch without arms or back, originating in Turkish form of pile of rugs for reclining.

DOCUMENT DRAWER. In desk cabinets, the small vertical drawers, usually found one on each side of the central compartment, in the interior or writing section. Often ornamented with carved colonnettes, etc. 442.

DOG EAR. Projecting rectangular ornament at the head of a door frame or panelling, found in early Georgian work.

DOG TOOTH. Ornamental detail, chiefly Gothic, in the form of repeated cones, like pyramidal dentils.

DOLE CUPBOARD. Ecclesiastical cupboard for food for the poor; disappeared after Middle Ages. 168.

DOLPHIN. Sea animal used more or less realistically in carving and painting on furniture, bronze and stone in architecture. 990.

DOLPHIN HINGE. English hardware used in cabinets; name suggested by its dolphin-like shape. See *Hardware.*

DOME BED. Canopy bed with tester in either full dome or arched shape. 104.

DOME TOP. Half round pediments of cabinets, etc., especially Queen Anne period; similar to hooded top.

DORIC. The primary Greek order of architecture. Heavy arrissed columns with simple details yield a sense of structural value. Roman Doric, lighter and more refined, retains much of Greek simplicity. See *Orders.*

DOSSER. Prior to the fifteenth century, a fabric cover or hanging on walls or behind the seats.

DIAMOND-POINT PANELS. (LOUIS XIII)

DIAPER PATTERN

DOLPHIN FOOT ENGLISH REGENCY

DOUBLE CHEST. Two sets of drawers, the lower usually slightly larger than the upper; chest-on-chest; tall-boy. 61, 512, 703-6.

DOVETAIL. Method of joining boards at the ends, as in a drawer or a case, made of interlocking tenons suggesting the form of a dovetail. Also a butterfly-shaped inset used to join boards lengthwise in table tops, floors, etc. See *Construction*.

DOWEL. Round wooden pin or peg fitted into holes in two adjacent pieces of wood with glue to hold them together. See *Construction*.

DOWER CHEST. The custom of providing a chest for the plenishing of a perspective bride, a hope chest, appears universally in most civilizations. The romantic aspects have inspired fanciful efforts in every style, but in some the production carries special interest. In the Italian work it is not easy to distinguish between the ordinary chest and those planned as dower. In later styles the intention as a bride's chest is plainly deduced from the initials, the inscription or the forms of ornamentation. Two distinct types are found in America—the Connecticut chest, and the Marriage chest of Pennsylvania. 25, 370.

DOWN. The under plumage of fowl, used in best upholstering for the filling of soft cushions.

DRAGON. Legendary beast used in more or less detail in furniture. Scaly feet and claws, fierce heads, serpentine coils, etc., are motives called after the dragon, being generally derived from Oriental art. Free renderings occur in Baroque carvings in Italy, France and Germany.

DRAKE FOOT. Three-toed foot occurring in 18th century furniture.

DRAPERY. In all historic styles the hanging of fabrics has been a prime device in decoration. Originating in utilitarian need, the technique has invariably run away with the object, making drapery an end in itself. The draping of cold stone walls by means of *Arras* or tapestries fostered the triumph of European weaving of the 15th, 16th and 17th centuries. Windows and doorways, thrones, canopies, beds, and chairs likewise inspired weaving and tailoring which too often subordinated the object to the form. Yet the manipulation of rich folds of handsome fabrics does produce effects of luxury not attainable by other means. Like good structural architecture reduced to ornament, this has led to the simulation of the effect of drapery in painting and wallpaper, carving and plasterwork. Witness linenfold panelling; the painting of swags and festoons, and the painting of textile forms and styles as wall decoration. 98 et seq.

DRAUGHT CHAIR. Large English wing-backed chair; wholly wood in Tudor, upholstered in later styles.

DRAW TABLE. Drawing, Drawer, Draw-out or Draw-top Table.

Refectory type table with a double top, the lower of which is in two sections which pull out at the ends to increase the length of the table. The original base must therefore be quite heavy to balance the extended table. First appears in both France and England in the sixteenth century; its highest development is in the Jacobean oak refectory tables of the 17th century. 496.

DRAW RUNNER. DRAW SLIP. Small piece of wood, freely inserted into a slot just under a fall front, drop lid, or slant flap, as on a desk or secretary. When the lid is dropped, the draw slip is pulled forward to support it. 439.

DRESSER. 1. A low chest of drawers with a mirror over, for clothing, storage and dressing. (American usage.) See *Commodes*.

2. Sideboard or buffet chiefly for the storage and display of eating utensils. European usage derived from *dressoir*. 885 et seq.

DRESSING MIRROR. Small mirror on standards, used in connection with table, lowboy or chest for dressing. Also *cheval*. 788 et seq.

DRESSING TABLE. Almost any form of table may be used as a dressing table when equipped with the customary mirror, drawers, etc. The use of types has varied considerably with the mode, eras of greater luxury producing more complex solutions for this function. See *Tables; Beau Brummel; Poudreuse.* 515, 562, 1014 et seq.

DRESSOIR. Buffet-cupboard-sideboard, usually with open shelves or racks for china. Late Gothic development of credence in France, Flanders and Germanic countries. The type became chiefly rural in England in the 18th century. Now identified as dresser. 584, 885 et seq.

DRINKING TABLE. See *Wine Table*.

DROP. Pendant ornament, either turned and hanging free, half turned and applied, inlaid, or carved into the *surface,* as the husk ornament in 18th century classical work. 158.

DROP FRONT. Desk front or leaf which falls forward for use. 465.

DROP HANDLES. Handles which hang pendant-like. See *Hardware.* 393 et seq.

DROP LEAF. Hinged flap or leaf on a table which when raised enlarges the top. 980.

DROPPED SEAT. Concave seat, in which the sides are slightly higher than the middle of the front and back. Also called Scoop seat. 332.

DRUM TOP. DRUM TABLE. Round library or center table with a deep apron, sometimes with drawers. The shape suggests a drum. 988.

DRUNKARD'S CHAIR. Deep, rather low upholstered armchair; 18th century England. 305.

DUCHESSE. French chaise-longue, or large upholstered chair and stool designed together to form a couch. Hepplewhite's version had two armchairs facing each other, with a stool or ottoman of the same level between. 821.

DUCHESSE BED. French canopy bed with full tester, fixed to the wall instead of to posts, the drapery hanging down to the bedding and floor.

DUCHESSE BED

DUCK-FEET. Incorrectly used term for Dutch foot; sometimes a three-toed or web foot. 13.

DUMB WAITER. Generally three or four circular trays graduated in size from the largest at the bottom, revolving about a central shaft; originated in England in the early 18th century; spread to France and Germany. They were generally placed near the hostess's end of the table, and carried additional plates and silver, dessert and cheese, and later liquor bottles and glasses. An American version for use *upon* the table developed as the "Lazy Susan," a revolving tray for condiments, etc.

DUMMY BOARD FIGURES. Boards cut out with the silhouette and painted figure of humans, animals and objects of furniture. They appear throughout the 17th and 18th centuries in England and the Low Countries. Since no use seems plausibly ascribable to them it is assumed that they were made and used merely as whimsical decoration.

DUST BOTTOM, DUST BOARD, DUST PROOFING. Thin wood panel used between drawers to exclude dust and hinder access. See *Construction.*

DUTCH COLONIAL. Period of Dutch colonization in North America, 17th century. Long Island, New York, and the Hudson Valley up to Albany were occupied by the Dutch long enough to leave a permanent character in houses and furniture. This is simplified Baroque; massive, stolid, unpretentious. Local woods were used almost exclusively; turning is common, usually deeply cut and with feet often eccentrically turned to produce a rudimentary cabriole foot called Dutch foot, spoon foot, pad foot or duck foot. There was some rude carving, but paint was a more common decorative medium. Distinctive are large cupboards called *KAS,* usually painted. 36.

DUTCH CUPBOARD. Large cabinet or buffet with open shelves above for display of plates, etc.

DUTCH FURNITURE. See *Netherlands.*

DUTCH INFLUENCE. In English furniture, the influence of the Dutch was so apparent as to give its name to the work of the William and Mary and Queen Anne periods; in fact most of the walnut styles between 1690 and 1735. See *England.* 511 et seq.

DUTCH FOOT. Generally, a club foot. Variations are the angular foot, the elongated foot (forming a point), and the grooved foot. 36.

DUTCH SETTLE. 18th-19th century settle with back pivoted to form a table.

EAGLE. Its use as a decorative motive goes back to farthest antiquity, but its revival from Roman and Byzantine designers in the Renaissance was sparing at first. From heraldry it was adapted to painting and carving; conventionalization brought out the familiar decorative uses. The eagle's head, wings, and claws in conjunction with mythological forms became rampant in Baroque and Rococo 18th century work. Empire style, deriving from Napoleon's Imperialistic art, employed the eagle widely in carving, bronzes, painting, and fabrics. American furniture after the Revolution favored the eagle on mirrors, couch feet, and finials. 20, 535.

EARLY AMERICAN. See *American.*

EARLY CHRISTIAN. Byzantine Art became permeated with Christian symbolism and remains of this period show wide use of church emblems, such as the circle, cross, crown, vine, dove, peacock, and Biblical figures. They survive in fabrics, mosaics, carvings in stone and wood, painting and metal work.

EASTLAKE. Sir Charles Locke Eastlake, 1793-1865, in an effort to introduce a more conscious design method into furniture, originated a style of furniture compounded of medieval outlines with ornament freely adapted from the Gothic, the Japanese and the special abilities of the machine. Cherry wood was the principal medium, embellished with metal and tile panels and conspicuous hardware. It was too eagerly seized upon by the newly-arisen machine-equipped shops, and such tastefulness as the style originally possessed was lost in the subsequent distortions. See *England, Modern.*

EASY CHAIR. Any large chair, so padded or upholstered as to be suitable for lounging. The spring and cushion chair is distinctly an invention of the 19th century, although the essential form may be patterned after chairs of the preceding century. The French Bergere is probably the prototype of all our easy chairs, although some variation came by way of the English Wing chairs and deep armchair of the 18th century.

EBENISTE (Ebonist). Ebonyworker; French for cabinetmaker. The craze for ebony in the early 17th century led master craftsmen, then called *huchiers,* to advertise their ability to work in this difficult wood. The name lingered to denote a cabinetmaker of masterful skill.

EBONIZE. The staining of native hardwood to resemble ebony.

EBONY (Diospyros). Tropical wood of general black color, heavy and dense in texture. Of those in current use, the blackest is the Gaboon ebony; the Macassar has stripes of light brownish orange and black brown.

ECHINUS. Greek egg-and-dart moulding.

ECLECTICISM. In design, the method of using and adapting at will the forms and motives of any previous period. It permits them to be modified or combined with other styles as freely as the designer's whim dictates, or it may follow rigidly the complete formula of an earlier style. Thus all modern copying or utilization of period styles is eclectic. Periods of eclecticism seem always to follow great periods of constructive designing. The major effort of the 19th century was eclectic, following the great burst of artistic energy of the 18th century. Yet, in retrospect it appears that, to a degree, even eclecticism takes on an original, constructive and unique aspect when viewed in the light of interpretation and adaptation to current needs and techniques. The various 18th century revivals were, in their day, eclectic in their use of ancient forms; yet today they appear as well integrated, distinctive schools.

EDGING. Thin strip of solid wood at the edge of a veneered panel, to protect the veneering.

EGG-AND-DART, EGG-AND-TONGUE, EGG-AND-ANCHOR). Carved enrichment of an ovolo moulding suggesting alternately eggs and darts. An ancient architectural ornament, it is one of the most frequent in carved woodwork of all lands after the early 16th century. *537*.

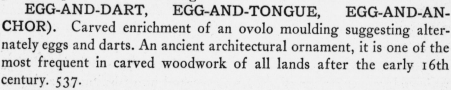

EGG · AND · DART

EGYPTIAN. Ancient Egypt left a fairly complete record of its daily life in the contents as well as the decoration of its tombs, thanks to the custom of supplying the dead with mundane articles planned to remind the soul of its former associations. From these we may conclude that Egyptian inventiveness supplied the shapes and models for most articles of furniture in ancient times. Subsequent to 1500 B.C. there appears a rich catalog of chests and sarcophagi, tables and stands, stools, chairs and folding seats, ingenious in design, sound in workmanship and with a superior sense of construction.

Folding seats had X-crossed legs with leather seats. Low stools with rush seats survive, and low chairs with stiff backs flowing easily into the seat line. The legs are more or less conventionalized animal feet, bull hoofs and lion paws supplying motives. Some beds were piles of quilts on frames, others folding-chair arrangements, but always with a yoke-shaped arrangement as pillow. Tables were commonly simple four-legged structures, well braced. Decoration was usually in paint; chairs were often plain white, while chests and sarcophagi were painted in strong colors with bands of geometrical decoration. The motives were largely animal forms; the various lion paws, heads and other details persisted in all subsequent decoration.

Wood being scarce in Egypt, the wood character was often made a feature, and there is evidence of the use of varnishes and natural finishes on sycamore, olivewood, yew and cedar. Inlaying and veneering were also known, employing for the former pieces of faience, semiprecious stones, ivory, mother-of-pearl, gold and other metals.

The substance of Egyptian furniture is the basis of most subsequent style. *919, 1029*.

438. AMERICAN DESK BOX with drawer on frame. Oak. 1675-1690.
Metropolitan Museum

DESKS

THE DESK FORM GREW OUT OF THE SLANTING SHELF DESIGNED TO HOLD A HEAVY BOOK. THE ADDITION OF A BOX OR DRAWER FOR WRITING MATERIALS, PLUS AN ATTACHED STAND, MADE THE DESK FORM AS KNOWN TODAY.

437. AMERICAN, about 1650. Oak Desk Box, gouge carving. *Metropolitan Museum*

441. ENGLISH, about 1700. Walnut Desk, showing fully developed type.
Anderson Galleries

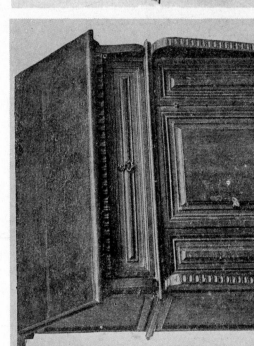

440. ITALIAN (FLORENCE), MIDDLE 17th CENTURY. Walnut Desk with closed-in base section.

436. JAPANESE READING STAND, about 1662. Gold lacquer. *Metropolitan Museum*

439. AMERICAN, 1700-1725. Pine Slant Top Desk on frame. The interior divisions and drawers and the lid supported on runners typify the developed form. *Metropolitan Museum*

DESKS

The Slant Front Desk appeared ge
in Europe and European Colonies
Eighteenth Century. The lighter typ
cabriole legs, were often called "
Desks."

442. (Left) AMERICAN, 1710-1725. App
Queen Anne influence. A detachab
box set on a lowboy.
Metropolitan

Lower Row, Left to Right:

443. AMERICAN. Mahogany, Middle
Century. *Metropolitan*

444. FRENCH, late 18th Century. Bu
cylindre (Louis XVI). Fruitwood
Anderson

445. FRENCH, middle 18th Century. Le
Rococo, Marquetry.

Right Hand Page, Top:

446. FRENCH, LOUIS XV, Boulle work.

Lower Row, Left to Right:

447. ITALIAN, ROCOCO, Mid-18th
Walnut.

448. SWEDISH, about 1760. Rococo
Figured Walnut.

443.

444.

445.

446.

447.   448.

with drawers below were kno
Europe as "Bureau," "Escritoir
"Scrutoire"; hence our term SECRE

449. (Left) AMERICAN, MAHOGANY
1775. Block front, shell blocking r
in the interior. *Metropolitan*

450. (Below) ENGLISH, about 1700. Walnut burl, the flat surfaces designed to display the elaborate grain. Note ledge upon which a book might rest. *Vernay*

451. AMERICAN, 1740-50. Bracket foot form closely related to 450. *Metropolitan*

(Right) FRENCH, Provincial style of Louis XV, probably late 18th Century. Hoof foot.

Ruseau

AMERICAN, late 17th Century. Ball foot of English type. Burl veneers.

Metropolitan Museum

454. ENGLISH, about 1720. Walnut. Serpentine front.

Vernay

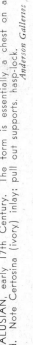

THE VARGUEÑO: TYPICALLY SPANISH DESK-CABINET ON STAND

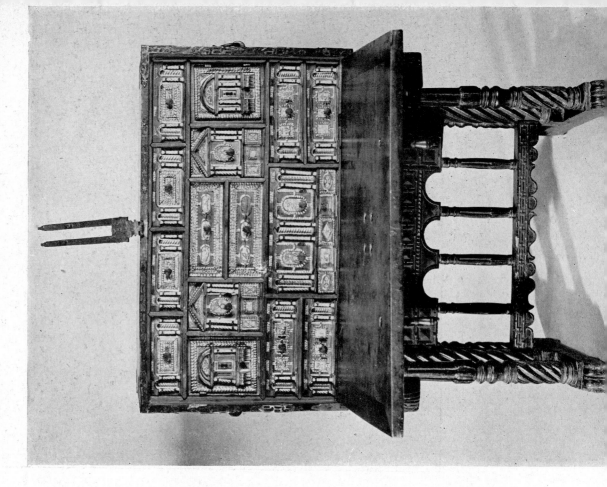

456. SPANISH, about 1600. Walnut, inlaid with bone. More advanced type than 455, typical arched base, spiral turning.
Anderson Galleries

455. ANDALUSIAN, early 17th Century. The form is essentially a chest on a stand. Note Certosina (ivory) inlay; pull out supports, hasp-lock.
Anderson Galleries

458. SPANISH, 16th CENTURY. Walnut, gilt and polychromed. (Closed view see No. 916.) *French & Co.*

457. ITALIAN (VENICE), 16th CENTURY. Certosina inlaid walnut (Collection of Count Depoli). *French & Co.*

459. ITALIAN, HIGH RENAISSANCE, 16th Century. Highly Carved Walnut. *Olivotti*

460. SWEDISH, Middle 18th Century. Influence of English Forms.

461. FRENCH, Louis XVI, 1774-1793. Black and Gold Japanese Lacquer with Gilt Bronze Mounts. *Metropolitan Museum*

462. ENGLISH, About 1700; Inlaid Panels in Chinese Taste. *Metropolitan Museum o*

463. ITALIAN, LATE 16th CENTURY. WALNUT WRITING CABINET WITH THE ARMS OF THE STROZZI FAMILY. (The Fall Front is Missing.) TYPICAL ANIMAL FEET. GADROONED BASE.

Metropolitan Museum of Art

464. ITALIAN, 16th CENTURY. "Stipo" hinged door instead of fall. Grotesque infant figures—"Bambocci" —on pilasters. *Olivotti*

465. ENGLISH, 1690-1700. Walnut, early form of scrutoire. *Metropolitan*

466. ENGLISH, 1760-1780. French Rococo influence, characteristically restrained. *Symons*

467. FRENCH, late Louis XVI, Acajou ("Secretaire a Abatta Late style of Riesener. *Anderson Gal*

ENGLISH. QUEEN ANNE, About 1700. WALNUT.
Metropolitan Museum

ITALIAN, 17th Century. Venetian Painted Landscape Decoration.
Metropolitan Museum

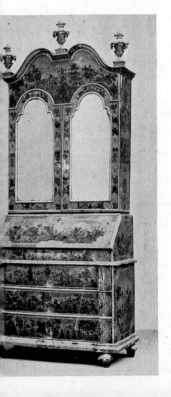

470. ENGLISH. ABOUT 1700. BLACK AND GOLD CHINESE LACQUER. BAROQUE MANNER.
Metropolitan Museum

471. ENGLISH, About 1715. WALNUT BURL.   *Vernay*

472. (Upper Right) FRENCH, Late 18th Century
Provincial Style of Louis XV.   *Ruseau*

473. (Lower Right) ENGLISH, Late 18th Century. Satinwood.   *Vernay*

474. (Above) ENGLISH; EARLY GEORGIAN. Double-hooded Cornice of Dutch Influence. Burl Walnut. Handles Indicate Three Portable Sections.

Vernay

475. (Top, Left) ITALIAN BAROQUE. Late 18th Century. *Olivotti*

476. (Left) AMERICAN, 1750-1775. Bombé or Kettlebase with Block Front.

Metropolitan Museum

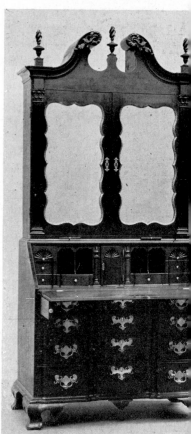

477. A RHODE ISLAND BLOCK FRONT, CLAW-AND-BALL FOOT.

478. (Top) ATTRIBUTED TO JOHN G

479. (Lower) MIRROR DOOR SECRETA
Owned by General Henry Knox.

AMERICAN SECRETARY-DESKS; MID-EIGHTEENTH CENTURY *Courtesy Metropolitan M*

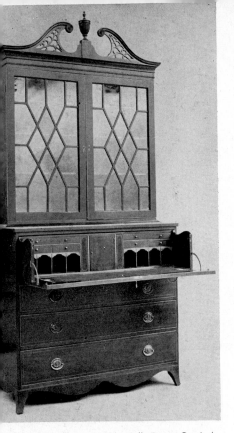

MERICAN. Drawer with Fall Front Carried
Quadrants. Dated 1798. *Metropolitan Museum*

480. AMERICAN, SHERATON STYLE MAHOGANY AND MAPLE. Gothic Detail
in Doors. The Fall Front Has Almost Disappeared. *Metropolitan Museum*

GERMAN, BIEDERMEIER STYLE, about
1826. Cylinder front.

MODIFICATION OF THE FALL FRONT AT THE END OF THE EIGHTEENTH CENTURY

484. ENGLISH, SHERATON CYLINDER FRONT
DESK for a lady. Amboyna with tulipwood
and satinwood bandings, about 1780.
Vernay

485. ENGLISH, SHERATON ROLL TOP DESK.
Mahogany. *Vernay*

486. FRENCH, LOUIS XVI ROLL TOP
Satinwood banded with mahog
with blue and white Basalt Pla
Saunier.

487. AMERICAN, 1780-1800. Tambour Desk of Hepplewhite style. Mahogany with satinwood inlay. Hinged writing bed.

All photos on this page courtesy Metropolitan Museum of Art

RICAN, Sheraton style made in New York t 1800. Mahogany.

489. AMERICAN, about 1800. Figured mahogany.

490. FRENCH, 20th Century. Rosewood and ivory.

10353

491. FRENCH, late 18th Century. Provincial style of Louis XV. Walnut. *Ruseau*

EGYPTIAN TASTE. A brief attempt was made to naturalize Egyptian forms and decoration around the turn of the 18th and 19th centuries. Napoleon's African campaign in 1798 brought it to France, where it was systematically organized and offered as a style, and the English designers took it over to some degree. As a feature of the Empire style, some details persisted. See *Empire.* 647 et seq., 749.

ELIZABETHAN. Loosely used, the term denotes the culture of England during the 16th century. The Tudor period is generally limited to the Earlier Renaissance work, with Gothic elements dominant; the Jacobean includes the period during which the Renaissance spirit was wholly absorbed into English Art. At Elizabeth's accession in 1558, the dominant Tudor forms of furniture were based on the perpendicular Gothic architecture; the arts as a whole possessed a homogeneity of spirit and design never after approached. Oak was almost universally used. Outlines were large, straight and severe, as in the Gothic, with an elaborate use of Italian Renaissance carving. Flemish craftsmen at this time came as refugees and brought French and other versions of the basic Italian Renaissance designs, and with them a host of novelties in the way of fabrics, metal treatment, intarsia, new woods and uses for furniture as well as the new decorative details. This process continued until at Elizabeth's death in 1603 the style had assumed a continental appearance but it was plainly imposed upon the older forms. The melon-bulbous leg, the Tudor rose and decoration by channelling, are the most easily identified characteristics. See *England.* 97, 152, 157, 496, 970.

ELLIOTT, JOHN, died 1791. Philadelphia cabinetmaker known to have made dressing cases and wall mirrors. 770.

ELM (Ulmus). The wood of this family has generally a very light brown color and a porous, oak-like texture. It appears to have been used for furniture by the Romans and there are surviving Gothic examples. It appears occasionally in English and a few continental styles, but principally in provincial work. English chairs of Elm, particularly with Elm seats, are common survivors of Georgian times.

Elms are used extensively today as decorative veneers. The odd figures of the American and English Elm and more particularly the Burl of the Carpathian Elm, make beautiful veneered surfaces.

EMBLEM. Symbolic and heraldic ornaments passed from their original connotation to a conventionalized, purely decorative use. Thus, coats of arms, personal insignia and monograms, cyphers and religious symbols are used ornamentally only, with no significance other than the association with the traditional form on which they first appeared.

The use of emblems is particularly characteristic of Elizabethan embroidery. 645.

HERALDIC EMBLEM

EMBROIDERY FRAME. Elaborate, often decorative frame used by dilettantes in the art of embroidery in France, England and elsewhere, 17th century and after.

EMPIRE. The neo-classic style of architecture and decoration created practically by edict of Napoleon. A committee of artists headed by David in the early years of the 19th century eclectically proposed a complete style based on the imperial forms of ancient Greece, Rome and Egypt. The furniture is rectangular, architecturally massive and excessively sumptuous, rich woods and metal mountings offsetting the rectilinear simplicity. Mahogany, rosewood, and ebony were the rule, with brass or gilt mounts in the forms of swags and festoons, wreaths and laurel branches, torches, mythological figures, and the Napoleonic emblems of the bee, the crown and the letter N; later sphinxes and other Egyptian figures were used. The tripod table and other Pompeiian details are common. Fabrics bore the same ornaments and were executed chiefly in hard textures and strong shades of green, yellow, blue and red.

The style spread over Europe along with the wave of classical knowledge, and most European and American work is strongly flavored with the Empire essence. It influenced in England men like Sheraton and Thomas Hope; in America, Duncan Phyfe's later work is all in the Empire manner. In Germany it grew into a rusticized version popularly known as Biedermeier. In short, whatever Napoleon's motive in inspiring the step, the fact remains that its spirit suited excellently the rising classicism, and its persistence for more than a generation indicates that it was generally acceptable. 647 et seq., 193, 83 et seq., 28.

EMPIRE (Late). The Second Empire in France produced after 1830 a wave of heavy rolled shapes in furniture, far from the classical and in general portraying an unwholesome mixture of Louis XV and earlier Empire forms. In America, Phyfe accepted this style which he termed "butcher furniture," and these remains, together with a considerable amount imported into the South (particularly around New Orleans) often appear in the antique market.

ENAMEL. On wood furniture, a hard glossy finish applied by brushing, then rubbed with pumice stone and oil to a satiny finish. On metal, enamels are baked on.

ENCOIGNURE. Small French corner cabinet. 183 et seq.

ENDIVE. Carved decorative motive, a variation on several acanthus leaves combined. Originally favored in work of the Louis XIV period, it was extensively used by Chippendale.

END TABLE. General current term for any small table used in relation to a couch, chair, etc. Small tables of all periods and original purposes are used now as end tables.

ENGLAND. The period distinctions of English furniture are somewhat indefinite due to the variety of labels according to monarchs, designers, typical woods, external influences, etc. Political and economic changes were so rapid after the 16th century that styles are known by their influencing sources as well as by their mature characteristics. More than any other detail, the use of specific woods establishes boundaries of English styles and a most convenient classification is MacQuoid's separation of the Ages of Oak, Walnut, Mahogany and Satinwood.

The Oak Era, most typically native, includes all the Gothic development from French sources after the Norman Conquest, through the reigns of the Tudors and the Stuarts. Thus furniture up to 1660 is reasonably consecutive in style; the basic Gothic forms persist, with a growing use of Renaissance details. British sailors and traders, encouraged by Henry VIII and Elizabeth to expand England's sphere of influence, went everywhere, bringing home ideas and riches. Under the less sure hand of the Stuart kings, there was confusion and revolt. James I and Charles I, Cromwell and the Puritan Commonwealth, Charles II and James II are lumped as Jacobean or Stuart or distinguished as Early Jacobean, Cromwellian or Commonwealth, Restoration, Carolean, late Jacobean. The latter, a transitional period, saw the rise to dominance of foreign forms.

The Walnut Age is one of foreign rulers as well as of foreign furniture styles, but it utilizes a domestic wood. Dutch Baroque came with William and Mary and flowered during Queen Anne's reign.

Mahogany, an imported wood, symbolizes the growth of wealth and world-power under an imported dynasty, the German Georges of the House of Hanover. The distinctions of the Georgian styles are purely chronological; the real classifications follow the names of the great architects, cabinetmakers, designers and artists. Their printed works and executed furniture tell us of the Anglicized interpretations of the Dutch Baroque, the French Rococo, the revived classicism of the dilettante archeologists, the waves of Chinoiserie. Chippendale, the Adams, Hepplewhite and Sheraton are only a few of the many great talents that made 18th century furniture synonymous with great design.

The Satinwood Era is least distinct, chronologically or as a school of furniture style. It represents the flowering of luxury and refinement; exotic, overdelicate and self-consciously sophisticated, it is more truly the transition from the great age to the debased eclecticism of the 19th century. It foreshadows all the groping of the Regency and Victorian periods.

MEDIEVAL

Medieval furniture in England, as elsewhere, was crude and sparse, typical of the dormant state of the arts everywhere.

GOTHIC

The Gothic age established a fairly universal system of furniture, solid and angular in outline, architectural in form and ornament. The development of furniture is marked principally by the passage from the hands of the carpenter to the specialized joiner or cofferer. The former

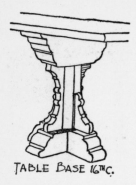

TABLE BASE 16ᵀᴴ C.

employed solid boards; the latter made framed panels. The coffer and its descendants,—ambries, hutches, cupboards (684) and sideboards represented most of the furniture; there were throne-like chairs, forms, joint stools, benches and trestle tables and little else. A small amount of beech and elm was used besides the ubiquitous oak, whose hardness set limits on the style of carving. Gothic structural elements like arches, tracery, bosses and deep mouldings were favored carved motives as were linenfold panels and zig-zags. The wood was either painted in colors or left raw. Wrought iron locks and keys, hinges and straps were conspicuous. 150, 684.

TUDOR-ELIZABETHAN

The reign of the Tudors, 1485-1603, covers the last phase of the Gothic style and the beginning of the Renaissance. In the reign of Henry VIII the secular power displaced that of the Church and domestic furniture began a robust development. Italian influences came with Italian architects, but only in details of ornamentation did furniture styles deviate from the established Gothic. Romayne work, scrolls and dolphins were added to the Tudor roses, palmetted bands and zigzags of the carvers' vocabulary. Intricate carving encouraged some use of walnut, more easily worked. Under Elizabeth this Renaissance-Gothic combination attained its height, distinct from any continental styles. Massive and large-scaled, the structural principles are simple and effective; joints are at right angles, well braced. The huge bulbous-melon-turning appears on all upright members; stretchers are square and low. Panelled chairs, draw-top tables, court cupboards, colossal beds with heavy wooden canopies are prodigally ornamented with grotesques, caryatids, foliated scrolls, strap-work, gadrooning, inlaying and other Italian exuberances. Inigo Jones brought Italian architecture; Italian workmen followed. Religious freedom and commercial advantages attracted French, Flemish, German and Dutch craftsmen, but their output appears strangely homogeneous. 97, 152 et seq., 196, 257, 368, 373-4, 496, 970-1.

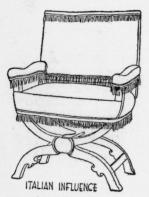

ITALIAN INFLUENCE

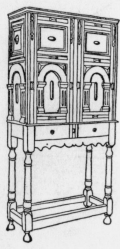

EARLY JACOBEAN

Under James I and Charles I, 1603-1649, the Renaissance continued to submerge the Gothic styles. The straightforward structure and simple outlines persist, but furniture grows smaller, lighter, less ornamented. Flatter carving used the Renaissance motives, including Ionic capitals, weak acanthus leaves (503), the guilloche and intertwined circles, palmettes, etc. The melon-bulb turning is conspicuously lighter (510). The gateleg table (976) appeared, and upholstery improved some chairs. The Italian X-chair, footstools, highly carved mirror frames, and turned chairs were common. 160, 164, 200, 208-9, 492 et seq., 759, 923, 972, 976, 992.

CROMWELLIAN OR COMMONWEALTH

The Civil War, 1649-1660, a Puritan revolt, substituted austere undecorated furniture for the ornate luxuries favored by the Cavaliers. Simplified turnings followed spool or sausage profiles (505). Ball- or bun-turned feet came from the Dutch. Carving, inlays, mouldings were simplified. Padding appears on the backs as well as on the seats of chairs and leather decorated in the Spanish manner is used. 119, 226, 383, 493, 505, 508, 922.

ELIZABETHAN

RESTORATION

Charles II returned in 1660 and ruled until 1685. From his refuge in Flanders he returned with continental elegances and ideas of luxury, and a train of French, Flemish and Italian craftsmen, who preferred to work in walnut. The court of Louis XIV shed some of its brilliance on the revived English court, and the rising Baroque lushness appeared. Restoration lines are everywhere lines of movement, instead of the static squareness of Early Jacobean work.

Distinctive are spiral turnings, double-curved legs, scrolled feet, large free curves, the Flemish Scroll, deep carving with the oft-repeated crown motive (517, 815), caning and upholstering with fine silks, velvets, brocades, embroideries, stamped leather. Veneering is a new feature, displaying large surfaces of selected grain with inlaid floral patterns—marquetry (389). Oystering—veneering with cross sections of small branches (520)—was a unique development. Lacquer and painted decoration after the Indian and Chinese example, known since Elizabeth, became a rage. Oriental themes and details were colorfully executed in inlay (462), paint and carving. Gesso, silvered or gilded in the Italian manner also provided brilliant showy surfaces. Even solid silver furniture was made for the court.

EARLY JACOBEAN

The demand for luxury created new species of furniture. Rest beds or daybeds (818), bureaux or desks (465), sofas, drawer-chests (386), wing chairs, mirrors, small tables and stands and great draped beds were accepted by the upper classes as required by the French standard of splendid living. The huge bed, hung with fabrics of absurd costliness and grandeur reached its zenith during this period (98). 207, 264, 267, 303, 386, 511 et seq., 846.

Grinling Gibbons' style of carving set the precedent for most decorative treatment during the ensuing half-century.

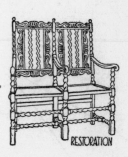

RESTORATION

LATE JACOBEAN

Often used to limit this period named for James II. His three-year reign ended with the Bloodless Revolution of 1688. The entire period, more properly called CAROLEAN after Charles II, is typically

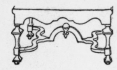

transitional; oak gave way to walnut, the innate structural simplicity to excesses of Baroque technique, native directness to foreign brilliance. 389, 687, 753, 815, 818, 831, 851, 924, 933.

WILLIAM AND MARY

Brought from Holland the full-blown Baroque style in 1688. Continuing the tradition of importation, the French architect Marot brought the rich style of Louis XIV; Christopher Wren worked in a chaste Italian manner; Dutch and English traders continued their Oriental importing; religious tolerance attracted weavers, painters, carvers, joiners. New types and processes produced a revolution in furnishing and the swing away from excessive grandeur to a simpler domesticity changed the scale and style. Smaller, more intimate rooms had lighter chairs, tables, chests. Chairs were comfortably padded and covered with needlework; legs were mostly turned and braced with serpentine stretchers (516). The Dutch club foot and the scroll leg inspired the rudimentary cabriole leg, but trumpet, bell, cup and bun turnings are more typical.

Surface treatment became vital in this epoch, partly due to the need of protecting the delicate veneers, partly to the love of fine finish. High polishes emphasized the carefully matched veneers. Lacquer and japanning still rose in popularity. Seaweed Marquetry (389, 696) suggests the minute intricacies of French Boulle work. Walnut is predominant but many other woods appear as veneers and for contrast in inlays. 465, 514, 518 et seq., 688, 696, 702, 752-4, 1008, 1046.

QUEEN ANNE

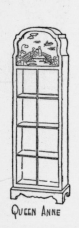

The reign of Anne, 1702-1714, carries on the Dutch inspiration, developing the elements of comfort, grace, elegance. There is little positive differentiation in the work of the years 1690-1720, but the tendency is toward a more English interpretation of the flowing Baroque outlines. Sleek and sophisticated, there is generally a unity of curved lines in Queen Anne furniture; a restraint of ornament and a better technical understanding of design. The cabriole leg is the outstanding detail, and its skillful association with other curves, as of seat outlines and back members of chairs, produces superb, distinctive designs (270-275). Improved technique made stretchers unnecessary after 1710 (528), and pierced back splats became more decorative. Marquetry was subordinated to fine walnut surfaces. Carved motives were the scallop shell, broken and C-curves (536), acanthus leaves. New habits introduced new furniture; tea drinking called for hosts of small tables. A craze for collecting china produced the china cabinet. Secretaries, bookcases, fire screens, mirrors, tall-boys, love-seats, etc., were moderate in size, beau-

tifully proportioned and ornamented with restraint and charm. 175, 270 et seq., 307, 392, 441, 462, 468, 470-1, 522 et seq., 789, 853, 930.

GEORGIAN

The furniture produced in the earlier part of George I's reign shows an orderly progression of the Queen Anne style, but two rising factors could not long be withstood: first, the coming of mahogany, and second, the trend toward magnificence bred by the new prosperity. Until about 1725 walnut was undisputed. More ornate features began to elaborate suave lines. Cabriole legs ended in animal details, as ball-and-claw (533) or hoof (532) feet. Lion masks (538), foliated scrolls, complex rock-and-shell ornaments, satyr (532) and other mythological forms were symptoms of the Rococo offshoot of the Baroque style.

The architecture of the great houses after 1725 was classic Italian in the Baroque manner, and the architects did not hesitate to design furniture in the same manner. Thus the classification of "Architects' Furniture"—pompous, florid, magnificent, denying the simple elegance of the earlier work. Full-bodied architectural pediments, columns, statuary distinguish the work of Kent, Ware, Langley, Vanbrugh. Gilding was favored while lacquer work declined. Bracket and pedestal bases and applied architectural details are typical.

GEORGIAN

Mahogany had been in some use before this time, but removal of import taxes in 1733 let it compete with walnut. As it excelled walnut in strength, ease of carving and resistance to decay, its popularity virtually drove walnut out of use.

Most significant about Early Georgian furniture is its completely English quality. The foreign elements, flowing into England for more than a century had become completely fused into a distinct national style. By 1730, the furniture was English, more so than the Dutch and German rulers. Style—and nomenclature—no longer follows the monarchs. 310 et seq., 404-5, 454, 474, 524, 527 et seq., 771, 833, 870, 993, 1005, 1038.

CHIPPENDALE

The name of Thomas Chippendale has become a convenient tag for the entire style of the Middle Georgian period. The reason for this widespread influence lies in his publication in 1754 of "The Gentleman and Cabinet-Makers' Director." Far from being the first book of this type, it had prototypes in works by the Langleys, Swan, Lock, Jones, Copeland, Johnson, the Halfpennys, etc.; but the Director alone was confined to furniture. It illustrated practically every type known, showing the average Early Georgian basis with variations after the more fleeting whims: French, Rococo, Gothic, Chinese. The book was so

THE "GOTHIC TASTE"

FRENCH ROCOCO

CHINESE CHIPPENDALE

enthusiastically received everywhere that its patterns became the current style of English furniture.

Of furniture in the style of the Director, Chippendale himself produced a minimum. Some of the designs are technically poor, while Chippendale's known work is invariably of superb craftsmanship as well as design. Furthermore, much of his work appears to have been done in collaboration with Robert Adam, whose classicism made the Director designs appear old-fashioned.

Chippendale's genius is most evident in the manner in which he amalgamates the various details of Rococo, Gothic, Chinese and other styles without sacrificing the unity of the design. With all the intricacy of rock-and-shell, fretwork or ribbons, there is always a strong outline and a dominating wood-structural sense that permits great vitality even to renditions or copies by lesser men. Consequently there are vigorous schools of Chippendale in America (See *Philadelphia Chippendale*), Scotland, where most literal copies were made, and Ireland, where the style was so liberally modified as to be recognizable as a distinct manner. (See *Irish Chippendale.*)

The Rococo taste came from France as the style of Louis XV, was greatly restrained in English work, but attained special splendor in gilt mirrors (776) and commodes (420). The eclecticism of the period also led to an abortive Gothic revival. Interest in Chinoiserie and Oriental themes came in periodic waves. All these details, surprisingly welded together, found their way into mahogany. 103, 131, 282 et seq., 305-6, 331, 422, 466, 542, 547 et seq., 705, 776, 856, 858, 1014, 1051.

THE BROTHERS ADAM

Are notable for their preoccupation with the refined classicism of Pompeii, to the exclusion of the Baroque-Rococo influence which had prevailed. They stopped at no detail as unworthy of their designing, so that furniture and all other interior fittings came under their sway. Classic symmetry was a revolutionary substitute for the naturalism of the older style; this, more than any other characteristic typifies the influence of the "Antique." Scale became fine, sometimes painfully, unstructurally, so. The square line framed in everything. Ornaments comprised swags and ribbons, fluting and paterae, rams' heads, sphinxes, griffins, chimerae, Greek key and honeysuckle and Vitruvian scrolls. Painting was used for whole surfaces as well as ornaments. Marble and scagliola, metal mounts and gilding, all contributed to the effect of rich elegance and refinement. 133, 338, 561 et seq., 774, 893.

Satinwood appears about 1760, and is coincidental with the refining influence inaugurated by the Adams.

HEPPLEWHITE

Is credited with modifying the classic influences into furniture of great charm and elegance. Cold angularity was softened into subtle curves. Chairs are his best designs, but there are excellent chests and commodes, sideboards, desks with cylinder tops, tall secretaries, sofas and settees, etc.

The Rococo influence shows in Hepplewhite's earlier work (555, 558) but his major work is in straight lines. Tapered legs end in spade feet. Chair backs were in five shapes: oval, wheel, heart, shield, camel, always filled with pierced splats in delicate designs, sometimes lightly carved. Typical motives are the three-feathered crest of the Prince of Wales, wheat, ribbons, fine swags, pateræ, etc. Hepplewhite employed decorative painting extensively, and sponsored the use of satinwood and fine inlaying.

In 1788, two years after Hepplewhite's death, his widow published his book, "The Cabinet Maker and Upholsterer's Guide," which had much the same effect on his reputation as the "Director" had had on Chippendale's—that is, the whole style is sometimes ascribed to him. 135, 138, 140, 180, 315, 322, 327 et seq., 389, 407 et seq., 420, 554 et seq., 706, 791, 865, 932, 975.

SHEARER

Collaborated with Hepplewhite and is credited with the familiar sideboard design (895). His drawings appear in "Designs for Household Furniture" (1788).

SHERATON

Is known as a designer and publisher of several books on furniture, more than as a working cabinetmaker. His book, "The Cabinet Maker and Upholsterer's Drawing Book" (1791), purports to show the "present taste in furniture"—probably indicating that many of the designs were not his own. The designs shown are, however, so good and so well thought out as to the details of construction that, like Chippendale forty years before, Sheraton served as master to the whole cabinetmaking industry, and his drawings epitomize the contemporary style.

The earlier designs follow generally the same classic antique forms as the Louis XVI style. Rectangular forms are nevertheless graceful; segmental curves are preferred to Hepplewhite's serpentines; many flat areas afford surfaces for inlay, and later porcelain plaques. Sheraton liked complicated mechanical arrangements—folding tables and disappearing drawers and secret compartments, all ingeniously devised and workably delineated. He covered the entire field of furniture then known, and in tremendous variety.

Closed
LIBRARY
STEPS
Open.

The French Revolution and the chaotic sequence of styles which followed were too much for Sheraton, as for everybody else. After some brilliant work on Directoire models, the Early Empire style confused him and his designs appear weak, overornamental, debased. He died in 1806. 137, 333 et seq., 484-5, 566A et seq., 838, 981 et seq., 988, 999, 1010, 1017, 1020, 1044.

It must be remembered that Chippendale, Hepplewhite and Sheraton, outstanding though they were, held no monopoly sufficient to name the period for them. They were the great lights of a vigorous style, but there were lesser lights and there were cabinetmakers with the craft and grace to execute the designs offered. The production of books on furniture was a thriving industry, and part of every gentleman's education was in architecture, the classics, and design. Among the contributors must be listed Chambers, Manwaring, Ince and Mayhew, Lock and Copeland and innumerable others.

The tremendous furniture output of the mahogany period can be largely lumped into the two types: the Baroque-Rococo, through 1755, and the Classic Revival, after that time. The former, known by fuller proportions, solidity, robust ornamentation, is exemplified in Chippendale's earlier work. The Classic work is piously symmetrical, fine-scaled, graceful to a fault, with a tendency toward the finicky. After that the *Age of Satinwood* lays the ground for the decline. In the quest for lightness, structure is lost; fine scale becomes mere thinness, novelty leads to the bizarre and eccentric. This is the trend of early 19th century furniture; the post-Sheraton period as laid down by Sheraton.

ENGLISH REGENCY

The name is applied roughly to the period 1793-1820, although these dates do not exactly cover the period during which George, Prince of Wales acted as Regent. The declining influence of Robert Adam gave way to an intensely literal archeological spirit. Roman types were reproduced wherever possible after the French Directoire and Empire models, or from the ancient sources. For such articles as ancient Rome provided no precedent, an assortment of Roman ornaments was combined or adapted. Bookcases like temple facades, couches after Roman beds, sideboards as bits of architecture were all so literally architectural that both scale and comfort were often lost, the artist's sense of rightness being sacrificed to the archeologist's enthusiasm. The Adams' typical compo ornaments and painting were discarded for metal inlays and applications; the ornamental features were directly Roman and Egyptian, bronzed or gilded, comparatively sparse and accepting large surfaces of unembellished wood.

REGENCY CHAIRS.

Thomas Hope and Sir John Soane were the foremost exponents of this English version of the French Empire style, but the taste was general enough to leave us drawings and work by Sheraton, Thomas Chippendale Junior, Ackerman and George Smith. The earlier phases of the style are, in a solid, scholarly way, interesting to the designer and student. It developed into a debased grotesque mannerism, conspicuously coarse and ineptly ornamented. 141, 361, 580 et seq., 874, 902-3.

VICTORIAN

The long reign of Victoria, 1837-1901, covered a multitude of artistic sins in furniture. Creative taste sank to a low ebb. The endless search for novelty produced revival after revival; after the Greek, the Gothic, Turkish, Venetian, Egyptian and back to Louis XV. They were all cheerfully misinterpreted, unstudied, caricatured. The introduction of machine processes created new idioms which Eastlake tried to adapt. Ruskin and William Morris led another revolt, equally ineffective at the time. (1093 et seq.)

ENGLISH COUNTRY FURNITURE

Foreign influences usually came in through the court and the aristocracy in the capital, and slowly seeped down through the country aristocracy to the middle classes (where such existed) or the artisans and tradespeople. In England this saturation process was slow. The lower classes were wedded to the simple forms, and the provincial gentry were conservative. Thus, oak furniture prevailed throughout the walnut age, and many characteristics of Good Queen Bess' time lived on in furniture of the following century. Stronger individuality and deficiencies in technique yielded novelty to the styles when they did come. The dates of much unascribable furniture are therefore in doubt. 885, 891, 892 show sideboards of essentially country type, using oak for details of walnut style; retaining some Jacobean details, some Queen Anne, they may date from the latter 18th century.

The Windsor Chair is a unique country development. Chairs, stools and tables with turned members, and many other articles of utility furniture reveal an innate respect for wood and pride of craftsmanship. 208-9, 225, 233, 239, 243-6, 300, 885, 890 et seq.

ENTABLATURE. The horizontal section borne by a column. Each order of architecture has its distinctive entablature made up of architrave, frieze, and cornice. See *Orders*.

ENTASIS. Slight swelling of a column at the middle designed to overcome the optical illusion of hollowness which appears in a perfectly straight column. See *Orders*.

ESCALLOP SHELL. Cockle shell. See *Shell Motive*. 449.

ESCRITOIRE (Scrutoire, Secretary). Writing desk with drawers, pigeon holes, etc. 441 et seq.

ESPAGNOLETTE

ESCUTCHEON. Armorial term for a shield-shaped surface bearing coat-of-arms, monograms, etc. In furniture, fitting over a keyhole or the back plate of a handle. They are usually of metal, but are sometimes ivory, bone, inlaid veneers, etc. See *Hardware*.

ESPAGNOLETTE. Female busts used as terminal ornaments on posts of cabinets, etc., usually arranged on the upper curves of volutes. Frequent in styles of Louis XIV, the Régence and Louis XV.

ETAGÈRE. What-not; a series of shelves supported by columns, used chiefly for the display of curios. Commonest in the 19th century, although graceful examples in exotic woods survive from the time of Louis XVI. 146.

EVOLUTE. Recurrent wave scroll used to decorate friezes and bands. 149.

FABRICS. See *Textiles*.

FACADE. Front, using the word in the architectural sense. The faces of chests, etc., were often treated to resemble architectural facades, particularly in the classic revivals. 374, 435, 881.

FACING. An economical, technically incorrect method of veneering by covering a thick cheap wood with a thin layer of better or more decorative wood. Rarely practised today.

FAKES AND FAKING. The fine art of counterfeiting antiques flowered with the recent craze for them. The problem would be a simple one if there were some criterion of the genuineness of antiques, but unfortunately the trade is permeated with practices varying from the faintly unethical to the completely fraudulent. The technique of faking has a partly legitimate parentage in the art of restoration. New parts are used to replace old or missing ones in old pieces and are then treated to present the same superficial aspect as the old parts. This is legitimate enough, but the seller must state that parts are replaced or restored. A good craftsman who knows the methods of restoration could take an entirely new piece of furniture and make it look antique. Honor alone can deter him from this fraud and compel him to start, at least, with a truly old original piece.

Some of the tricks are admirable in their ingenuity. Fine birdshot makes wormholes; a heavy chain wears off edges; acids and rusty nails stain wood, and burying a board in a barnyard for three months ages it a century.

See also *Antiques, Copies, Restorations, Reproductions.*

FALDSTOOL. Portable folding seat, like a camp stool (262).

FALL FRONT, FALL. Drop lid or drop front, as in a cabinet-desk or piano. Sometimes slant front. 459.

FALL LEAF TABLE. Drop leaf or flap table.

FAN. Radiating design suggesting a fan used in chair backs (18th century English), a fan-shaped filling, upright or reversed. Windsor chairs with flaring spindles and curved top rails are called FAN BACKS. 250.

FAN DESIGN-ADAM COMMODE

The fan motive is used in inlaid and painted decoration on 18th century furniture. 578.

FAN LIGHT. Elliptical or half-round over-window or over-door with radiating design of muntins or leading.

FANCY FURNITURE. Tables, chairs, etc., usually small, intended more for ornamental purposes than for utility.

FARTHINGALE CHAIR. English chair, period of Elizabeth and James I. It was without arms in order to permit the then fashionable wide dresses called Farthingales, to spread in all directions.

FASCES. Roman decorative motive depicting a bundle of rods with a projecting axe. Recurs in most classical revivals as Louis XIV and the Empire.

FASCIA. A broad flat moulding; a facing band.

FAUN. Mythological demi-god, half man, half goat, used instead of a caryatid. Italian and French Renaissance; Adam.

FAUTEUIL. French upholstered armchair. The sides are open, while the sides of the Bergere are upholstered solidly. 326.

FAUX-SATINE (False Satinwood). Cypress crotch, which yields very beautiful veneers similar in color and texture to satinwood crotch.

FAVAS. Honeycomb-like detail characteristic of Louis XVI decoration.

FEATHERED. Certain grains, particularly of mahogany and satinwood, are referred to as feathered when cut to show a plume-like figure.

FARTHINGALE CHAIR

FEATHER BANDING. Herringbone inlay.

FEATHER EDGE. Edge of a board thinned off, as in panelling.

FEATHERS. Feathers, plumes and bird wings are used as ornamental details in Egyptian work, in the period of Louis XIV, Hepplewhite and subsequent styles. 336.

FEDERAL. American period, coincidental with the early years of the Republic, 1780-1830. Beginning marked by the Revolution or end of Colonial period; the decline by the deterioration in taste after the early stages of the Empire influence. The style is completely classical, traces of antique Pompeiian and Greco-Roman design coming through Adam, Hepplewhite, Sheraton and Regency influences from England; Louis XIV, Directoire and Empire influences from France.

The Federal period is the period of Duncan Phyfe. His earliest work echoes the English Masters; after 1800 stronger French qualities bring his work to its highest distinction. The Directoire-Classic influence so evident in late Sheraton and English Regency is also the basis of Phyfe's best style. Samuel McIntire excelled in Adam interpretations.

The Directoire influence was followed by the heavier Empire. By 1830 the decline had set in; furniture was heavy and coarse.

Federal furniture is predominantly mahogany. Some curly maple was used to imitate the satinwood of European models. Cherry and other fruit woods are common in less splendid furniture; rosewood was used in more costly work after 1820. Maple and pine were stained to imitate rosewood, notably in the chairs of Lambert Hitchcock. Veneering is general. Brass feet and casters, brass ring handles and, to a lesser extent, brass applied ornaments were used. Of the latter, the commonest form was the eagle; the national bird is almost symbolically Federal. China and glass knobs were later used as drawer pulls.

Feet and legs were mostly turned, reeding being more typical than fluting. Lions' paws were carved on feet, lions' heads on handles; lyres, swags, festoons, delicate acanthus leaves suggest the Directoire. The Empire style favored cornucopiæ, pineapples, spiral carved turnings with leaves and mostly heavy scrolls as brackets, table and mirror supports, bed ends, etc.

The Federal era was marked by great interest in architecture and archeology; leading citizens like Thomas Jefferson brought this enthusiasm to a high pitch. Interiors and furniture reflect in pure outlines and refined detail the classic stateliness of Palladio and Vignola and their European followers. See *American, Phyfe.* 65, 79.

FESTOON

FESTOON. Scallop-like series of loops as a rope, chain of flowers, drapery, etc., painted or carved for decoration; swag. 413, 420.

FIBER. In furniture, specifically, an African fiber sometimes used in cheap furniture as a filling for upholstery in place of hair.

FIDDLE BACK. Chair back whose splat resembles a violin. Queen Anne. 277.

FIDDLE BACK (Veneer). Parallel curly grain in wood as maple, mahogany, walnut, koa and others, like the finely marked sycamore selected for violin backs. See *Woods.* 1109.

FIDDLE BRACE BACK. Windsor chair with two spindles radiating from a projection back of the seat up to the top bar (240).

FIELD BED. Canopy bed of smaller proportions. Planned in the 17th century as one to be carried about, the name came to signify the less monumental types with curved canopy and comparatively low turned posts.

FIELDED PANEL. Panel formed by moulding, grooving or bevelling around a plain surface. Also a panel made up of smaller panels (158).

FIGURE. In wood, certain characteristic markings other than the customary straight grain. These are spoken of as crotches, burls, butts, curls, mottles, feathers, waves, crossfire, etc.

FIGURE DECORATION. Human, animal and mythological figures are used in most styles of decoration, more or less conventionalized. They are adapted to the embellishment of structural parts, as brackets, columns, legs and arms of tables and chairs. They are also used as motives in every form of flat decoration. See *Ornament*.

FILIGREE. Wire work in delicate ornamental patterns. 141.

FILLET. Small band or fascia used for separating mouldings. Also a small cleat or ledge for supporting loose shelves.

FINIAL. Decorative terminal placed vertically to accentuate a point or the ending of a structural feature, such as a post, pediment, or intersection. 61, 470.

FINISH. Generally refers to the process of polishing or preserving the wood in furniture. It originates in two needs: first the desire to embellish and decorate, second the need of protection of the perishable material from the ravages of use and time.

The decorative impulse seems the older. The ancient Egyptians, Chinese, Mesopotamians and Romans used color and design on most of their furniture. The Chinese perfected their lacquer at a very early date. This is an opaque shellac process with many rubbed coats yielding a surface of great depth and durability. The Egyptians used pigment and polychromy more as we know it and their methods, together with gold and bronze leafing, were handed down through the Romans and the Byzantine artists to the Renaissance decorators.

Less elaborate work in the Early and Middle Ages appears to have been untreated; apparently common usage suggested polishing with oil or wax, which method continued in use until the end of the 17th century. Woods were exposed to the light until they darkened somewhat, then were rubbed with oil and beeswax.

Varnishing had been known to the Egyptians, but disappeared until the early 18th century. Martin, a French carriage painter, made a transparent varnish about 1740. This "Vernis Martin" so brought out the beauty of the wood that more exotic woods were sought in order to display the beauty of the treatment. The English finishers relied on their oil and wax process and on shellac which, rubbed smooth, produces a satiny finish, and very little English furniture before the end of the 18th century was given the "French Polish" or high gloss produced by rubbing and polishing gums.

It seems probable that varnish as we know it did not appear until American finishers dissolved resins in hot oils, about 1848. In cheaper work these varnishes were applied without rubbing, producing a cheap sticky looking effect.

Finishing has enjoyed much study in recent years. Synthetic lacquers (having nothing in common with Chinese Lacquer) developed out of nitro-cellulose compounds. They make a tight skin or film and yield beautiful finishes. At present, new finishes for special purposes are being developed constantly.

FINIALS

FIR. Family of pine trees. American varieties most used for furniture and construction grow on the West Coast in tremendous trees yielding long, wide boards. The wood is very soft, highly resinous and not susceptible to good finish; its use in furniture is therefore limited to interior parts.

FIRE SCREEN. Metal spark guard.

Also a panel on a pole adjustable to any height to ward off the direct heat of the fire. 842.

FISH TAIL. Carving on the top rail of a banister back chair.

FITMENTS. Articles made up and fitted to the walls of a room, as cabinets, bookcases, panelling, fireplaces, and built-in work in general (English usage).

FITTINGS. Metal mounts, handles, etc., applied to the completed piece of furniture. See *Hardware*.

FLAG (Flagg). Rushes used for weaving seats of chairs. 12.

FLAMBEAU. Flaming torch used as decoration.

FLAMBOYANT. Brilliant, sometimes overdecorated. Specifically the late Gothic of Northern Europe which tended to excessive ornamentation. 150, 367.

FLAME CARVING. Finial of a vase, spirally or naturalistically carved to represent a flame; from the Italian Renaissance. 61, 703.

FLAP; FLAP TABLE. English term for drop leaf.

FLEMISH. See *Netherlands*.

FLEMISH SCROLL. Baroque double scroll on chair legs, etc. The lower curve is a C-scroll separated from the upper, a reversed C-Scroll, by a right angle. 514.

FLIP-TOP TABLE. Double top dining or card table which unfolds like a book, supported either by pivoting about to the opposite axis, by a swing leg or by a runner. 502.

FLITCH. Part of a log which is sawed into veneers; the bundle of veneers when cut.

FLOWER BOXES. Ornamental boxes for the growing and display of flowers. During the reign of Charles II a craze for horticulture came to England from Holland. This prompted the designing of handsome boxes in which the bulbs and roots were grown indoors, and for two centuries fine examples were produced in veneers and japanned decoration.

FLUSH BEAD. Bead moulding sunk into the surface.

FLUTES, FLUTING. Hollows or channels cut perpendicularly in columns. In furniture flutings are applied to pilasters, legs, friezes, aprons, etc., particularly after the 16th century. Good flutes are close together and deep, with a sharply scooped curve for the ending. The ridge between the flutes is a fillet (430).

FLY RAIL. Swinging bracket which supports a flap or drop leaf.

EST, 1600-1625.   *Charles of London*

TUDOR - ELIZABETHAN (1558-1603).

STUART (James I, 1603-1622; Charles I, 1622-1649).

CROMWELLIAN OR PURITAN: 1649-1660.

Gothic shapes, essentially carpenter work, were embellished with Renaissance ornamental details.

The wood was invariably oak.

eft) WAINSCOT CHAIR, CROMWELLIAN.
ight) JOINT STOOL, JACOBEAN, CA. 1625.
opsen Manor Collection.

Courtesy Anderson Galleries

495. COURT CUPBOARD, Melon-Bulb Turning.   *Charles of London*

496. DRAW TABLE, LATE ELIZABETHAN. Ionic Capitals on Bulbous Turnings.   *French & Co.*

SQUARE, HEAVY OUTLINES WITH LARGE AREAS O
COMPLEX CARVING, RENAISSANCE IN ORIGIN, TYPIFY TH
FURNITURE OF THE REIGNS OF JAMES I AND CHARLES

497. CROMWELLIAN GATE-
LEG, about 1650.   *Stair*

498. EARLY JACOBEAN
WAINSCOT CHAIR.
French & Co.

499. SIDEBOARD, JACOBEAN.
Charles of London

500. RUSH LIGHT HOLDER.

501. COURT CUP-
BOARD, dated
1626.

502. FLIP-TOP TABLE, Middle 17th Century.

503. CARVED CHEST, Italian Influence, 1600-1610.   *Charles of Londo*

JACOBEAN AND CROMWELLIAN

SOMEWHAT LIGHTER FORMS AND SIMPLER DETAIL CHAR-
ACTERIZE THE FURNITURE OF THE MIDDLE 17th CENTURY

504. BED, CA. 1620.
Stair & Co.

505. GATELEG TABLE, typical Cromwellian
turnings. Copsen Manor Collection.
Courtesy Anderson Galleries

506. CHILD'S CHAIR, about 1650.
Metropolitan Museum

507. CREDENCE TABLE, about 1640. *Anderson Galleries*

508. LEATHER CHAIR, CROMWELLIAN.

509. CHEST, walnut, Italian style,
about 1665. *Anderson Galleries*

510. TABLE, EARLY JACOBEAN.
Anderson Galleries

511. CHAIR, about 1680.
Anderson Galleries

512. MARQUETRY CHEST-ON-CHEST, QUEEN ANNE.
Anderson

513. WALNUT CHAIR, Back and Leather Sea[t] 1675.

514. (Center) WILLIAM [&] MARY TABLE, Walnut C. 1690.

515. (Below) SILVERED MIRROR, 1700.
DRESSING TABLE, Walnut and Ash Burl, about 1690.
TABLE OR BRACKET CLOCK, about 1695.

516. WALNUT CHAIR, C. 1690.
Symons

517. (Below, Center) JAM[ES] WALNUT CHAIR. Re[?] crown motive a symbol [of] Restoration.

518. SMALL CHEST-ON-S[TAND] WILLIAM AND MAR[Y] 1690.
CLOCK, CHARLES II. by William Clement, L[ondon] 1680.
Photos Courtesy Anderson G[alleries]

Baroque lines in forms of large opposed curves, full moldings and vigorous contours prevailed in English work of the late Seventeenth Century. The style spread from Italy through France, Flanders and Holland.

519. STOOL, WILLIAM AND MARY.

520. WILLIAM AND MARY TALLBOY, OYSTERED.

521. CABINET, WILLIAM AND MARY.
Courtesy Anderson Galleries

522. SMALL WALNUT CHEST, CA. 1710. With writing top. *Metropolitan Museum*

523. SECRETARY, with broken Pediment. About 1710. Walnut. *Vernay*

524. ARMCHAIR, about 1730.

525. (Center) WALNUT CHAIR WITH SHAPED STRETCHER, CA. 1705.
Courtesy Anderson Galleries

526. (Lower Right) WING CHAIR, Walnut base, about 1705. *Cavallo*

527. WALNUT, Gilt, about 1710.
Anderson

529. PINE BOOKCASE OF BREAKFRONT TYPE, CA. 1745.
Anderson Galleries

530. IRISH WALNUT CHA
1730. *Anderse*

528. WALNUT, about 1710. *Anderson*

531. WINDSOR CHAIR with
Queen Anne style.

532. SILVERED SIDE TABLE, carved Gesso, CA. 1725. Cabriole
legs ending in hoof feet.

533. MAHOGANY SIDE TABLE with marble top. Claw and
CA. 1745.

ENGLISH FURNITURE OF THE EARLY EIGHTEENTH CENTURY SHOWS THE ASSIMILATED CONTINENTAL FORMS MERGED INTO A UNIFIED AND DISTINCTIVE NATIONAL STYLE

RED GESSO MIRROR, CA. 1710.
Ginsburg & Levy
SOLE TABLE, style of Kent, CA.
Buttfield
NER CHAIR, Walnut, CA. 1700.

537. MIRROR IN CARVED GILT FRAME, CA. 1735.
Vernay

538. FOLDING CARD TABLE (Concertina) with Lion Masks. Guinea holes. C. 1730.
Anderson Galleries

539. LACQUERED CLOCK CASE in Chinese taste. Made by William Giscard, Ely, about 1725. *Anderson*

540. WALNUT CHAIR, suggesting the Windsor form. CA. 1720. *Vernay*

541. SECRETARY, carved bracket feet. *Vernay*

543. HANGING SHELVES, yew and mahogany, C. 1765.

544. (Upper Right) GILT MIRROR, Chinese painting in Rococo frame, CA. 1755. *Vernay*

545. (Right) TILT-TOP TABLE, scalloped edge, CA. 1735. *Cavallo*

546. (Lower Right) MAHOGANY WRITING TABLE, Middle 18th Century. *Vernay*

542. SWING-LEG TABLE, mahogany, about 1730-1740. Early Chippendale. *Metropolitan Museum of Art*

CHIPPENDALE DOMINATES THE MAHOGANY PERIOD

553. BOOKCASE. Lattice pediment with Gothic detail. *Anderson Galleries*

547. GILT ROCOCO MIRROR, CA. 1760.

548. TEA TABLE with scrolled base. CA. 1760. Mahogany. *Vernay*

549. CHINESE CHIPPENDALE CHAIR.

550. LADDER BACK CHAIR.   **551.** CHIPPENDALE, Gothic taste. *Vernay*   **552.** EARLY WING CHAIR. *Anderson*

557. RENT TABLE, Mahogany, CA. 1790. ARMCHAIR, Leather, CA. 1790. *Vernay*

558. DRESSING TABLE, CA. 1790. French influence.

559. (Below) CHAIR OF HEPPLEWHITE STYLE, plume detail.

560. MAHOGANY WRITING TABLE, tambour top.

HEPPLEWHITE AND THE SATINWOOD PERIOD

ROCOCO INFLUENCE DECLINED AND YIELDED TO SEVERE CLASSIC TYPES.

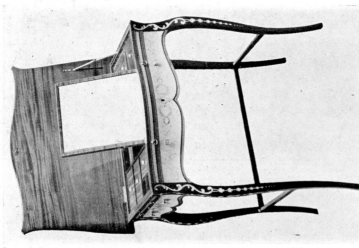

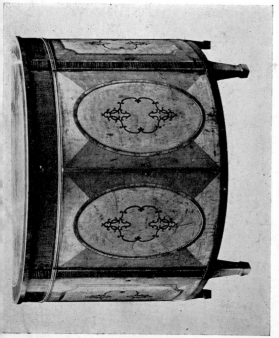

554. SATINWOOD COMMODE, INLAID, CA. 1785.

555. ARMCHAIR, Hepplewhite style, French inspiration. mahogany, CA. 1770.

556. BOOKCASE, harewood with painted decoration, CA. 1790.

Courtesy Arthur S. Vernay

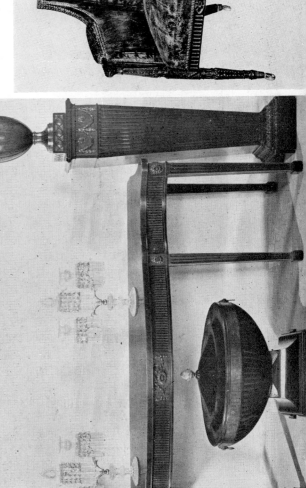

THE BROTHERS ADAM AND THE CLASSIC REVIVAL

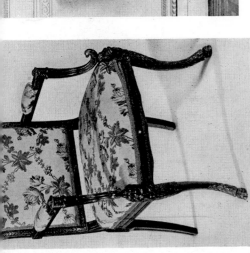

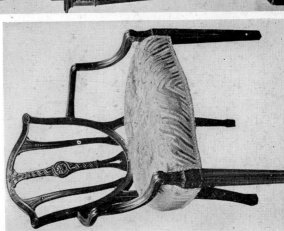

566A. COMMODE.
Vernay

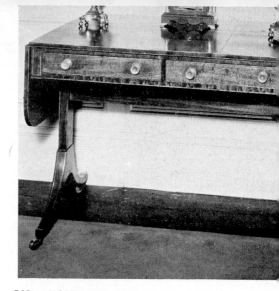

568. MAHOGANY SOFA TABLE, CA. 1790.

567A. SECRETARY BOOKCASE, CA. 1785. Mahogany and satinwood with typical painted panels. From the collection of Lord Leverhulme. *Courtesy Anderson Galleries*

569. LADIES' DESK, CA. 1790. Mahogany. *Anderson Galleries*
570. MAHOGANY ARMCHAIR.
Vernay

571. BAG - SEWING
Satinwood.

572. ARMCHAIR, C.
Metropolitan

ALL BOOKCASE-COMMODE,
nted, CA. 1810.
Vernay

SHERATON

CLASSIC DETAILS OF ANCIENT
ART INSPIRED EUROPEAN DESIGN
AT THE END OF THE EIGHTEENTH
CENTURY.

SHERATON'S DRAWING BOOKS
SHOWED ADAPTATIONS OF
CLASSIC FORMS TO FURNITURE
AND INFLUENCED MOST FURNI-
TURE DESIGN FROM 1800 TO
1830.

577. HAREWOOD COMMODE, C. 1800.
Metropolitan Museum of Art

RNER BASIN-STAND, mahogany.
Anderson Galleries

578. PEMBROKE TABLE, satinwood, inlaid, CA. 1805.
Anderson Galleries

576. SECRETARY, CA. 1780. Gothic
tracery, shallow pediment.
ARMCHAIR with cane back.
Vernay

NTED CHAIR, CA. 1800.
Anderson Galleries

579. MAHOGANY ARMCHAIR, CA. 1790.
Vernay

580. MAHOGANY FALL-FRONT BUREAU, about 1810. The style is essentially Louis XVI but detail and workmanship are English.   *St. James Galleries*

582. MAHOGANY SIDEBOARD with typical turned and reeded legs.   *Anderson Galleries*

581. CARD TABLE, inlaid rosewood, 1820.   *Colc*

583. ROSEWOOD CABINET, CA. Wire grilled front.   *V*

FOIL. Point at the intersection of two arcs. Gothic decorative detail used in the trefoil, quatrefoil, cinquefoil, etc.

FOLDING FURNITURE was made from earliest times, folding chairs and couches being found in Egyptian tombs. Their mechanical aspects always excite more enthusiasm in the mechanic than in the artist, as few folding pieces present a very attractive appearance. Sheraton's special ingenuity led him into very complex designs, but generally speaking, the mechanical demands preclude the possibility of a coherent substantial design. 256.

FOLIATED. Leaf ornaments.

FOLIO STANDS. Folio size books being more common prior to the 19th century than since, provision for their storage was made in deep cases. The top surface was generally tilted and adjustable for folios to be rested upon.

FOLD OVER. Desk leaf which doubles over to a table surface. Found in French table desks, Sheraton desks and American secretaries. 480.

FOOTBOARD. Panel in the lower end of a bed, or the entire end.

FOOT-RAIL. Front stretcher of a chair.

FOOT-STOOL. Low foot rest related to a chair.

FOOT WARMER. Box-shaped footstool with holes for radiating heat from a hot brick placed within. Sometimes decoratively carved in Early American work.

FORM. Old English term for bench or seat, usually long and backless (924).

FOUR POSTER. **FOUR POST BED.** American term for beds with the corner posts elongated. Probably the field bed or low canopy bed descended to the four poster by simply omitting the canopy. 99 et seq., 108, 123.

FRAME. Border or case for pictures, mirrors, etc. Also the wood skeleton of an upholstered chair. Also, in case joinery, the use of framing parts as a skeleton in place of merely joining the panels of a carcase together.

FRANCE. GOTHIC, approximately 1100-1450.

Up to 1400 French furniture was indistinct from the whole Gothic style of Northern Europe. This was essentially ecclesiastical. Secular art and architecture was in the minority and domestic work the smaller part of that. Gothic art has the quality of uniformity: architecture, woodworking, the metal crafts, etc., are homogeneous, designed directly from the same impulse, using the same ornaments and motives; a local, non-imported product, scarcely susceptible to outside influence. Social conditions were unsettled; people of high estate lived a semi-nomadic life while the submerged classes were too poor to afford or require furniture.

LATE GOTHIC COFFER

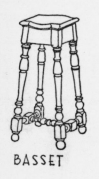

BASSET

The nomadic, unsettled life established the chest or coffer as the pre-eminent article of furniture. A portable catch-all for bedding, clothing, valuables, it also served as a bench, a serving table, a bed for retainers and other extemporaneous devices. At first mere planks with heavy iron reinforcements, its weight was the measure of strength. About the 14th century some genius invented the framed-in panel, a stout frame with thin filler-panels, which lightened and strengthened the whole structure. There were armoires, cabinets or cupboards; stools and forms, rude tables, chiefly demountable trestles and elementary seat structures. Oak predominated. Carving developed with the style, utilizing architectural details, conventionalized flora, grotesques. Painting was undoubtedly resorted to for decoration; polychromy for picking out moldings and ornaments and representational painting in panels. 150, 367, 584, 677-8, 680-1, 683.

With the rise of a semblance of political organization in the 14th century there arose in France a few individuals capable of dominating or subduing their neighbors and rivals. They acquired wealth and satellites. To their rude courts they imported from Italy and Spain artists, materials, methods and motives and at a later date, rulers. Thus, a fairly well defined France was ruled between 1453 and 1515 by Louis XI, Charles VIII and Louis XII. Their arts and architecture were persistently Gothic, but with decorative details of Italian flavor.

The chest, now more sedentary, became larger to serve as buffet or sideboard and acquired a permanent base. With sides raised it became the bench and then the sofa; fabrics and cushions were piled upon it. Permanent tables were still unknown, except minor specialized forms such as the *lectern* for reading, the *pupitre* for writing, the *demoiselle,* a kind of dressing table, and the *basset,* a very small square or round stand, like a tall stool. Beds were merely rough frames upon which were hung the many draperies; or *lit clos,* huge boxes with wooden panels. Seatings are described as of three types: the *faudesteuil,* the *banc* and the *chaire.* The *faudesteuil* (English fold-stool) was an X-type conceivably deriving from the Roman curule chair, and seems to have had implications of royalty. The most important *banc* is the ponderous *archebanc,* a coffer set either immovably before the fire or as an integral part of the bed, backed on to the side to serve as clothes closet and bed steps. Lesser *bancs* are the *bancelle,* the *escabeau,* the *selle* and the simple *forme* or *fourme.* The *chaire,* never quite the same as the English chair, had a throne-like importance, was quite immovable and mercilessly uncomfortable.

The cabinet appeared as an extension of the wainscoting. The various cupboards, armoires, etc. were fundamentally the same in their ancestry and evolved by regional and personal distinctions into the entire family of closet forms. It is just as reasonable to ascribe their origin to the coffer equipped with doors in front in place of a top lid.

Besides oak, other native woods were either slightly used or did
not survive so well; these may have been beech, chestnut, maple, pine
or elm. Walnut came into extensive use in the 15th century. Pieces
with ebony and ivory inlays are known after this date, but may have
been imported. Iron hinges, locks and straps were essential and highly
decorative features of the designs.

Gothic architecture about the year 1500 was still vital, evidenced
by such structures as the Hotel de Cluny in Paris, the Palais de Justice
at Rouen, the Chateaux of Amboise, Blois and many others. Yet in
all occurs a suggestion of classic Italian decoration. Woodwork followed closely with the adoption of antique vases and candelabra,
acanthus and rinceaux motives.

THE EARLY RENAISSANCE: FRANCOIS I, 1515-1547

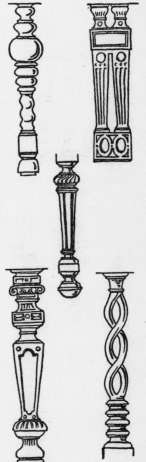

The Renaissance rolled into France in great waves of Italian influence during these years, assimilated and merged into a coherent style
There were incidental influences: Spanish marquetry (derived from
the Moors); German and Flemish details via craftsmen brought to
the court from the North. Walnut waxed and rubbed to a deep finish
became the dominant wood. Polychromy became rare. Surface carving
covered everything and high relief carving of plastic character was
carried to the point of distorting the outlines. Ebony was so prized
that a cabinet maker became—and still is—an *ebeniste*—a worker in
ebony. Hardware disappeared as part of the design. The homely Gothic
vegetable ornament yielded to the olive, the laurel and the acanthus,
although the latter became the endive, never to disappear.

The use of the architectural orders as decoration on furniture was
formulated in a work dated at Lyons, 1572, by Hugues Sambin, carver
of Dijon. Sambin's plates were the model for a great school of
"Huchiers." This guild brought cabinets to their highest development
in France. These were architectural compositions in bulk, but with
irregular, jagged outlines and Baroque architectural embellishment.
Pilasters were commonly used as decoration, often with circle or lozenge
panels. This diamond shape, elaborated into stars and other geometric
forms, remained a favorite ornament for nearly a century and persisted in the provinces after that.

The catalogue of ornaments of this period is most extensive. Grotesque figures growing out of almost equally grotesque foliage spread
over everything; swans and dolphins, sphinxes, chimeræ, griffins, masks
and mascarons, caryatides and atlantes—were carved in high relief.

The TABLE is conspicuously new during the period of Francois I.
From a disappearing utilitarian device it became an architectural entity.
The bases, vigorously carved after Italian models, had greater license
in ornament and scale. Smaller tables appeared.

The bed assumed a more recognizable form in the structure of four posts which carried the various draperies and curtains. The sheer carpentry of the bed became in the reign of Francois I a monumental affairs of pillars and canopy. The wood posts were extravagantly carved.

Chairs were scaled down from the monumental, and were even designed to yield comfort to women. The exaggerated costume of the time suggested the *Caquetoire,* a light armless chair similar to the farthingale chair of England. About 1580 straw seated chairs were in use. The flat squab cushions or *carreaux* indicate the trend toward comfort. 167, 201, 205, 216, 219, 254, 261, 376, 585 et seq.

THE HIGH RENAISSANCE

The style of Francois I prevailed with variations through the reigns of Henri II, Catherine d'Medici and Francois II, Charles IX, Henri III and Henri IV of Navarre. Fierce religious wars upset the logical sequence of furniture evolution and accelerated changes by the in-and-out movement of courtiers, craftsmen and architects. It was a violent period. The Gothic root withered and died—at least in the capitals. In the provinces it persisted due to the rise of a powerful middle class. Wealth and security seeped down through the classes. Merchants, artisans and peasants enriched their houses with furniture inspired by that of the local nobles. In adapting these luxuries to their needs they omitted much of the ornamentation, they substituted available woods and fabrics, they scaled the gigantic pieces down to their rooms and tempered the designs to their skill. The result is the school of French Provincial Furniture, known in France as *Mobilier Rustique,* as distinguished from *Meubles de Luxe.*

The height of the Renaissance in France may be judged from the work executed in Paris between 1550 and 1610. The engravings of du Cerceau reveal the supreme development of the cabinet. The *armoire à deux corps* or double bodied cupboard had the upper section narrower than the lower; pilasters, panelled and decorated with flat carving, framed the doors which were often panelled geometrically, such as with stars and diamonds in bold relief. Broken pediments crown many of these structures. Cartouches and flat strapwork carving prevailed over the purer Italian decoration. Table bases were involved compositions of columns, balusters, carytides and scrolls. Chairs were architectural in scale, except the unimportant types which remained stiff and uncomfortable. This phase is sometimes labelled the style of Henri IV, but it cannot be precisely distinguished from the work executed under Louis XIII. 172, 173, 927, 963, 968-9.

LOUIS XIII, 1610-1643

Gaudily splendid, monumental, overpowering, the furniture of this epoch reflects a rich parvenu imperialism. The names of the period are the great in their fields: Mazarin, Molière, Corneille, Rubens, Descartes, Pascal. A period of great power, it brought the High Renaissance to a vivid climax. Walnut and ebony were the principal woods. Panels, columns and pilasters of semi-precious stones or moulded stucco panels were introduced into cabinets. Marquetry came from the Low Countries. Tortoise shell and gilt bronze contributed to the lavish air. Carving is in the Flemish style: rich and turgid. Turning is used not only for legs of all types of furniture, but also for applied ornament. Turnings with complex profiles are distinctive of the style, but not so much so as the elaborate geometric panels and deep moldings. This vigorous panelling, likely of Flemish origin, is probably the outstanding clue to Louis XIII furniture.

Cabinets are the pièce de résistance. They cover the whole range from little coffers covered with embroidered velvet to colossal structures carried on twelve ornate supports. They are now no longer necessarily vertical; the buffet form as we know it appears in Guyenne and Gascony with drawers below. The *Bureau* is new, evidently adapted from the cabinet by the addition of a fall front although the name derives from the cloth used to cover earlier writing tables. Tables with expanding tops for dining are another novelty of the period of Louis XIII. These either were hinged flaps or telescoping types; the bases were commonly turned legs with elaborate detail, although the classic vase or slab shapes are frequently used. The H-stretcher is typical. There is a great variety of small tables, some oval, round or octagonal, but chiefly oblong. Beds were still great masses of fabric covering the rough wooden structure.

Chairs are generally low, possibly due to the current headdress and ruffs. The word *fauteuils* appears in inventories, but uncertainty exists as to whether it indicates the type so called after the period of Louis XIV. The most important change in seatings occurs under Louis XIII in the permanent nailing-down to seats of fixed upholstery. Leather was commonly used for upholstery and silver or gilt nail-heads were decoratively applied, either close together or in the daisy pattern. 170, 590 et seq., 816, 850, 886, 928, 1033, 1045.

LOUIS XIV—1643-1715—BAROQUE

Louis XIV came to the throne of a self-consciously powerful France, and with deliberation proceeded to focus it into the center of the world. The Gobelin tapestry factory was transformed into the "Manufacture Royale des Meubles de la Couronne." Under Le Brun's direction Jean

LOUIS XIV

and Daniel Marot, Bérain, Le Pautre, Leclère, Andrau, engraved designs for furniture. The outstanding cabinetmakers of this period were Boulle, Oppenord, Cucci, Caffieri, Peter Golle. It is significant that these are not French names but Italian, Flemish, Dutch. Yet the product was French; clearly welded into a positive style, for all its foreign roots.

The style of Louis XIV is distinctly Baroque, the robustly exaggerated manner emanating from the Jesuit architecture of Italy. It is sumptuous, large in scale, masculine for all its lavish decoration, completely symmetrical. The straight line predominates; curves are restrained within severe outlines, lending formal dignity. Panels are simple rectangles, occasionally hollowed at the corners, or with semi-circular tops, or inset circles and ovals. They are always defined with strong mouldings of classic quality. Carving is rich and plentiful, employing animal forms of nature and mythology to express the current love of allegory. Masks, satyrs, lions' paws and heads, sphinxes, griffins, dolphins, acanthus in endless variety; water lilies, oak, laurel, olive leaves; weapons, musical instruments, agricultural implements, ribbons, festoons, swags, knots. Architectural details were sparingly used for small furniture prior to 1680.

Woods were rich and varied. The simple oak and walnut and even ebony lacked magnificence; elaborate marquetry panels formed large surfaces. Almond, holly, box, pear and other woods were toned by fire but this did not suffice and Boulle perfected marquetry of tortoise shell, brass, horn, pewter, tin, ivory and bone and mother-of-pearl in intricate detail. Bronze appliqués were imposed upon the whole. Painting was liberally resorted to, strong colors such as red and green being favored. Gilded and silvered furniture was substituted where real gold and silver were prohibitive—although an incredible amount of metal was used for small furniture prior to 1680. The gilding was exceptionally fine and further distinguished massive armchairs and tables.

The *"Chinese Taste"* became a rage; first with the collection of porcelains and finally in the effort to duplicate the lustrous depth of Oriental lacquer. *Martin* perfected the process of varnishing known as *Vernis-Martin,* of great brilliancy and solidity.

Changed manners affected the forms and variety of furniture. The coffer had completely disappeared, and the monumental cabinet of Louis XIII declined. Outside of Paris, cupboards, while developing in the general form, were ornamented in the old style of Louis XIII. In fact, the entire ornamental system retained much from the earlier 17th Century. In Normandy a narrow, graceful form for the storage of bonnets is known as *Bonnetière.* "Bookcase cupboards" had doors fitted with iron wire grilles. The most important piece of receptacle furniture after the period of Louis XIV is the commode, stemming either from the table with drawers or the coffer on legs, fitted with drawers.

Boulle's name is attached to some famous commodes, irrational and pretentious. Others exhibit the curved leg and doe's foot destined to become the cabriole leg.

Beds achieved new heights, literally and figuratively. The woodwork was still a skeleton for the manifold draperies consisting of as many as thirty-three distinct parts. Some arrangements of suspended testers were known as "duchess-beds" and "angel beds." The canopy of the first hung completely from the ceiling while the tester of the angel bed was shorter than the bed and had side curtains looped to the wall. In these types, the actual bed frame or stead was a detached unit becoming handsomely treated in its own right. The rest bed or chaise-longue was a logical product of this age of luxury.

Of tables, the newest form under Louis XIV is the console type. Decorative tables having become immovable due to the great weight of the stone tops and elaborate bases were set permanently against the wall, the hidden side left undecorated. The architectural console became common as a base. Free standing tables with the double console were developed. Table legs were also turned or flattened balusters. Important types such as these were gilded, but natural or painted woods were used for smaller tables suitable to carry trays, for coffee, candelabra or writing stands; there were toilet tables and night tables and specialized game tables and desks of various types.

SEATS: The etiquette of seating is in this period the philosophy of royalty. Thus in order of importance range the arm chair, chairs with backs, joint stools, folding stools, hassocks with gold gimp, hassocks with silk edging. The Louis XIV throne chair was majestic indeed; high, wide and handsome, it stood upon a dais with several steps. It was solid silver, draped with crimson velvet. The back was eight feet high, draped with full gold embroidery carried by caryatides, fifteen feet high. This was the model for important armchairs. They always had stretchers, first H-shaped, later the serpentine X. Legs were scrolled or flat or turned balusters; the arms were well molded and swung into the back with great curves. The "Confessional" was the first of the Bergère type, or fully upholstered easy chair. The armless chairs follow the caquetoires of Louis XIII. The sofa was the most important seating invention of the period. The first was a rest bed or canapé, almost bed in shape and upholstery; the word sofa appears about 1680, and the later sofas were less fully upholstered. Caning for chairs grew in popularity and straw-seated turned chairs, called *chaises a la capucine* were used in the palaces as well as in peasant homes. 302, 426, 597 et seq., 779, 852.

RÉGENCE

Louis XIV died in 1715, but long before this a modification of his style set in. The transitional period is marked politically by the regency

of Philippe d'Orléans from 1715 to 1723, when the young Louis XV became king. The term Régence loosely describes the transition from the high style of Louis XIV to the feminine style of Louis XV. The massive square grandeur of Louis XIV relaxes into softer outlines and freer ornament. Curves at first only modify the rectangular forms in corners and ornamental details; later structural members as legs and stretchers are shaped into flowing lines.

The craze for Chinoiserie is responsible for much of the ornamental character of the Régence and Louis XV styles. Louis XIV's explorations and commercial exploitation of the Far East brought to Europe Chinese porcelains, jade, decorations depicting formalized landscapes and figures. The technique somehow suggested the use of natural forms in decorations, and rocks, shells, flowers and birds became the basis of a manner dubbed "Rock and Shell"—Rocaille et Coquille; years later this was unsympathetically contracted into ROCOCO, by which name we characterize furniture and manners emanating from this age, having a florid, gaily absurd manner.

The cabriole leg—*pied de biche* or doe's foot—was no novelty but in the Régence became the characteristic shape. It was so curved as to make the vertical line flow evenly into the horizontal of the apron. The typical curve is that of the cross bow.

Ornament was less classical, discarding mythology for nature, though ribbons, foliage, shells and scrolls are usually symmetrically arranged. Chair backs have pierced carved splats. In general the wider range of ornament has delicate movement austerely restrained within clear architectural outlines. The lighter touch also applies to materials; ebony and walnut are too somber and yield to fine veneers of polished rosewood and lighter colors.

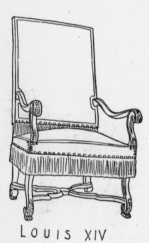

LOUIS XIV

Robert de Cotte, Bérain, Marot, Mansart, Boulee and others carried over the grand tradition; younger men then in their early phases created novelties destined to be the elements of the Louis XV style. But the styles of the Régence is epitomized in the work of Charles Cressent. His supreme creations are commodes, whose cabinetwork is important only as a base for superbly chased bronze appliqués. 118, 178, 604 et seq., 883.

LOUIS XV—ROCOCO

The ultimate in decorative furniture is, to many critics, that produced in France between 1700 and 1760. Louis Quinze furniture avoided like a plague the appearance of symmetry and the right angle. Every device was employed to alleviate the rectangle. In plan or elevation no piece of furniture is permitted straight lines . . . only flowing lines, everything was rounded so that the eye might follow any line without perceiving the junction of planes. Ornaments were drawn from shells, flowers, musical instruments, pastoral objects like shepherd's

REGENCE

crooks and baskets, all naturally and unconventionally rendered. Chinese themes were capriciously misinterpreted. Architecture alone was rejected as a source of ornament.

Marquetry and inlaying assumed primary importance. For large veneer surfaces, rosewood, satinwood, amaranth and tulipwood were used, while marquetry was made up of most of the exotic varieties known today. Mahogany rose to great popularity and the native fruit woods, notably cherry and plum, were used in Paris as well as in the provinces.

Painted furniture grew in demand through the middle years of the reign, the brightest reds, greens, yellows and black being emphasized with fillets painted in gold and contrasts. Lacquering processes were studied, although much woodwork was actually sent to the Orient to be decorated. The delays incidental to this procedure encouraged the development of varnishes whose depth rivalled that of the Oriental lacquers. The Brothers Martin with their *Vernis Martin* were phenomenally successful. Gilding, only slightly less popular than during the Louis XIV period, covered console tables and mirrors, chairs and small tables.

Metal appliqués were universal. The costliest pieces were chiefly decorated by this means. But in more modest furniture the bronzes were all functional, being handles, lock escutcheons, keys, feet or fillets to protect weak veneers. That both Meissonier and Caffieri were metal workers before they made furniture is evidence of the importance of this decoration to the style.

Marble of many colors made tops for commodes and tables: onyx and alabaster were used for small pieces. Imitations of stone were variously successful. Small China plaques were let into table tops and inlaid in mahogany panels. Mirrors likewise were set into panels.

The types of furniture follow closely those described previously as originating during the Régence. The commode type was expanded into many forms, among them slant-front desk types. Tables for every purpose shared one common feature—the cabriole leg. Expanding dining tables "of the English kind" came from England about 1770; other types were developed earlier. The small tables or *ambulantes* have great variety. Console tables were architectural fixtures, the most typical having legs which came together to a point at the base. Special tables were designed for every game. Dressing tables of wide variety, writing tables (bureaux), work tables, etc. make a long list of table shapes.

LOUIS XV

Comfortable chairs, chaise longues and sofas were dimensioned to the human frame and shaped for luxurious ease. Chair backs and seats were low, modified to the current costume and habits. The bergère was made with solid sides and loose down cushions. Armless chairs, designed for voluminous skirts, were popular as they had been a century before. Cane chairs were important and often had loose cushions

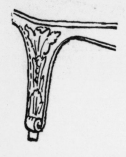

of lemon or red morocco. Straw or rush chairs appeared in great variety and imagination.

Chaise-longues are significant in this luxurious time. Ladies received *en déshabille* in their boudoirs, and the furniture designed to accommodate this pose varied between a small bed and a large chair. Turkish inspiration provided types of "sophas" or full length beds with backs on three sides and the large "ottoman."

Beds developed along more modern concepts, since specialized bedrooms were smaller and warmer. This permitted the diminution of the completely enclosed bed. Though the canopy and draperies were retained, they were minor or decorative, and were generally supported on four posts. The *Duchesse* bed had a flat canopy as long as the bed, with the counterpane falling to the floor at the foot. There were straight side draperies. The "Angel Bed" had equal headboard and footboard, while the half length canopy hung from the ceiling and had two looped back draperies at the head. The "Polish Bed" had the head- and foot-board but instead of the high tester had a curving dome carried on four iron rods, with four curtains looped up at the corners.

Of the cabinetmakers of the period, Jean Francois Oeben is supreme particularly for his marquetry. Phillippe Caffieri, Meissonier, Oppenord, Oudry and many others developed superb techniques to meet the demands of a style essentially unstructural. 276, 308, 312-3, 414, 417-8, 445-6, 610 et seq., 757, 820, 835, 842, 859, 905, 998, 1019 et seq., 1026, 1054, 1068.

LOUIS XVI, 1774-1793—THE CLASSIC REVIVAL

The inevitable revolt from the curved line came long before Louis XVI. But here again the old king outlived the taste he fostered. Some time after 1760 the curve-weary demanded pointedly a return to simple forms and straight lines. The answer came from Italy in an intellectual movement not unlike the early Renaissance—the imitation of antiquity.

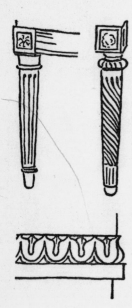

Excavations in Greek and Roman ruins had been in progress for many years but the unearthing of Pompeii and Herculaneum set off a new spark. Ancient architectural forms became the basis of furniture design as they had been in the Renaissance. The architectural spirit demands recognition of supports, so legs are truthfully expressed as sheer vertical members, forming right angles with the aprons, etc. The vertical is emphasized by fluting and grooving; the architecture suggests bases and capitals in the form of mouldings and feet. Curves where used are cut-off segments of ellipses or circles; in legs they are gradually straightened out entirely. Panels are important in their flatness and absence of decoration, being set off by exquisitely studied mouldings. Ornament is classic, mathematically symmetrical and recalls all the forms of Louis XIV; laurel and acanthus, egg-and-dart, oak leaves and Greek palm leaves, fretwork, rinceaux, ribbons, etc. Fluting was partially filled in (cannellated) the filling ending in small vase turnings or torch effects. Bound arrows, lyres, swans, urns, wreaths, festoons, fanciful animals, etc. were adapted from Greco-Roman sources. Brass galleries were applied to tables, commodes and bookcases: delicate brass or gilt moldings framed drawers. Ornament varies from the earlier style in its delicate scale, its tactful proportion and the complete denial of the sinuous line.

Mahogany was the preeminent wood. Rosewood, tulipwood, and others were combined in geometric marquetry, arranged as diamond and lozenge patterns. Ebony returned to favor. Black and gold lacquer was popular and much painted furniture of grayish white, gray green and similar soft tones was used. Sèvres China plaques were inset into desks, cabinets, etc.

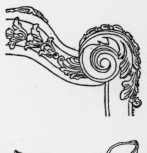

Jean Francois Riesener was the great master of the era. Oeben's pupil, he later married his widow. David Roentgen, known only as David; Georges Jacob, and his son, called after the Revolution, Jacob Desmalter; Etienne Avril, Martin Carlin, Leleu, Saunier, Schwerdfeger, Lalonde, Aubert and innumerable others created masterful designs. A few, as Montigny, Levasseur and Severin, copied or adapted the style of Louis XIV and the technique of Boulle. Others, as Beneman and Weissweiler, worked so closely to the antique architectural ideal that they actually created the later Empire style.

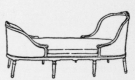

The character and function of the individual pieces scarcely varied from the lines established under Louis Quinze. Commodes, chairs and sofas, desks and tables merely assumed straight lines. A few new shapes appear in chairs by Aubert, excessively classical; such are the curule chairs and seats and sofas with roll backs, Roman tripods for tables, and a glazed commode called the vitrine for the display of curios. Beds are smaller following the styles set earlier, with the angel bed the dominant type.

Fabrics were of small patterned silks, (small patterned) tapestries and the whole range of Louis XV materials. The vogue for printing cotton and linen created the Toile de Jouy. 104-5, 120-1, 146, 149, 319-21, 325, 413, 415, 421, 427, 431-2, 444, 461, 467, 483, 486, 617 et seq., 777, 795, 823, 836, 843, 860-2, 907-8, 995, 1000-4, 1021, 1027-8.

DIRECTOIRE 1795-1799, CONSULATE 1799-1804

The period of the Revolution 1789-1795 was chaos. A somewhat authoritative government, the Directory, assumed control in 1795. Directoire is essentially Louis XVI simpler, adorned with the symbolism of the Revolution—the Phrygian caps, arrows, pikes, triangles, wreaths, clasped hands, the fasces and lictor of Rome, etc. There were "Patriotic Beds." It is improbable that any considerable quantity of furniture was produced during this troubled era, short at best, so that it is difficult to construe a full style out of the few scattered remains. Simplicity, grace, directness, charm; straight lines with restrained classic double curves; the swan, lyre, stars, in addition to the antique and Revolutionary symbols are the index of decorative motives. Woods were more often native fruitwood, walnut, oak, than mahogany, now that foreign trade was difficult.

For the most part the old cabinetmakers continued in their work: Reisener, David, Jacob, Beneman. Two young unknown designers, *Percier* and *Fontaine,* worked under Jacob and in their hands lay the evolution of the developing style. 124, 127, 317, 323, 326, 355, 429, 625 et seq., 825, 837, 866, 936, 939, 1066-1069.

EMPIRE, 1804-1815

The classic Revolution became Imperial under Napoleon in 1804. His absolutism reached into the arts and the wavering Directoire style was galvanized by edict into a solid formulated manner. Percier and Fontaine's first work, issued in 1801, expressed a system of archeological copying and adaptation in the grand manner.

The Empire differs from the Louis XVI in the degree to which it absorbs classic forms whole and undigested. It took the few vestiges of ancient furniture literally, and tried to stretch them over the whole field of furniture without modification. The discriminating scale of Louis Seize was lost completely; architectural forms were taken whole rather than as motives for decoration. Absolute symmetry, cubic rectangular or geometric shapes, heavy solid proportions, characterized all pieces. Large surfaces were flat and plain, free of moldings or panelling to emphasize the highly polished wood grain. The ornamentation consisted almost exclusively of bronze or flat gilt appliqués (the invention of Gouthière in the preceding era) molded into stiffly formalized relief, and tacked on. These motives included military symbols as the sword and shield, arrows and wreaths and winged figures, torches and the whole catalogue of ancient symbolism, all coldly archeological and precise. Napoleon invented a few of his own symbols: the bee and the letter N. Cornucopiae, palm leaves and laurels were stiffened and added to the list; in fact, nothing available to the Greco-Roman researchers was overlooked. Carving was entirely avoided except for the arms and posts of chairs and table legs where they could be transformed into lions or griffins or caryatides.

Mahogany was the overwhelming favorite. The rich deep red color was favored, along with rosewood and ebony, and other woods were stained in imitation. Knot elm, thuya and similarly burled veneers were equally rich. Marble is classic and was therefore acceptable. Fabrics were always deep and rich in color, primary reds, greens and yellows, deep browns; all in hard textures, with large imperial patterns or diaper patterns with the usual stars, etc.

Tables are invariably round, generally on a pedestal or tripod base. Tops are often thick marble or porphyry slabs. All cabinet furniture was designed as miniature architecture. Desks vary from table types with superimposed banks of drawers in temple-facade form to the large cabinet type almost flat with fall front. The drop front type evolved under Louis XVI as *Bonheur du jour* was popular. Beds of the "Angel" type were first favored but the typical Empire bed is the boat style with richly scrolled ends of the same height.

Chairs and sofas are stiff and clumsy and supremely uncomfortable. The shapes are forced copies of the Greek and Roman ceremonial seats, unwillingly rendered in wood instead of the original stone and bronze. The chaise longue developed a rather new type—the Recamier type and the Méridienne. With the eclipse of Napoleon the impetus and the style disappeared together. 128-9, 357, 434, 646 et seq., 822, 867, 931, 1061, 1083.

PROVINCIAL FRENCH

The foregoing classification of French styles is essentially Parisian. The great body of people in the provinces were only partly aware of or interested in these developments. The local styles were of course constantly modified by the new influences, but the degree of acceptance was always subject to local conditions. These include degree of wealth, climate, available materials and skill, and local customs and prejudices. As a whole, the provincial furniture is honestly designed for family life, as distinct from the *meubles de luxe* of the capital, and in its restrained scale, constructional quality and charm forms a distinct body of styles.

The bourgeoisie and peasantry of the 17th century acquired wealth but continued to live simply. Their furniture comprised only the essentials: a closed bed, a few straw-bottomed stools, a cupboard or hutch. The few additional pieces of the 17th century were receptacles: wardrobes, cabinets, various forms of buffets. In Flanders, the Gothic forms persisted. The wealthier provinces like Burgundy and Gascony adopted the style of Louis XIII enthusiastically and have clung to it ever since. The long reign of Louis XIV witnessed in the provinces little more than a development of Louis XIII, but the style of Louis XV struck so responsive a chord that the 18th century became known as "Le Siècle de Louis Quinze." In many sections they continued to make furniture in this mode until the end of the nineteenth century. Louis XVI was only partially accepted, the classic details being imposed upon the curved Louis XV forms. The Empire style simply passed the provinces by.

The buffet and cupboard forms are the most important provincial types. They evolved out of sheer utility and had characteristic shapes and names in different regions. The armoire likewise developed in variety according to local usage. Beds were more or less closed in according to the climate; those in Provence were open at an early date,

while the mountainous sections of the Vosges, Auvergne and Savoie retain the *lit clos,* a room within a room. Straw-seated chairs were treated with innate distinction everywhere, some distinctly minor forms are interesting. The Pannetière or bread box is universal as are wall shelves and knife boxes.

Local types of decoration often survived even when the design books from Paris suggested new ideas. Normandy long exhibited traces of her Viking ancestry. Alsace shows Germanic or Swiss traces in painting; the metal workers of Provence and Limousin developed handsome steel mounts as hinges and handles. The available woods make for variations; oak in Normandy with brass fittings; walnut and the fruitwoods trimmed with polished steel in Lorraine; walnut in Savoie; even the imported tropical woods in the Saintonge region, all tend to differentiate not only the technique of carving but the whole style of the piece. 177, 228, 230, 423-4, 430, 452, 472, 491, 634 et seq., 872, 884, 888, 1052.

INFLUENCE OF
LOUIS XVI STYLE

PROVINCIAL LOUIS XIV

FRENCH FURNITURE AFTER THE EMPIRE

PROVINCIAL LOUIS XV

The Nineteenth Century was in France as elsewhere a period of aesthetic indetermination. Styles floundered from outright copying or eclecticism, to misbegotten attempts at conscious organization. After Napoleon there was a tepid Restoration, no more successful in art than in politics. Follow an abortive Gothic revival, a heterogeneous Louis Philippe manner, various resurgences of the classic spirit and finally a series of outright "Styles" in the limited sense of the word. The French response to the intellectual-artistic rebellion of the 1880-1900 period was the Art Nouveau. It attained a vogue and a mild success in silver and ceramics but its furniture, as illogical but not so charming as Louis Quinze, was less appreciated. (990.)

MODERN FRENCH

The unorthodox French approach to design has been a spur to advanced thought the world over and the French government has provided further impetus with the great Expositions. The International Exposition of Decorative Art in 1925 evoked tremendous interest in the various schools of design operating in Europe. The French designers exhibited well developed tendencies in two schools; one, which may be designated as the Romantic, offering handsomely presented shapes reminiscent of traditional forms; the other, entirely forward-looking, based on "form follows function," a social-engineering concept. 490, 796, 808.

FRANCIS I. King of France 1515-1547. Builder of Chateaux of Blois, Chambord and Fontainebleau. In them the Renaissance has its first great French expression. It was really a mingling of flamboyant Gothic and Italian Renaissance ornament, more Italian than French. Walnut was favored in the South, oak in the North. Cabinets, tables and chairs were rich and profusely carved and inlaid.

FRENCH BED. Roll end bedstead without posts.

FRENCH FOOT. Scrolled or spiralled foot, ornamented as with a dolphin. Also a slightly swept-out foot as used by Hepplewhite. 407.

FRENCH POLISH. Process of finishing wood with a high gloss by padding-on successive films of shellac in spirits.

FRET. Fretwork, Fretting (Latticework). Interlaced ornamental work, either perforated or cut in low relief on a solid ground, usually in geometric patterns; also the tracery of glazed doors and windows. A Chinese importation, it was sparingly used on the Continent but taken up avidly by the Georgian masters. Particularly characteristic of Chippendale's Chinese manner, it was also adapted to his Gothic designs. 481, 543, 553.

Flat fretwork, as painted and inlaid, comes down from the Greek and is also a feature of Arabian and Moorish design.

FRIESIAN, FRIESLAND. Scratch carving in simple geometric designs, as the wheel. In early American work it is found as decoration on rude pine Bible boxes, spoon racks, etc. (437.)

FRIESLAND CUPBOARDS. Important cabinets with rich carved cornices in the Baroque Style, made in Friesland (Netherlands) in the 17th century.

FRIEZE. Central part of the entablature, between the architrave and cornice. A flat member, it is usually the surface most decoratively treated with formal ornament, inscriptions, painted or inlaid detail. See *Orders*.

FRINGE. Ornamental edging used in upholstering furniture; made of twisted threads, yarns, tassels, etc. of silk or other materials, often with metal.

ENGLISH FRETS

FRISE (Frieze). Heavy woolen or linen and cotton cloth with a nap used for upholstering.

FRUIT WOOD. The woods of the various fruit trees have always been used for small furniture, especially in provincial work. These woods are usually hard and durable and polish well. Pear, Apple and Cherry are most used of this class.

FRUIT MOTIVE. Motive in Italian and Tudor carving; also in Grinling Gibbons' work.

FUNCTIONAL. In general use as applied to furniture, serviceable, utilitarian, designed primarily for use rather than decoration. Specifically, in modern design the school which eschews the decorative nature of furniture in order to emphasize its special utility. It is the outgrowth of Sullivan's edict that "form follows function." Only those factors which directly concern function may be accepted as elements of the design. Analysed closely it will appear that pure functional design tends to restrict the outward expression of functional forms into the narrowest bounds, resulting in abject poverty of aesthetic interest. On the other hand the scope of room composition is emphasized.

Due to the conflict between functional and decorative approaches pseudo-functionalism in furniture is rampant. Fake structural forms and construction methods lack both straightforward functional design and the intrinsic beauty of traditional forms. See *Modern, International Style*.

FURNITURE. American usage limits the word to movable articles, equivalent to the French "meuble" or German "möbel." In England the term is more inclusive, embracing every type of equipment, whether portable or built-in. Thus "chimney-furniture" includes the accessory furnishings of the fireplace: fenders, andirons, tools, etc. The room panelling and built-in fittings are also furniture.

Decorative Furniture includes all types of more or less utilitarian pieces to which is applied some effort of beautification. In former times every article of use was treated ornamentally except the crudest utilitarian objects. Modern practise has discarded much of this decoration, and even furniture has been exempted from the erstwhile need of elaboration; the decorative aspect of rooms is conceived to be a matter of composition of abstract elements, rather than an association of many objects of individual ornamental claims. Most furniture today is designed in the terms of modern utility but with the decorative aspects of former periods. This cannot be correctly called *period furniture* since it modifies proportions, woods, finishes, structural methods, purpose, or other features which in a true period copy should follow the example of the original.

FRENCH RENAISSANCE
THE EARLIEST RENAISSANCE INFLUENCES FROM ITALY
MERELY IMPOSED CLASSIC DETAILS ON GOTHIC STRUCTURES

584. DRESSOIR, 15th Century. Oak. Pure Gothic with portrait medallions, the earliest Renaissance detail.
From the Brady Collection, Courtesy Anderson Galleries

OAK CHAIR, 16th Century. Moldings, panels and carving are pure Italian Renaissance, but the structure is Gothic.
French & Co.

586. WALNUT CREDENCE, 16th Century. Style of Henri II. Details are Italian High Renaissance.
Brady Collection, Courtesy Anderson Galleries

"CAQUETOIRE" — A small Armchair about 1600.

588. "ARCHEBANC-COUCHETTE"—Oak chest of Gothic form with Renaissance ornament, served as coffer, or couch. Henri II, Mid-16th Century.

589. WALNUT CAQUETOIR with medallion, about 1600

590. "CHAUFFEUSE." Walnut.
Anderson

591. BURGUNDIAN TABLE. Walnut with typical turnings, H-stretcher.

592. WALNUT ARMCHAIR c⟨ Moquette. *Fr*

LOUIS XIII
HIGH RENAISSANCE
1610-1643

593. LARGE CUPBOARD from Gascony. Twisted pillars and diamond point panels.

594. WALNUT CABINET in Burgundian style.
Metropolitan Museum

595. OAK DRAW-TOP TABLE with gadrooned apron. Brady Collection.
Courtesy Anderson Galleries

596. WALNUT DRAW-TOP TABLE of earlier style, about 1600.
Anderso⟨

97. CONSOLE TABLE in natural oak. Square baluster legs.

598. BOULLE CABINET, CA. 1680.

LOUIS XIV
BAROQUE
1643-1715

599. ARMCHAIR. Walnut, tapestry cover, cabriole leg. End of period.
Metropolitan Museum

600. ARMCHAIR. Walnut, gilt, velvet cover, square baluster legs. About 1680-1700.

T PEDESTAL.

603. CLOCK by Boulle.

602. WRITING TABLE of Boulle Work.

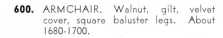

604. CARVED OAK OVER-MIRROR PANEL. Combination of straight and curved lines in simple architectural outline is typical of the Regency work. *Metropolitan Museum*

605. MEDALLIER. Rosewood and gilt bronze cabinet by Charles Cressent.

606. CLOCK in rosewood and satinwood with gilt ornaments, by Cressent.

607. COMMODE of rosewood veneer. Mainly baroque but with a tendency to lighter detail.

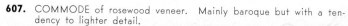

REGENCY
TRANSITIONAL
1715-1723
The curved line became prominent in the later Louis XIV work and dominated all design until after the middle of the Eighteenth Century.

608. CANE SOFA of beechwood. Typic ornament.

609. STOOL of walnut, covered with bro

NED BEECHWOOD
IR.   *Anderson*

ROR, gilt wood.

NSOLE TABLE, painted
, C. 1740.
          French & Co.

613. ARMCHAIR by Louis Cres-
son. Gilt frame, wine-col-
ored velvet.
          Metropolitan Museum

LOUIS XV
ROCOCO
1723-1774

614. COMMODE, Coromandel
lacquer in Chinese style.
Gilt mounts.

616. WRITING TABLE of violet
wood with gilt-bronze
mountings. *Anderson Galleries*

A, walnut frame.

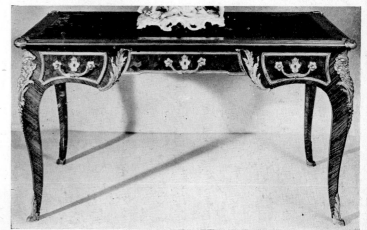

LOUIS XVI
CLASSIC REVIVAL
1774-1793

617. KINGWOOD SECRETARY.

618. TRUMEAU, painted.
Anderson Galleries

619. CARVED DETAIL.
Metropolitan Museum

620. A C A J O U
CHEST by
J. P. Du-
santoy.

621. D E M I -
L U N E
C O M -
M O D E.
Tulipwood.
Anderson Galleries

622. ARMCHAIR by F. Milet.
Metropolitan Museum

623. CANAPE.

Anderson Galleries

624. PAINTED ARMC
Anderso

CARVED AND GILT MIRRORS.

PAINTED CHAIR, FRUITWOOD TABLE.

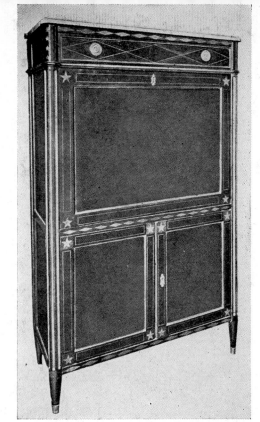

625. DROP FRONT ESCRITOIRE. Mahogany with brass inlay.

626. BUFFET TABLE. Mahogany. Beginning of style.
Anderson Galleries

WRITING TABLE. Acajou and brass.

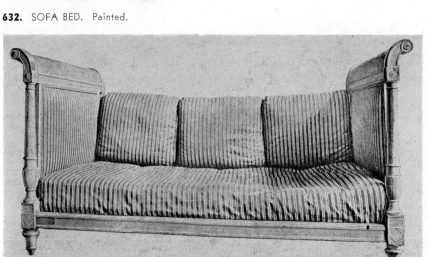

630. CLAVECIN by Erard Freres, Paris, 1802. **633.** WRITING CABINET.

"ATHENIENNE."

632. SOFA BED. Painted.

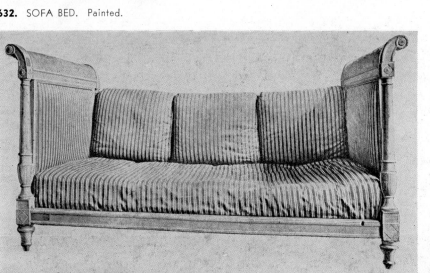

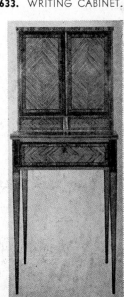

634. COFFER FROM HAUT-VOSGES.

635. SMALL GILT MIRROR. *Ruseau*

636. SIDEBOARD-DRESSOIR FROM LORRAINE.

PROVINCIAL FRENCH

styles did not always follow the Parisian influence im
diately, if at all, but often clung to accepted fo
which were developed with great individuality.

637. BURGUNDIAN CUPBOARD in oak, diamond point panels, 17th Century.

638. (Below) CHAIRS AND COMMODE from Normandy, late 18th Century.

Courtesy Angelo Romano, Ltd.

639. CREDENCE SIDEBOARD of walnut wood—from Arles.

640. WALNUT KNEADING-TROUGH, from Arles.

641. ALSATIAN BUFFET CABINET.

S XVI COMMODE, fruitwood with marble top. *Anderson Galleries*   **642.** LYRE BACK STRAW SEATED CHAIR.

TWOOD SIDECHAIR. Classic influence.
IS XV COMMODE, WALNUT.   *Ruseau*

645. FRUITWOOD SIDECHAIR, Directoire.   *Anderson*

648. ARMCHAIR, with bronze mounts. *French & Co.*
Tapestry cover.

649. "BONHEUR-DU-JOUR"—MAHOGANY SECRETARY
with flat gilt bronze ornaments.

652. CONSOLE. Caryatides in bronze.

Butsfield

647. MAHOGANY TABLE, Sphinxes on base.

Metropolitan Museum

646. ARMCHAIR, about 1800.

THE EMPIRE STYLE

650. CABINET IN EGYPTIAN STYLE.

651. (Right) TABLE WITH GRECO-ROMAN DETAIL.

653. FLEMISH OAK COFFER, 16th Century.
Anderson Galleries

654. INLAID WALNUT TABLE, Swiss 15th-16th Century.
Anderson Galleries

655. BIBLE BOX, Norway, dated 1691. Oak. FLEMISH TABLE, late 16th Century.
Anderson Galleries

IN THE SIXTEENTH CENTURY THE RENAISSANCE SPREAD FROM ITALY AND FRANCE INTO
THE GERMANIC COUNTRIES

656. BOXWOOD and EBONY CABINET, German, 17th Century.

657. DOUBLE VIRGINAL, by Hans Rucker, dated 1581. Dutch.
Metropolitan Museum of Art

658. CABINET, South German (Augsburg), 16th Century.

660. GILT ROCOCO MIRROR, South German, late 18th Century.
Charles Henders

661. BOMBÉ COMMODE, 18th Century, South German Baroque.
Charles Henders

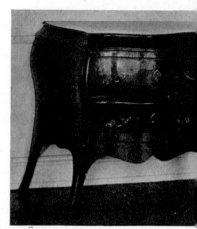

659. SACRISTAN CHEST from Austria (Salzburg). Double bodied buffet type of fine baroque outline, inlaid, middle 18th Century.

662. TABLE from Lubeck, Germany, about 1700.

BAROQUE IN GERMANIC LANDS

663. CHAIR OF LOUIS XV INSPIRATION, South Germany, late 18th Century. *Charles Henders*

664. GERMAN ROCOCO. Frederick the Great's Writing Table in the Rococo Chinese manner.

665. ARMCHAIR of Regence South German, early Century. *Charles*

666. VITRINE, OR CURIO CABINET, South German, CA. 1800.

667. CYLINDER DESK of mahogany and bronze. By David Roentgen. End of 18th Century.
Clock and Candlesticks of the period.

668. MARBLE - TOPPED COMMODE from Alsace, CA. 1795. By David Roentgen.
Charles H. Henders

THE CLASSIC REVIVAL IN GERMANY

The Paris styles of the end of the Eighteenth Century were enthusiastically copied in the furnishings of the more luxurious German houses.

669. (Lower Left) LOUIS XVI INFLUENCE IN SOUTH GERMAN ARMCHAIR, CA. 1785.   *Courtesy Charles H. Henders*

670. (Center) BIEDERMEIER SIDE TABLE, CA. 1810.

671. (Right) LOUIS XVI STYLE ARMCHAIR. Gilt.
Charles Henders

672. LATE EMPIRE BED, Munich, CA. 1820. Mahogany and Ormolu.

673. ARMCHAIR AND TABLE, Munich, CA. 1820.

674. HIGH CABINET with desk drawer. Mahogany. Fr[...]
Munich, CA. 1820.

BIEDERMEIER — THE EMPIRE STYLE IN GERMANY

675. WALNUT SOFA with printed wool cover. Frankfort-am-Main, CA. 1820.

GOTHIC FURNITURE

676. SOUTH GERMAN, LATE GOTHIC TABLE, 1450-1500.

677. FRENCH, BENCH IN LATE GOTHIC STYLE, CA. 1520. Pierced ornament on ends.

678. FRENCH OAK COFFER with carving representing tracery windows and spiral pillars. Late 15th Century.

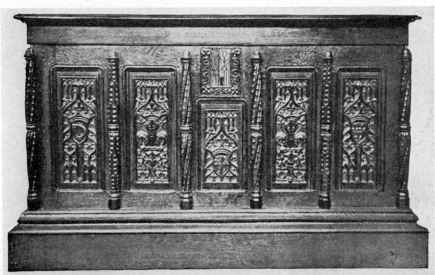

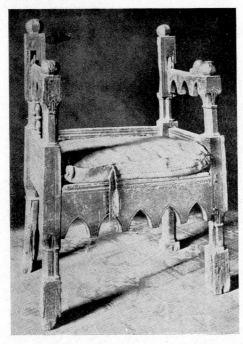

679. ITALIAN GOTHIC ARMCHAIR, 14th Century.

680. (Left) FRENCH GOTHIC OAK STALL, CA. 1500.

French & Co.

681. (Right) CREDENCE OR BUFFET, French oak, CA. 1500. The flamboyant style, with well developed joinery and pierced ironwork.

682. SWEDISH CHEST with metal straps.

683. FRENCH GOTHIC CHOIR BENCH, walnut, C. 1500.
Anderson Galleries

684. ENGLISH, GOTHIC CU[
oak, Middle 16th Century.

685. BEDSTEAD FROM TYROL, CA. 1500.

686. SWEDISH CUPBOARD with
panels and typical iron wor
1558.

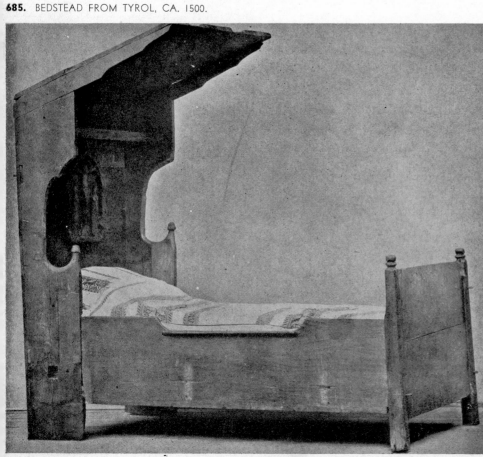

GABOON. (a) Ebony of the blackest variety which comes from the Gaboon region of Africa.

(b) A light, inferior mahogany from the Gaboon region, known in Europe merely by this name.

GADROON. Ornament carved on edges either of flat areas or turnings resembling short convex or concave flutes or ruffles. It is common in Elizabethan work, Italian Renaissance work and all styles influenced by Italy. A characteristic decoration of bulbous supports in Elizabethan carving. Chippendale used it extensively for borders and top edges. 117, 463, 496.

GALLERY. Small railing of metal or wood, or a raised rim, around the tops of tables, cabinets, buffets, etc. (146.)

GALLOON (Galon). Narrow tape used as gimp in the finishing of uphostery.

GAME TABLES. One of the earliest specialized types of tables developed for games, as dice, cards, chess or draughts, backgammon, etc. Sixteenth century examples have needlework tops in patterns required for the various games; the ultimate development occurred in 18th century England. See *Card Tables*. 1049 et seq.

GARGOYLE. Grotesque figure originally used in architecture as decorative rain spout. Best known in Gothic examples, it was adapted for purely ornamental purposes in some medieval and Renaissance woodwork.

GARLAND. Floral decoration, freely arranged.

GATELEG TABLE. The whole classification of tables in which one or more drop leaves are supported by a leg or gate which swings away from a central fixed structure. According to Nutting the gateleg must have a stretcher; if the stretcher is lacking the type is known as "swing leg." Gatelegs were made with as many as twelve legs, and appeared in every style during the 17th century. (497, 505.)

GEOMETRIC PATTERN. Abstract design based on simple mechanical lines, such as squares, triangles, circles, etc. 437, 457.

GEORGIAN. In England the period of George I, George II, George III—1714-1795.

The first three Georges ruled an England of swelling importance, but in which their personal influence was not great. The interchange of ideas with the rest of the world, the wealth and growing leisure and fine living promoted the adoption of modes and manners from abroad, as well as the products of the ingenuity of native designers and craftsmen. The rising importance of individual designers made their personal styles the fashion, so that unlike the period of Louis XIV, we think of a given period as that of Chippendale, Hepplewhite, Sheraton or the Adams. Naturally much of their material overlapped, was interchanged or borrowed from the same sources, so that we are at a loss to find an

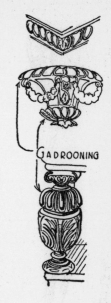

GADROONING

JACOBEAN GATELEG

adequate name for the whole period. For that reason they are often lumped as Georgian.

Early Georgian usually begins with the passing of Queen Anne, 1714, and includes the style up to the ascendancy of Chippendale about 1745. The style is a heavier, richer Queen Anne, substantial and not excessively Rococo. There is much gilding and lavish upholstery. Chairs and tables have brass casters. Decorative details include the scallop shell on cabriole legs, eagles' heads on chair arms, satyr heads, lions' and ball-and-claw feet, hoof and paw feet; cabinets were of solid architectural proportions. Mahogany was used, but some walnut work was still done.

Later Georgian styles are better known as Chippendale, Hepplewhite, Sheraton, etc. See *England*. 527 et seq.

GERMANY. The Teutonic peoples derived their first ideas of furniture from Rome, there being evidence of turned members of chairs and tools drawn from Roman models. Scandinavian elements of rich open-work carving, dragons and intertwined floral decorations occur on earlier medieval coffers. Chests on high legs, with sloping lids like a gable roof display both Celtic and Byzantine ornamentation. Other chests are embellished with many iron bands. Construction and decoration is elementary Romanesque and crude. (682.)

The Gothic architectural influence reached domestic furniture early in the 15th century, but the Romanesque tradition remains in peasant work for several centuries. Chests decorated with mingled Romanesque and Gothic motives occur in low Saxony, in Holstein, in the Hartz mountains and elsewhere sufficiently to indicate that the type was general in the Netherlands, Northern France, Scandinavia, England and Alpine lands. (942 et seq.)

The later Gothic stage saw the evolution of chests with doors, variations known as credences, dressoirs, etc., in the lower Rhine district, parallel to the various cupboards of Flanders, France and England. Linen-fold decoration was universal. The post-and-panel method of construction was the great contribution of this age to cabinetwork and from it developed all the drawer and cabinet forms.

There is a distinct line of demarcation between North German and South German types, due both to the nature of the accessible woods and the exposure to outside influence. North German work employs oak and follows the intricate ornament of the Scandinavian countries. South German work is in fir and pine and exhibits North Italian influences coming both via the Alpine countries and Flanders.

In South German work occurs a wide range of coffers and cupboards in all stages of evolution, with the carved ornament freely Gothic of the flamboyant school. Green and red paint emphasized the planes. Box settles, turned chairs of a type common in England two

GEORGIAN CABRIOLES

GERMAN ROMANESQUE

centuries later and trestle tables are of well developed type. A distinct form of bedstead has square posts and side pieces and a short wooden canopy at the head. 222, 676, 685.

THE RENAISSANCE

The free cities of Southern Germany had a flourishing trade with Northern Italy, and the first signs of the Renaissance appeared there. Woodcuts of furniture by Peter Flötner of Nuremberg appeared about 1542 showing Italian Renaissance details and there are cupboards extant, probably of his workmanship, which show a mature appreciation of the Lombard forms. Classic ornament and intarsia are employed. Flötner's austere style was the prevalent type for a generation, but after 1580 the richer plastic decoration, with a larger vocabulary of ornaments, becomes the rule. Pilasters taper toward the base; heavily projecting consoles, lion motives, scrollwork and cartouches appear and the trend toward the exuberant richness of the Baroque has begun. Examples of about 1600 from Ulm, Frankfort-am-Main and Augsburg are parallel in the elaborate late Renaissance tradition to the work of Flanders and Northern France. Veneered panels of walnut and ash and intarsia enrich the fir and pine surfaces. Augsburg had a specialized cabinet industry and the earliest Baroque forms appeared there about 1620. Elaborate joinery, as mitering, broken corners, undulating mouldings, all superseded carving. Chairs were four-legged board types, folding chairs, and later, armchairs with square legs. Turned baluster legs displaced the latter in the Late Renaissance. This style clung to much of the South German work until after the mid-17th century.

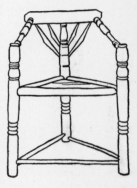

In North Germany oak furniture continued to be made in the Gothic structural tradition through 1550. Cologne and Muenster were centers of cabinetmaking and carving and there the Early Renaissance first appears in the work of John Kupfer and Aldegraver. In Luneberg and Schleswig-Holstein restrained Italian ornament was merged with the Gothic. Schleswig-Holstein early produced the more exuberantly carved cupboards with metal ornament and scroll-work, while other regions followed with the imposition of late Renaissance ornament upon late Gothic shapes. The corner cupboard appeared about this time in Dithmarshen.

The bed with carved posts and canopy frame appeared in North Germany about the middle of the 16th century. Chairs for state uses were inlaid with ivory and silver. Lesser ones were elaborately carved and turned. Cabinets were of wide variety and were decorated with elaborate carving, architectural features and intarsia panels. In these particulars, the High Renaissance remained the source of much German cabinetwork until the later 18th century. 94-96, 656, 658.

BAROQUE

The substitution of bold-scale mouldings, surfaces and shapes for excessive applied plastic ornament differentiates the Early Baroque of Holland from the late Renaissance styles of Germany. This took place about 1660 but the austere Dutch curves were speedily enriched in Nuremberg, Augsburg, Frankfort and other centers of German skill. Frankfort cupboards were richly curved, lush in outline and modelling as a whole. To the north, Hamburg walnut cupboards of 1680 were severely, vigorously architectural with heavy cornices and high raised panels. Pointed ovals, bases with drawers and large bun feet, with richly carved enclosed leaf, flower and fruit ornament characterize these excellent ornate structures.

Spiral turned legs are universal in earlier Baroque tables and chairs, but about 1690 the cabriole leg was widely accepted, indicating the penetration of the forms evolved in the court of Louis XIV. The Augsburg cabinetmakers followed the French lead with both ebony and Boulle tortoiseshell. The court of Frederick I was furnished with pure Louis XIV forms; from this time on all the palaces borrowed directly from Paris while the lesser houses lagged with the older styles.

This is particularly true of the Régence. This transitional style was readily taken up in the royal castles of Germany and inspired lower caste furniture for many years later. Few new forms appear in important work; it is henceforward essentially French, with a variable time-lag. Burgher furniture along Régence lines form a fairly national style in South Germany; inlays after Boulle, and intarsia in ribbon patterns are characteristic. Bombé commodes and high chair backs with smooth wooden splats are common. 395-7, 659 et seq., 760.

ROCOCO

The Rococo style of Louis XV permeated German cabinetmaking through the period 1730-1790. Spreading from Belgium and Lorraine, spheres of French influence, the lavish naturalism of the French court styles was brought into Bavaria by the architects Cuvillies, Knobelsdorff and Couven. The decorative sculptors Johann Hoppenhaupt and Johann August Nahl luxuriated in magnificent carved decorations for backgrounds and furniture alike. Consoles, mirror frames, commodes, chairs de luxe and canapés were embellished with birds, fruit and flowers, garden tools and musical instruments, carved, gilded and painted in the French manner. North German palaces vied with those of Munich. Frederick's New Palace in Potsdam, like the Solitud near Stuttgart, others in Munich, Wilhelmthal and the Electors' castles on the Rhine and the Main being masterpieces of the style. It is noted however, that most of the *meubles de luxe*—the bronze mounted commodes and writing tables, etc., were actually made in Paris.

ROCOCO COMMODE

The German Rococo on its own initiative indulged in more unrestrained fantasy than its prototype. The bombé shapes and loaded cornices are less airy, more solidly brilliant; possibly excessive in the best work of Wurzburg and Mayence. Chairs bear strong resemblance to the simpler Dutch and English types, although the German cabriole shape is distinctive. Bright paint colors carved furniture of Bavaria and Austria. 281, 401, 663-5.

EMPIRE
1810

GERMAN CLASSICISM

The Classic influence arrived after 1770 through both French and English channels. The German cabinetmakers made writing tables and commodes, chairs and cupboards in the familiar proportions and some of the austerity of the Parisian manner. The classic straight lines were more floridly ornamented. David Roentgen surpassed many of his French contemporaries with his cylinder desks, commodes, writing tables, etc., using light mahogany, superb marquetry and ormolu mounts. As in France, the classic continued in essence to be an urban style, the provinces retaining the exuberant curves of the Rococo, but about 1800 the influence of Hepplewhite and Sheraton had penetrated these strongholds. The middle class furniture of Napoleonic Germany has an appreciable style of its own, its later phases being known as Biedermeier. The early years of the century produced a group of designs of light graceful furniture, classic in form but devoid of excessive ornament, executed in light mahogany, pear, ash, cherry, and poplar. The smooth veneered surfaces of the Empire style are common but the proportions are better and there is a livable human quality. Painted furniture was also popular.

BIEDER- MEIER

BIEDERMEIER

After 1830 the style settled down recognizably to express easy comfort on a lightly classical foundation. Light native woods, light birch, cherry, pear and apple, maple and ash were displayed to advantage, without other ornament, in commodes and chests, tables, large secretary-desks and cabinets. Curved chairs and sofas were upholstered with horsehair, calico and rep and bore infinite variety of graceful ornament based on swans and griffins, cornucopiae and domestic flowers and fruits. Gothic bits were added to the ornamental repertoire about 1840. But there was no solid Gothic revival. This style is so dominantly middle class, so comfortably gauche that it took its name from the comic-paper character Papa Biedermeier, who expressed his simple political views in Fliegende Blatter.

The growing comfort and wealth of the mid-century period undermined this simplicity and brought various Neo-Rococo and merely lavish picturesque effects. The weakening of the genuine feeling for style is

VIENNA
1810

evidenced by the acceleration of the changes in style and, by the end of the century, pure eclecticism permitted Renaissance, Turkish and Far Eastern, Neo-Empire and neo-everything styles to come and go with individual whims. 433, 435, 482, 666 et seq., 879, 1067.

MODERN

The essential philosophy of the Modern International style grew largely in Germany where an early appreciation of the revolutionary ideas of William Morris led to the growth of the Jugendstil. This "Youth Style" as a German "Art Nouveau" produced little directly, but established a system of thought and art training rather more comprehensive, unified and progressive than in other countries. After the war, the movement toward greater simplicity and functional form found its prophets in Germany, in leaders like Gropius, Mies van der Rohe and Bruno and Max Taut.

GESSO. Plastic preparation used for raised decoration. In Italy it was extensively employed on furniture in the Middle Ages and after. It was never very extensively used elsewhere, although gilded it was popular for a time under Charles II in England. 532.

GIBBONS, GRINLING (1648-1721). English carver and designer. John Evelyn brought him to the notice of Christopher Wren who employed him as a carver on St. Paul's and Windsor Castle. His work and influence are the basis of English carving after that time. Most typical of his work are the garlands and festoons, birds and animals and other typically Baroque details exquisitely executed in rich high relief. The carving was usually done in pine, limewood or similar close textured woods, later nailed to the panelling and gilded on mantels, panelling, ceilings, overdoors, and important furniture. He combined superb draftsmanship, a remarkable sense of composition and inspired craftsmanship.

GIBBS, JAMES, 1682-1754. English architect, disciple of Palladio. Like many of his contemporaries he designed the furnishings as well as the structure. His "Book of Architecture" (1728) was one of many on the subject.

GILLINGHAM, JAMES, Born 1736. Philadelphia cabinetmaker, produced simple furniture of fine quality.

GILLOW, Firm of. English cabinetmakers first known about 1728, who constructed much furniture during the 18th and 19th centuries.

GIMP (Guimpe). Narrow flat tape, more or less ornamental, as a trimming or finish on upholstery and drapery.

GIRANDOLE, GIRONDOLE. Wall bracket or chandelier, often with a mirror back. Later in the 18th century the mirror was made cir-

GIRANDOLE

cular and convex—and was used alone. Sometimes called Bulls-eye mirror. (766.)

GLAZED DOORS. Doors fitted with glass, often with a lattice pattern of woodwork, or tracery. 567A.

GLAZING. In painting, glazing is the application over the finish paint of a thin wash coat which is then wiped off, thereby modifying or subduing the base color. It produces a mixed, soft tone. Glazing is definitely not polish, or the application of a gloss, as on chintz.

GLOBE STAND. Wood or metal stand of pedestal, tripod or other shape designed to hold terrestrial or celestial globes. Like other objects of scientific interest they were given serious artistic treatment in the 18th century.

GLUE. Adhesive material of various kinds, used in veneering, joinery, etc. Good glueing provides the tightest joint of wood known. A proper glue joint will break less readily than the wood it holds together, but this implies good glue, good joining and accurate fitting. Much study is now being given to adhesives for wood, with the object of producing waterproof joints, by a simpler process than the customary hot-glue method.

GOBELIN. French family of dyers, established 15th century, began to make tapestries in 1529. In 1662 their factory was purchased by the government and transformed into an upholstery manufactory under the direction of the painter Le Brun. This actually marks the beginning of the period of Louis XIV. During the 18th century they made chiefly tapestries, and in 1826 they added the manufacture of carpets. The industry is still conducted by the state. 302.

GLOBE · STANDS·

GODDARD, JOHN. Latter half 18th century. American cabinet-maker worked in Newport, R. I. with his son-in-law John Townsend. Produced distinct form of block-front desks, cabinets, secretaries, chests, etc., with shell carving. Bracket feet, usually ogee in shape and finely carved or in clustered shapes are also typical. 410, 449, 478, 1016.

GONCALO ALVES. Dense hardwood from Brazil. Color is light tan with red-brown stripes, with some curl.

GONDOLA (Gondole). Chair or sofa whose back curves downward continuously to form the arms, so called because of its supposed resemblance to an 18th century gondola.

GOOSENECK. Double curved arch of the pediment of highboys and the like. Also called swan-neck or broken arch. 701.

GOSTELOWE, JONATHAN—1744-1806. Philadelphia cabinet-maker; produced distinguished mahogany furniture of Chippendale Baroque influence. A man of property and education, he made furniture of the finest type for a rich clientele. Nutting rates his identified work ahead of that of Savery. (405).

GOOSENECK PEDIMENT

GOTHIC. To the Romans, Gothic symbolized the barbarians of the North. To the Renaissance artists the name implied the unclassical,

SWISS · 15th C

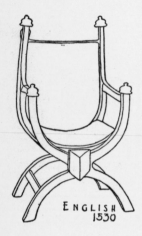

ENGLISH
1530

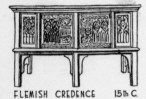

FLEMISH CREDENCE 15th C.

rudely home-made efforts of the Dark Ages, when men had lost the classic touch. Yet today the Gothic is regarded as having the primary greatness of a complete, spontaneous art system. The reason lies in our recognition of the underlying impulse; the deep need of people to construct, beautifully, the things they require out of the materials at hand. The only stable power of the time being the Church, the chief artistic expression was ecclesiastical. The cathedral was the triumph of Gothic art. Secular and domestic expressions lagged far behind. Gothic domestic furniture is therefore almost an anomaly.

Gothic architecture grew from the Romanesque, the style of Christian Europe between 800 and 1200. Vestiges of ancient Rome, particularly the round arch, were crossed with Byzantine showiness and the ancient semi-barbaric themes of the Teutonic peoples; debased architectural forms with naturalistic and geometric ornament. The Gothic structural system developed in stone the notion of the skeleton framework. The great pointed arches, the pillars and buttresses are decorated with mouldings and details of unique and logical type. These details were carried through into the detached wood furniture. Altars, screens and other ritual furniture were magnificent, in complete harmony with the architecture.

Secular Gothic art stemmed from the castles of the feudal barons. Such governing powers as they were able to seize and to hold were largely personal matters. The state of semi-continuous warfare kept them moving about; their furnishings and their material wealth went with them from castle to castle. With mobility as the basis, chests and coffers were the principal articles of furniture: these carried clothing, bedding, valuables; they could be used as beds and seats for the retainers. Later, chests were mounted on feet or stands, but it was not until the 15th century that there appears a consistent type of furniture foreshadowing the various cupboards, chests and cabinets. These were invariably of oak. Earlier types were plank boxes, heavily bound with iron straps and locks, often with gabled tops. Later flat-top chests had sides ornamented with carved representations of architectural forms. Finally the logic of the stone skeleton of buildings was applied to furniture; a sturdy framework held panels of thinner wood, which in itself created an ornamental type. The panels were further ornamented with linen-fold, tracery or painted designs. (See *Chests.*)

Chairs were almost a royal prerogative. Under nomadic conditions, folding chairs were carried only for the lord and his lady; when court was set up, a throne-like structure of canopy and dais was literally the court. Below sat the lesser ones, importance diminishing as distance grew.

Beds were chiefly textile; curtains and canopy and bedding were easily transportable. The framework of exposed wood appeared after security warranted such permanent structures. Beds retained their enclosure character until rooms became small enough to afford privacy and warmth. (See *Beds*.)

Tables as such did not exist. For dining, boards were set on trestles . . . hence "set the table."

All this furniture, usually of unpolished oak, borrowed its decorative character from church art. Carving in oak makes for large scale, not too fine detail. Familiar floral forms, vines and leaves, with grotesque animal and human representations were often humorously rendered. Simple structural embellishments as grooves, mouldings and panelling are typical. In later Gothic work these were scaled down to represent architectural arches, tracery, façades. Cusped arches, trefoil, quatrefoil, etc.; ogee curves and deep, full mouldings are essential in the style everywhere. Painting later became general.

The Gothic as a style had extremes of type according to locale. In Italy there never was a true Gothic; Italian Gothic was merely the imposition of a few Northern motives on a persistent classic taste, diluted with Eastern (Byzantine and Saracenic) forms and motives. Spain was Moorish through the early Gothic stages; even in her 15th Century Gothic a strong quality of Oriental light and shade is evident. France was scarcely a political entity. The style centered in the Ile-de-France types and spread with local variations from north and south. The Teutonic and Scandinavian lands worked in individual styles. The rise of secular nationalism came with the Renaissance, when church influence in politics and in art waned. 150, 165, 168, 198, 203, 204, 222, 367, 369, 492, 584, 654, 676-686, 909, 942 et seq., 967.

NEO GOTHIC DETAIL

GOTHIC REVIVALS. England had a brief interest in the Gothic after 1740, and ornamental forms, fondly imagined to be in the "Gothic Taste," were incorporated into furniture by Chippendale and others. Cusped arches, ogee curves and similar rudiments were accepted as Gothic: there was no further effort or understanding of the whole concept of Gothic structure. 55.

In the mid-19th century another revival gained more momentum. Architecture profited chiefly; the Gothic became the accepted style for churches and, somewhat less, for schools. In furniture in America, England and France it remained only a source of a few ornamental motives (879). Somewhat later William Morris and his school fostered an abortive attempt to reintroduce Gothic handicraft methods to combat the machine development. (1093).

GOUGE CARVING. Rudimentary form of decorative carving found in cruder styles, as the Gothic in Spain and England. Usually simple chisel marks in rhythmic repetition. 437.

GOUTHIERE, PIERRE (1740-1806). French bronze worker (ciseleur), famous for unsurpassed metal mounts for cabinets.

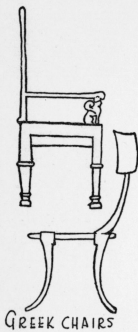

GREEK CHAIRS

GRIFFIN (FRENCH)

GRAIN. Wood fibers tend to assume characteristic arrangements. When boards are cut the cross sections of the fibers reveal these arrangements in patterns, which the cabinetmaker employs in the design much as the pattern or texture of fabric is used in draping and tailoring. See *Woods*.

GRAINING. Process of painting to resemble the color and figure of wood.

GRANDFATHER'S CHAIR. Large upholstered English wing chair.

GRANDFATHER'S CLOCK. Tall clock case. 62.

GRANDMOTHER'S CLOCK. Floor clock of smaller dimension than grandfather's clock.

GRECO-ROMAN. Refined decoration style of late classical antiquity, roughly 200 B.C.-200 A.D. Appeared in 18th century through the excavations of Herculaneum and Pompeii, and formed the basis of the 18th century classical revivals. In itself a free mixture of styles of Egypt, Greece and Rome, it was liberally misunderstood and misnamed.

GREEK, ANCIENT. The Golden Age of Greece, 1200-300, B.C., has left scant remains of furniture, but vase pictures and sculpture show many well developed types of beds and couches, chairs and tables. (188.) In literature we find references to "chests of cedar . . . gilt and inlaid with ivory." Chairs were gracious in outline with sweeping curves on legs and backs. The form often suggests bronze rather than wood. Couches were elongated thrones, suggesting Egyptian origin, like much other Grecian furniture. Tables were low and portable, even as they occur in Asia Minor today, and bronze animal legs and feet are found. Chests or coffers are found in a distinct architectural-roofed shape, decoratively painted.

Turning, inlaying, carving, painting, incrusting with precious stones, gilding, etc., were widely practised, and construction methods were good. The native olive and cedar, yew, box and ebony seem to have been employed, and upholstery with silken cushions was known before 300 B.C.

GREEK FRET. Greek Key pattern; repeated square hook shaped forms as a band decoration.

GRIFFIN (Gryphon). Mythological beast, half eagle, half lion. Grotesque, occurring in much late Italian Renaissance, French Renaissance thru Louis XIV, and the work of Adam and Sheraton, and again in the Empire Style.

GRILLE. Metal (rarely wood) lattice work used in bookcase doors, cabinets. They were of brass or gilt wire in a variety of woven patterns and often had fabric curtains behind them. (182).

GRISAILLE. Painting in various gray tints, representing solid bodies in relief. Fashionable in furniture decoration of the late 18th century. (567 A).

GROS POINT. French coarse stitch embroidery used for upholstering chairs, etc.

GROTESQUES. Fantastic figures or part figures as decoration.

GUERIDON. Small French table for candles and small articles. 1068.

GUILLOCHE. Continuous running or band ornament of interlacing circles, found in every style after the Assyrian.

GUIMPE. Gimp.

GUINEA HOLES. Scooped out corners in 18th century English card tables as receptacles for coins. 538.

GUMWOOD. Three species of gumwood are used in furniture: sweet, tupelo, and black gum. Sweet or red gum has a pinkish hue, especially in the sap wood. Tupelo has a tan-gray color, while black gum is the lightest, and has the most decided figure. All gums are susceptible to warping unless they are very carefully kiln-dried. They are commonly used for structural parts in less expensive cabinetwork, as they are strong and stain easily to resemble mahogany or walnut.

GUILLOCHES

HADLEY CHEST. Early American chest, first found in Hadley, Mass. Typical tulip carving over front rails as well as the three panels. Often with a drawer.

HAIG, THOMAS. Partner of Chippendale.

HAIR CLOTH. Fabric woven of horsehair, colored or small-figured, typical of middle 19th century upholstery. A mixture of horsehair and linen was used by the 18th century English upholsterers.

HALF COLUMN. Engaged column against a flat surface or rounded pilaster. (429).

HALF-HEADED BED. Short posted bedstead without canopy.

HALFPENNY, W. & J. 18th century English architects and designers.

HALF-TURNING. Turned members sawn in half, lengthwise,— usually applied to a flat surface as ornament, particularly in English and American Jacobean, Italian and German Renaissance. 379. Also used as spindles in chairs (Jacobean) with the smooth side to the sitter's back.

HALL CHAIRS. Formal, ornamental chairs, originally named by Manwaring.

HALL CLOCK. Grandfathers' or any tall clock case.

HALL TREE. Stand or framework, wood or metal, for coats and hats, etc.

HALVING-IN. Method of joinery. See *Construction.*

HANDLE. Knobs or pulls on drawers and doors. The types and materials have varied in all periods to such an extent that handles constitute a sure index to the period of a piece of furniture. Wood, metal, glass, ivory, etc., have been adapted and designed in characteristic forms; the better the designs the more harmoniously related was the hardware to the case, as to size, spacing, shape, material. See *Hardware*.

HANGINGS. Bed and window curtains and portable wall coverings. Medieval construction provided no finish for interior walls, so that men of wealth carried with them to their various transient abodes hangings which provided grace and comfort to the harsh castle interiors. Bed curtains and window curtains were variations of these same draperies, as these were still architectural features. The latter were almost always plain fabrics, such as fustian, but the wall hangings early took on highly decorative character. The conventionalized patterns of medieval weaves became tapestries, which in turn became in the hands of the French weavers, representations of paintings, including the representation of a gilt frame.

Leather hangings of Spanish or Saracenic origin, with typical stamped embellishment and coloring, were popular on the Continent during the 16th and 17th centuries.

Papers pasted on the wall displaced textile hangings very largely in the 18th century.

HANGING SHELVES, BOOK SHELVES, PLATE SHELVES. Oldest surviving examples of these types are found to be of crude type, particularly in England and France. The latter are exclusively Provincial and are of middle 18th century character. English oak shelves of early Jacobean date are carved abundantly, with double-arch shapes. 18th century shelves developed with the craze for china-collecting: Chippendale's school produced jig-sawed variations on Chinese themes with Gothic accents. (543) Hepplewhite's book illustrates simple types, some with turned uprights. Many of these types have survived, made of mahogany or satinwood with inlay and painted decoration. American hanging shelves after 1750 are of similar style, usually plainer. The country types of pine are rarely decorated but show inventiveness in decorative outlines.

HARDWARE. Fittings of metal were originally intended to strengthen the heavy board construction of chests, etc., and early became decorative features as well. Earliest Gothic chests have beautifully wrought iron straps and corners, hinges and locks, hasps and keys. As stronger joinery became the rule the metal fittings were allowed to lapse into decorative desuetude. Renaissance furniture relegated hardware to an inferior place; brass and bronze replaced iron, and mounts virtually disappeared. Functional details as hinges and locks were subdued, largely through technical improvements. Gothic hinges had exposed leaves which were fashioned into decorative shapes as the dolphin, cock's head, loop, and H-hinges. These designs persisted espe-

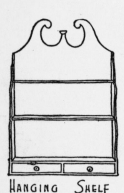

HANGING SHELF

cially in ironwork and in rural districts, but sophisticated Renaissance work used butt hinges, concealed like the countersunk locks, etc. This left only keys and key plates and handles as decorative members; these were fine in scale and delicately wrought, often chased. Handles or pulls

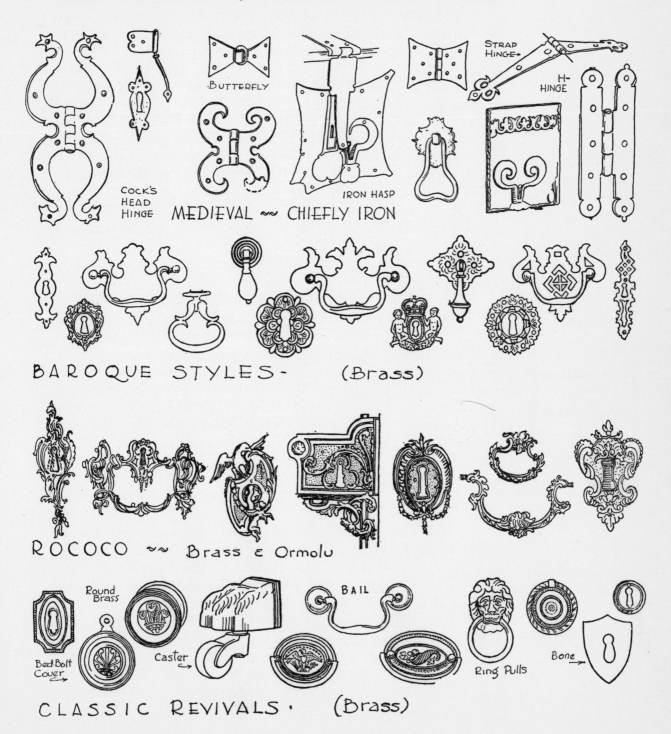

COCK'S HEAD HINGE　　·BUTTERFLY　　IRON HASP　　STRAP HINGE→　　H-HINGE

MEDIEVAL ～～ CHIEFLY IRON

BAROQUE STYLES - (Brass)

ROCOCO ～～ Brass & Ormolu

Round Brass　　BAIL

Bed Bolt Cover　　Caster　　Ring Pulls　　Bone →

CLASSIC REVIVALS · (Brass)

were either knobs or drop handles. Pear, tear and ball shapes were common drops, while bails were gracefully formed and fitted with ornate escutcheons or back plates. Later Baroque and early Georgian work employed silver extensively.

The Rococo style revived interest in metal work. Bronze appliques were a mainstay of the ornamentalist, and much of the effect of Rococo furniture derives from the contrast of exquisitely chased bronze and gilt metal against the background of fine veneer. Handles, key plates, etc., were particularly fine. Chippendale's handles were ornate Baroque-Rococo compositions and form an essential contrast with the mahogany.

The Classic Revivals brought new hardware designs, severe in outline and fine in scale. Ring handles were general in Regency and all Empire styles, and decorative metal appliques of classical themes were universal. Mirrors were metal ornamented, and galleries and beadings of brass were common.

Late 18th century handles began to utilize glass, ivory, and porcelain. These remained throughout the 19th century. The turn of the century featured copper and leather and modern styles added chromium, aluminum and the plastic materials.

HAREWOOD. Greenish gray wood. Actually sycamore or in America curly maple, stained or dyed to a thin gray tone. Originating in England in the 18th century, it was used chiefly for inlays and decorative veneering. Widely favored in modern work in France, England and America, in spite of its tendency to lose the dye and to assume a greenish cast. 577.

HARLEQUIN TABLE. Table invented by Sheraton in which the center part rises automatically when the leaves are raised, revealing fittings and compartments for toilet articles or writing materials. Recently adapted to bar and cellarette uses.

HARVARD CHAIR. Three cornered chair with all turned members; Early American (17th century) version of a Gothic type found throughout the Continent in late Gothic and Early Renaissance stages.

HASP. Hinged part of a hinge lock, used decoratively in Gothic and Spanish cabinets. 455.

HASSOCK. Thickly stuffed upholstered footstool showing no wood.

HEADBOARD. The entire head section of a bed; or the boards within the head framework.

HEART AND CROWN. Baluster back chair whose cresting has cut-outs of these shapes.

HEART-BACK. Shield back chair, Hepplewhite type.

HENRI II, HENRI III. Medici kings of France whose Italian preferences imposed Italian forms upon the French Renaissance-Gothic of Francis I. Their style was a complete Baroque Italian one but more highly carved and decorated, featuring interlaced strap-work, delicate reliefs, cartouches, etc., etc. 586 et seq. See *France*.

HENRY VIII. The first English monarch to look away from England's insularity, Henry VIII literally imported the Renaissance into England. The lessening of church influence affected design of furniture and the influx of Italian motives enriched the heavy, severe furniture of earlier days. For the most part shapes remained Gothic, but unquestionably Italian ornamentation appeared. See *England*.

HEPPLEWHITE, GEORGE. Died 1786. It is known that he worked for the firm of Gillow, and that he began to make furniture in London about 1760. He collaborated with the Adams much as did Chippendale, and produced furniture in a more rational, simple version of their taste. Some of his work modifies the earlier French styles; his later output develops the classic outlines. 554 et seq. See *England*.

HERCULANEUM. The excavation of the Roman city of this name after 1719 revived interest in the decorative arts of the Romans. This persisted throughout the 18th century, particularly as the inspiration of the classic styles of Louis XVI and the Adams.

The name specifically was applied by Sheraton to a type of upholstered chair in the antique style.

HERRERA. Spanish architect, reign of Philip II—1556-1600; his name applied to the style of the period, noted for austere, harsh design. A reaction to the brilliant Plateresque style preceding it, it was followed by the even more exuberant Baroque called Churrigueresco.

HERRINGBONE. Inlay banding in which the alternately slanting grain produces a chevron or herringbone effect. Louis XIV and Queen Anne particularly.

H-HINGE. One with exposed, long flat leaves which when opened, resemble the letter H.

HICKORY. Strong, tough, elastic American wood, good for bent parts, or parts where thinness and strength are required. Oak color and texture; it is too hard to work easily.

HIGHBOY. Tall chest of drawers, usually in two sections, the upper chest being carried on a table-like structure or lowboy with long legs. The form is essentially English, the earlier chests on turned stands appearing in the early 17th century. Transported to the American colonies, it developed with William and Mary and Queen Anne influences into the unique and characteristic highboy of Colonial America of the 18th century. 31, 687-706. See *Chests, Tallboy*.

HIGH RELIEF. Deep surface carving. See *Relief*. 173.

HIP. Same as knee, in speaking of the part of a chair or table leg of cabriole shape. More exactly, the horizontally elongated part of a cabriole leg above the line of the seat rail as found on English chairs from 1700 to 1760.

HITCHCOCK

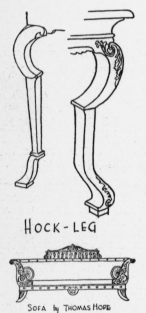

HOCK-LEG

SOFA by THOMAS HOPE

HISPANO-MORESQUE. Spanish style with Moorish influence.

HITCHCOCK. The Hitchcock chair is an American type, 1820-1850, named after Lambert Hitchcock of Connecticut. The typical form derives from a Sheraton "Fancy Chair" and has a typical "Pillow Back" or oval-turned top rail, splayed turned front legs, a rush or caned seat enclosed in thin wood strips. Most often these were painted to simulate rosewood, with a unique powdered-gold stencil of fruit and flowers. 336, 337. See *Chairs*.

HOCK-LEG. Cabriole leg with a curve and angle under the knee.

HOGARTH CHAIR. English chair, early 18th century of the Decorated Queen Anne Style. Has hoop back and pierced splat, with a heavy-kneed straight cabriole leg.

HOLLAND, HENRY. English architect, 1746-1806, fostered the use of Greco-Roman details.

HOLLY (Ilex). Hard grayish white wood, among the whitest of all woods, with small flecked grain. Used primarily for inlays, it has been favored in modern work for larger surfaces.

HONEYSUCKLE. Basis of conventional ornament; the anthemion of Greek origin, it was revived with other classicism in the Renaissance in every form of decoration. See *Ornament*.

HOOD (Hooded top). Shaped top, usually curved, on a highboy, clock case, etc. See *Bonnet-Top*. (468).

HOOF-FOOT. Hoof-shaped base of a leg, representing principally the goat hoof on a cabriole leg. See *Feet, Cabriole*. 452, 542.

HOOP-BACK. Chair back whose uprights and top rail form a continuous curve. Bow back in Windsor chairs. (331).

HOPE, THOMAS, 1769-1831. English writer, architectural dilettante, who was influenced by the Empire designs of Percier and Fontaine. His book "Household Furniture and Interior Decoration" (1807) formulated an archeological classicism for furniture which was not well received, but which nevertheless epitomizes the classical massiveness of the period.

HOPE CHEST. Dower chest; traditional form of furniture for storage of trousseaux. See *Chests*.

HORSE. Primitive trestle or stand to support table top or board.

HORSESHOE ARCH. Arch whose curvature is more than a half-circle. Occurs in Moorish decoration.

HORSESHOE BACK. In Windsor chairs, outward sweep at the base of the bow of the back. 251.

HORSESHOE TABLE. English Wine Table, 18th Century.

HOUSING. In Joinery, grooving of one piece of wood into another.

H-STRETCHER. Typical stretcher construction, as in some Windsor and Chippendale chairs. A stretcher from front to back leg on each side is connected thru the middle by a third member. (591.)

H-STRETCHER

THE HIGHBOY

THE CHEST MOUNTED ON A STAND BEGAN TO ASSUME IMPORTANT SPECIAL CHARACTERISTICS IN ENGLAND AFTER THE RESTORATION. THE TYPE APPEARS ELSEWHERE IN EUROPE BUT DEVELOPED MOST DISTINCTIVELY IN ENGLAND AND AMERICA BETWEEN 1680 AND 1800.

Photographs Courtesy Metropolitan Museum of Art

690. AMERICAN, 1680-1695. Gumwood highboy. Owned by the Mitchell family of Port Washington, L. I.

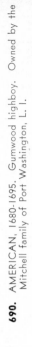

687. ENGLISH, 1660-1685, CHARLES II WAL- NUT CHEST-ON-STAND with seaweed marquetry.

689. AMERICAN, CA. 1700. Painted decoration on pine, black ground with colors.

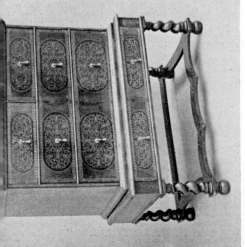

688. ENGLISH, CA. 1695. William and Mary oak highboy with panelled drawers.

691. NEW ENGLAND, 1710-1725. Walnut burl veneered on birch.

692. CROTCH WALNUT VENEER, 1700-1720. Trumpet turned legs.

693. WALNUT HIGHBOY. Strong cornice moldings conceal drawer. 1710-1725.

694. PENNSYLVANIA SPICE CUPBOARD. Walnut. CA. 1700.

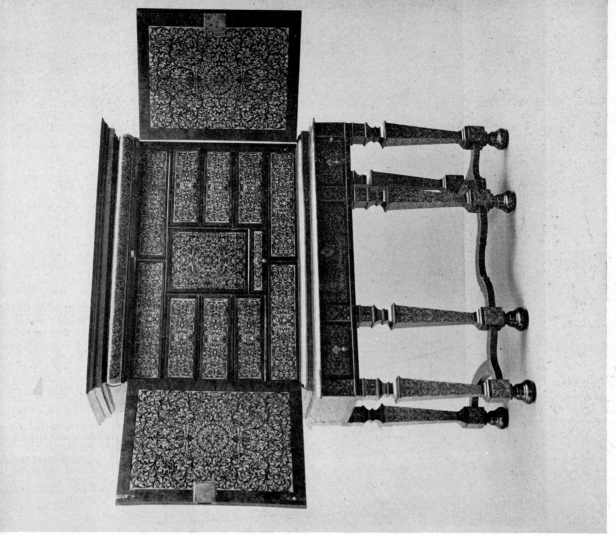

696. ENGLISH, CA. 1690. Highboy of William and Mary style, following silhouette of contemporary French Cabinets of Louis XIV style. The all-over pattern of seaweed marquetry to which all surfaces are subordinated suggests the intricate inlays of Boulle work.

Photographs Courtesy Metropolitan Museum of Art

695. JAPANESE CABINET on two stands, lacquered wood with mother-of-pearl and porcelain decoration, 1663-1741. The general appearance and the use suggest the interplay of ideas at great distances.

697. DUTCH CABINET, early 18th Century, showing bonnet top chest set on cabriole legs.
Anderson Gallerie

698. (Left) NEW ENGLAND, 1725-1750. Swan neck pediment, fluted pilasters, gilded shells burl walnut, inlaid. The highly developed type shows the persistence of the Queen Anne tradition. *Metropolitan Museum*

699. FLAT-TOP NEW ENGLAND HIGHBOY o figured maple, Mid-18th Century.
Anderson Gallerie

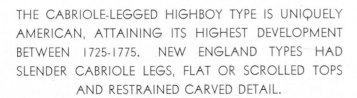

THE CABRIOLE-LEGGED HIGHBOY TYPE IS UNIQUELY AMERICAN, ATTAINING ITS HIGHEST DEVELOPMENT BETWEEN 1725-1775. NEW ENGLAND TYPES HAD SLENDER CABRIOLE LEGS, FLAT OR SCROLLED TOPS AND RESTRAINED CARVED DETAIL.

700. PHILADELPHIA CHIPPENDALE; 1770. Open scroll top.

701. (Right.) ELABORATELY CARVED HIGHBOY, from Philadelphia, 1760-75.

702. ENGLISH HIGH CHEST, Ca. 1700. The English Highboy followed this type generally. The bracket foot is of later date. The marquetry is the height of the art.

Photographs Courtesy Metropolitan Museum of Art

THE PHILADELPHIA HIGHBOY HAD SHORT LEGS AND ROCOCO ORNAMENT OF CHIPPENDALE ORIGIN. BOTH WALNUT AND MAHOGANY WERE USED. SOME OF THE BEST EXAMPLES OF THIS TYPE ARE THOSE MADE BY WILLIAM SAVERY.

703. RHODE ISLAND
TYPE, 1750 - 1775.
Cherry, block front
with shell, cabriole
foot.
Metropolitan Museum

704. MASSACHUSETTS
TYPE. Maple.
Anderson Galleries

THE DOUBLE CHEST, or CHEST-ON-CHEST

705. ENGLISH TALLBOY,
CA. 1760, with desk
drawer. Mahogany.

706. ENGLISH, CA. 1790.
Harewood, inlaid.
Hepplewhite School.
Photographs Courtesy
Anderson Galleries

ONAROLA CHAIR, WALNUT,
Century.
French & Co.

708. UMBRIAN WALNUT CABINET.

. TUSCAN WALNUT CABINET-TABLE, 16th
Century.

711. WALNUT DANTESCA CHAIR, 16th
Century.   *Courtesy French & Co.*

712. WALNUT CHOIR STALL, WITH
CANOPY, 17th Century.

LNUT ARMCHAIR, LEATHER
ER.
French & Co.

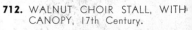

713. CASSONE, 15th Century. Wood, Carved and Gilded.
Courtesy Metropolitan Museum of Art

LNUT MONASTERY REFECTORY TABLE, 16th Century.

715. FLORENTINE TABLE, WALNUT, 16th Century.

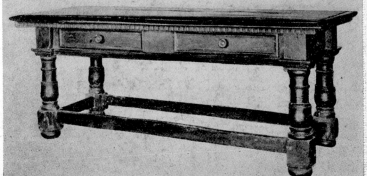

717. FLORENTINE WROUGHT IRON TORCHERE 16th Century.

716. VENETIAN CARVED WALNUT TABLE, 1610-1640.

ITALY
THE HIGH RENAISSANCE
1500 - 1600

• • •

718. "STIPO"—WALNUT WRITING CABINET, 16th Century.

719. FLOR IRON TORC

720. WALNUT SIDEBOARD, FLORENCE, 16th Century.

Metropolitan Museum

721. WALNUT ARMCHA Century. Velvet and En Fr

723. TUSCAN CARVED WALNUT BENCH, 1600-1630. Hinged Seat, Derived from Cassone.

724. TUSCAN CARVED W PRIE-DIEU, 16th Centu

722. FLORENTINE ARMCHAIR

725. TUSCAN WALNUT CABINET, EARLY 17th CENTURY.

726.
SILVERED
WOOD
TORCHERE,
17th Century.

729.
VENETIAN
TORCHERE.
Silvered
Wood
17th Century.

AGONAL WALNUT CENTER TABLE. Tuscany, 16th Century.

728. TUSCAN TABLE WITH TWIST TURNINGS, 16th Century.

730. SIDE CHAIR.   *French & Co.*

731. MADIA OR SIDEBOARD, Bologna, 16th Century.

732. WALNUT SIDE CHAIR.

733. VENETIAN WALNUT SETTEE, 17th Century.

734. GILT MIRROR. *Cavallo*

736. VENETIAN BED, Mid-18th Century. *Metropolitan Museum*

737. TUSCAN ARMCHAIR, CA. 1680.

735. BAROQUE CUPBOARD, CA. 1

BAROQUE AND ROCOCO IN ITA

Seventeenth and Eighteenth Ce

738. (Lower Left) LATE 18th CENTU CLASSIC INFLUENCE.
Angelo Roma

739. VENETIAN BAROQUE CHAIR. Walnut. 17th Ce
Anderson

740. SEDAN CHAIR, painted, C. 1775.
Olivotti

741. GILT TABLE, CA. 1785. Style of Louis XVI.
Anderson Galleries

742. GILT MIRROR in classic style of Louis XVI, CA. 1780.
Cavallo

CLASSIC REVIVAL

Late Eighteenth Century

743. SMALL ROCOCO MIRRORS, early 18th Century.
Lavezzo

744. BOMBE CHEST with miniature chest, CA. 1750.
Cavallo

745. CHEST OF LOUIS XVI STYLE.
Cavallo

ITALIAN EMPIRE

1795-1825

746. MIRROR IN DIRECTOIRE STYLE. *Lavezzo*

747. CONSOLE AND MIRROR IN STYLE OF LOUIS XVI. White and gold. *Olivotti*

748. (Lower Left) GILDED AND MARBLE-IZED CORNER TABLE, after style of Louis XVI.

749. WIRE-GRILLED CABINET OF WALNUT. Egyptian-Empire form. *Cavallo*

750. (Lower Left) ARMCHAIR, FALL FRONT DESK, AND STAND of Empire character, CA. 1815. *Cavallo*

751. LYRE BACK CHAIR detail, CA. 1810.

HUCHIER (French). Cabinetmaker, chiefly one who makes fine cabinets by the panel method of construction.

HUNTING-CHAIR. Sheraton design with a slide in front upon which to rest the feet.

HUSK. Drop ornament—such as the cornflower or catkins of shrubs, arranged in diminishing series. From classical times down.

HUTCH. From the French *Huche*. A chest or cabinet with doors, usually on legs. An early form descending from the Gothic and disappearing after the 17th century. Its principal interest is as progenitor of the chest—court-cupboard sideboard. The type was common in France and Italy and particularly in Early Jacobean England, whence it came to America. (150).

IMBRICATION

IMBRICATION. Decoration resembling fish scales adapted from the antique Roman in the Italian Renaissance.

INCE AND MAYHEW. English firm of cabinet-makers and upholsterers; published "Universal System of Household Furniture" (1762) illustrating their designs. Many of them were based on Chippendale's work and much of the actual furniture is in a debased Chippendale manner.

INCISED LACQUER. Decoration carved into lacquer which has been built up in layers of sufficient thickness.

INCISED ORNAMENT. Deeply cut engraved or carved work, the entire being cut *into* the surface rather than raised from it.

INITIALS. Initials, monograms, etc., were favorite decorative devices from ancient times. Conventionalized letters of monarchs' names up to Napoleon, were frequent in state furniture. Personal furniture such as dower chests, toilet cases, writing boxes, etc., were often monogrammed. 373.

INLAY. Designs formed in wood thru the contrast of grains, colors and textures of wood, metal, ivory, tortoiseshell, etc., inserted *flush* into the wood. The process is one of the oldest of the arts, the Egyptians surpassing many later peoples in their skill. Ancient records indicate that this was the most prized of the woodworker's arts. In the Renaissance the earlier work appears to have been inlaid into the solid wood; only later reappears the ancient method of assembling the small pieces comprising the whole design in veneers, and laying and glueing them to the background wood. 152, 389.

INITIALS

INTAGLIO. Carved design cut into the surface differing from cameo cut on which the design is raised from the surface.

INTERNATIONAL STYLE. Modern functional manner, so called from its freedom from nationalistic traditions of decoration and its development along similar lines in many countries. Inspired purely by material and purpose, which today vary only slightly in different lands, furniture tends to assume a similar appearance everywhere. See *Functional, Modern.*

INTERRUPTED ARCH. Arched pediment, the center or top part of which is cut away.

INTERRUPTED PEDIMENT. See *Broken Pediment.* 523.

IN THE WHITE. Any cabinetwork or woodwork in the raw state, before the wood is finished.

INVERTED CUP. Turning profile of cup shape typical of Jacobean and later work. See *Turnings.* 689.

IONIC. Greek and Roman order of architecture, distinguished by double voluted capital. See *Orders.* 97, (496).

IONIC

IRISH CHIPPENDALE. Type of mahogany furniture probably made in Ireland by local craftsmen in the middle 18th century after designs in Chippendale's published works. It is solid, rather heavy in form and ornamented with disconnected flat carving. Lion masks and paw feet are characteristic.

ITALY. If we divide man's history into the Ancient era, the Middle Ages, and Modern times, we must look for the source of the arts of the Modern world to Italy.

Geography made Italy the heir of the Roman Empire; it also gave it the seat of the Church, and dominance of trade operations through the Middle Ages. The feudal system and its Gothic church art never flourished in the lively trading cities of Italy, Venice, Genoa, Rome, Milan, Florence.

Exploration and commerce engendered a spirit of free inquiry, and the Renaissance was born. Established dogma, pat, static ideology quivered before the heretic questionings of mathematicians, geographers, artists, poets and philosophers. These rediscovered the works of the ancient Greeks and Romans and fostered the cult of Humanism, the glory of individual Man. This was the *Renaissance,* a rebirth, a new conception of the exploring mind. At first the church opposed it as revived paganism; then turned toward it gradually. The material blessings were accepted most readily. The classic pagan arts were less difficult to Christianize than the philosophy. Italian church art, never truly Gothic, vied with secular art to reproduce and interpret the glories of Greece and the grandeur of Rome.

The chronology of Italian furniture is therefore based on the unfolding of the Renaissance. For convenience the following distinctions of period may be observed.

(1) The *Pre-Renaissance* period, 1100-1400. Insincere, misunderstood Gothic on a base of classic Romanesque, Byzantine and Saracenic art.

(2) *Quattrocento,* 1400-1500. The early Renaissance, a style of classical purity, simplicity.

(3) *Cinquecento,* 1500-1600. The High Renaissance. First half was the great period of the Renaissance.

(4) *Baroque,* 1560-1700. The counter-Reformation in art, a Jesuit movement.

(5) *Rococo,* 1700-1750. Secular prettification of the Baroque.

(6) *Foreign influence,* 1750-1900. All the eclectic revivals; the impulses originating chiefly in France and England and including the classic styles of Louis XVI, Hepplewhite, Adam, etc.; Directoire, Empire, Middle 19th century, etc., in freely modified versions.

PRE-RENAISSANCE

Italian furniture of the Middle Ages, unlike the homogeneous Gothic style shows the classic-Romanesque basis, enriched with Byzantine and Saracenic motives. Crusaders, sailors, merchants and explorers brought influences from the Near and Far East and Africa. Wealth and power being largely in the hands of the rich merchant families, their palaces displayed a cosmopolitan, secular style, but only a minimum of furniture was needed.

The chest (Italian *Cassone*) as elsewhere was all-important, but continued to be made of planks and heavy boards long after the superior framed-panel construction was the rule in France. In the Piedmont and other localities touched by the Alpine styles appear evidences of Gothic details, as pointed arches, etc. (204, 679), but their Gothicism is superficial. Venice had pierced tracery carving, with Persian overtones. Flat surfaces were painted with landscapes or textile patterns, sometimes raised with Gesso and sometimes inlaid with Mosaic and marble (Cosmatesque work) or with ivory or bone in fine geometrical patterns (certosina) in Moorish style.

The Italian climate discouraged the enclosed bed, in place of which Oriental fabrics and rugs were used, probably with light four-post frames. 204, 679.

QUATTROCENTO

Renewed interest in ancient art endowed all furniture of the Early Renaissance with an architectonic outline. Chests and cupboards, heretofore box-forms, had bases, pilasters and cornices, scaled down from architecture; the architectural profile is a distinguishing Renaissance feature. Their bases were pedestals, solid to the floor, rather than feet. The chest-type was modified into new shapes for specialized purposes. The "Cassapanca" was a cassone with back and sides to form a settee; cushions were added for comfort. The "Credenza" was a low sideboard with doors and drawers.

Chairs were principally straight rectangular structures (sedia) large and dignified and uncomfortable, with flat arms at right angles to the backpost; the seats were padded at an early date. The X-chair shows many variations; from the Moorish folding chair came the Savonarola chair (707) interlacing curved slats with carved wooden back and arms, often with certosina ornament. The Dante chair (711) had four curved legs continuing into arms; with a fabric or leather seat and back. "Sgabelli" were wooden side chairs; some had three legs dowelled into the seat, with a flat board back; others had bases of two carved slabs.

Tables derived largely from the long trestle type, with turned baluster legs or shaped slabs (714), but four-leg types with box stretchers appeared early (715). There are many incidental table forms.

Austerely restrained surfaces in the early phase became highly decorated as the period waxed. Ornament was purely classic in character, with pilasters and scrolled volutes, fine mouldings enriched with egg-and-dart, dentils, etc.; panels with foliated scrolls, delicately carved. Gilding and polychromy in strong colors, landscapes and conventional painting decorated flat areas and mouldings.

A few general characteristics run through almost all Italian furniture of the 15th and 16th centuries.

(1) The wood is universally walnut, oiled or waxed to a deep, rich tone.

(2) Ornament is sparing, but increases progressively from the simplest early style to a highly decorative character later. Paint and gesso, even inlay are less common in later work, while carving becomes the principal resource for decoration.

(3) Proportion is architecturally large and stately, proper to large rooms; even chairs were larger than in modern usage, so that most Renaissance furniture is over-large and uncomfortable by current standards.

Italian furniture is distinguishable by local styles. Tuscany, centering in Florence, led in the Early Renaissance. Her style was refined and nobly restrained. Siena is noted for painted and gilt furniture, while in Lombardy the certosina inlay was favored. Venice produced inlays in vari-colored woods (intarsia) and later turned to highly decorative painted work of capricious form. Genoa and Liguria are known for distinctive four-door cupboards. Rome developed the rich style of carving which came to dominate all Cinquecento furniture. 197, 210 et seq., 253, 256, 258, 370, 707 et seq., 844 et seq., 881-2, 964-5.

CINQUECENTO

High Renaissance furniture developed consistently out of the early style, adding, embellishing, expanding types and decoration. Dignified formal richness is achieved by bold carving, free and brilliant, utilizing the whole vocabulary of classical decoration. The acanthus leaf has infinite variety; likewise guilloches, rinceaux, flutings, animal forms, gargoyles, caryatids, scrolls and volutes, imbrications, gadrooning, paterae, moulded panels, pilasters and architectural cornices, intarsia, etc. Newer are cartouches, strapwork, turned rosettes, broken pediments. Paint appears less frequently, gesso is rare, carving in positive relief abundant.

The large, formally bare room of the Quattrocento became richer, fuller, more sparkling; though in similar scale, chairs were made more comfortable by cushions, tables were used in greater variety, beds were built as four-post frames, chests had animal feet, sideboards appeared in divers shapes, and the whole catalog of furniture grew. Carving was universally rich but judicious. The period was indeed one of the golden ages of furniture. 108, 110, 117, 206, 255, 259, 371-2, 381, 388, 390, 425, 440, 457, 459, 463-4, 716 et seq., 832, 925-6, 962, 980, 1031, 1034.

BAROQUE

The Baroque style consists chiefly of an exaggerated, emphasized fullness of size, scale, and proportion. It is not necessarily overrich in ornament, although lavish carving is typical. So is unorthodox treatment of accepted Renaissance features, as ornate broken pediments, tremendous scrolls, profuse sculpture, deep mouldings, theatrical effects of light and shade. Twisted turnings, broken and reversed curves, inlays and appliqués of brilliant materials—marble, ivory, gilt, bronze, all contribute to the rich effect, but the classic architectural silhouette vanishes.

The style is a logical outgrowth of the High and Late Renaissance. Its exaggerations are characteristically the aftermath of a good mature style in its decadence. (The period 1560-1800 is often called in Italy "Decadenza.") The great architects, Vignola, Palladio, Michelangelo witnessed and promoted the transition; among their successors Bernini most crystallized the change. The architects' part in the evolution of the Baroque was stimulated by the Counter-Reformation, the movement fostered by the Jesuits to win back the Catholics wavering toward the Protestant movement. The means was partially this showy, theatrical dramatization of the power and wealth of the church. Paradoxically, the effect on furniture was most pronounced in the secular product, and that most sustained in the Northern lands from which the Reformation flowed.

The distinctive features of Baroque furniture are apparent after 1580, and as such set a fashion for state apartments and *meubles de luxe* in France and England and the Germanic countries. Its splendor rendered it incapable of being scaled down or simplified; it furthermore was usually a group-design, so that the individual pieces are often either downright ugly or meaningless or unbalanced by themselves. A design was studied not as a unit of furniture, but as a composition of wall and ceiling, architectural features and chairs, mirrors and candelabra and consoles, all one indissoluble picture. The detached furniture elements are therefore apt to be illogical, even absurd.

The earlier Baroque, 1560-1650, is a purely Italian outgrowth of the Late Renaissance; the later phrases show French, Flemish, Spanish, Dutch and English traits. Italian Baroque foreshadows the style of Louis XIV, and later echoes it. Wall furniture flourished in this formal atmosphere; tall cabinets, console tables and wall seats superseded the cassone. The dominating cabinet, a great architectural structure, came from France. Sculptured bases, with cherubim, mermaids, lions, eagles and negroes in composition with scrolls, shells and leaves were gilded and polychromed. The middle sections had small panels veneered or moulded or carved within restrained outlines; the top features again burst forth in a glory of pediments, involved in profile and loaded with carved ornament.

Table bases in the same style carried tops of marble, pietra dura, scagliola, or painted imitations. Chairs with flowing outlines, excessively carved and gilded, were upholstered with large-patterned velvets, silks and stamped leathers; nail heads were arranged in decorative patterns. Mirrors were larger, particularly as to frames, which were most intricately carved.

Beds of the earlier styles were still four-posters, light and graceful. As the style wore on the panels were made larger to permit more painting area for landscapes and robust floral compositions. 112, 114, 309, 400, 403, 469, 475, 733 et seq., 758, 761, 848, 974.

ROCOCO

Italy's declining commerce reduced wealth, and the declining quality of craftsmanship and materials in this period is significant. The best craftsmen found profitable occupation in France, Germany and England. The movement was not one-way; to Italy flowed the technique and ideas of the expanding nations. The later Baroque, and more particularly the *Rococo* are cosmopolitan, Italianized. By 1675 the general scale of furniture was smaller, prettier; gracefulness supplanted grandeur. Still lavishly decorated, the motives favor foliage and ribbons, rocks and shells, Chinese forms, all increasingly naturalistic. Asymmetry and the curved line were the rule. Capricious gaiety is the tradition of the early 18th century. Regence and Louis XV influences from France, William and Mary and Queen Anne from England were exaggerated, distorted, often badly designed and unsuitably adapted. The effect was theatrical, romantic, superficial and charming.

Venice alone retained some of her prestige and wealth, and therefore led in the production of furniture. Consequently, most Italian

Rococo work is described as Venetian. Painting over inferior wood and joinery achieved effects cheaply; using not only formal motives but landscapes and marble—and even wood—imitation. Bombé commodes and fancifully wavering outlines in chairs and mirrors, sofas and beds are recognized as vulgarized Louis XV. 115-6, 179, 181, 186, 278, 280, 284, 316, 402, 736 et seq., 793, 857, 1002-3.

THE CLASSIC REVIVAL

The Classic Revival came well after the excavations in Pompeii and Herculaneum had stirred the revolt toward ancient simplicity in France and England. Almost at the end of the 18th century, Italian classicism was able to borrow from the mature Louis XVI, Adam and Hepplewhite styles. Rejecting the cold formalism, it achieved symmetry and brilliance with paint, marquetry, marble and gilding. Louis Seize was interpreted in designs by Piranesi, Pergolesi, Albertolli. Milanese commodes inlaid with light wood are typical. 111, 318, 324, 447, 741 et seq., 701, 873, 906, 996, 1025.

THE EMPIRE STYLE

The *Empire* style substituted the heavier Roman, Greek and Egyptian forms for Greco-Roman airiness. This style, engendered by imperial command, has less national distinction than any prior; the general description of its traits applies as well to the Italian as to the French. More walnut was used, and less ormolu. The imperial manner lingered long after Napoleon's fall; it was in fact the accepted formal style for much of the 19th century. In less important work Italy followed the swiftly successive eclecticisms of France and England during the 19th century. 148, 185, 194-5, 343, 344, 352, 365, 746 et seq., 778, 783, 824, 991, 1084.

ITALIAN DIRECTOIRE

ITALIAN DIRECTOIRE

Italian Directoire carried the use of ancient themes even farther, emphasizing the light grace of Pompeii. Swans and lyres, scrolls and fine detail are used more exuberantly than in French furniture. 344, 353, 356, 428, 751, 826, 876, 878, 1039, 1058, 1074.

IVORY. Elephant tusks, and less properly the tusks of some other animals have been used for decorative and small utilitarian articles since prehistoric times. Egyptian sculptures in ivory are among the finest remains of their art and Early Christian, Mohammedan and Far Eastern and Gothic Ivories also reveal the skill lavished on this material.

Its use in furniture is ancient, but size limits it to decorative features. Inlays, mounts, ornamental plaques, small caskets, etc., were used by the Egyptians, Romans and Byzantines, among others. In the 18th century its use for ornamental details was revived and again in details of some modern work, notably the designs of the more elegant French school. 455.

JAPANESE STAND - 1637

MEDIEVAL JAPANESE CHEST

JACOB, FRANÇOIS GEORGES. Cabinetmaker, late Louis XVI, Directoire and Empire periods. Made furniture for Napoleon. 320.

JACOB, GEORGES. French cabinetmaker, period Louis XVI. Father of François George Jacob.

JACOBEAN—from the Latin Jacobus (James). General term for English styles up to 1688. *Early* Jacobean comprises reigns of James I, 1603-1625; Charles I, 1625-1649, and The Commonwealth, 1649-1660. Late Jacobean covers the Restoration period, including Charles II, 1660-1685, and James II, 1685-1688. The period represents the growth of foreign influence and the passing of the oak styles. Furniture becomes lighter and more adaptable, with ornament changing from Early Renaissance types to Baroque. 154 et seq., 592 et seq., 972. See *England.*

JAPANESE. Japanese domestic usage requires but little furniture. Chests and cupboards are invariably built-in, with sliding panels as doors. For sleeping, mats are unrolled on the floor and seating is similarly on mats. Tables are rare, being extremely low and portable. Such furniture as appears is usually lacquered and highly polished. Japanese lacquer is flecked with gold and decorated with fine-scaled flower, animal and landscape motives.

JAPANNING. The art of coating surfaces of wood, metal, etc., with various varnishes, dried in heated chambers. The process dates from remote antiquity in the East, but reached Europe only about 1600. In France it attained remarkable excellence under Louis XIV, who installed in the Gobelin factory Leymoyne and other artists to imitate the Oriental styles, which they called *laquage.* The Dutch traders developed a considerable commerce in lacquered work, even carrying European furniture to China to be decorated. They also tried both taking Dutch "joyners" to China, and bringing Chinese artists to Holland. The latter seems to have been more successful. The extensive traffic between the Dutch and the English as well as that between the courts of Charles II and Louis XIV created a vogue for "Japanned work" in England, and the years of Charles II's reign and later produced quantities of cabinets, mirrors, screens, etc. The earlier work in both France and England was in high relief which gave way to flatter decoration of flowers and foliage in Georgian times. It was called also "Bantam Work" and was incised as well as flat. The technique declined toward the last part of the 18th century, such work as was designed by Robert

2. WILLIAM AND MARY TABLE. Oystered walnut. With Dutch coffer, velvet covered and mounted with brass.
Brady Collection

753. CHEST-ON-STAND, CA. 1685. Walnut base with Spanish foot.
Anderson Galleries

THE LOWBOY IS NOT A DISTINCT TYPE AS TO FORM OR PURPOSE. IT DERIVES FROM THE TABLE WITH SEVERAL DRAWERS, OR FROM THE CHEST PLACED UPON A STAND, AND IS VARIOUSLY USED AS DRESSING TABLE, CONSOLE, WRITING DESK, SERVING TABLE, ETC.

754. OYSTERED WALNUT VENEER CHEST on legs of Flemish scroll shape. Period of William and Mary.

755. AMERICAN LOWBOY of William and Mary style. Burl walnut, about 1700.
Metropolitan Museum

756. PHILADELPHIA LOWBOY of mahogany, 1760-1775. Style of William Savery. The Chippendale ornament was Rococo, derived from the French style of the years 1720-1750.

Photographs Courtesy Metropolitan Museum of Art

757. FRENCH, style of Louis XV. Mahogany with gilt bronze moun... This Rococo style of ornament i... fluenced the English designers a... so spread to America.

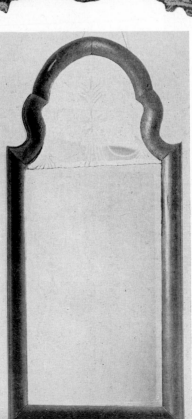

759.

Ginsburg & Levy

760. GERMAN, 17th Century.
Carved wood, gilded.
Metropolitan Museum

58. ITALIAN, 17th Century.
Wood, carved and gilt.
Metropolitan Museum

759. JACOBEAN ENGLISH
MIRROR of small pieces
leaded together.

761. VENETIAN MIRROR, early
16th Century. Carved and
polychromed.

762. (Lower center) AMERICAN
QUEEN ANNE STYLE.
Ginsburg & Levy

MIRRORS
17th Century

763. AMERICAN, late 17th Century. *Metropolitan Museum*

764. SWEDISH, late 17th Century.
Walnut. Baroque form with
pierced ornament.

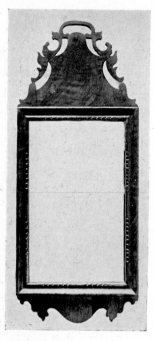

765. AMERICAN, WALNUT, C. 1720. *Weil*

766. AMERICAN, GIRANDOLE. About 1790. French influence. Pine and Composition, Gilded. *Metropolitan Museum*

767. AMERICAN, Mid-18 Century.

768. AMERICAN, Mid-18th Century. Gilded Ornament on Walnut. *Henry Weil*

769. AMERICAN, Mid-18th Century. Mahogany, Gilt Ornament. *Metropolitan Museum*

770. PHILADELPHIA, 1756-1761 Label of John Elliott. *Metropolitan Museum*

771. ENGLISH, Early Georgian

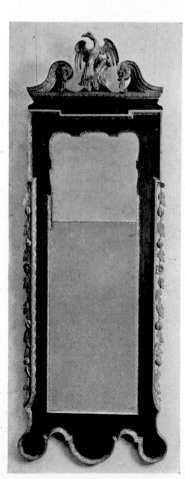

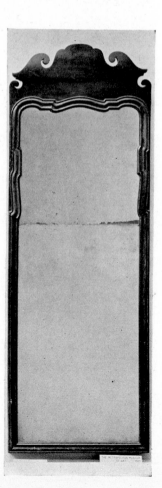

ENGLISH GILT ORNAMEN-
TAL MIRROR, CA. 1775.
Vernay

773. GILT OVAL MIRROR with Roc
ornament, C. 1760.
Ve

774. GILDED MIRROR of Adam design. English, classic
influence. *Vernay*

775. AMERICAN, early 19th Century. Gilt mirror of classic
French style: *Metropolitan Museum*

776. ENGLISH GILT MIRROR of Rococo Chippendale
style, CA. 1750. *Vernay*

780. AMERICAN, CA. 1810. Gilt.
mirror of French style. *Wei...*

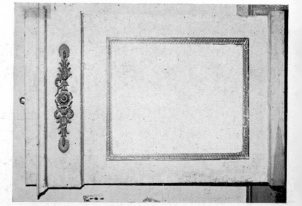

781. ITALIAN, late 18th Century.

779. TRUMEAU of the period of Louis XIV. Carved and painted.

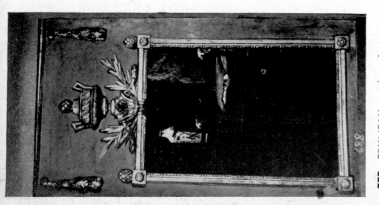

777. TRUMEAU, style of Louis
XVI. Painted and gilt. *Ruseau*

786. ITALIAN EMPIRE. C. 1810.   *Weil*

787. AMERICAN. Ca. 1810.

782. ITALIAN, EARLY 18th CENTURY.   *Cavallo*

785. AMERICAN. GILT WITH PAINTED DECORATION. Ca. 1800.   *Weil*

783. ITALIAN EMPIRE. Ca. 1815.   *Lavezzo*

784. AMERICAN. C. 1815.   *Weil*

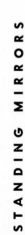

791-792. ENGLISH, 1780-1795.

795. FRENCH, C. 1790.

790. ITALIAN EMPIRE, CA. 1815.

794. GERMAN, BIEDERMEIER, CA. 1820.

789. ENGLISH, CA. 1700. *Vernay*

788. ENGLISH, CA. 1710.

STANDING MIRRORS

793. ITALIAN, 18th Century. *Metropolitan Museum*

Adam for this medium being inferior to the Queen Anne and earlier Georgian work. See *Lacquer*.

JEWELLING.   Surface carving to simulate jewels. 155.

JIG SAW.   Saw for cutting interior work, such as pierced work, fret work, lattice work, etc. Originally operated by a treadle, it was one of the first machines to which power was applied. As a consequence jig-sawed detail is typical of the earlier machine age of the 19th century. Inevitably it ran away with its designers and an easy characterization of the period 1830-1890 is by this lacey wood ornament. Not only furniture but facades of houses were draped with better or worse decoration of this type. 4.

JOINERY.   The technique or mechanics of furniture and woodwork. Joinery is to the interior designer what masonry is to the architect. It is the oldest term for the craft, and literally means the joining together of pieces of wood. See *Consruction*.

JOINT STOOL.   Jacobean stool with turned legs, originally with mortise and tenon joints. 494.

JOINT STOOL

JONES, INIGO, 1573-1652.   Leading architect of the Early English Renaissance. Apprenticed to a joiner and sent to Italy to study, he was imbued with the spirit of classical architecture as exemplified by Palladio. On his return to England, he inspired the use of these forms, under the patronage of Charles I. He designed furniture in the current Baroque Italian style.

JOUY.   Printed fabrics, usually on fine cotton, produced at Jouy near Paris by Philippe Oberkampf, from 1760 to 1815. The patterns were most commonly realistic designs on classic themes, with charming compositions of all classical ornaments, fruit and flowers with plaques and landscapes. These prints are extensively reproduced today, and also serve as models for fabrics printed with subjects of timely interest. 124. See *Oberkampf*.

STYLE of INIGO JONES

JUGENDSTIL.   Decorative style in Germany roughly contemporary with L'Art Nouveau in France about 1895-1912. Rebellious and self-conscious, it failed to materialize as a substantial or mature style in furniture.

KAS.   Dutch cabinet or sideboard; appears in the Dutch American colonies of New York and the Delaware Valley; sometimes carved walnut, also pine, cherry or maple, panelled and painted with rather primitive ornaments of vases and flowers. 166.

KAUFFMANN, ANGELICA, 1741-1807.   Swiss painter and decorative artist. Came to London in 1766 where she executed murals and ceilings, many designed by Robert Adam. Her classical compositions appear as decoration on much painted furniture of last third

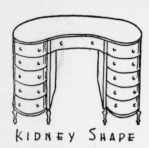

KIDNEY SHAPE

KNEEHOLE DESK

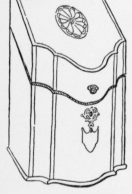

KNIFE BOXES

of the century, whether inspired by her work or actually painted by her being uncertain. Her husband was Antonio Zucchi, likewise a painter of murals and decorations under the auspices of the Brothers Adam. Their influence on the work of Hepplewhite, Sheraton and others is unmistakable. 567A.

KENT, WILLIAM, 1684-1748. English architect and furniture designer of the Golden Age, probably the first English architect to make a practice of designing the movable as well as fixed furniture of his rooms. His work is insistently architectural, employing columns, entablature and pediments on cabinets and bookcases; his side tables and desks and most smaller pieces become heavy and massive as a result of this ornamentation. 535.

KERF. A saw cut. Sometimes on curved work a series of saw cuts against the grain, not quite through the board, permitting the bending of the wood into curved shapes.

KETTLE FRONT. Swelling or bulging front of a case, Baroque. Inspiration occurring in 18th century English and American work. 48.

KEY PATTERN (Greek Fret). Ancient Greek band ornament of interlacing lines at right angles. Carved on middle Georgian and inlaid or painted on English Regency furniture. See *Ornament.*

KIDNEY TABLE, Bench, etc. Oval shaped with concave front, applied to dressing- or writing-tables, etc. Appears in 18th century furniture of France and England. Especially favored by Sheraton. 1049.

KILN DRIED. Lumber which has been dried by artificial means in warm chambers. The heat is regulated to prevent the too sudden loss of moisture, avoiding checking, warping and other defects. Besides speed, kiln drying is superior to air drying because the remaining moisture content can be precisely controlled.

KINGWOOD. Conspicuously marked dark reddish-brown wood similar to rosewood, used for inlays and veneers in flat work, periods of Louis XV, Queen Anne, Late Georgian.

KLISMOS. Ancient Greek chair.

KNEADING TABLE. Utilitarian furniture of the provinces of Europe, now used as tables and side tables. Provincial French ones are particularly decorative. 640.

KNEE. The upper, convex curve or bulge of a cabriole leg, sometimes called Hip.

KNEE HOLE. Desks, chests, or bureaux are sometimes built with an opening in the center, between the two banks of drawers; so called because they make room for the sitter's knees. Sometime this space is filled part way from the back with a door compartment. 1015.

KNIFE BOX, KNIFE CASE. Box-cases for table silver usually in pairs, stood on buffets or side tables in 18th century English dining rooms. They first appear at the end of the 17th century, made of walnut with sloping lids and curved fronts. The later ones of mahogany were often inlaid and mounted with silver. In the late 18th century a vase form appears, often of satinwood. 567, 896.

KNOB. Handle of wood, metal, glass, etc., usually turned, always with a single stem, distinctive to the various styles. Elaborately chased metal gilt knobs feature Louis XVI furniture. Small wooden and ivory ones were used in fine 18th century English work, and large glass and china knobs were used on 19th century work in the United States. See *Hardware.*

KNOB-TURNING. Turning of knobs in series used on some 17th century work.

KNOCKED DOWN K. D. Constructed in sections to be easily assembled after shipping.

KNOP. Bunch of leaves or flowers. Also the old spelling for knobs, occurring as a swelling or vase shape on a turned shaft.

KNOTTY PINE. In good old work the knotty parts of pine were scrupulously avoided, only the clear wood being used except where painted. The removal of paint revealing these in renovated panelling and furniture, it is mistakenly assumed that the knots were purposefully chosen. Wide advertising has created a vogue for knotty pine, but it does not follow that this is historically correct or good. 529.

KNUCKLE. Carving on the outside end of chair arms, principally of Chippendale and Windsor types.

KNUCKLE JOINT. Joint as at separable leaves of a drop leaf table, resembling a finger joint.

KOA. Dense, dark-brown hardwood from the Philippines having pronounced stripes and cross stripes like curly maple.

LABURNUM. Hardwood, moderately durable, yellowish in color with brown streaks. It takes a high polish. In ancient Rome it was known as Corsican Ebony. It appears on veneered surfaces in the furniture of the Louis XV period and in English post-Restoration furniture. In the latter the branches or saplings were cut transversely and matched to produce the concentric markings known as "Oyster Shell." See *Oystering.*

LACEWOOD. Australian oak having fine regularly spaced flakes yielding a lace-like appearance. See *Woods.*

LACQUER. Oriental lacquer is a high dense finish acquired by tedious padding up and rubbing down of many coats of spirit shellac. This has nothing in common with modern lacquer, which is a compound of cellulose derivatives. These dry so rapidly that they must be sprayed by compressed air. Such lacquers now possess many qualities not found in varnish or shellac finishes, such as resistance to heat, moisture, and acids. They can be rubbed to a clear satiny finish which emphasizes the beauty of the wood; they are also made opaque, like paint, and tinted to any shade. In speed, ease of handling and resistance to wear they are more economical and probably more efficacious than older materials as varnish and shellac. See *Finish*.

LADDERBACK

LADDER BACK. Chair back with horizontal slats or rails resembling a ladder. Common types in Pilgrim furniture, and in the simpler Chippendale work. 229 et seq., 291.

LADIES' DESKS. Lighter and smaller desks on legs, developed in France and England after 1690. See *Desks*. 442.

LAMBREQUIN. Drapery around the top of a bed.

LAMINATE. The building-up of layers; in wood panels three, five or more layers are laid alternately across the grains for strength and durability. See *Veneers, Plywood*.

LAMPADAIRE. Pedestal in the classic manner, designed to hold a lamp or candles; French Empire.

LANCASHIRE CHAIR. English spindle-back chair of curved lines. The seats are rush.

LANCET. English Pointed Gothic arch.

LANDSCAPE PANEL. Wood panel with the grain running horizontally.

LANGLEY, BATTY AND THOMAS. English architects, early 18th century. Their published early designs were after the grandiose French manner. Batty Langley was one of the leaders of the earliest Gothic revival.

LANNUIER, CHARLES HONORÉ. French cabinetmaker who worked in New York, 1805-1819. Favoring the Directoire-Classic manner, much of his work may be erroneously credited to Phyfe. 125.

LANTERN CLOCK. Shelf clock suggesting the shape of a lantern; late 17th century English, often in brass. Also called *Birdcage* clock.

LATHE. Machine for shaping turned parts by the application of cutting edges against the revolving wood. See *Turning*.

LATTICE. Carved criss-cross pattern in cut-out work, found in chair backs, highboy pediments, etc. Metal is sometimes used for lattice chair backs. 71, 286, 481.

LAUREL. Hard wood of deep brown color. Best known for furniture is East Indian laurel, having a pronounced wavy grain.

LAURELLING. Decorative banding of laurel leaves, usually on a half-round moulding.

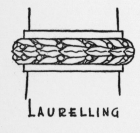

LAURELLING

LAZY SUSAN. Revolving tray for condiments, American. See *Dumbwaiter*.

LEAF. (A) Conventionalized or naturalistic leaves are among the earliest and most continuously used decorative forms. The acanthus leaf is the basic floral decoration; it lends itself to infinite shapes and variations. The laurel leaf, water leaf and other shapes occur constantly in decoration.

(B) *Drop Leaf* is the hinged part of a table, desk, etc.

(C) *Loose Leaf* is inserted into the opening of an extension table to provide additional surface.

LEAF SCROLL FOOT. Base of a leg with foliated design. 616.

LEATHER. The tanned skins of animals. Furniture uses chiefly those of cattle, calves, sheep, goats, and pigs. These are treated in many ways for strength, permanence and decorative interest. Dyeing and surface-coating yield an unlimited palette, and a great variety of textures are a product of manufacture as well as of nature. The heavier skins of cattle—steers, cows, etc., which are too thick for upholstering, are split into several thicknesses. The topmost or buff, extremely thin, is reserved for choicest small articles. The following layer or top-grain is the choicest for upholstery, accepting the flaws and irregularities, the vestiges of bruises and scratches on the living animal, as part of the beauty of the material. The succeeding layers, having no such natural surface, are treated with imitations of top grain or of the characteristic surfaces of other hides as pig, ostrich, walrus or snake, or with pebbling, glosses, etc. Such mechanical treatment is superficially more perfect, or more regular, than the natural hide. In such leathers the fiber is looser and therefore weaker. Skins, sometimes not tanned and with the hair not removed, were used in the most ancient periods, before weaving was known, and after for its strength and availability. There seems never to have been a time when it was not used for seats, but it comes into special favor in styles of the masculine character. All the earlier Renaissance types, particularly the Spanish and English especially favored leather upholstery. Special processes of embossing, tooling, painting, and gilding leather were disseminated by Spanish craftsmen in the 16th and 17th centuries. Everywhere chests, coffers, chairs, screens, etc., were covered with leather and studded with nail-heads arranged in decorative patterns (213). Table and desk tops have been covered with leather since Renaissance times (546) as have been decorative features and accessories, as handles. Oxhide and calf were supplemented in the late Louis XIV work by Morocco, a fine goat leather which was also favored by Chippendale and subsequent designers, but cattle-leather has always maintained its pre-eminence by reason of its strength and size. Today the many methods of surfacing leather for texture and color make it more desirable than ever. 65, 71, 214, 263, 283, 360, 508, 833, 912, 921, 960, 1007.

LEATHERETTE. Artificial leather made of cellulose-coated cloth embossed with familiar leather textures.

LE BRUN, CHARLES, 1619-1690. French architect, painter, designer; first director of the State Gobelin factory. A great organizer

SPIRAL   FLUTED

TURNED   CABRIOLE

FURNITURE LEGS

LIBRARY STEPS

LINEN·FOLD PANEL

as well as a great artist, his personality is the dominant force in the vigorous style of Louis XIV. He brought together French, Flemish and Italian artists and coordinated their work and styles. His mastery is reflected in the magnificent royal works of the age.

LECTERN.   Ecclesiastical reading desk of wood, metal, or stone.

LECTUS.   Roman beds or couches. The lectus lucubratorius and lectus cubicularius were respectively fitted with and without incidental conveniences as reading desks, receptacles for things at hand, etc. The lectus triclinarius was a lower couch, used when dining.

LEG.   Legs of furniture are in the various styles among the most distinctive features as guides in determining time and place of origin. A few general types have their individual styles and imitations, such as the cabriole, turned, tapered, fluted, concave, animal, etc., etc. See style headings.

LE PAUTRE, JEAN, 1617-1682.   French designer, school of Louis XIV; published "Livre de Miroirs, Tables de Gueridons," and other works on furniture, which influenced design in Flanders and England.

LIBRARY STEPS.   Various devices for providing access to the higher shelves in libraries. They appear frequently in England, latter 18th century, in many forms, chiefly combined with benches, tables, etc. The ladder part unfolds, sometimes providing a handrail.

LIBRARY TABLE.   Large table with drawers usually in pedestal form. English name for any flat top desk usually known in America as pedestal or knee-hole desk; often provided with space for books. 1005 et seq.

LIGNUM VITAE.   West Indian wood, the heaviest known. It was used for veneering in the late Stuart period.

LIMEWHITENED.   Sixteenth century painted furniture was first bleached with a solution of lime. The removal of the painted surface at later dates exposed this whitened surface which is sometimes referred to as "pickled finish."

LIMEWOOD.   Light-colored, close-grained wood which cuts equally well across as with the grain, rendering it excellent for carving. Favored by Grinling Gibbons.

LINEN-FOLD.   Gothic ornamental panel treatment representing the folds of linen, probably originally after the folded napkin on the chalice in the Catholic ritual. It appears to be exclusively a North-European motive, abundant in Gothic 14th, 15th and 16th century remains from Gothic France, the Netherlands and the Teutonic countries. In England it survived another century along with the persistent Gothic quality of the Tudor, Elizabethan and Jacobean styles. It is invariably executed in oak, in panels of seats, armoires, cupboards, chests, etc. 165.

LINEN PRESS. Two boards closed together by pressure of a large wooden screw. Linen placed between the boards and pressed down while damp came out smooth. Linen presses are seen in Dutch paintings of the 17th century, and some survive from the period of Charles I. Some 18th century types were made part of the chest of drawers planned to hold linens.

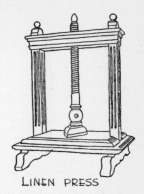

LINEN PRESS

LION MOTIVE. One of the most ancient decorative symbols, probably typifying the royal nature of the furniture of early peoples. In Egypt lion paws and heads, alone, were terminal decorations, rather naturalistic. In Gothic representation they appear more as grotesques or in heraldic shapes, the symbolism of lion couchant and rampant being represented in the carving and painting of furniture. Renaissance work employs the lion sporadically, although the paw and head were almost uninterruptedly used. The Empire style revived its use to a great extent, probably as much for symbolic as for historical or decorative interest. Brass castings of heads and paws appear frequently; handles of the lion-and-ring form are typical. 435.

LIP MOULDING. Small convex moulding around drawers, originally intended as a dust stop in Queen Anne and early Chippendale case work.

LISTEL. Same as Fillet, a flat, plain moulding.

LION MOTIVE

LIT-CLOS. French "closed-bed"; panelled enclosure of wood around a bed, sometimes free standing, sometimes in a corner. Chiefly provincial French. 17th-19th Centuries.

LIVERY CUPBOARD. Early English food cupboard. Livery is probably a contraction of *delivery*. Food was stored here and distributed to the household and to the poor. Ventilation was a necessity, often provided by grilles of wooden spindles, or tracery. See *Cupboards*.

LOBE. Section or profile in rounded form.

LOBING. Gadrooning.

LOCK, MATTHIAS. English carver and furniture designer. Published in collaboration with Copeland several books on Ornament between 1752 and 1769. Early work a flamboyant Rococo character, later almost exact copies of the Adam style.

LONG CLOCK. Grandfathers', hall or tall clock.

LOOP-BACK. Oval chair back; also Windsor bow back, without arms.

LOOP HINGE. Early type of hinge consisting of two intersecting loops.

LOOSE SEAT. Same as slip seat; separate wood frame, upholstered and let into the framing of the chair seat.

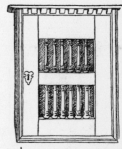

LIVERY CUPBOARD

LOO TABLE. Oval table designed for the old game of Loo.

LOPER. Sliding arms which support the fall or drop front or lid of a desk. Also the sliding runners of an extending table.

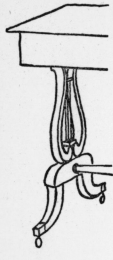

LYRE

ENGLISH
1770

BIEDERMEIER

LOTUS. Ancient flower ornament. The principal Egyptian floral motive, it appears in more or less ornamental uses in all ancient work, and may have been the basis for many later flower decorations.

LOUIS QUATORZE. Louis XIV, king of France, 1643-1715. Greatest period of French achievement, furniture style is marked by Baroque magnificence. Masculine character declined after 1680; proportions reduced, lines softened. Latter part was the Régence. 597 et seq. See *France*.

LOUIS QUINZE. Period of Louis XV, king of France, 1715-1774 marked by culmination of feminine Rococo style; dainty scale-free naturalistic ornament, rounded surfaces and flowing lines. 610 et seq. See *France*.

LOUIS SEIZE. Period of Louis XVI, King of France, 1774-1793, marked by revival of ancient classicism; severe rectangular lines, architectural ornament. 617 et seq. See *France*.

LOUNGE. Type of couch in late 19th century work, often with one end high as a pillow.

LOVE CHEST. 18th Century Pennsylvania Dutch Chest, with the initials of the bride and groom. 25.

LOVE SEAT. Double chair or small sofa. Queen Anne and later. Also "Courting Chair." 50.

LOW BOY. English low chest or table with drawers. Beginning in Jacobean times by raising a chest on a stand, it continues through English and American work of the 18th century in various forms as dressing tables, side tables, etc. 752 et seq.

LOW RELIEF. Carving or built-up work, not highly raised from or sunk into the ground. 151.

LOZENGE. Diamond shaped. Panels, overlays, inserts, etc., of this shape occur in Renaissance work of all descriptions. 588.

LUNETTE. Semicircular space. In furniture, a half-moon shape filled with carving, inlay, or painting. In Gothic oak furniture lunettes were carved, while in English late Georgian work they were often inlaid or painted with fan-shaped designs.

LYRE MOTIVE. A naturalistic representation of the lyre figures in Greek decoration, and was adapted by the Renaissance artists. It appears sporadically in all design, and was featured strongly in a free form in Louis XIV and Louis XV decoration. In the style of Louis XVI it occurs in symmetrical form, and in comparative forms in England. Sheraton employed it conspicuously as did the entire school of the Empire and Empire influence in England and America. Duncan Phyfe designed table supports, chair backs, mirror standards, etc., with this motive, delicately executed, with brass wires representing the strings. It is also found in Biedermeier work in Germany and in Italian furniture of the early XIX century. 351, 642.

6. BOOKSHELVES BY DJO BOURGEOIS, PARIS.

7. LIVING ROOM FURNITURE DESIGNED BY MAXWELL FRY
AND JACK HOWE, FOR HEAL AND SON, LONDON.

LIVING ROOM FURNITURE DE-
SIGNED BY RUSSELL WRIGHT.

site Page

(Left) LOUNGE CHAIR DESIGNED
BY MARCEL BREUER.

(Right) ARMCHAIR, AMERICAN.
WALNUT, CANE BACK.

LIVING ROOM FURNITURE DE-
SIGNED BY GILBERT ROHDE.

site Page

(Left) NEST OF TABLES IN SYCA-
MORE. COURTESY RENA ROSEN-
THAL.

(Right) DINING ROOM CABINET
DESIGNED BY GILBERT ROHDE.

(Right) DINING ROOM FURNITURE
DESIGNED BY GILBERT ROHDE.

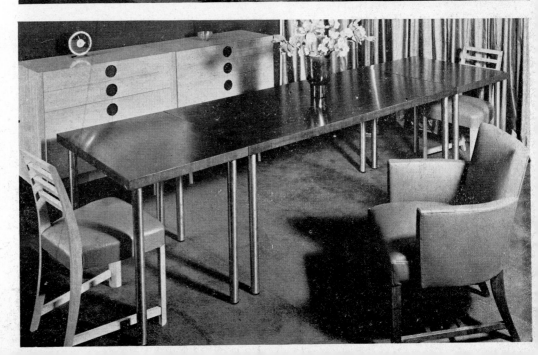

osite Page

(Left) BUFFET IN ROSEWOOD DE-
SIGNED BY JOSEPH LOTTO.

(Right) DRESSING CABINET IN
QUILTED MAPLE DESIGNED BY
JOSEPH LOTTO.

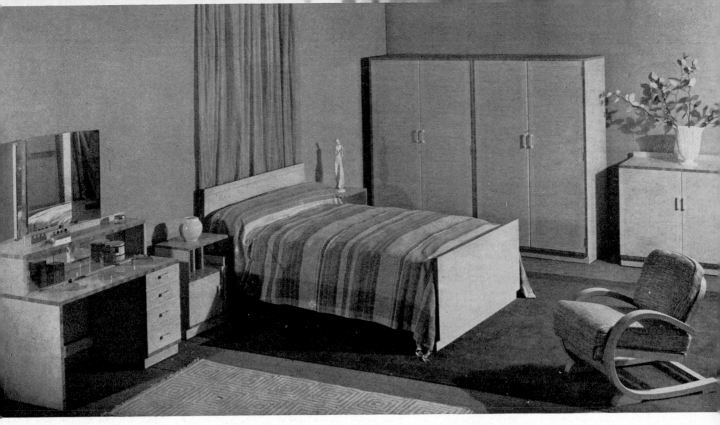

807. BIRCH WITH ZEBRAWOOD EDGINGS, BY CHRISTOPHER HEAL, LONDON.

808. BEDROOM FURNITURE OF WHITE SYCAMORE BY MAURICE BARRET, PARIS.

WEDEN; INLAID CABINET.

810. ENGLAND; COCKTAIL CABINET IN INDIAN LAUREL. DESIGNED BY E. MAXWELL FRY.

GLAND: DINING ROOM FURNITURE IN PEAR-WOOD AND SYCAMORE, DESIGNED BRIAN O'RORKE.

Courtesy Heal & Son, London

812.
ITALY: FURNITU
ARCHITECTS M
OPOCZYNSKY AND
QUALI.

813. FURNITURE OF SYCAMO
SIGNED BY MARCEL B
FOR HEAL & SON, LO

WALL CASES CANTILE
FROM THE WALL TO
THE FLOOR CLEAR; CHA
BENT SYCAMORE PLYWO

*Photographs
The Architectura*

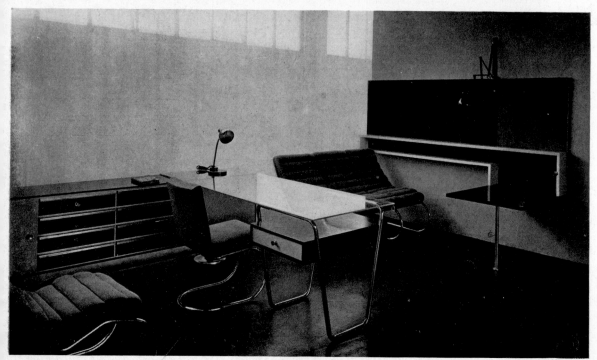

814. ITALY. WRIT
TABLE AND CAS
BIANCHETTI AND

MACASSAR. Dutch East India port from which is shipped the striped ebony called Macassar.

MADRONE. Brown-red burl of sound, regular texture and figure, from the Pacific coast.

MAGNOLIA. American tulip-tree: wood is light straw color with slight figure. Suitable for exposed parts of furniture and face veneers.

MANWARING, ROBERT. English designer and furniture maker. Published "Cabinet and Chair Maker's Real Friend and Companion" in 1765. Heavy and highly ornamented chairs, resembling those of Chippendale are shown. There seem to be few surviving pieces with his mark. 287.

MAHOGANY. Reddish brown wood of medium hardness, great strength and among the most beautiful for texture, ease of polishing, variety of grain and figure. Today mahogany includes several botanical species, chiefly the *Swietenia* of the West Indies, South and Central America, and the *Khaya* of Africa. The American mahoganies were the first known. The Spanish explorers were quick to appreciate its splendid properties, and its early importation and use in cabinetwork is attested by the 16th century date of some fine Spanish Renaissance remains. Other countries were slower to use it. Queen Elizabeth is said to have been interested in some mahogany brought by Sir Walter Raleigh, but no headway was made against the domestic oak and walnut until the 18th century. In 1733 the heavy tariff against mahogany was modified, and it rapidly supplanted other wood in fine work, retaining its ascendancy for many years. The Cuban and San Domingan varieties were preferred; these had a hard firm texture which nevertheless carved well. Its original light color changed gradually to a deep rich lustrous tone, and the various figures, as crotch, rope mottle, fiddleback, etc., stimulated the designers' imaginations. Later, Mexican and South American mahoganies came into the market, each with special characteristics. The African varieties were accepted as true mahogany in the later 19th century. They are lighter in weight and softer in texture, with rarer appearance of the beautiful eccentric figures, but they have distinct features, such as fine stripings and cross-fire markings which recommend them. Philippine trees as the tanguile and lauaan are not recognized as true mahogany, although referred to as Philippine Mahogany.

Mahogany is the essential ingredient of the great 18th century school, which MacQuoid calls the Age of Mahogany. Not alone England, but France, Spain, and Italy used the wood more or less continuously since that time. The Empire period featured it extensively; the Federal period in American work is essentially a mahogany style.

Each style developed a special treatment of Mahogany which is significant. Georgian England had a light red-brown tone, the result of polishing with bee's wax, slightly red-tinted. Empire mahogany was rich red, highly polished. Until very late years a popular misconception in America held mahogany to be a blackish red wood, the result of universal dark staining and over-varnishing in American furniture practice.

MAIDOU. East Indian wood prized for decorative veneers, both in the long grain and the fine, even burls resembling Amboyna.

MAPLE. The *Acer* family is the distinctly American wood. While known in Europe in a few varieties, its preeminence in the Western Hemisphere is due to its prevalence, its fine structural properties and its decorative interest. The early Colonists were quick to recognize and use maple, and we have the example of much early American maple furniture as a guide to its use. There are hard and soft maples, with varied figures and textures, as curly, birds' eye, wavy, blister, and quilted figures, usable in the solid lumber or as veneers. It varies from very hard to medium, with a high ratio of strength and resistance to shock and splitting; it works well and can be polished very smooth.

The texture of maple is very hard and smooth, the fibers and pores being exceptionally small. It is almost white in color in the harder varieties, the softer maples being light tan or yellow-brown. Recent furniture practice has been to stain or glaze maple to a red-brown shade which purports to be the color of Early American antiques; this is neither accurate nor beautiful and it is to be hoped that commercial producers will soon abandon it and utilize the true light beauty of the wood.

MARBLE. Marble furniture remains from Egypt, Greece and Rome are not uncommon, whether resulting from a considerable use or its ability to survive being conjectural. Ceremonial chairs or "Thronos" from classic Greek times are known and inspired the "curule" chair of the classic revivals. The type was copied by the Romans in elaborately sculptured chairs of state. Remaining Roman table bases indicate that these likewise were handsomely adorned and combined with bronze, used as supports for marble tops. The Romans undoubtedly used the highly colored Italian marbles as well as the classic white, while Byzantine remains show a preference for these colors. The Italian Renaissance revived the use of marble, neglected by the Gothic designers, and the process of inlaying marbles into wood or stone surfaces was either revived or re-discovered. Baroque Italian and, to a greater degree, French work of the 16th and 17th centuries favored marbles, and in the magnificent furniture of Louis XIV and XV it appears most frequently as tops of buffets, commodes, tables and side tables. The Italian precedent did not reach England to any considerable degree until the 18th century; after 1720, however, the vogue for marble grew. At first only white marble was imported and it became customary to stain this to represent the costlier varieties. About 1738 colored marbles native to England were employed in furniture, and the search abroad was for still more exotically hued stone. After 1750 porphyry, lapis lazuli, alabaster and other semi-precious stones were used as tops. With the diminishing scale of furniture toward the end of the century the use of marble tops waned; the decline was also hastened by the new skill in coloring and veining *Scagliola,* a composition. The Adams used these imitations extensively.

Italy, with a declining aristocracy, carried marble effects so far that whole rooms and their furniture were painted to simulate highly figured marble.

The Empire style revived the classic use of marble. It survived the style and was probably most characteristically used in the furniture of the 19th century throughout Europe and America. The styles of Louis Philippe, Victoria, and the marble-topped era in the U. S. favored the dull tone of gray and white marble. Dressers, washstands, tables and commodes were generously covered with the stone, the habit persisting almost to the end of the century. 533.

MARBLING. Wood painted to simulate marble was probably used in all times, but we have actual examples surviving from the 17th century in Italy, France and England, and later throughout Europe. Painted columns, commodes and tables were often combined with real marble.

MAROT, DANIEL. Architect and designer of furniture, born in Paris about 1660, died in Holland about 1720. Studied under Lepautre and Boulle; went to Holland to escape religious persecution; under patronage of the Prince of Orange he designed important public and residential work. As architect to William III of England he issued many designs, but to what extent they were executed is not known. Much detail of Hampton Court Palace bears his characteristic form, whether it was his actual design or not. Marot's style is the quintessence of the later style of Louis XIV. His designs for Boulle typify his ability to compose extravagant detail into an architectural whole. His fireplaces and wall treatments likewise incorporate the richest assortment of motives into sound compositions. In lesser hands the effects are garish, but Marot's designs employing all manner of rinceaux and festoons, animal and geometric forms, with every color and texture, are firmly held together. His talent inspired Dutch, French and English artists for almost a century. Chippendale, Kent and most other designers of the age appear to have profited by his work in no small measure.

MARQUETRY. Inlay of contrasting wood into a background of veneer. See *Inlay*. 389.

MARQUISE CHAIR (French). Wide bergère armchair, completely upholstered. 323.

MARRIAGE CHEST, COFFER. See *Dower Chest*. 370.

MARTIN, GUILLAUME, SIMON ETIENNE, JULIEN AND ROBERT. French carriage painters to court of Louis XIV, who invented a varnishing process to simulate the popular Oriental lacquer. Known subsequently as Vernis Martin, this brilliant transparent finish was universally employed. See *Vernis Martin*.

MASK. Decorative motive of great antiquity, representing a human or animal face, distorted, conventionalized or naturalistic. Found in practically all European styles. 532.

MATTRESS. Thick pad or cushion, filled with feathers, down, spring, hair, wool, cotton, etc., and placed upon the springs of a bed. The loose cushion of an upholstered chair (Squab or Carreau) is sometimes called mattress.

MAYHEW, T. (See Ince and Mayhew). English designer.

McINTIRE, SAMUEL, 1757-1811. Woodcarver of Salem, Mass. Distinctive style and superb craftsmanship distinguish his mantelpieces, overdoors, and other carvings for furniture and architectural embellishment. 868.

MEANDER PATTERN. Same as Greek Key. See *Ornament*.

MEDALLION. Circular, oval, square or octagonal plaque painted or carved with decorative figures, ornament, etc. French Renaissance and Italian work used medallions of stone set into the wood; the Adams used cameo-like medallions of pottery or painted wood.

MEDIEVAL. See *Gothic*.

MEISSONIER, JUSTE AURELE, 1693-1750. French designer; developed Rococo style to greatest extravagance. Introduced Italian features as broken shell-shape curves. Published "Le Livre d'Ornements."

MELON-BULB

MELON-BULB. Thick bulbous turning, typical of Elizabethan and Jacobean furniture. Thicker, more ornate types are early; later forms were smaller and not carved. Found less typically in Continental styles. 495.

MENUISIER. French word for cabinetmaker or joiner.

MERIDIENNE. Short sofa unique to the French Empire period. It had one arm higher than the other. 867.

MERIDIENNE

METAL FURNITURE. The ancients left remains of much furniture in bronze and iron, though its greater durability rather than favor may account for the excess of metal relics over wood. Egypt, Assyria, Greece and Rome used bronze in a magnificent way, and among the best evidences of their styles and craftsmanship are table bases, chairs, torchères, etc. In India, China and Japan, likewise, brass, bronze and iron articles of great antiquity are found and yield a clue to the artistic power of dead ages.

Ironworkers in the Middle Ages attained superb skill, and executed in this medium almost every article of furniture then known. In addition wood pieces were both ornamented and reinforced with a prodigious amount of wrought iron straps and bands, hinges, locks and handles. 369, 682, 99, 165, 401, 417.

In the earliest phases of the Renaissance in the Mediterranean countries the skill of the medieval ironworkers survived, and in Spain and Italy there are iron chairs, bedframes, torchères, table structures, etc., of superb design and technique. 717. Wholly metal furniture declined during the later Renaissance, but the use of metal details as accessory to wood increased to the point where in the mid-18th century it represented the principal means of ornamentation. Modern times and machine processes have rendered us essentially metal-minded, and the quest for a metal furniture technique is as old as the movement to create furniture in current moods. The metal bed, both brass and iron, of the late 19th century is the example par excellence of the trend and its success. It seems entirely logical and proper to make such structural frameworks of metal, but the memory of the tasteless creations of tortured brass and steel is enough to forbid at this time much experiment in this medium. Chairs of tubular steel answer supremely the contemporary cry for forms readily adapted to cheap machine production. Their shapes are peculiarly expressive of the material and the process. They are exceedingly comfortable, easy to handle and to keep in good condition. Many other articles of furniture may likewise be made wholly or in part of this strong light material, but design ingenuity and public demand are still far behind the technical possibilities. 796 et seq.

Sheet metal work is likewise in a tentative state. Excellent utilitarian cabinets, chests of drawers, bookcases, etc., are possible technically, but timid taste and the exigencies of commercial production have retarded the development of other than office furniture.

METAL MOUNTS. See *Hardware*.

MEUBLES. French for movable furniture.

MEUBLES DE LUXE. The luxurious furniture which set the standards of most great styles. The extremely decorative furniture in the great rooms of continental palaces was really built more for show than for use; its large scale, its profuse ornamentation and extreme cost, render it unsuitable as inspiration for the design of average modern furniture.

MIDDLE AGES. See *Gothic*.

MIRROR FRAMES,

MIRRORS. Looking glasses of polished metal were known in ancient times, but the mirror of silvered glass appears in the early Renaissance. It was costly and available in small sizes, so that the important frame both exaggerated its size and emphasized its value. In Italy the typical form was a rich architectural profile of simple shape; in the north the frame was elaborately outlined and richly carved. Jacobean mirrors, the earliest English types, were small and heavily framed in the Italian manner. Some were framed in smaller bits of mirror leaded together. The carved wooden frame predominated with the advent of the Grinling Gibbons type of carving. The Louis XIV style inspired larger mirrors with firm architectural outlines, richly carved and gilded or silvered. Under Louis XV these assumed irregular shapes in lighter frames. English mirrors of the Chippendale school were in the Rococo manner, with a constant tendency toward greater size; these were often pieced together in intricate frames. The classic types, as the characteristic Adam mirrors, were very large and of simple shape, outlined in thin gilt frames of Pompeiian inspiration. Trumeaus, of this time, were mirrors set into the panelling of rooms as overmantels, etc. Smaller mirrors were in general use for dressing; these were frequently mounted on stands. In America the elaborate Rococo mirrors were simulated in jig-sawed outline. The later classic revivals produced mirrors of strong architectural feeling. 758 et seq. Picture frames have in general followed the style of mirror frames.

MISSION. Spanish Missions in Southwestern North America (California, Mexico, etc.) were built by missionaries and Indians of native materials in a crude substantial style. The furniture was heavy and square. In the early 1900's the Arts-and-Crafts movement, reaching America from England appropriated the heavy, home-made air of the missions, using heavy square oak, with crudely obvious mortise-and-tenon jointing (usually faked) and finished with a smoky or fumed dark stain. Upholstery was of leather; for ornament appliqués of hand-hammered copper, large nail heads or simple cut-out patterns were popular. The style lacked charm or subtlety; its clumsy weight and decorative poverty quickly condemned it, by 1913 it was extinct.

MITER (Mitre). Joint in a moulding where it changes direction, usually at 90 degrees.

MIXING TABLE. Side or serving table arranged with compartments for bottles, etc., and a flat work space for mixing drinks. See *Wine Tables.* 899.

MODERN FURNITURE. Modern furniture and decoration has come into being through the same processes that in other times were responsible for the organization of other styles. To analyze these processes is to define those social, economic and emotional changes that distinguish one time and one place from another. The appraisal or even description of a style demands detachment, perspective. To write at this moment in a summary or conclusive vein about modern furniture —meaning in the largest sense, the special contribution or characteristic production of the first third of the twentieth century—is therefore more in the realm of journalism than of permanent record. As a record of the time and its customs, contemporary furniture is still a fragmentary and incoherent document. Its acceptance is still far from universal and its characteristics are largely those of personal schools, either of designers or of the fashion promoters that are an essential factor in the sale of merchandise. Yet there are certain well-defined tendencies, favored materials and techniques that may be accepted as the ingredients of the formulating style, and there are reflections in both contemporary architecture and in the story of earlier approaches to modern furniture, that reveal the outlines of the future picture.

The impulse or urge to design along other than historical lines appears to have originated in England about the middle of the nineteenth century, when a rebellious group of young artists, including William Morris, Ruskin, Rosetti, Philip Webb, Burne-Jones, Madox Brown, Faulkner, and Marshall set out to design and manufacture interior decorations. Their particular revolt was against the dead classicism which then dominated all the arts, the heritage of the eighteenth century; they took up the challenge of the new machine and sought to cancel it and its effects. All this was to be accomplished by a return to naturalism, to the medieval concept of humanity, nature and brotherhood. The whole movement is inextricably combined with a poetic nostalgia for the Gothic, as it typified the good old days. The Pre-Raphaelites discarded all painting after the fifteenth century; Ruskin denounced the "foul torrent of the Renaissance." In furniture, textiles, metal work and all the other accessory arts, they attempted to restore the theory of hand processes, and designed accordingly. This phase dwindled into the rapturously self-satisfied aestheticism of the Oscar Wilde school, and its output offers little inspiration to the designer beyond its freedom from the clichés of the time.

The fundamental concept of good materials, honestly expressed with fine craftsmanship, of undisguised form influenced by function, stands out above all the poetic obscurantism. This feeling, which the originators expressed so gropingly, spread to the continent and evoked in Holland, Germany, Austria, the Scandinavian countries, and France a system of radical thought. The teaching of art, particularly of design and applied art, was transformed, and various new movements followed to develop the nationalistic trends. Based uniformly on the naturalistic approach, as distinguished from the classical, these movements did not always appear to recognize the true forces that inspired them, and developed along many tangents. The English Arts-and-Crafts movement had its parallels in L'Art Nouveau of France, the Secession of Austria, and the Deutsche Werkbund.

The first tangible expression of a modern approach to furniture occurs in the exhibition in 1894 in Brussels. Here Henri van de Velde emerged as the genius of L'Art Nouveau, and his 1895 Paris exhibition of four complete rooms established the style. Though an advocate of functional design, he somehow confused the "line of force" with the peculiar whiplash curve which has come to symbolize L'Art Nouveau. At the Paris International Exposition of 1900, Van de Velde's style was a sensation; its very brilliance proved its undoing. Commercial copyists of varying degrees of skill adopted and manipulated the typical curved line *ad nauseam;* its furniture and large scale work it quickly became graceless, forced, tiresome; its vogue in decorative glass and metal-work lived on, but was sterile.

German craftsmen and designers accepted Van de Velde enthusiastically, and in 1902 he opened a school—the Bauhaus—at Weimar, under the patronage of the Grand Duke of Weimar. Another school at Darmstadt had Peter Behrens, Hans Christiansen, and Ludwig Habich working under Josef Olbrich. The various forces coalesced in the first decade of the 1900's into the Deutsche Werkbund, aimed at consolidating the active forces in art education and production. For the most part, their design was simple and unaffected, sound in construction theory and practice.

In Vienna, the Secession was organized in 1896 by Josef Hoffman, Roller, Klimt, Moser, Olbrich and others. It pioneered in the application of the English Arts and Crafts. In 1903, the Wiener Werkstätte appeared. Architects, mostly pupils of Otto Wagner, formulated a coherent style, and by the time of the World War, their thought dominated house design and decoration in Europe.

Design in Sweden enjoyed intelligent direction of an artists association, responsible for the employment by Orrefors Bruck of Simon Gate and Edvard Hald. The co-operative associations have been a force in the classification of design ideas, and today Sweden produces outstandingly good furniture.

Design in the United States followed a curious roundabout procedure. In the nineteenth century, the applied arts had little or no encouragement other than from the commercial producer. The decline of the Victorian and the rise and fall of Eastlake left the manufacturers with a vague notion of design as mere fanciness, applied ornament, gimcrackery and untrained individuality submerging craftsmanship and perception. The Chicago Exposition of 1893 led architecture into the paths of inspired classicism, and for thirty years thereafter, Ancient Rome alone inspired all major design. Furniture followed with eclectic copying of all the major historical styles, scaled down, misinterpreted, unintelligently adapted. In the 1920's the vogue for good reproductions improved the tendency, but the major output of furniture was unskillfully designed after the Brothers Adam, the Louis periods, Chippendale, Tudor, Italian, and other historical motives.

Among the architects there were, however, a few exceptions, working on personal interpretation of historic forms, or completely iconoclastic.

Of the former, the free Gothic of Bertram Goodhue, the Romanesque of H. H. Richardson and the classic variations of Burnham and others in Chicago are milestones of individuality. Of the iconoclasts, Frank Lloyd Wright and Louis Sullivan were almost alone in recognizing the potentialities of the new age of steel construction and its child, the skyscraper. Alone they sought new external expressions for this technique. Their productions are recognized today by their vitality and sincerity, but at the time the classic movement was too strong. Sullivan, disappointed, died in 1924. Wright worked in Japan and elsewhere, and is today hailed as a prophet even in his own country. Their recognition in Europe, however, was almost immediate, and the advanced schools did not hesitate to build on their constructional premises. To the German Schools in particular the work of Sullivan and Wright suggested an honest approach to essential design, and their architects and designers show this influence profoundly.

Sullivan's work was principally in commercial structures in the Middle West; Wright, besides several excellent business buildings, designed many houses in the Great Lakes region, as well as farther West. The time was between 1907 and 1912. Interior furnishings were largely in the styles designated as Mission, Craftsman, Arts and Crafts, English Cottage types, etc. They all had simple, crude outlines, and were almost invariably of oak, exaggeratedly heavy, stained or fumed to a deep tone. The joinery was elementary and largely faked, always obvious. Decoration was meager; besides excessive copper hinges, handles, and straps, it was by means of cut-out shapes. Textiles were coarse and dull in color, and leather in dark browns, reds and greens provided a dingy palette. The resulting interiors were dark and morose; their lack of suavity and grace damned them and undoubtedly was responsible for the rejection of the whole idea—house and all.

The Mission style was based loosely on the few primitive articles of furniture left by the Spanish Missionaries in the Southwest, crossed with strains of the glorified amateurishness of the English Arts-and-Crafts School. The English had largely discarded this, and were elaborating on the fin-de-siècle shapes, reviving motives of the seventeenth century that favored oak. The French, Germans, and Austrians still based their work on L'Art Nouveau: liberal tastes permitted the borrowing back and forth of new ideas. Original tendencies were brewing, but were still indistinct and largely a matter of personal eclecticisms, tinged with bizarre overtones.

Thus, there appear two divergent impulses in early twentieth century European design: one a matter of decorative interpretation, recasting the ornamental forms of all bygone times in a new idiom; the other a simple rationale of construction and functional necessity, inspired by essential architecture alone, often referred to as the International style.

The more decorative school may be regarded as an unorthodox merger of many types of decoration. It enunciates no major principles, but strives merely for fresher individuality, more original ornamental forms than mere copies of historical examples, good as they may be. It respects the continuity of the old, offering only to embellish it with new and more personal detail. It is pleasant and well-mannered, often elegant; it employs beautiful materials and works them with accomplished craftsmanship. Fine woods and metals, ivory, glass and the new synthetic materials are used according to the designer's fancy. The forms often suggest older styles: there are reminiscences of Empire solidity, Directoire lightness and grace, Chinese and Hindu conventionalization, Chippendale and Neo-Grec; the designer is generally free to take old patterns at will, subduing ornament, exaggerating some details, emphasizing surface material and proportion. The individual pieces have the distinction and decorative unity that characterizes fine furniture of all ages. Their arrangement in rooms, in association with floor, wall and window treatment, is more or less orthodox. Essentially a matter of decorative stylism, it is chic, stylish, suave. Striving for originality sometimes leads it into bizarre shapes and color schemes, but the critique will be one of personal taste. The German and Austrian forms of this style grew directly out of the earlier decorative schools. The Wiener Werkstätte, the various Werkbund and conventional schools on the Continent developed a clear style during the several decades during which American schools were concerned with the canons of formal historical periods. The leaders of the style bear familiar names: Josef Hoffman, Bruno Paul.

This progressive influence barely touched America until after 1925, although a few designers, such as Joseph Urban, Paul Frankl, Winold Reiss, were conspicuous in the post-war years for their originality and untraditional approach. But their work was personal and limited to personal contact; the current European sources were a closed book to the commercial producers and hence to the country at large. Small objects—pottery, porcelain, metal work, textiles, book printing, and binding, followed European inspiration in the same manner as fashions in women's dress, but furniture and architecture styles were pure archeological research.

The Paris Exposition of Decorative Art in 1925 threw into dismayingly sharp relief the general back-sightedness of American applied art. The United States had nothing to show. The exhibits of the European designers stirred a spirit of inquiry, and in 1926 and 1927 the trend of European design began to appear in America. It was unfortunately treated as a unified style; the copyists set to work with more enthusiasm than judgment. Indiscriminately, any motive, form or arrangement of colors that had no precedent labelled their new concoctions Modernistic, Futuristic, Moderne, Modernique, Art Moderne, in much the same way that a compo swag made a chiffonier Adam, or a scrolled iron leg made a cookstove Queen Anne. In other words, the same external details by which essentially twentieth century utilitarian articles were tricked into a semblance of historic types, were used to qualify these pieces as contemporary art.

At this point it is important to go back to consider the more revolutionary development which produced a widely divergent style. Prior to the Great War the steel cage system of construction was, so far as its influence on design in Europe little more than a philosophical possibility. The social and economic upheaval of the war brought a new interpretation of function and utility. In Germany, France, Holland and elsewhere appeared a new simplified, wholly untraditional style. Mies van der Rohe, Walter Gropius, Le Corbusier, Mallet-Stevens, Marcel Breuer, Aalto, are today the exponents of Louis Sullivan's edict that "form follows function." The simple, undecorated utilitarian form is considered adequately beautiful, if designed with honest respect for the materials and new conveniences that serve our needs. It is, therefore, logical to design the implements of daily use in accordance with their special conditions. Lighting by electricity creates new problems and new possibilities; we should therefore discard the electrified-candlelight technique of lighting and design according to the new possibilities. Steel tubing can be bent into elastic shapes for light comfortable chairs, but it may be contrary to the nature of the material to work it into the traditional shape of chairs. Thus, the style attaches less value to the designer's preoccupation with aesthetics in the established sense. It presupposes an essential, basic beauty in objects designed precisely to their required use and whose final shape is nothing more than the expression of this use and of the materials of which it is composed. By this strict criterion most furniture is dismissed as beautified, not beautiful; its non-essential ornament is hung on, not implicit in the major design, hence detracts.

This viewpoint leads directly to the composition of rooms. Designers of interiors of this school feel that we must discard the notion of a room as the inside of a box, with the walls to be treated as continuities which enclose certain given activities. Rather, each wall may be regarded as the background of a specific purpose. The new furniture is therefore more closely integrated with its architecture than heretofore. The architect-decorator conceives his room not alone as planes of walls and ceilings, doors and windows, but in terms of the actual factors essential to human occupancy; artificial light and ventilation, the functions of storage and seating, sleeping and eating. The relationship of these varied elements and functions is the true basis of the design of the component parts.

The name, "International Style" has been applied to this school because of an obvious similarity in the output of designers in all lands, Japan as in Germany, Italy or the Argentine. This is easily ascribed, aside from the general disregard for nationalistic tendencies, to the fact that the essential materials are no longer local. Steel and concrete, glass and rubber, are marketed on international plans, and no process or material may long be restricted to one region. Thus the whole of the style is not uniformly applicable to every place and condition, and the same judicious selection must be governed by local conditions.

The fact remains that no style can long escape the establishment of clichés by which the ununderstanding classify and recognize it. An unfortunate characteristic of the functional style has been the uncompromising use of angles and straight lines: the mechanical line has alone been identified as the functional line. This is not necessarily true, either from facility of production or use, but it earned for modern furniture the condemnation of being harsh and uncomfortable. Of recent years the proponents of the functional manner have displayed greater ease of manner which renders the typical forms more generally acceptable. It seems safe to predict in the immediate future a widening response to the logic of this style as the truthful and unaffected expression of the age, because it serves it best.

The excessive simplification will of itself create obstacles, since most furniture is produced to be sold. New sales demand new markets, but much selling must be in old markets. Furniture must therefore become obsolete, or out-of-style, to reopen these markets, and the speeding-up of the process of obsolescence is part of the stylist's job. The fashion element will probably operate to introduce extraneous factors or to play up minor details. In this light, the truthful development of a style may be retarded, if not rendered impossible, by these capricious elements.

In the ten years following the first imports of European modernism, America has sampled most of the movements and manners current abroad. It seems odd that the simplest solutions have been the last arrived at. The earlier modern work was often really bizarre, unnecessarily different. To the unbiased observer it merely exchanged ornaments, and the new ones were rarely as praiseworthy as the historical. There was small virtue in its mere rebelliousness. Too much picturesque novelty, too little craftsmanship; too much sales promotion by material manufacturers, too little critical objection by the consumer, all contributed to the hoop-la merchandising of the style. If the style had an idiom, it was slang.

Presently—about 1930—reticence, sobriety, taste became characteristic. Exhibition work as shown at the Metropolitan Museum in New York, the Chicago Exposition and other displays indicated a clearer concept of the objective, a mature approach to rational furniture design.

This furniture is characterized by simplicity, directness of purpose and material, absence of applied decoration, and an effort toward simple bulks, eliminating projections, mouldings, deep shadows. It is generally low, and planned to give the impression of being an integral part of the room. This applies principally to storage furniture as chests, cabinets, bookcases, etc. Beds are reduced to the simplest terms of bedding supported on frames with minor panels as head- and foot-boards, if any. Couches and chairs stress comfort, ease of handling and maintenance. Tables are of wide variety—dining tables are chiefly expanding types, often with resistant tops of synthetic materials, and bases are sometimes of metal. Small tables display much ingenuity in the use of new materials as well as glass, metal and wood. Mirrors tend to cover large areas of wall, unframed, sunken or set in simple molds.

Of materials, wood is consistently favored for most purposes. More than ever fine veneers are available through the improved techniques of making plywood, and design around the possibilities of wood grain has largely supplanted surface ornament. The various synthetic materials, compounds of casein, phenol-resin, ureas, etc., provide Bakelite, Formica, Micarta, Catalin, Plastacele, Lumarith, and numerous others which are used in furniture as resistant tops, decorative panels, handles, ornaments, etc. Of metals, stainless steel, aluminum, chromium-plating and new plating processes on other metals commend themselves for their ease of maintenance. Textiles featuring synthetic yarns are generally used, often in combination with wool, silk, cotton, etc. Colors are clear and clean; patterns are simple, chiefly introduced in the weaving.

There is occasional mention of machine processes. Furniture making is still a craft. The machine is a tool, and properly handled it can perform many operations better than the hand. But *it cannot make a piece of wood furniture*. The ultimate perfection of the piece lies in the joinery, a hand process which attained its ultimate perfection one hundred and fifty years ago. Upholstering is similarly a handicraft and even the finishing of wood is a point of manual skill. The glib advocate of "machine processes for the machine age" must hereafter design in some material and method that renders the machine more universally competent than it is now. When that time comes, furniture will assume its distinctive appearance, without discussion as to whether it should recall the glories of Greece, or demonstrate the fantasy of an H. G. Wells trip to Mars.

MODILLION. Projecting brackets, usually enriched with carving, at regular intervals under the cornice in the Roman Corinthian, Composite and Ionic orders.

MOHAIR. Upholstery fabric, originally made from the hair of the Angora goat. The Moors introduced it into Spain, whence it spread to England and Northern Europe. It is mentioned in English inventories of the 17th century, but these appear to have been woven partly if not entirely of silk.

MONEY DISHES. Scooped out saucer-like spaces in card tables for holding money or counters. Also called *guinea holes*.

MONEY MOTIVE. Decoration of flat overlapping disks like scaling.

MORESQUE. Moorish; the style of decoration left in Spain by the Moors, in which high color, abstract geometric patterns of fine detail, and gilding are features. See *Spain*. 914.

MOROCCO. Goat leather, used in fine upholstering in Louis XIV, Chippendale and other styles.

MORRIS CHAIR. Large easy chair of the late 19th century with adjustable back. Loose cushions forming the seat and back rest within a wooden frame. Said to have been invented by William Morris.

MORRIS, WILLIAM, 1834-1896. English artist, architect, poet; formed in 1862 firm of Morris, Marshall, Faulkner & Company for practice of decorative arts. Chiefly motivated by a free interpretation of the medieval, Morris was a leader of a group of liberals in art and politics who tried to stem the tide of machine development by fostering handicraft designing in simple naturalistic forms, producing textiles both printed and woven, wall papers, carpets, furniture, stained glass, metal work, book-printing and binding, etc., embracing the whole field of design. This thought was the springboard for the development of subsequent European and American design philosophy, which after many divergent movements is now crystallizing into a truly contemporary school. 1097.

MORTISE. Hole or slot in wood, into which the tenon or tongue fits; one of the most important joints in woodworking.

MORTLAKE. English tapestry mills established near London by James I in 1619, discontinuing during the reign of Charles I.

MOSAIC. Decorative inlays of small pieces of wood, glass, stone, etc., conventional or pictorial in effect; Roman and subsequent.

MOSS. Vegetable growth from the South, used as upholstery stuffing in inexpensive furniture.

MOSS EDGING. Heavy pile cording used as a decorative edging in upholstery; first appears in Italy, France and England late in the 17th century.

MOTHER-OF-PEARL. Hard inner layer of shells. Its brilliant color after cutting and polishing has suggested its use for inlays since the 16th century. First applied in the East, it was adopted by the French, Dutch, English in the 17th century. In England it often replaced tortoise shell in Buhl work. Early 19th century work in England and America abounds in mother-of-pearl inlays. 383.

CAVETTO
OVOLO
TORUS
ROLL
SCOTIA
CYMA RECTA
CYMA REVERSA

MOULDINGS

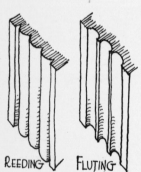

REEDING FLUTING

MOTIVE (Also Motif).   Distinctive feature or element of design or ornament; theme.

MOTTLED.   Spotted, speckled or blotchy figures in veneers.

MOULDING (Molding).   A shaped profile applied to a continuous member to emphasize the difference in planes or to provide decorative bands of light and shade. Any break in a continuous flat surface may be considered a moulding if it is designed to catch light and shade as an accent or embellishment. Certain general types of mouldings have been in use since the earliest architectural decoration. These are broadly classified as (1) *flat* or angular, (2) single curved (3) compound curves. All types are variously embellished. The flat or angular types include (1) the band, face, or facia, continuous flat members, raised or sunken into and parallel with the main surface; (2) the fillet, listel, or regula, a narrow band, usually projecting; (3) the chamfer or bevel, an inclined band; (4) the splay, a large bevel.

The simple curved mouldings are (1) the cavetto, a concave moulding of a quarter circle, though the section may be flatter or more elliptical; (2) ovolo, the reverse of the cavetto, a convex quarter circle or flattened shape; (3) the flute, a semicircular groove which may be flatter; (4) the torus, a convex bulging shape of approximately a half circle; (5) the astragal, a small torus or bead; (6) the Scotia, a hollow moulding of more than the quarter circle of the cavetto; (7) the roll moulding, about three quarters of a circle. The compound mouldings are the (1) Cyma Recta, (2) the cymatium and the (3) Cyma reversa or ogee, all serpentine or double mouldings, and (4) the Beak mould, with the upper part concave and the lower convex.

Historically, certain ornaments have been used for specific profiles, the styles varying chiefly in technique. For example, the egg-and-dart is classical for the ovolo, wreath forms for the torus, bead-and-reel for the astragal; anthemion and acanthus for the cyma recta, water leaf for the cyma reversa.

The Gothic mouldings were deep hollows, generally roll mouldings with fillets. The ornaments were less often continuous than spasmodically applied, or at the terminals of the shape.

MOUNTS.   Metal fittings or ornaments applied on furniture. Most important in the style of Louis XV, when bronze appliqués were responsible for most decorative effects. Some mounts are utilitarian, as handle and key plates, hinge ornaments, corner and angle protection, for inscriptions, etc. 674, 149.

MUDEJAR.   Mixed Moorish-Christian style of Spain 1250-1500. Marking the transition from Mohammedan to Christian art by partial assimilation of Gothic and Renaissance forms. Some Moorish traits still persist. See *Spain.*

MUFFIN STAND.   Small tier stand for plates, used in tea service in England and America.

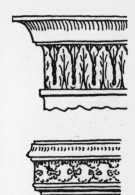

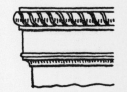
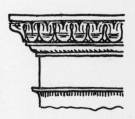

ORNAMENTED
MOULDINGS

MULE CHEST. Evolutionary type of coffer or chest with one or more drawers beneath the lid section. 380.

MULLION. Vertical bar dividing the panes of a traceried window. In furniture the tracery in glazed doors of bookcases, etc. 132.

MUNTIN (Munting). Inside vertical members of a door or window frame, such as the divisions between the glass or wood panels of a door.

MUSICAL INSTRUMENTS. The less portable instruments as pianos, organs, etc., have been treated as furniture because they could not be stored away. From the Renaissance to the present we have examples of elaborate casework designed for these instruments, and in late years the phonograph and radio have been added. The tendency is to simplify the cases for the instruments to the minimum, avoiding the architectural or decorative cabinet idea. In the past however some notable forms as the spinet shape have developed around instruments.

MUSIC STAND. Table with inclined top for holding music in front of the player. Decoratively treated in 17th, 18th centuries, English and Continental work.

MYRTLE. Light tannish-yellow wood with fine burly markings, excellent for fine inlays and veneered work; from the Pacific coast.

MUSIC STAND

"N." Napoleon's monogram, used as a decorative motive in French Empire style. Occurs in bronze mounts; also is embroidered or woven on chair backs.

NAILS (Upholstery). Nails with ornamental heads are used for finishing in upholstery work. In some styles they are arranged to make patterns, as the daisy pattern in the French period of Henry II, and on screens, coffers, etc. Large nail heads are characteristic of Portuguese and some Spanish work. 213.

NECKING. Narrow moulding or collar around the upper part of a column or post.

NEEDLEPOINT. Upholstery covering of woolen threads embroidered upon canvas.

NEO-CLASSIC. Revivals of interest in the ancient manner, such as the Renaissance, Adam and Empire styles. See *Classic*.

NEO-GRECQUE. French term for classicism of Louis XVI, based on Greco-Roman style of Pompeii.

NEO-GREEK. Classic Greek influence in early 19th century, particularly American work of late Empire style, 1815-1845.

NEST OF DRAWERS. Quantity of small drawers or boxes contained in a case; a diminutive chest of drawers, chiefly English, 18th and 19th centuries.

NEST OF TABLES (Nested Tables). Set of several tables, graduated in size so as to fit one over the other. 800.

NETHERLANDS. The Low Countries, now Holland and Belgium, shared the homogeneity of Gothic art. Flanders as an entity produced only slight variations from the typical oak styles. In the 16th century it was under Spanish rule, and was thereby exposed earlier than other Northern lands to the Mediterranean Renaissance. Italian influences likewise came up via France. Elizabethan England and South Germany thus, through propinquity felt the repercussions of the Italian Cinquecento, and imposed upon their current Gothic forms the lush Italian plastic and inlaid ornamentation (152).

Antwerp, Brussels and Liège had important furniture makers early in the 1500's. Vredemann de Vries' book, about 1600, shows compositions with architectural pilasters, scrollwork, grotesques, and robust applied ornaments in beds (106) and cupboards, credences and tables and chairs.

Flemish Late Renaissance cupboards are distinctive. Square panels are boldly moulded and carved (169) table and chair legs are recognized by the use of blocks interrupting the turned parts (215, 1035). The method of upholstering betrays Spanish origin, and is reflected in English Jacobean work.

HOLLAND
BAROQUE

The Baroque came into Northern Europe through Flanders. The painter Rubens' house, built after his return from Italy in 1613, shows bold scale and a rich architectonic conception. Furniture is in the same spirit. Four-door cupboards of oak, panelled with ebony, are square and firm, the cornices adorned with cartouches and leaves. Chairs become broader to accommodate the spreading costumes. Dutch Early Baroque, according to the paintings of the old masters is simpler, quite devoid of plastic ornament, but full scaled and restrainedly embellished with deep mouldings. Walnut became important after 1660, and inlays or exotic veneered panels enriched the surfaces. Twisted turnings are universal; oval bulb legs and bun feet are equally popular. The great "Friesland" cupboards are unique. Portuguese influences are present in chairs with embossed leather. The Dutch traders brought bits of styles from everywhere but the Oriental touches are most interesting. Chinese porcelains, collected avidly, demanded cupboards of their display. Chinese Lacquer was imported and imitated endlessly. But nothing exceeds in importance the development of the cabriole leg, partially inspired during this period by the Chinese. From India the Dutch borrowed the arcaded chair back. Dutch imports and exports of the latter 17th century are the real basis of English Baroque furniture of the Walnut Era.

Dutch power waned early in the 18th century, and Flanders was virtually a French province after 1700. Henceforward French style of Louis XV dominates Dutch and Flemish furniture.

NIGHT STAND. Night table, Somnoe.

NIGHT TABLE. Bedside table.

NORMAN. Style of the French conquerors of England after 1066; a rugged, bold, large scaled manner basically Romanesque, employing the sparing ornament and hard outlines of medieval fortress architecture.

NORMANDY. Furniture of the province of Normandy, in France, has a simple, refined rustic character somewhat reminiscent of the product of Colonial New England. See *Provincial French*.

NOTCHING. Simple form of decoration found in primitive woodwork.

NULLING. Quadrant-shaped (in section) carved ornament, similar to gadrooning.

NURSERY. Furniture specially designed for infants and small children, including bassinets and cribs, bath-tables, high chairs, diminutive chairs and tables, toy chests and wagons, etc.

OAK. Coarse textured, hard, durable wood valuable for woodworking. It occurs everywhere in the temperate zones, in a wide range of varieties. The northern part of Europe was originally covered with oak, so that practically all Gothic work is in this wood. Its displacement by walnut and other woods in Germany and Europe north of central France occurred in the 17th century. It is the typical wood of all the Gothic styles, of the Tudor and Jacobean styles in England, and the early Renaissance in Flanders and Germany.

OBERKAMPF, CHRISTOPHE PHILIPPE, 1738-1815. French textile manufacturers, creator of the Toiles de Jouy. See *Jouy*.

OCCASIONAL TABLE. Small table for incidental use, as coffee and tea tables, end tables, book tables, lamp tables and other less definite uses.

OEBEN, JEAN FRANÇOIS (died 1765). French ébeniste, an outstanding designer of Louis XV Rococo style. Made celebrated "Bureau du Roi" completed by his pupil Riesener. 421.

OGEE. Classical moulding having a cyma or double curve; also two S-shaped curves, the convex curves meeting at a point or fillet, as used in the sides of an arch. Ogee-headed panels are found in Georgian casework, and in the tracery of bookcase and cabinet doors. See *Mouldings*. 405.

OGEE BRACKET FOOT. Cabinet foot with cyma reverse profile, found in American and some English work, late 18th century. 405. See *Goddard*.

OGIVE, OGIVAL. Pointed arch, distinctly Gothic.

OLIVE WOOD. Hard, close grained wood, greenish yellow in color with irregular dark markings. It takes a high polish. It has been used by the Mediterranean peoples since time immemorial, as indicated by Egyptian, Greek and Roman remains and documents. It is found as inlays and veneers in furniture of the French Renaissance, and of England after late Stuart times. English Regency and Continental Empire styles favored the burl figures. Ash burl is often substituted for the olive.

ONION FOOT. Oval-shaped cabinet foot.

ONLAY. Overlay; decorative applique, as of veneers.

OPPENORD, GILLES MARIE (1672-1742). French cabinet-maker and designer, Louis XV style.

ORDERS. The orders of Architecture are the standardized ornamental types of columns, with their associated bases, capitals, pedestals, entablatures, etc. They are based on the Greek and Roman remains, having been originally classified by Vitruvis during the reign of Julius Caesar. He defined three Greek orders, the Doric, Ionic and Corinthian, and five Roman orders, the Tuscan, Doric, Ionic, Corinthian, and Composite, reducing the proportions and profiles of each surface, moulding and ornament to exact rules. Later Roman and Byzantine work deviated increasingly from these standards until they were completely lost, to be rediscovered and revitalized in the Renaissance.

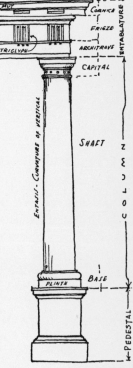

DORIC ORDER

The significance of the orders in furniture design lies in the application of architectural forms by Renaissance designers. Case furniture of all types was profiled with base and cornice mouldings, and increasingly the column form was used as applied and, later, free standing ornament. Vertical members like table legs were made into miniature columns. The whole structural significance of the orders was lost in their universal use as applied ornament. This idea of trying to make a piece of furniture resemble a scale model of a building reappears in every revival of classicism. In contrast is the homogeneity of the design whose ornamentation is an essential part of the whole structural method, exemplified in Gothic and French Rococo furniture.

ORIENTAL. It is almost equally true of all Eastern countries that furniture in our sense is scarcely known or needed. They are largely warm lands where living goes on out-of-doors. Sleeping and sitting is on mats; tables are hardly needed, being low, simple portable structures when used at all. Receptacle pieces, as chests and coffers are not common, being chiefly built-in in form. Coffers for special storage are small and portable and are made of such varied materials and so ornamented as to exclude them from the furniture class.

The Far East—China and Japan—has always excelled in lacquer decoration so that outlines are simple through sheer neglect of the possibilities of decorative profiles. India favors inlaying and turning, both fine in scale and delicately worked, but unimportant in general bulk or artistic interest. Fine spindled arcades of Hindu style occur in 17th century Portuguese work and the motive appears in continental and

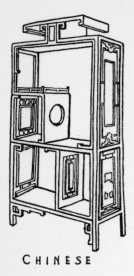

CHINESE

18ᵗʰ CENT JAPANESE

English chair backs, beds, etc. Hindu work generally appears in natural wood, as teak, sandalwood, lightly polished.

Near Eastern work of Mohammedan origin is generally unimportant in form and poorly constructed, but characterized by infinitely detailed inlaying and light surface carving. These are almost always geometric in outline, due to the religious injunction against the representation of living things. Inlays of pearl and metal, as well as of vari-colored woods, are most common. The outlines are of primitive form, unchanged for many centuries. Trays, small chests, low stands and similar small pieces are typical.

ORIENTALWOOD, ORIENTAL WALNUT. Australian wood of the laurel family; brown with blackish stripes and cross-figures and mottles. Polishes well and generally desirable for furniture. Also called *Queensland Walnut.*

ORMOLU. "Or-Moulu"-gilded brass or copper mounts for furniture principally used by the French ébenistes of the 18th century, and the followers of their styles. 149.

ORNAMENT. The term ornament applies to every manner of embellishment to make one surface contrast with another whether consciously applied or intrinsic in the nature of the material or design. Ornament is achieved by means of color, texture, or relief. Certain more or less conventionalized forms used as the basis of ornamental designs are called motives.

Color ornament may be contrast in surfaces, or it may be applied to a surface in the form of designs. These may be painted or inlaid; in textiles, printed, woven, embroidered, etc. Texture, or the quality of the surface may be varied by the combination of woods, metals, etc.; in fabrics of monotone color the weave may be interrupted or varied; woods are inlaid with metals or other woods for contrasting texture; metal and glass surfaces are varied to yield contrasts. Relief ornament is accomplished by cutting into or building up the background surface in forms of recognizable design. This implies carving in high and low relief, scratch and gouge carving, moulding, etc., also their imitations in composition, stucco, applied relief ornaments, etc.

Motives are produced spontaneously, or borrowed and modified by peoples at various times. The manner of treating ornamental motives is always characteristic of a people or their style and serves as an index to the style. Certain motives have been used since dim antiquity, yet the individual variations are an unfailing guide to the time and place. Motives are classed as abstract or naturalistic. Abstract forms grow from simple imaginative use of lines, as circles, triangles, dots, crosses, etc., in rhythmic repetitions. Naturalistic ornament derives from the representation of visual things, chiefly plants and animals. These may be realistic or conventionalized, according to whether they truly pictorialize the object or merely symbolize it in more or less recognizable simplification.

The simplest structural form may be considered ornamental, if it is adapted in the slightest way to uses other than pure structure. Thus an arch is ornamental if any other than the true stone structural principle is employed. A column treated with bases, capital, fluting, etc., is *ornamented* but the use of the column itself in furniture is *ornamental*. All architectural forms reproduced in furniture may be considered ornament. The use on furniture of ornaments planned for the embellishment of buildings is similarly architectural, but the scaling down process has developed a distinct sequence of ornamental forms. Certain styles as the Renaissance and other classical revivals which look backward to ancient times, employ these architectural forms; others like the Gothic and phases of the Rococo derive their ornamental character from the deft manipulation of lines, planes, color and organic details.

Ancient Egypt conventionalized its flora and fauna in paint and sculpture. Animal forms as bull feet and lion heads and paws, and flowers like the lotus were used on furniture. Greece and Rome enlarged the list, developing the acanthus leaf, the water leaf, lions, eagles, ox skulls, flowers and fruits in garlands and festoons, mythological or partly real animals and figures as chimerae, grotesques, satyrs, caryatids, etc.; also compounds of lines as flutings, dentils, scrolls, volutes, etc.; and repeated motives in rhythms like rinceaux, eggs-and-darts, guilloches, undulating vines, etc.; also breaks in planes and surfaces, as mouldings, panels, coffers. Gothic art deviated from these conventionalized classes by working out at first hand a series of naturalistic representations of familiar fruits and flowers, grotesque animals, etc., in combination with mouldings; also all-over patterns, diapers and other rhythmic repeat designs. The Renaissance scrapped the Gothic system and resurrected the ancient patterns but quickly changed them to their means and fancy, so that Renaissance classicism is usually distinguishable from the antique. The Baroque-Rococo styles carried modification to the extreme of losing sight of the source and creating a wholly distinct category of ornaments. Revival after revival has only used the old as a starting point; the ornament of every period is finally the index to that period.

OTTOMAN. Upholstered seat or bench having neither back nor arms, so named after the Turkish influence in the early 18th century.

OUDRY, JEAN BAPTISTE. 18th century French designer; as director of Gobelin works after 1736 influenced Rococo style.

OVAL BACK. Chair shape, best developed by Hepplewhite somewhat after French precedent. 321, 332.

OVERLAY. Ornamental veneer applied upon the surface, rather than inlaid into a veneer surface.

OVERSTUFFED FURNITURE. Chairs, sofas, etc., in which the wood frame is completely covered by the upholstery, only minor decorative woodwork being exposed. 1096. See *Upholstery*.

OVOLO. Convex classical profile, usually the full quarter of a circle. When enriched with the egg-and-dart moulding it is known as "echinus." Both the plain and garnished types occur in much Renaissance detail. See *Mouldings*.

OYSTER PIECES, OYSTERING. Veneers cut as cross sections of roots and branches of some trees, as walnut and laburnum saplings, lignum-vitae, olive-wood and some fruit woods. The irregular concentric rings resemble oyster shells. A favorite device of the English designers from the end of the Jacobean period to the end of the 17th century. 389.

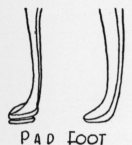

PAD FOOT

PAD FOOT. Simple flattish end of a cabriole leg, similar to club foot without the disk at the base. 274.

PADOUK. Vermillion, or Andaman redwood; a heavy brilliant wood from Burma, having the texture and polish of rosewood. Appears to have reached Europe early in the 18th century and to have been used extensively by the French ébenistes. In England the solid wood was used for fretwork.

PAGODA. Temple or sacred tower in Burma and China. The Chinese influence popularized their distinctive sweeping roof shape as the crowning motive for cabinets, canopies, etc., in England and France, 18th century. 288.

PAINTED FURNITURE. Any opaque colored finish on wood, hiding the actual wood grain, whether lacquer, enamel or simple paint, decorated or plain. The practise of painting furniture is very old. Most Egyptian relics are painted, and much of the furniture of the Far East is finished in lacquer. Medieval furniture was liberally polychromed; in this age appeared the practice of painting common woods in imitation of rarer ones.

PAGODA TOP

Painted furniture became popular in Italy in the 17th century, probably through the influence of the Oriental trade, and spread to the rest of Europe. Most 17th century work on important furniture was after Oriental motives, although several distinct styles grew independently, as the Alpine type of painting in Switzerland and Alsace, and work in Scandinavia. In the 18th century the free Baroque decoration spread from Italy and painted furniture everywhere followed these lines, using lighter, brighter colors. In England most painting continued to be called Japanning. The Louis XVI style brought delicate pastel shades, greys and white, and much late 18th century furniture is so painted. Painted furniture reached its apogee in the Italian work of the late 18th century, generally called the Venetian style. 25, 412, 469.

PALISANDER. French name for rosewood, particularly the straight grained varieties from India.

PALLADIO, ANDREA, 1518-1580. Italian architect; formulated a free version of the classic orders which he used in domestic architecture in Northern Italy. His published work most strongly influenced architecture in England and America. Several features as Palladian windows and columns perpetuate his name.

PALMATED. In Stuart oak furniture, a running band of half circles containing a crude leaf form, resembling palmettes.

PALMETTE. Conventional representative of the palm leaf. First known in Assyrian and Egyptian work, and adapted in subsequent styles. 495.

PANEL. Board held in place by a framework of rails and stiles which are grooved to receive it. The sunken panel has its surface beneath that of the framework, the edges of the panel not necessarily moulded. The flush panel has the same height as the frame, and is usually moulded; the raised panel is always moulded. Modern plywood boards are spoken of as panels. Panelled effects are sometimes secured by framed mouldings, or painted frames.

PANEL BACK CHAIR. Wainscot chair. 196 et seq.

PANETIÉRE. Bread Box, especially decoratively treated. French Provincial.

PAPIER MACHE. Moulded compound sometimes used as a base for small Japanned and lacquered articles, late 17th and 18th centuries. In the early 19th century it had a great vogue in Europe and America; tabletops, boxes, trays, etc., of papier maché being decorated with Eastern designs. 1098.

PARCEL GILDING. Method of applying gilt to carved or flat surfaces in which only parts of the design are gilded. Early 18th century English.

PARCHMENT PANEL. Linen-fold panelling.

PARQUETRY. Mosaic of woods laid over a ground in geometric patterns, in which respect it differs from marquetry which is in more representational designs. Often inlaid directly into the solid wood. It occurs in Italian and French Renaissance work, and in England during the Walnut period; again briefly at the end of the 18th century and in the Regency period. 421.

PATERA. Small round or oval carved ornaments. In the latter half of the 18th century the classic revivals, as the Adam and Louis XVI styles, brought paterae to the decoration of friezes, chair splats, mirror crestings, and many other places. 564.

PATINA, PATINE. Color and texture of the surface produced by age and wear. In wood furniture the varnish, shellac or oil has a tendency to deepen yet retain transparency; edges wear smooth and sharp outlines are softened. These characteristics may be duplicated to some extent but a fine patine is a most essential characteristic of good antiques.

PEAR DROP HANDLE. Small brass pendant drawer-pull, typical of late 17th century English work.

PEAR DROP ORNAMENT. Frieze decoration in Hepplewhite and Sheraton work. A series of small arches ending in pendant ornaments. 473.

PEAR WOOD. Hard, close-grained wood; takes a fine polish. Found chiefly in provincial furniture, especially in France, Austria and South Germany, 18th and 19th centuries. The color in old pearwood furniture varies from light, warm tannish pink to a medium tobacco brown. The best furniture pearwood comes from the Tyrol. It is also used extensively for inlaying, often stained black to imitate ebony.

DOUBLE-HOODED PEDIMENT

PEDESTALS. Stands for vases, candelabra or lamps, sculpture or other objets d'art appeared as decorative adjuncts during the Renaissance. They are found in block form and in simple shaft types, resting on bases of solid or branched form. In some styles they have been adapted to utilitarian purposes as the sideboard-pedestals of 18th century England, fitted with warming chambers, provision for storage of silver, liquor, etc. Banks of drawers carrying flat top desks are called pedestals.

SWAN-NECK PEDIMENT

PEDESTAL TABLE. Table, usually round or oval, borne on a single central column or pillar with spreading feet. Pedestals are also used in pairs. Ancient Roman types were made in bronze. The type recurs extensively in late 18th Century English designs, chiefly by Sheraton, after whom Duncan Phyfe modelled some superior designs. 981 et seq.

PEDIMENT. In classical architecture, the triangular top over a portico, or gable end. In furniture, a similar feature at the head of cabinets or other tall pieces. The pediment came to furniture with the rest of the architectural repertoire. Italian furniture after the XVI century, French after the XVII, and English furniture at the end of the XVII centuries employ this feature in the classical triangular and rounded forms, and as Baroque broken pediments. In these the line stops short before the apex, leaving a gap for an ornamental finial. The swan neck pediment consists of two opposed flat S curves. 173, 175, 178, 567 A, 641, 698, 702.

SWAN-NECK PEDIMENT

PEG. Wood pin or dowel run through a hole in the corresponding member as a fastener or joint. Peg generally implies an exposed peg; such a joint is not necessarily better than the universal blind peg or dowel. They are used as decorative notes in reproductions of simple sturdy furniture, as Colonial maple, etc.

PEMBROKE TABLE

PEMBROKE TABLE. Small rectangular drop leaf table with drawer, the leaves supported by brackets in the frame. Earliest recorded made by Chippendale for Garrick about 1771. Named after Earl of Pembroke. 578.

PENDANT. Hanging ornament, or drop. 158.

PENNSYLVANIA DUTCH. Eastern Pennsylvania was largely settled in the 18th century by German and Swiss peasants, with a sprinkling of Swedish and Dutch. Uninfluenced by the English styles of the seaboard, they reproduced the homely straightforward cabinetwork of their homelands, adapting the traditional ancient forms and methods to their slightly changed needs and materials. Using the native pine, maple, walnut, cherry and other fruit trees, they simplified rather than expanded the ornamental vocabulary of their ancestors. Turning and shaped-outline sawing, as scallops and zigzags, and scratch-and-gouge carving and simple vigorous moulding were employed but most decorative effects were obtained by painting. Clean colors were used and embellished with naïve, fanciful motives of fruits and flowers, animals, people, names and dates, etc. The usual range of farmhouse chairs and tables, chests, cabinets, beds, etc., occur but there were in addition some unique types. Brides' chests are outstanding; work boxes, kneading tables, hanging cabinets and boxes for pipes, spoons, spices, etc., are distinctive and comparatively unknown in settlements of other national origins. The basic imported types were only slightly changed with the passing of generations and outside influences scarcely touched them for almost 150 years. This quality of slow change, as well as the directness and naïveté of the designs, is typical of all peasant or rural styles.

The name is corrupted from the word "Deutsch" or German, as these Teutonic people described themselves, rather than from any Holland Dutch association. 18-20, 24-26.

PERCIER, CHARLES (1764-1838). French architect. In collaboration with Fontaine formulated the Empire style in their books published in 1801.

PERGOLESI, MICHEL ANGELO. Italian decorative artist. He arrived in England about 1770 and worked for Robert Adam as a painter of ceilings, walls, furniture, etc., in the classic manner. Published a series of "Original Designs," painting motives.

PERIOD FURNITURE. Furniture of a distinctly recognizable style, period in history, school or time. The special characteristic of historical periods may be woods or finishes; manner of inlaying, painting, carving; distinctive bulks or details as legs, posts, frames, hardware, or many of the details which distinguish the style of one place or time from another. The characteristic types of a place may be borrowed by another of the same or another time, producing through its interpretation another style. Thus the Gothic period has distinct character in separated lands; the Gothic of Italy, France, Germany, Flanders and England are separate and distinct, yet have certain points in common. The Renaissance as a major period is separable into Early, High, and

Timeline: 1400   1500   1600   1700   1800   19oo

ITALY — RENAISSANCE · BAROQUE · ROCOCO · CLASSIC
QUATTROCENTO · CINQUECENTO · BAROQUE · DECADENZA → FOREIGN STYLES. · EMPIRE DIRECTOIRE · VENETIAN ROCOCO

SPAIN — PLATERESQUE · HERRARA · DEJORNAMENTADO · CHURRAGUERESQUE · FOREIGN STYLES.

FRANCE — FLAMBOYANT · FRANCIS I · HENRY IV · LOUIS XIII · LOUIS XIV · REGENCE · LOUIS XV · LOUIS XVI · EMPIRE · DIRECTOIRE · CONSULATE · NAPOLEON · LOUIS XVIII · LOUIS PHILLIPPE · NAPOLEON III · ART NOUVEAU

NETHERLAND — ITALIAN AND SPANISH INFLUENCE

GERMANY — FRENCH AND ITALIAN INFLUENCE · REGENCE · BIEDERMEIER

ENGLAND — HENRY VIII · TUDOR · ELIZABETHAN · ELIZABETH · JACOBEAN · JAMES I · CHAS I · JAMES II · STUART · CHAS II · WILLIAM AND MARY · QUEEN ANNE · WILLIAM · CROMWELLIAN · RESTORATION · AGE OF WALNUT · GEORGE I · GEO II · GEORGIAN · GEO III · GEORGE IV · VICTORIA · CHIPPENDALE · ADAMS · HEPPLEWHITE · SHERATON · AGE OF MAHOGANY · SATINWOOD · REGENCY · EMPIRE · VICTORIAN · EASTLAKE · MORRIS · ARTS AND CRAFT

AMERICA — EARLY COLONIAL · LATE COLONIAL · FEDERAL · EMPIRE · VICTORIAN · PHYFE

Late, with minor separations in various countries, but it must also be classified by the country which lends its furniture distinctive traits. The Baroque, Rococo and Classic styles are large classifications of Period Furniture, too comprehensive to be descriptive; therefore the further distinction of exact time and place.

PHILADELPHIA CHIPPENDALE. Distict school of middle 18th century centering in Philadelphia, then a center of Colonial wealth, and following the elaborate style of Chippendale in fine mahogany, with some walnut and maple. Rich carving is characteristic. The outstanding names are Savery, Gostelowe, Randolph, Affleck, Tufft, Folwell, Trotter. Notable are highboys and lowboys and chairs of characteristic Chippendale outline. 53, 60, 405.

PHILADELPHIA SCHOOL

PHYFE, DUNCAN. Duncan Phyfe's earliest work was done in Albany in the Adam-Hepplewhite style of sound but undistinguished design. Arriving in New York about 1790 he built up an excellent trade with his exquisite workmanship and designs based on the Sheraton-Directoire manner. His productions in the best style cover about 20 years; there is little in any furniture, American or European, to excel in beauty or technique the grace of these interpretations. After 1820 the Empire styles bore down too heavily even on his mastery and from that date on there was a steady decline in both artistry and quality. Phyfe died in 1856.

Phyfe's earlier work was almost exclusively in mahogany, meticulously chosen. After 1830 he used much rosewood. The lyre motive commonly associated with Phyfe appears in chair backs and table bases. Delicately carved lines were favored with fine reedings or flutings to accentuate lightness. Carvings of leaves, plumes and animal motives were lightly executed after the Pompeiian example. 76 et seq., 349, 904, 984, 1042, 1070.

DUNCAN PHYFE

PICKLED FINISHES. Cloudy white patina over light wood, originally produced by the removal with vinegar of the plaster base of painted wood. Old English painted furniture usually had a pine structure for reasons of economy. The rough surfaces were smoothed out with plaster which remained when the top paint fell away. The effect is now widely reproduced on many woods. Also see *Limewhitened.*

PICTURE FRAMES. See *Mirrors and Frames.*

PIE CRUST TABLE. Small table, usually round, with edge carved or moulded in scalloped outline. 51, 1076.

PIED-DE-BICHE. French deer's foot; slight curvature applied to a leg, ending in a cloven foot. Forerunner of the cabriole leg first occurring in late Louis XIV-Régence Work and in contemporary English furniture.

PIER GLASSES AND TABLES. Wall mirror hanging between windows or in a narrow space, usually over a table of console type. See *Mirrors.*

PIER GLASS and TABLE

PIETRA DURA. Hard composition of fragments of marble and other fine stones, usually arranged in designs and highly polished for use as table tops, etc. Italian Renaissance et seq.

PIGEON HOLES. Manifold small compartments in desks and cabinets for papers, etc. (465).

PILASTERS. Rectangular or half round pillar or column placed against a surface. 477.

PILGRIM. The style of the New England Puritans, 17th century. 1-7.

PILLEMENT, JEAN, 1719-1808. French decorative painter known for Chinese compositions.

PINE. The pine chiefly used in furniture is the soft pine, generally the white pine of the Northeastern states, the sugar pine of Idaho and the soft pine of the Pacific Coast. European pines are used locally; Spain, Italy, the Alpine lands, the Scandinavian and North European countries produce distinct varieties. By reason of its availability, its ease of working and satisfactory performance pine is among the first woods chosen, especially for provincial or rustic work. This trait is distinctive of pine; it is invariably associated with simple country furniture, with the exception of its use, inspired by economy, as a base for painting or veneering. Of the latter, 18th century English work is the outstanding example since the loss of the paint leaves an interesting whitish patina. (See *Pickled Finishes; Limewhitened.*) The knots were allowed to remain where they were intended to be painted over; knotty pine was probably never deliberately used for decorative effects prior to the age of reproductions. In Spain the reddish pine of the mountainous sections was used in inferior cabinetwork; in Italy likewise. Alpine cabinetmakers traditionally used pine for chests, cabinets, etc. It was either painted entirely or in decorative patterns. The same with local variations is true of all Northern Europe, and the style appears in America in the Dutch, Swedish and German settlements. New England pine was usually left raw, or treated to an oil finish which produced a dark tone, or occasionally painted.

Pine carves very easily for which reason it was extensively used by early Georgian cabinetmakers. In other places carving still was rare, so that finely carved pine is not common. Early 19th century America developed many processes of painting on pine in imitation of other woods. 132, 166, 369, 887.

YELLOW PINE is very hard, golden yellow in color with strong dark streaks. It is not satisfactory for furniture.

PINEAPPLE. Conventionally rendered fruit motive used as finial, particularly in early 19th century American bedposts.

PLANE WOOD. Maple leafed, or London, plane tree is the English sycamore, a very white, tough, hard wood used in England for painted chairs and structural members subject to strain.

PLAQUE. Ornamental medallion of metal, porcelain or other material, circular or elliptical in shape and inserted into the woodwork of cabinets and other furniture in the 18th century. Sèvres and Wedgwood are the best known names of makers in France and England. Bronze plaques in the antique manner were used in Empire and Regency work. 486.

PLASTICS. Synthetic materials are molded or used in sheets, bars, etc., in modern furniture because of their ability to resist many agencies ordinarily destructive to finished wood. Compounded variously of phenolic-resins, ureas, casein, or other substances, they require no further finish, as they are produced in many colors. Small objects as radio cases, boxes, handles, ornaments, etc., may be molded wholly of plastics; other parts, like table tops, are produced by veneering sheet plastics to a wood body. Handles and ornamental features are cut or turned from bars. Among the better known plastics so used are BAKELITE, MICARTA, and FORMICA.

PLATEAU. Platform or stand on low feet used in the center of dining tables to raise the center decorations above the table level. They appear toward the end of the 18th century, and were variously made of painted wood, papier maché, glass or metal.

PLATE PAIL. Receptacle for plates, pail shaped, usually of wood with a brass handle. They were necessitated by the long distances between dining rooms and kitchens in the 18th century. They were usually made with lattice sides to permit warming, and with a slot or open side to allow easy access to the plates. 484.

PLATE PAIL

PLATERESQUE. Period 1500-1556 in Spain; reign of Charles V marked by brilliant style, suggesting silversmith's work—"platero." See *Spain*.

PLATE WARMER. Sideboard pedestals of George III's time were fitted as plate warmers by lining with tin and fitting with an iron heater. Later they were made as separate articles of furniture. See *Pedestals*.

PLINTH. Block, square or octagonal, used as base of a column; also the base of a chest when solid to the floor.

PLUM WOOD. Yellowish wood with deep brown-red heart, hard and heavy. Old furniture of country origin is sometimes found of this wood.

PLYWOOD. Several thicknesses or plies of wood glued together so that the grain of any one ply is at right angles to the grain of the adjacent ply.

Wood is weak across the grain, strong the long way of the grain. Thus the alternation of grains produces the maximum strength of the material all ways. The cross-grain fiber weakness, the tendency to expand and contract from heat and moisture are counter-balanced in the

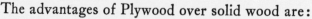

PLYWOOD

various plies, so that inch for inch of area and thickness plywood has much greater strength than solid wood.

Plywood is made in two ways: (1) *Veneer Construction,* in which several thicknesses of veneers are glued together, (2) *Lumber core,* with a thick central layer of semi-porous wood to which are glued thin veneers at right angles, equal in number and thicknesses on both sides. Thus, a 5-ply plywood panel 13/16 inch thick might have a basswood *core* 5/8 inch thick; on each side is glued a veneer *crossbanding* 1/16 inch thick, at right angles to the core; then a face veneer on each side, about 1/20 inch thick, at right angles to the cross banding. Odd numbers of thicknesses are the rule.

The advantages of Plywood over solid wood are:
(1) Its greater strength in every way.
(2) Its comparative freedom from warping, checking, swelling, etc.
(3) Its use of woods with no structural strength as face veneers for more decorative results.
(4) The lower cost when fine face veneers are used, compared to solid lumber in fine woods.
(5) The ability to match grains and make many panels of a finely figured wood and to use the grains more freely.
(6) Its superiority in curves and shaped work.

The disadvantages of plywood are:
(1) Danger of improperly glued veneers separating, causing blisters, open joints, etc.
(2) Comparative difficulty of repairing dents, burns, etc. In solid wood such injuries to the surface can be planed off, but thin veneers cannot be scraped through.

The first danger is now being overcome by exhaustive research in the subject of adhesives. New gluing processes, either by casein or phenolic-resins under great pressure insure freedom from moisture-damage.

Plywood has been known for centuries, since it was first realized that applying a thin veneer to a thicker backing would cause the backing to curl; this was overcome by applying the veneer to both sides, counter-balancing the pull. The weakness was always in the adhesive. Technical research since the World War has made plywood so superior that today the overwhelming bulk of good furniture has its flat areas all of plywood.

POLE-SCREEN. Small fire or draught screen adjustably mounted upon an upright pole. See *Screens.* 838-41.

POLISHES. The process of obtaining a smooth and glossy finish on wood by means of friction and a polishing material is as old as furniture. The early methods were chiefly by applying a film of oil or wax and rubbing it to a satisfactory surface. In the early 1700's the

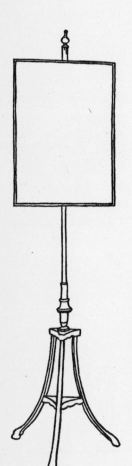

POLE SCREEN

French began to apply successive films of dissolved shellac by means of a pad, producing a hard glossy shine known as French Polish. See *Finish*.

POLLARDED WOOD. Pollarding is the removal of the crown or top branches of trees leaving the main stem intact. This produces a peculiar grain in the wood. In France walnut is pollarded, while in England oak, poplar, willow and elm are so treated.

POLYCHROME. Multi-colored. Polychromy in furniture, or the embellishment by paint, is the most ancient decorative device. Egyptian remains are trimmed with simple bandings, ornamental figures and representational pictures, all in strong color. The practice undoubtedly was favored in other ancient styles. In medieval furniture the mouldings were commonly picked out with color and gold. Medieval Italian practice favored whole surfaces of color, often over raised figures of gesso. Northern European furniture was often wholly painted in red or green; in some rural sections, such as the Alpine lands, a picturesque style of painted decoration still survives. The Renaissance made much of polychromy; in the earliest phases color was sparingly used in furniture, but by the 15th century decorative painting on cabinets, coffers, etc., was the rule. In its later phases, particularly in the Baroque style, paint and gilding were extensively used to emphasize profiles and to embellish whole areas with fantasies in the typically extravagant manner. 25, 114-6.

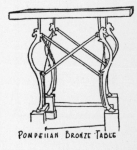

POMPEIIAN BRONZE TABLE

POMPEII. The buried cities of Italy preserved a complete record of ancient Roman life. The excavations at Pompeii and Herculaneum, begun in 1753, stirred enough interest in the classic arts to terminate the Baroque-Rococo rage and inaugurate the period of the Classic Revival. French and English architects studied the ruins and from their reconstructions formulated the Neo-Classic styles known as Louis XVI, Adam, Hepplewhite, Sheraton, etc. See *France, England, Rome, Adam*.

POPLAR. Pale yellow, smooth textured soft wood, light in weight and lacking in structural strength. Used chiefly for interior parts in furniture and cores in plywood; slightly, in imitation of better wood. In England in Stuart times used for wall panelling.

POUDREUSE (French). Powder-table, usually small. 1019 et seq.

PRIE DIEU. Chair with high back and very low seat, used for kneeling in prayer. The back has a shelf to carry the book; the seat is cushioned and is hinged to form a receptacle for books. Italian 14th century and later. 724.

PRIMA VERA. White Mahogany; light straw-colored wood whose texture and working properties are similar to Mahogany. From Central America.

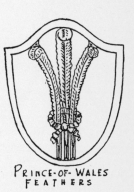

PRINCE-OF-WALES FEATHERS

PRINCE OF WALES PLUMES. Decorative motive of three ostrich feathers, symbolic of the Crown Prince of England; favored by Hepplewhite as the filler-design of chair backs. 336.

PURITAN. Of furniture, the 17th century New England style. The English Puritans revolted against the worldliness of the Court and substituted simple, functional forms as in the English Cromwellian style.

PURPLEHEART. Dense hard wood from Caribbean South America. Violet or purplish, it is used for inlay and ornamental purposes. Also called Amaranth, Violetwood.

QUADRANT. Metal device of quarter circle shape used to support fall fronts in some desks; English and American, late 18th and 19th centuries, generally brass. 481.

QUARRIES. Small panes of glass, square or lozenge shaped used in the doors of bookcases, 18th and 19th centuries.

QUARTERED. Method of cutting the log into four quarters thru the center, and then into parallel boards in order to produce a grain having a cross section of the rays. See *Woods*.

QUATREFOIL. Gothic form made from the conventionalized four-leaf clover, the four intersecting curves being enclosed in a circular shape.

QUATTROCENTO. Early Italian Renaissance, 1400-1500, characterized by development of classic architectural formality. Dignified austere furniture, chiefly in walnut. See *Italy*.

QUEEN ANNE. English ruler 1702-1714 during whose reign the Netherlands-Baroque strain imported by William of Orange continued to develop producing chiefly walnut furniture of excellent style. Chiefly identified by the developed cabriole leg, the best types are chairs, china-cupboards, secretaries, etc. 522 et seq. See *England*.

QUIRK. Narrow groove moulding, a sunken fillet or channel.

RABBET (Rebate). Rectangular slot or groove in joinery. Also a recess in the meeting stiles of cabinet doors so that one shuts against the other to form a dust-proof joint. See *Construction*.

RACK. Stand or frame for various purposes as book rack, magazine rack, hat rack, music rack. It may be either a piece of furniture in inself, or part of another piece. Decorative racks for various purposes are found in many styles, and possess charm and interest to collectors typical of such minor furniture.

Letter Racks in England were vertical strips of wood ornamented with fretwork, etc., with hinged leaves to hold letters.

Spoon Racks were primitive affairs while wooden spoons were in use; after Elizabeth spoons of soft metal as pewter came into use, but were too soft to be kept in a drawer. The spoon rack therefore grew in importance in lesser homes.

REST-BEDS...DAYBEDS OR CHAISE-LONGUES

ELONGATED SEATS FOR BRIEF REST PERIODS APPEARED IN THE SEVENTEENTH CENTURY. THE ADDITION OF COMFORTABLE UPHOLSTERY AND CUSHIONS MADE THE "CHAISE-LONGUE" POPULAR IN THE EIGHTEENTH CENTURY.

1680. [Scroll leg and stretcher with crown.]
Anderson Galleries

816. FRENCH, about 1635 (Louis XIII). Walnut.
Anderson Galleries

817. ENGLISH: QUEEN ANNE STYLE, about 1715. Walnut.
Anderson Galleries

818. ENGLISH: CHARLES II. Carved walnut with cushions of Crewel embroidery.
Anderson Galleries

819. AMERICAN: Middle 18th Century. Dutch influence. *Weil*

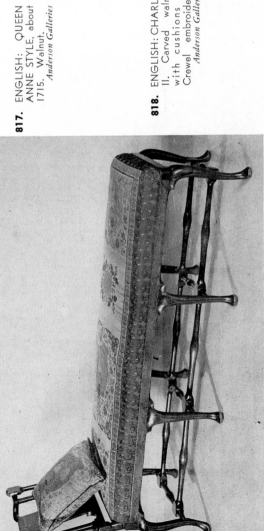

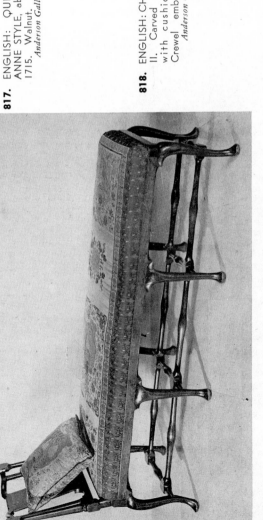

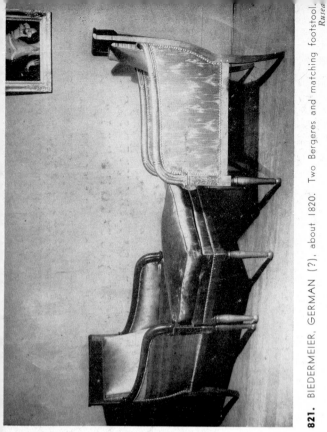

821. BIEDERMEIER, GERMAN (?), about 1820. Two Bergeres and matching footstool.
Rusea

823. FRENCH; PERIOD OF LOUIS XVI. Painted frame.

820. ITALIAN OR SOUTH FRENCH: STYLE OF LOUIS XV, about 1770. Painted and gilt; cane back, damask upholstery.
Anderson Galleries

Rusea

822. FRENCH, EMPIRE STYLE, about 1815. Separate chair and long foot stool.

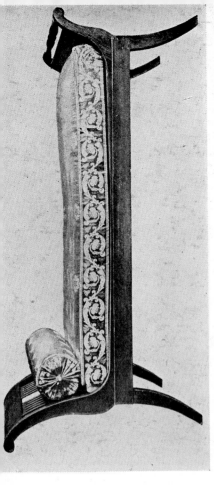

825. FRENCH, DIRECTOIRE, about 1800.

Lavezzo

824. ITALIAN, EMPIRE INFLUENCE, about 1820. Gilt frame.

CLASSIC SHAPES TYPIFY THE LINE OF REPOSE IN EARLY 19th CENTURY DESIGNS

826. ITALIAN DAYBED; GREEK DETAIL OF DIRECTOIRE INFLUENCE. Painted frame and upholstered ends. This style was equipped with ordinary bedding. Date about 1810.

Cassard Romano

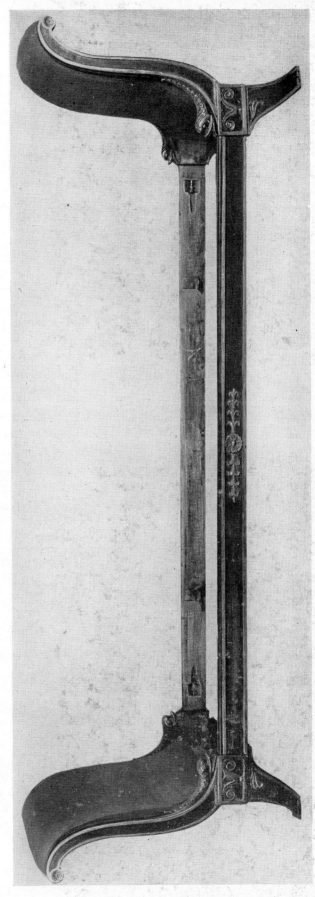

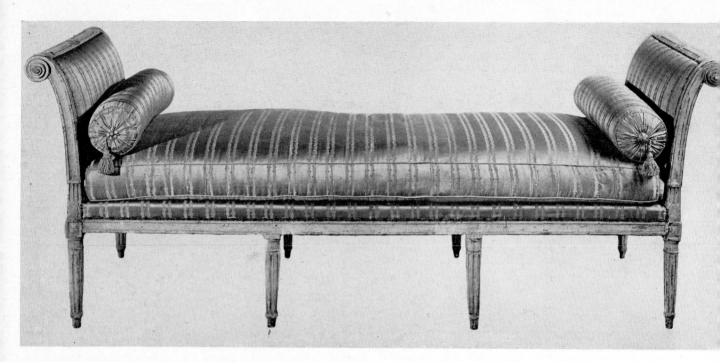

827.   (Above) DAYBED, LOUIS XVI, about 1790.   Painted white.   *Anderson Galleries*

828.   (Below) DAYBED, AMERICAN, about 1800.   Sheraton style.   Mahogany.   *Ginsburg & Levy*

RADIATES. Carved or inlaid rays, as in a shell or fan motive.

RAILS. Horizontal members of framed furniture. In beds, the long side pieces. In casework the framing which holds the sides together.

RAKE. The angle of a slanted or splayed member, as a chair back or table leg which is not strictly vertical.

RAMP. In chairs of Portuguese, Queen Anne and corresponding American types, a sudden curve ending in an angle at the end of the post. Characteristic of the type called Hogarth chair.

RAM'S HEAD. Classic decorative carving, borrowed from ancient Greece and Rome and used in all styles employing antique ornament, as Louis XIV, Adam, etc. Probably originally a symbolic representation on sacrificial altars. 195.

RANDOLPH, BENJAMIN. Philadelphia cabinetmaker of the period of the Revolution; made chairs in the Chippendale manner as well as the typical Philadelphia highboys.

RANDOM JOINTS. Joints in either veneer or solid board walls or floors, in which there is no attempt at matching either grain or width of boards.

RANGE TABLES. Several identical small tables planned to be used together as one long table.

RAT CLAW FOOT. Sharp skinny claws grasping a ball, as the decoration of a cabriole foot; English, after 1740; also found in American work.

RAYONNANT. Middle period of the Gothic Style, about 1225-1420. Radiating lines form typical ornament.

READING DESK, READING STAND. Small table with top adjustable to hold a book. Found in 18th century English work chiefly, although similar bookstands, occurring in later Renaissance work on the continent, evolved from the medieval lectern. See also *Bible box*. 436.

REBATE. Rectangular groove cut in wood members to permit the insertion of a tongued member, in joining frameworks.

RECAMIER. Chaise longue shaped like ancient Roman bed or reclining couch with gracefully curved high end. Directoire and Empire styles, named after Mme. Recamier. 824.

RECESS. Niche, alcove or any depressed or sunken surface.

RECESS CABINET. Tall shallow cabinet designed to be set within a recess or niche; late 18th century English. 144.

RECESSED STRETCHER. Middle or cross stretcher of chair or table set back from the front legs. See *H-Stretcher*. 250, 267.

REDWOOD. Red-brown wood from Pacific coast, too soft for most furniture construction. The burls are highly decorative, and are sometimes known as Sequoia.

REEDINGS. Two or more beads set closely in parallel lines, either flush with or raised above the surface it decorates. It is the reverse of fluting. Late 18th century. 480.

REFECTORY TABLE. Long narrow table so-called after the refectory or dining room of the monks in ecclesiastical institutions of the Middle Ages. Heavy stretchers are close to the floor. 714.

RÉGENCE. French period covering the end of Louis XIV's reign, until the accession of Louis XV, about 1680-1725. It is marked by the transition from massive straight lines to the gracious, curved, intimate style of Louis XV. 178, 604 et seq.

REGENCY. English period, roughly 1793-1820, during which George Prince of Wales, later George IV, acted as Regent. Furniture style is marked by declining classic influence of Pompeiian studies, and increasing use of Roman, Egyptian and earlier Greek styles. It coincides with the Directoire and Empire style. 141, 362, 580 et seq. See *England*.

RELIEF. Raised ornament or sculpture in which the carving is raised or cut above the background. Various styles are characterized by high or low relief carving.

RENAISSANCE (Renascence). Literally a "rebirth" of interest in the culture of ancient Greece and Rome, the Renaissance terminated the medieval Gothic styles. Instead of continuing the Romanesque-Gothic development in the arts it went directly back to classic sources and adapted the ancient architectural and decorative themes. The movement began in Italy, attaining its major momentum in the 15th century; it spread to Spain and France in the 16th century largely through church and political contacts. Flanders, a Spanish colony, imported the Renaissance early in the 16th century. It spread to England in a gradual way over a period of a century, being slowly imposed on the firmly entrenched Gothic art. The same was true in Northern Europe; Gothic art yielded slowly to the classic forms in the Germanic countries. By the middle of the 17th century de luxe furniture everywhere was clearly Italian classic; but Gothic traces persisted in lesser furniture for another century.

Early Renaissance Italian furniture is marked by simplicity of outline and detail, a definitely architectural profile with classic mouldings and sparing ornament of classic acanthus, rinceaux and animal forms. This developed by the enrichment of ornament and outline, and general elaboration. It was this later phase which first reached other countries, so that the earliest distinctly Renaissance features in France, Flanders and England are quite elaborate. There never had been a true Gothic feeling in Italy and the classic themes were therefore purer than in the North, where essentially Gothic shapes and mouldings remained, to be modified with more or less Italian details.

Roman orders in the form of colonettes and pilasters were applied to furniture; these carried the full complement of bases and cornices, pediments, etc., so that cabinets, etc., were scaled down architectural compositions. Where the Gothic had depended on free renditions of familiar flora, naturalistically applied, Renaissance ornament was highly conventionalized. With greater variety, it was more stylized.

The great change in furniture came in the increased variety of types. Secular life in the Middle Ages had been, for the nobles, a rather nomadic affair; for the peasants, poverty stricken and insecure. With the change in political conditions came economic improvement, security, and a substantial middle class. Home life improved; furniture became essential and developed into many new forms. Practically all types of furniture appeared, at least in rudimentary forms, between 1500 and 1700; older types assumed shapes now recognizable as social conditions and customs approached the standards of modern times.

RENT TABLE. 18th Century. English round or octagonal pedestal table with drawers marked with days of the week or dates. They were used by the landlord as a sort of filing arrangement in collecting rents. 557.

RENT TABLE · G 1765

REPLICA. Reproduction or copy of a piece of furniture, usually old or of historic period; accurately copied from the original in all details of material, technique, detail and finish. See *Reproductions*.

REPOUSSÉ. Decorative sheet metal work in which the design is hammered forward from the back.

REPRODUCTIONS. "Reproductions" in furniture refers to copies of old pieces of historic styles. Good reproductions follow the original in all details of material, method and detail throughout; it is a moot point whether the finish and patina with all the marks of wear should be duplicated. An accurate copy if made in the period of the original would be a replica. But if made later it would be a copy or reproduction and if sold as a genuinely old piece, it would be a fake. Commercially made pieces which merely follow the general external form without regard to material or the technique are copies; more or less accurate, they are called reproductions only by commercial courtesy.

REST BEDS. All types of chaise-longues, daybeds, and couches planned for repose during the day hours in preference to the formal bed. Appearing in France during the early Louis XIV period, when beds had become excessively large and formal, it was at first merely a cushioned settee or bench. Called couches in England, they took form with one high end; these were caned or rush-covered, with loose cushions thrown over. In Régence France they were more comfortably upholstered. England reflected these types in Restoration and Queen Anne "daybeds," which uniformly were of extended chair form. The Louis XV epoch produced the most luxurious styles, feminine in scale and ornamental character. In the ensuing period the chaise longue developed as a combination of two or three pieces, sometimes two bergeres with a footstool between, or a large bergere with lengthened footstool. The daybed form was developed from the simplified bed and appeared in Italy and France at the end of the 18th century. *See Chaise-Longue, Daybed, Sofa, Couch.* 815-828.

RESTORATION. Period in English history, succeeding the Puritan Revolution, beginning in 1660 with the restoration of the monarchy of Charles II and ending in 1688 in the Bloodless Revolution. It is the first part of the Age of Walnut. Ornament is highly decorative, gay and frivolous, lighter than the preceding styles but still simple and rectangular in the main, although lesser structural members as stretchers, arms, crestings, etc., are given highly curved and scrolled ornament. Strong French influences came with the immigration of craftsmen, and the Flemish forms were brought by the returning nobles. The decorative forms include spiral turnings, moulded geometric panelling, floral scrolls, carved crowns and scroll feet. Grinling Gibbons' rich deep carving is representative.

The wealth, security and social aspirations of the time are reflected in the free use of changed forms in tables, chairs and cabinets. They are no longer portable and are more decorative. Daybeds and luxurious upholstery became common.

The Baroque influence appears in Restoration sweeping curves and generous ornamentation which caused oak to be replaced by the more easily worked walnut. 511 et seq.

The period is also referred to as *Carolean, Late Jacobean.*

RESTORATION CHAIR. A typical form with high caned back, turned legs and richly carved scroll design on front stretcher and top rail. 264.

RESTORATION OF ANTIQUES. Old furniture may ethically be restored to its original condition, which may include the addition of minor or missing parts. The danger in buying "restored" pieces is that the greater or most characteristic original sections have been replaced around a few unimportant relics, as the use of an old table top upon a new base. The distinction becomes a fine one and is another pitfall in the path of the antique collector.

RHODE ISLAND SCHOOL. 18th century American style centering in Newport, R. I., and chiefly in the manner of John Goddard and his son-in-law, John Townsend. The block front in chests, secretaries, desks and dressing tables is practically unique; other features are the Rococo shell, the steep scroll pediments, ogee bracket feet with fine shallow carving. Mahogany predominates, but some maple, walnut and cherry was used. 48, 61, 410, 703.

RIBAND, RIBBAND. Ribbon ornament. In some Chippendale chairs the splats simulate elaborately arranged ribbons. Ribbons in bows or knots were important in Louis XVI decoration and were characteristically treated in German Rococo work of the 18th century. 287.

RIBBON. See *Ribband.*

RESTORATION CHAIR

RIBBON STRIPE. In wood, a straight banded grain effect, common to mahogany, walnut, and similar woods with a long straight grain and bands of alternate soft and hard textures. 1105.

RIESENER, JEAN FRANCOIS, 1735-1806. French cabinet-maker, period Louis XVI; learned craft under Oeben. Celebrated for his marquetry work. (413).

RINCEAUX. Continuous ornament of spiral or wavy form, sometimes called the branching scroll when intertwined with stems and leaves. 372.

RISING STRETCHER. Serpentine or X-Stretchers curving up toward the intersection; found in Louis XIV and allied styles. 270.

ROCAILLE. Earlier term for Rococo.

ROCKING CHAIR. The rocker is a curved slat fastened to the feet of a chair to permit it to be rocked back and forth. It is practically peculiar to America and is fundamentally a rustic or inelegant type, dating chiefly after 1800. Several unique types were evolved in New England, such as the Salem Rocker, the Boston Rocker, etc., having high comb backs and thick scroll seats. These were characteristically painted and decorated in the fruit-and-flower manner popularized on Hitchcock's chairs—a delicate stencilled ornament somewhat in the Biedermeier manner. 237.

ROCOCO. A phase of European art of the 18th century, reactionary to the classical spirit. In France, Louis XIV furniture and decoration had been characterized by a solid pompous classic grandeur. The succeeding style of the early Régence years lightened these forms by the introduction of curves generally symmetrical and exquisitely balanced, and contained within a rectangular framework. These gave way to an extravagantly free naturalism, accepting curved irregular forms as their basis. Rocks (rocaille) and shells (coquilles) provided the decorative forms in the gardens of Versailles, and were translated into carved and painted ornaments for interior decoration; the name, at first "rocaille" became "rococo" many years after the style had waned.

ROCOCO ORNAMENT

SWEDISH   ROCOCO

Rococo forms are most characteristically asymmetrical, elaborately ornamented with flora and fauna borrowed literally from nature. Leaves and flowers, intertwined with rocks and shells, outline irregular shapes in which the dominant structural form is rarely openly expressed. Associated curves flow together with astonishing rhythms, irregular but not restless, delicately balanced for all their lack of symmetry. Inevitably these imaginative compositions are more successful in those pieces whose structure is less intimately associated with utility. Mirrors and small tables, consoles and chandeliers lend themselves readily to audacious outlines, but such structural forms as chests, chairs and important tables are founded on a rectangular basis. Accordingly these were treated to elaborate surface ornamentation designed to lead the eye away from the rectangular joints. Applied ornaments of gilt bronze, gilded carving, lines of color or inlay were used to draw lines together in curved sequences. The earlier work in France by such master ébenistes as Meissonier and Caffieri is exquisitely graceful, charming and playful; after 1750 it declines into excessive ornamentation, glitter and restlessness, which pave the way for its replacement by the classical severity of the style of Louis XVI.

Elsewhere the style persisted variably for an undefinable period. The German countries accepted and adopted it as the basis of most 18th century work; a glittering Rococo distinguishes the interiors of most palaces and important structures long after some of the classical features of the Louis XVI style were accepted. In England the Rococo tendencies were cheefully absorbed by all designers, and imposed upon more local forms in all degrees of ingenuity, together with minor notes of Gothic and Chinese reminiscences. Here the classic revolution inspired by the Brothers Adam swept away this gay freakishness, but in much of the most esteemed work of Chippendale, Hepplewhite, and other masters there remains the clear Baroque freedom of the Rococo. 115, 179, 181, 311 et seq., 414 et seq., 446 et seq., 491, 610 et seq., 842, 858, 998.

RÖENTGEN DAVID, 1743-1807. Known as David.

Outstanding French cabinetmaker, period of Louis XVI. Born a German, his principal shop was at Neuwied, but he catered chiefly to the French court. 667

ROLL TOP. In desks, a tambour or flexible cylindrical hood which is drawn down as a lid. 667.

ROMAN (Ancient). Etrurian bronze remains show an early conventional style similar to the archaic Greek rigid lines and austere decoration. Later Roman work, indicated by bronze and stone remains and painted and sculptured representations show that Rome in her great period borrowed and interpreted all the known styles rather than created her own. Egypt, Greece and the East contributed basic forms which were amalgamated and enriched in infinite variety to serve the luxurious, urbane standard of living. In general the evolution of the style began with a severe, rigidly limited list of pieces, expanding in size and adding ornamentation and delicacy. The last phase, amply revealed in the buried cities of Pompeii and Herculaneum, show the late Alexandrian-Greek traits, referred to as Greco-Roman.

Chairs appear in four types: *Curule* with square seat, and legs in X-shape (originally a folding stool, the back was added later); *Bisellium* a double chair or settee, the wood frame of turned members, or carved to represent horses' or mules' heads; *Solium,* a throne-like chair with back, for the head of the household; *Cathedra,* chair for the exclusive use of women. Skins or pillows with rich fabrics were used loosely.

ANCIENT ROMAN

Beds and couches, *Lectus,* had the general form of beds known today, with a platform of cushions carried on turned legs, often inlaid, painted or mounted with metals. A pillow rest at one end served as an arm rest as well, for the couch was also used for dining, which was done in a semi-reclining position.

Chests or cupboards known as *armaria* for the storage of arms, probably were the origin of the "armoire."

Tables were of all shapes, bronze remains suggesting round, tripod types, and rectangular shapes resting on carved slabs or pedestals.

There were in addition a great many styles of tripods, pedestals, stools, etc., of which the forms are conjectural. They employed many means of decoration and finish; carving, inlaying, turning, metal appliqué, painting, engraving, veneering, varnishing, etc. It seems probable that the ancient Romans employed the metals, woods, ivory and stones known then, much as we now import and utilize such products from the whole world. 961, 985.

ROMANESQUE. European style following the fall of the Roman Empire, roughly 500-1100 A.D. Architecture followed debased Roman style, stiff and barbaric, using coarsely rendered animal and plant forms. Chaotic life encouraged little furniture making. The style is most significant as the parent of the great Gothic style. 95, 203, 947.

ROMAYNE WORK. Ornamental form of human heads carved upon roundels or medallions, deriving from the Italian and occurring among the earliest Renaissance ideas in English, French and Flemish Gothic furniture. 151.

ROPE MOULD. 18th century decorative moulding quarter or half round, spirally channelled to simulate a rope. Also called cable mould.

ROSE. The rose motive highly conventionalized is an ancient one, and recurs in simple form in most styles. The full rose was adopted as the Tudor badge in England after the 15th century and frequently appears carved in simple form as a decoration on furniture. In Louis XV and other Rococo work the naturalistic rose is common. 157.

ROSETTE. Rose shaped patera or disk ornament.

ROSEWOOD. Several species of tropical woods from India and Brazil are grouped as rosewood, so called from the odor of the newly cut wood rather than its color. It is heavy, dense, resinous and of a deep red brown color, richly streaked and capable of being highly polished. It was used in fine European furniture of the 18th century as veneers and ornamental inlays; in the 19th century the solid wood was used extensively for furniture in Europe and America. The French "Palisander" is the Indian variety. The German "Rosenholz" is generally called "Tulipwood" in England and America.

ROTTEN STONE. Soft finely powdered stone used with oil in polishing wood.

ROMANESQUE

ROSETTES

ROUNDABOUT CHAIR. Chair with a leg in front, one in back and two on the sides. The back, rather circular, is carried on three legs. Found in English and Continental and American work of the 18th century. (38.)

ROUNDEL. Any ornamental disk, or motive enclosed in a circular shape as a rosette, medallion, patera, etc.

ROUTING. Decorative engraved lines made by a portable revolving spindle.

ROYCROFT. Establishment at East Aurora, N. Y., in early years of 20th century, founded by Elbert Hubbard on the ideas of William Morris. Produced furniture of Mission-English Arts and Crafts type.

RUDDER. The rudder, butterfly, or flap is a support for the leaf of a drop leaf table, similar to a ship's rudder in outline. 977, 17.

RULE JOINT. Hinged joint, as between a table top and flap, which leaves no open space when the leaf is down.

RUNIC KNOT. Interlaced ornament typical of early Northern European work, as the Celtic, Scandinavian, German Romanesque, etc.

RUNNER. Sometimes the rocker of a rocking chair. Also a guide strip for a drawer either on the side or the bottom.

RUNNING DOG. Continuous ornamental band or wave motive, also called the Vitruvian Scroll. 149.

RUSH. Rush stalks were used in medieval times as a covering over stone floors. Later they were plaited into mats. These were sometimes used as beds in the Tudor period.

Rush seats in chairs and stools are known to have been made by the Egyptians. Probably they were always used after this time, but remains are scant. 18th century chairs with rush bottoms survive everywhere in Europe and America, being also known here as "flag" seats. 228.

RUSTICATION. Architectural treatment of masonry in which the joints are marked out as grooves. This effect is simulated in furniture of architectural character of the 18th century.

RUSTIC FURNITURE. Garden furniture of the 18th century was decorated with details resembling the natural growth of trees, as drawn by Chippendale, Halfpenny and Manwaring. The latter designed chairs utilizing the whole smaller branches.

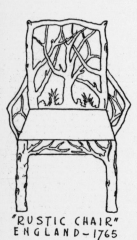

"RUSTIC CHAIR"
ENGLAND—1765

SACK BACK. Windsor chair with double bow back.

SADDLE SEAT. Chair scooped away to the sides and back from a central ridge resembling the pommel of a saddle. The best examples occur in Windsor chairs with thick pine seats. 235.

SAFE. Strongbox, usually of metal; in old times of heavy wood with metal straps. Sometimes applied to food cupboards of vermin-resisting construction.

SCREENS

ONG THE EARLIEST IMPORTS
M THE FAR EAST, ORIENTAL
REENS HAVE BEAUTIFIED
OPEAN INTERIORS SINCE
SEVENTEENTH CENTURY.

829. CHINESE CARVED COROMANDEL SCREEN. CHIEN-LUNG PERIOD, 1736-95. Pattern in
separate panels.
Courtesy Anderson Galleries

830. JAPANESE PAINTED PAPER SCREEN; TOKUGAWA PERIOD, 1603-1867. The pattern is
continuous over 6 panels. Collection William Rockhill Nelson Gallery of Art, Kansas City,
Missouri.

832. ITALIAN, 17th Century.
WOOD SCREEN. *Lavezzo*

831. ENGLISH SCREENED SETTEE, 17th Century. Elm and
oak. *Vernay*

833. ENGLISH LEATHER SCREEN, Mid-18th Century.
Pastoral scenes painted in oils in the French manner.
Vernay

ENGLISH LEATHER SCREEN, Rococo Style of Early 18th Century. Family portraits of successive generations painted in oils.
Vernay

835. FRENCH, PERIOD OF LOUIS XV. Small paintings of pastoral designs, with large panels of damask. *Symons*

836. FRENCH, STYLE OF LOUIS XVI. Brocaded silk panels in wood frame, carved and gilded. *Symons*

837. FRENCH, DIRECTOIRE STYLE. Paper panels printed with classic designs in wood frame. *Symons*

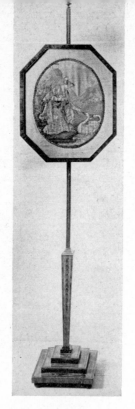

838. ENGLISH, winged panels, turned mahogany shaft with brass mounts. CA. 1785.   *Symons*

839. ENGLISH, satinwood pole, decorated, CA. 1790.   *Vernay*

840. ENGLISH, painted, style of Robert Adam, CA. 1780.   *Vernay*

841. AMERICAN, CA. 180[hogany.

POLE SCREENS

842. SOUTH FRENCH, 1725-35. Height of Rococo style, carved and gilded.   *Metropolitan Museum of Art*

843. FRENCH, PERIOD OF LOUIS XVI. Beauvais tap[in gilded frame.   *Anderson Gal[*

CHEVAL FIRE SCREENS

SALEM ROCKER. New England rocking chair after 1800. Has heavy scrolled seat and arms, a lower back than the Boston Rocker, light straight spindles and a heavy top rail with scroll.

SALTIRE. X-form stretcher. 267, 1036.

SAMBIN, HUGUES. 16th century French designer, cabinet-maker, carver, engraver; his engravings show the development of Renaissance forms in Burgundy, where the Italian influence had practically obliterated the Gothic. Much work of the rich Burgundian Italian type is credited to him or his followers. His Book of Designs was published in 1572. 173.

SANDALWOOD. Hard yellow-brown wood from Southern India, distinguished by its fragrant odor. Used in Oriental (chiefly Indian) woodwork and furniture.

SAN DOMINGAN. One of the best qualities of mahogany, heavy and dense. Turns dark after long exposure to light.

SAPELE. African hardwood resembling mahogany with fine stripe and uniform color.

SARACENIC. Influence of Mohammedan design, reaching Europe after 700 through Spain, and during the Middle Ages through the Italian trading centers. Motives are fine-scaled, abstract interlacings or geometric forms and some conventionalized floral details. Inlaying with ivory, bone, brass and stones is typical. 457. Fine fabrics were first brought to Europe from Saracenic sources. See *Italy, Spain*.

SATINWOOD. Light honey-colored, hard-textured, fine-grained wood susceptible to a high polish. Best varieties from Ceylon and India, but also found in the West Indies. Historically, most favored in later 18th century English work; its use marks the transition from the Baroque solidity of Chippendale to the lightness of Adam, Hepplewhite, and the later designers.

SATYR. Mask motive representing the head or whole figure of mythological Satyr. It occurs profusely in Greco-Roman work and in all classical revivals. 401.

SAUNIER, CLAUDE CHARLES. French cabinetmaker, late Lous XV, early Louis XVI Periods. (995)

SAUSAGE TURNING. Continuous turning similar to the spool turning, frequent in 19th century American furniture; similar to 17th century rustic turnings in Germany. 231, 910.

SAVERY, WILLIAM, 1721-1787. Philadelphia cabinetmaker who worked in a highly ornamented Chippendale style, probably the most elaborate produced in Colonial America. His highboys and lowboys are outstanding examples of American cabinetmaking; some maple and mahogany chairs and serpentine chests of drawers attributed to him are quite simple. It is probable that some of the work loosely identified as Savery's was made by other Philadelphians of the date, or later. 60, 700-1. See *Philadelphia*.

SAVERY LOWBOY

ROMANESQUE· NORWAY

ROMANESQUE — SWEDEN

SAVONAROLA CHAIR. Italian Renaissance X-shaped chair of interlacing curved slats and wooden back, carved or inlaid with certosina work. 253, 707.

SAWBUCK. Table frame or base having X-shaped supports. The type occurs in Gothic work in Northern Europe and in the early Renaissance in Italy. By this name is generally implied the rustic American type common in New England, although the most decorative examples appear in the Swedish and German-influenced furniture of the Delaware Valley. 967.

SCAGLIOLA. Hard plaster composition containing bits of marble, granite, alabaster, porphyry or other stones. It is capable of being highly polished and therefore is suitable for use as tops of tables, chests, etc. It is likely that the Romans used it but the process was lost until the early 17th century. After that time Italian workmen carried it over Europe and it is exceedingly common in English Georgian work. Robert Adam employed Scagliola constantly for many decorative and utilitarian purposes.

SCALE. Relative size; proportion of a piece to its surroundings, to other pieces, etc.

SCALING, SCALE PATTERN. Imbrication; a surface ornament resembling the scales of a fish. Frequent in 18th century carving throughout Europe, it occurs often in conjunction with carved shells and acanthus leaves.

SCALLOP. Carved shell ornament after the escallop shell. Typical of Spanish work where it is used alone; also common in the Rococo style as a center of floral ornament. 545.

SCANDINAVIAN. Sweden, Norway and Denmark sustained a unity of artistic expression through the Middle Ages. From the age of the Vikings there survived a system of intricately interlaced ornaments, birds and beasts and vines, vaguely suggesting the Romanesque, the Celtic, and even Far Eastern design (947). Gothic architecture came in French, English, and Germanic forms, but the ornamental system of the lesser arts was not seriously affected.

In the seventeenth century some quality of Renaissance work cropped out in Scandinavia, but it was a tentative exploratory gesture. (945) Chiefly a rural people, the southern decorative styles were accepted slowly and modified greatly to adorn the basic native furniture. In the 18th century the nobility imported extensively from Germany and England. The mixed strains were handled with grace and artistic insight. As the style filtered down to the lower classes the ornamental motives of Louis XV and Rococo England were pleasantly adapted to the honest pine chests and beds and cupboards. Painting, and to a lesser extent carving, are freely used on flat areas (942 et seq.).

The aristocrats followed closely the patterns of the Baroque-

Rococo-Classic Revival, but an unmistakable local quality is present in most renditions in these manners. The Empire style had longer life than elsewhere, developing under the patronage of the Bernadotti family into a gracious, refined style which lasted into the 20th century. The modern Swedish style is an orderly progression from this school, retaining much of the clean-lined simplicity which it acquired in a century of development, discarding much of the synthetic archeological ornamentation.

SCHOOL. Style, era, period, manner; type of a given time, place or designer.

SCISSORS CHAIR. Folding X type of chair, known in Egyptian, Roman, Byzantine and Italian Renaissance work. In medieval times it was actually a folding chair, but the type became solid as furniture ceased to follow its owner about in his rovings. See *Faldstool, Dante Chair, X Chair, Savonarola Chair,* 253 et seq.

SCOOP-SEAT. Dipped or dropped seat, one in which the front rail is slightly concave to fit the body. 332.

SCOTIA. Hollow or concave molding, approximately quarter round. See *Mouldings.*

SCRATCH CARVING. Crude form of carving done with a V-chisel. 161, 375.

SCREENS. Screens as furniture are ornamental frames or panels for protection from observation, draught, or the heat of a fire. The framework has variously been covered with leather, paper, textiles, etc., and may be made in only one panel or of several leaves or panels hinged together. Small one-panel screens have been decoratively treated to serve as fire screens; these usually stand on a pair of feet and are called Cheval screens. The type known as "pole screen" has a smaller panel, fixed to an upright pole upon which it may be raised or lowered. These frequently had tripod or pedestal bases.

The earliest known screens occur in China in the 2nd century B.C. Some of these were made with mica or glass panels to permit a sheltered enjoyment of the view, others were carved and inlaid with jade and metals. Screens from this time on were painted with landscapes, texts, memorable events or simple scenes of everyday activity; others were covered with embroidered silks, using natural forms and inscriptions. These were often made of many panels, some having as many as forty. The Japanese screens more characteristically are of 6 panels, with the landscape pattern spread entirely across the whole, instead of each panel being framed and decorated independently as were the Chinese.

In Europe the screen developed from sheer necessity in the draughty halls and tremendous fires of the Middle Ages. Records indicate that Edward II had screens, but of what material we are not aware. Henry

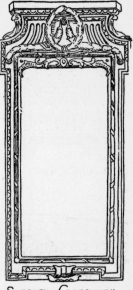

SWEDISH CLASSICISM.

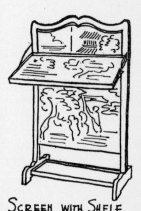

SCREEN WITH SHELF

VIII's inventory lists "scrynes of purple Taphata frynged with purple silke, standing uppon feete of tymbre guilte silvered and painted." Among the possessions of Charles I sold after his execution were "china skreens"; the rage for Oriental screens spread until they were common throughout England. Leather-covered screens came from the continent and were likewise highly decorated with pastoral scenes, Chinese pictures and characters, birds and flowers or formal diaper patterns typical of the Spanish and Flemish leatherwork. Wood, leather, textile and Oriental screens appear on the Continent after the Middle Ages. In France the period of the Régence produced handsomely panelled and carved wood screens. With the feminine character of the style of Louis XV screens were often curved at the top and covered entirely with tapestry, embroidery, or other textiles matching the hangings and chair coverings; some were painted canvas with the fashionable pastoral scenes; some with Coromandel lacquer and many with "India paper" with small flower and figure patterns. Mirrors were often set into the upper part.

Under Louis XVI the classic rectangular shapes returned, with fabric panels set within carved and gilded frames. Later, during the Directory, large panels of painted papers were used, in the Japanese manner but employing timely pictorial motives.

Shelves were sometimes added to screens, either fire or tall screens, as aids in reading or writing. (829 et seq.)

SCROLL LEG

SCRIBANNE. Secretary-commode made by the Dutch and Flemish and imported into France, middle 18th century.

SCRIBING. Method of fitting together surfaces whose profiles are not identical straight lines.

SCRIPTOIRE, SCRITOIRE. See *Secretary*.

SCROLL. Ornament of spiral or convolute form.

SCROLL FOOT. Curved foot, not fully articulated with the block above, as in a cabriole leg. 933.

SCROLL TOP. Broken pediment formed by two S or cyma curves; also Swan neck. 701.

S-SCROLL. Double curved scroll, as a swan neck. 514.

SCRUTOIRE. Enclosed desk for writing. See *Secretary*. 43.

SEAT. The whole class of seat furniture comprising chairs, stools, sofas and settees, chaise longues, etc.

AMERICAN SCROLL-TOP

Specifically it refers to the horizontal surface of a chair or similar piece of furniture.

SEAWEED MARQUETRY. Delicate interlacing designs in inlay suggesting marine plant life. Originating in Italy, the type was best developed in England, late in the 17th century. 389.

SECESSION. Style in design originating in Vienna about 1896. Precursor of the later "Modern" Austrian style, it followed no accepted types, modifying the French Art Nouveau and other reactions to traditional style. More than most of its contemporaries the Secession style was generally applicable and had elements of grace, directness and an easy charm now identifiable in the *Wiener Werkstätte* creations. Josef Hoffman, Moser, etc., were early exponents; the influence came to America through designers like Joseph Urban, Paul Frankl, and others. See *Modern*.

SECRET DRAWERS. Small, hidden compartments in old chests, bureaus, desks and the like for private or valuable papers. Rarely very secret, but the old cabinetmakers delighted in providing these difficult-of-access places.

SECRETAIRE—SECRETARY. Fall front desk, sometimes with drawers below and bookcase above. Sometimes refers to a drawer in a chest, fitted with a fall front. In Europe usually called Bureau. 468 et seq., 491, 523, 541, 617, 625.

SECTIONAL FURNITURE. Furniture made in units which complement each other, but which present a finished appearance if used separately. Bookcases, desks, chests, cabinets, etc., are arranged to form large units when placed together. 806.

SEDAN CHAIRS. Enclosed portable chair borne on two long poles carried by two men. They appear in Italy after the Middle Ages and their use spread with the growth of luxury during the 16th, 17th and 18th centuries. They were often elaborately decorated and luxuriously upholstered. 740.

SEGMENTAL ARCH. Arch made of less than half of a circle, the curve ending sharply. 62.

SERPENTINE STRETCHER

SEGMENTAL CORNERS. Panel corners broken by curved lines, typical of Régence work.

SEGMENTAL PEDIMENT. Unbroken curved pediment, the arc of a circle.

SELLA. Ancient Roman name for most seat forms; also occurs in Early French Renaissance usage.

SERPENTINE. Waving or undulating surface. A serpentine front, as in a commode, has the center convex or protruding while the ends are concave. 405. Reversed serpentine fronts have a more complex curve. Serpentine stretchers are X-type with curves. 267.

SERPENTINE FRONT

SERRATED. Zigzag or saw-tooth ornament of Gothic origin; a form of notched dentil.

SERVING TABLE. Side tables in dining rooms; generally higher than an ordinary table, and fitted with drawers for silver. 897.

SETTEE. Light open seat about twice the width of a chair with low arms and back, sometimes upholstered. 18, 50, 844 et seq.

SETTLE. All wood settee with solid wood ends, and occasionally a wooden hood; Tudor times and later in England, generally of oak; in America of pine, rarely of maple; sometimes walnut in Pennsylvania.

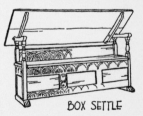

BOX SETTLE

Usually built solid to the floor, and sometimes with a hinged seat over a box. 11, 846.

SÈVRES. Porcelain objects from the manufactory at Sèvres, France, established 1756 and taken over by the government of Louis XV in 1759. Made plaques, medallions, etc. which were used as decorative inserts on furniture as desk fronts and table tops, particularly favored in the highly decorative styles.

SEWING TABLE. Small work table, usually with drawers or lid top, fitted with spool racks, etc., and often with a cloth bag for sewing material. They are mentioned in 17th century inventories, but are not common until the mid-18th century, after which they appear abundantly. Excellent designs by Sheraton, Hepplewhite, Duncan Phyfe, and others are extant; they are equally common in Louis XVI, Empire and Biedermeier work. 79, 571, 1061 et seq.

SGABELLE. Wooden side chair of the Italian Renaissance based on primitive three-cornered stools. Early types had three legs wedged into solid seat, with board back. Later elaborations had scroll-cut slab bases, sometimes with drawer or hinged lid, and elaborately pierced and carved back panel. The style persists, especially in provincial work in all European countries. 258 et seq., 942.

SHADED MARQUETRY. Method of shading or toning marquetry with hot sand.

SHAKER FURNITURE. The Shakers, a religious sect, founded independent communities in the mid-nineteenth century. Chiefly rural and self-sustaining, they produced their own furniture, simple and straightforward in design, soundly constructed and often well-proportioned and charming in detail. Almost unornamented and invariably of local woods as pine, walnut, maple and fruit woods, the Shaker productions are among the best of the rural American types.

SHAPED WORK. In cabinetmaking all large-surface flat work made in other than flat planes is known as shaped work. Such curved swelling or serpentine planes are made in forms or cut out of the solid. The latter requires wide boards, which are apt to crack.

SHAVING STAND, MIRROR, GLASS, TABLE. Various types of stands with adjustable mirrors planned as dressing or shaving stands for men. They appear on the Continent in the late 17th century, and most versatile forms were developed in Georgian England. 404.

SHEAF BACK. Typical small chair of France, late 18th and early 19th century, having a delicate back resembling a graceful bundle of rods spreading out in fan shape. They usually had straw seats.

SHEARER, THOMAS. English cabinet maker and designer, late 18th century. No identified furniture of his workmanship is known, but his drawings are a large part of "The Cabinetmakers London Book of Prices and Designs" (1788). His style is light and simple, slightly in the vein of the Brothers Adam. It undoubtedly influenced Hepplewhite to a great degree, and subsequently much of the work in America. Shearer appears to be the inventor of the sideboard in one piece with the flanking pedestals; this type and his ingenious dressing tables were freely praised by Sheraton. No chair designs are known to have been made by Shearer. See *England*. 895.

SHELLAC. Natural resin soluble in alcohol. The mixture may be brushed on or padded on and dries quickly, after which it is susceptible to fine satiny polish by rubbing down. The padding produces the high gloss brittle finish known as French Polish. Shellac finishes are easily damaged by moisture and heat.

SHELL MOTIVE. Various shells appear as ornament in all styles, but the scallop-shell (cockle-shell) form is most common, especially in Italian and Spanish Renaissance furniture. The Rococo style is actually based in part on the use of the shell ornament. In Queen Anne furniture the shell is typically placed on the knee of cabriole legs; Chippendale used it as a central theme in carving. Rococo shells are perforated; Louis XV style uses pierced shells as a center for two acanthus sprays. In later 18th century work the conch shell form is used as an inlay motive. 30, 176, 269, 470, 701, 756.

SHELL (LOUIS XV)

SHELL TOP. Cupboard of half-round recessed plan, whose round top is a half dome carved with ribs to simulate a shell. Excellent examples in middle 18th century English work and somewhat later in America. 176.

SHERATON, THOMAS, 1750-1806. English cabinetmaker, preacher, scholar, his fame rests less on his actual work as on the style that grew from his book, "The Cabinetmaker and Upholsterer's Drawing Book" published in 1790. This was a compendium of all known designs available to Sheraton and was published more as a catalog or book of directions for the aid of craftsmen; but the designs in it came to be accepted as Sheraton's own work and the whole style accredited to him. He also published "Designs for Furniture," "The Cabinet Dictionary" (1803) and had begun "The Cabinet-Maker, Upholsterer and General Artists' Encyclopedia," but had only reached the "C's" when death overtook him in 1807.

Sheraton's designs are largely in the straight, classic manner, after Hepplewhite, Adam and Shearer. Chair backs are mostly rectangular; legs are fine, tapered squares. Delicacy and grace mark most of his work; he was influenced by the Directoire and this influence is transmitted to American work through Duncan Phyfe. See *England*. 58, 71, 137, 182, 333 et seq., 341 et seq., 485, 566A et seq., 1009.

SHEVERET. Writing table, late 18th century, France.

SHIELD BACK. Typical chair back form of Hepplewhite, having double-curved top rail and a half-ellipse below, filled with various

SHIELD BACK

openwork designs as vase forms, three feathers, swags and ribbons, etc. 327.

SHOE.   On wooden turnings a small turned disk or fillet under a scroll; also a metal cup terminal for a foot. Brass shoes were favored in 18th century English work after Chippendale, and often are part of the caster.

SHOULDER.   Name sometimes applied to the top or thick section of the cabriole leg, also called knee or hip.

SHOW CASES.   Furniture in cabinet form but usually with glass sides, used to display curios and collections. English show cases after 1685 follow the general shape of cabinets when used for larger objects, as ship models. The later ones, for smaller objects, resemble more a glass box on a stand.

SHOW WOOD.   The exposed wood parts of an upholstered chair, such as a wood arm, post, frame, apron or leg.

SIAMOISE.   Late 19th century upholstered sofa or double armchairs, with the seats facing back and front; an S-chair; so named after the Siamese twins. Also called tête-à-tête.

Also a fabric popular during the Louis XV and Louis XVI for cushions on straw chairs.

SIDEBOARD AND BUFFET.   Originally a literal *side-board,*—accessory to the large trestle table or board during the service of meals. In Elizabethan England this piece acquired importance, and borrowed from the Italian and French credences and sideboards the partial enclosure of doors and drawers. The Italian version, developed from the chest, was a solid cabinet, though a lighter type—*madia* (731)—resembled the hutch type of Gothic France. The latter contributed to the court-cupboard which distinguishes the Jacobean style.

In 17th century France, the Italian form reached a high state, particularly in the provinces. (883) Great double-bodied cabinets are characteristic. The upper part provided for the display of plates, spoons, tankards and other vessels (636, 888, 886) on open shelves. This style spread to rural England, where the *dresser* (often Welsh dresser) is still current (885). The American dresser (887) flourished similarly in country houses.

The true sideboard form of open shelves (154, 499) was incidental to the court cupboard. Late in the 17th century it took on the typical long narrow shape (890 et seq.) with shallower drawers. By the mid-18th century under Adam and Chippendale it was almost a simple table, but an essential part of the sidewall composition were the additional narrow cabinets in which were kept silver, plates, liquor, often warming devices. Upon these were carried knife boxes. (893)

Shearer was probably the first to combine all these elements into one piece. (895) Hepplewhite, Sheraton and others of the period de-

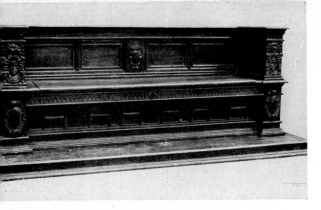

ALIAN "CASSAPANCA," 16th Century. Walnut.
Metropolitan Museum of Art

845. ITALIAN BENCH WITH BALUSTER BACK, 16th Century.

EARLY SETTEE FORMS

846. ENGLISH CARVED OAK SETTLE WITH LOOSE CUSHION, CA. 1660.

Stair & Co.

848. ITALIAN SETTEE, 17th Century. Baroque form.
A. Olivotti & Co.

ENGLISH, CHEST-SETTLE OF EARLY FORM.
Charles of London

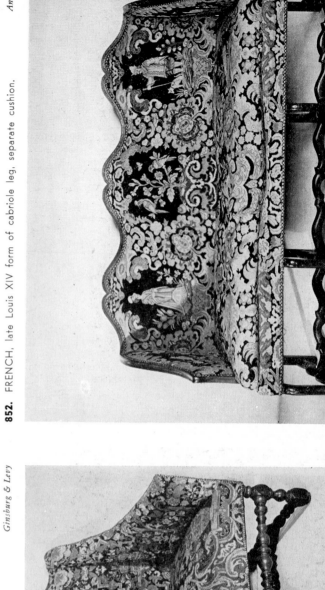

849. SPANISH, 16th Century. Padded velvet seat and back.

Brady Collection. Courtesy Anderson Galleries

850. FRENCH, Middle 17th Century. Heavily padded upholstery on framework of spiral turnings.

Anderson Galleries.

EVOLUTION OF THE SOFA TYPE

851. ENGLISH SOFA OF LATE JACOBEAN DATE, Flemish style.

Ginsburg & Levy

852. FRENCH, late Louis XIV form of cabriole leg, separate cushion.

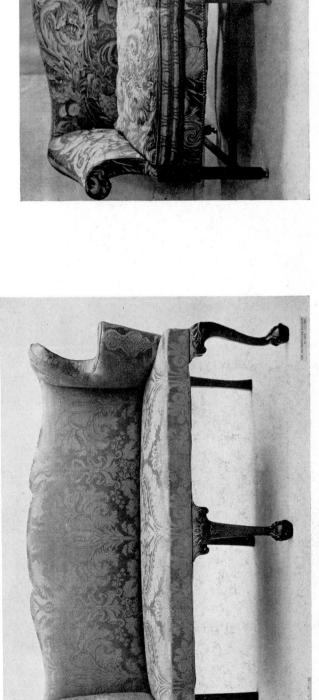

854. ENGLISH, Chippendale's Chinese manner, CA. 1750.

856. ENGLISH, CA. 1760. Chippendale's sofa designs of this period were essentially the same as the earlier forms.

853. ENGLISH, CA. 1710. Developed style of Queen Anne.

855. AMERICAN, 1750-1775. Early Georgian style of American make. *Metropolitan Museum of Art*

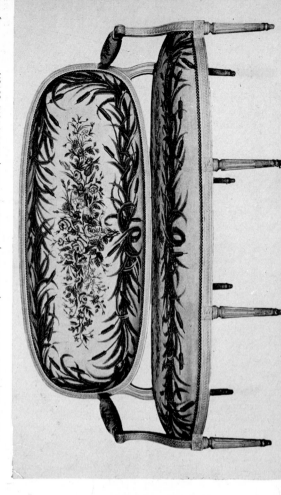

858. ENGLISH, CA. 1760. Chippendale's French style.

Vernay

860. FRENCH, CA. 1785 (Louis XVI). Painted frame, needlework cover.

Symons.

857. ITALIAN, Mid-18th Century. Louis XV influence.

Lavezzo

859. FRENCH, CA. 1765. Louis XV style. Walnut and brocaded silk sofa by Pierre Laroque.

Anderson Galleries

861. FRENCH, 1775-1790. Early style of Louis XVI, the curved plan indicating transitional style from Louis XV.

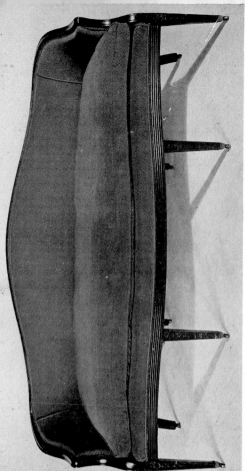

864. AMERICAN, end of 18th Century.
865. ENGLISH, HEPPLEWHITE STYLE.

Anderson Gallerie.

866. FRENCH, DIRECTOIRE, fruitwood frame.

Anderson Gallerie

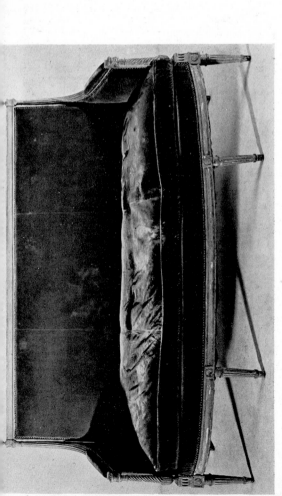

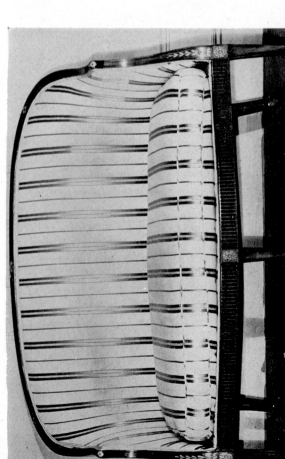

862. FRENCH, CANAPE, LOUIS XVI OR DIRECTOIRE.

Anderson Galleries

LATE EIGHTEENTH CENTURY SOFAS

863. ENGLISH, 1780-1790.

Colchester Galleries

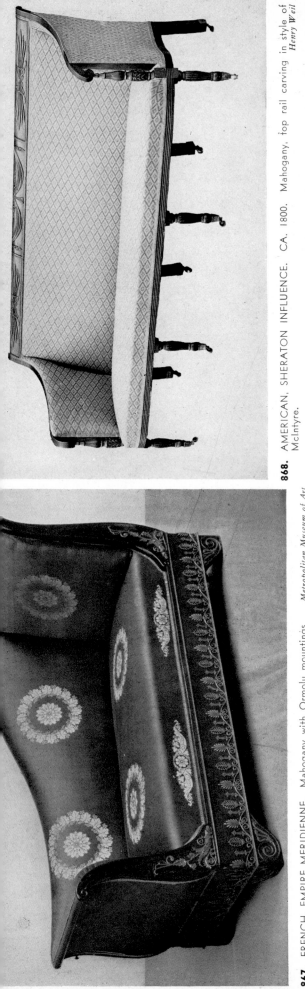

868. AMERICAN, SHERATON INFLUENCE. CA. 1800. Mahogany, top rail carving in style of Henry Weil. McIntyre.

Metropolitan Museum of Art

867. FRENCH, EMPIRE MERIDIENNE. Mahogany with Ormolu mountings.

869. AMERICAN, MAHOGANY SOFA by Duncan Phyfe, New York, CA. 1820.

Courtesy Anderson Galleries

SETTEES

DECORATIVE SHOW-WOOD C
ACTERIZES THE MORE FO
SETTEE AFTER THE SEVENTE
CENTURY.

870. ENGLISH, 1730-1740. Early G
Settee of double chair form, gi
decoration, lion masks.
Metropolitan Museu

871. AMERICAN, 1800-1810. Painted
of Sheraton style, made in New
Metropolitan Museu

872. FRENCH (PROVENCE), late 18
tury. Settee with straw seat an
cushions.

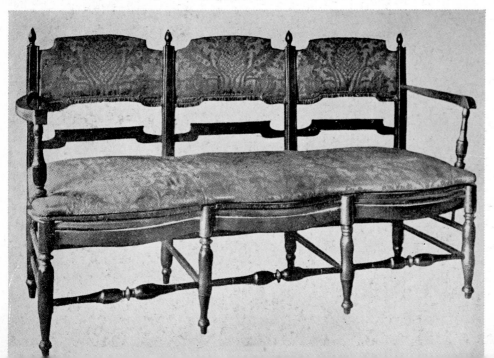

873. ITALIAN, end of 18th Century. Painted Settee.

Metropolitan Museum of Art

874. ENGLISH, REGENCY. Inlaid Rosewood Settee.   *Colchester Galleries*

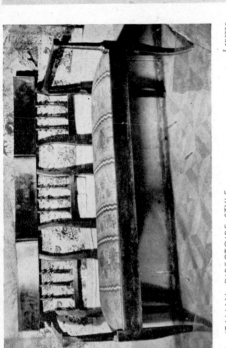

877. AMERICAN, CA. 1770. Miniature Love Seat of ladderback type from Philadelphia. *Weil*

Lavezzo

876. ITALIAN, DIRECTOIRE STYLE.

880. AMERICAN. Mid-18th Century. Windsor Settee.

875. AMERICAN, WAGON SEAT TYPE with splint seat. Early 19th Century. *Weil*

879. GERMAN, CA. 1820. Biedermeier Sofa with Gothic tracery detail.

878. ITALIAN, DIRECTOIRE INFLUENCE, 1800-1810. Settee with swan-and-lyre motive. *Cavallo*

881. TUSCANY, 1490-1500. Sacristy Cupboard of carved walnut. *Metropolitan Museum of Art*

882. EARLY RENAISSANCE CREDENCE of walnut, with drawers. *Olivotti*

THE SIDEBOARD-BUFFET TYPE

STEMS LARGELY FROM THE ITALIAN RENAISSANCE CREDENZA, AN OUT-GROWTH OF THE COFFER-CHEST.

THE SIDEBOARD IN RURAL DEVELOPMENT BECAME THE PLACE TO STORE AND DISPLAY THE EATING UTENSILS.

883. FRENCH, PROVINCIAL REGENCY STYLE. Buffet cupboard usually found as base of sideboard.

884. FRENCH (SAINTONGE), UNDER-CUPBOARD of late Louis XV style.

885. (Lower Left) ENGLISH DRESSER, Queen Anne style, West of England, 18th Century. Oak and Elm.

886. (Lower Right) FRENCH (GASCONY) DRESSER-BUFFET of walnut. Diamond point panels indicate a date CA. 1650 of the Louis XIII style.

(Right) PINE DRESSER, with bracket base. Middle 18th Century.
Anderson Galleries

(Lower Right) PROVINCIAL FRENCH DRESSER, 18th Century. *Ruseau*

NEW ENGLAND PINE DRESSER, CA. 1710-20. *Ginsburg & Levy*

890. JACOBEA[N]
SIDEBOAR[D]
twisted legs
1660.

891. OAK DRE[SSER]
(Welsh?), w[ith]
England, ear[ly]
Century.
Anderson

892. QUEEN A[NNE]
STYLE SIDEB[OARD]
of oak. Pr[obably]
middle 18th C[entury]
Anderson C[ollection]

893.   SIDEBOARD AND PEDESTALS WITH URNS, Adam design, CA. 1770. This composition later evolved into the single Sideboard.

894. (Top) AMERICAN, 1790-1800. Sheraton influence. Mahogany.　　*Metropolitan Museum*

895. (Bottom) ENGLISH, CA. 1780. In Shearer's manner. Tambour doors.　　*Vernay*

896. (Above) SMALL SIDEBOARD with deep drawers for bottles. Typical knife-boxes and wine cooler.

897. (Right) NARROW SERVING-TABLE OR SIDEBOARD, late 18th Century.
Vernay

NGLISH SIDEBOARDS OF HE LATE 18th CENTURY

OMBINED ALL THE FEATURES OF THE
PARATE PEDESTAL-SIDEBOARD GROUP-
INGS.

898. ENGLISH SIDEBOARD-BUFFET, end 18th Century.

899. AMERICAN MIXING TABLE, C. 1790-1800. Sheraton influence.
Metropolitan Museum of Art

900. ENGLISH SIDEBOARD with gallery of drawers, wine cooler below. C. 1790. *Vernay*

901. AMERICAN, late 18th Century. Mahogany and satinwood.

SIDEBOARDS OF THE EMPIRE PERIOD

902. ENGLISH REGENCY SIDEBOARD with glazed display cabinet. *Vernay*

904. AMERICAN EMPIRE SIDEBOARD by Duncan Phyfe, dated 1812. Tambour doors. *Ginsburg & Levy*

903. ENGLISH REGENCY SIDEBOARD, 1810-1820. Mahogany. *Symons*

SERVING TABLES

PARTAKE OF THE CHARACTER OF SIDEBOARDS, COMMODES OR SIDE TABLES.

905. (Left) FRENCH, late Century "Vitrine" for play of utensils.

906. (Below) ITALIAN, end 18th Century. *Lav*

907. (Left) FRENCH DEMI-LUNE SERVING TABLE, late Louis Mahogany. *Anderson Gall*

908. (Below) COMMODE, Louis XVI. Mahogany and bronze. *Sy*

CATALAN CHEST, late 15th Century. With Gothic tracery and moldings and typically Spanish spacing of panels.

(Center) CABINET WITH STAND, 16th Century. A rudimentary Vargueno. Inlaid walnut.

(Below) CARVED WALNUT ARMCHAIR, 17th Century. Typical broad arms, embroidery, bullion fringe, nail heads. Collection Conde de las Almonas.
Courtesy Anderson Galleries

912. (Above) ARMCHAIR, with suspended leather seat. 17th Century.
French & Co.

(Below) WALNUT TABLE, 17th Century. Characteristic turnings and iron stretchers. *French & Co.*

914. SPANISH CHEST, late 17th Century. Moorish influence.

915. WALNUT WRITING TABLE, early 17th Century.

916. VARGUENO, early 16th Century.   *French & Co.*

917. ANDALUSIAN GILT MIRROR, 17th Century.

918. WALNUT ARMCHAIR, late 17th Century.
French & Co.

signed fine examples of this shape. Sheraton favored a metal back rail, and drew many sideboards suggesting the old three-part grouping. All designers of the period indulged in shaped fronts, the simple bow and serpentine yielding to combinations of curves. Many late 18th century American sideboards show these traits.

In the late 18th century the sideboard produced many offshoots, such as the winetable, the mixing table (899) and various serving arrangements. (905) (76) (56)

Empire sideboards tended to great bulk and solidity, utilizing the entire available space. In addition there were frequent superstructures for the display of plate and china. (903, (572)

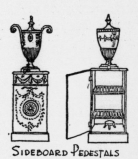

SIDEBOARD PEDESTALS

SIDEBOARD PEDESTALS.   See *Pedestals.*

SIDE CHAIR.   Chair without arms, usually small. Early types were evolved either by adding a back to a stool, called in Italy Sgabelle, or by omitting the arms of a more important chair. The latter type often appeared in the 16th and the 17th centuries to accommodate the wearers of the voluminous skirts, and are variously known as "farthingale" chairs and "cacqueteuses."

SIDE RAILS.   The long narrow boards or rails which connect the head- and footboards of beds.

SILVER.   Silver was used in regal furniture in ancient times, and again in the great work of the 17th century in France and England. Louiv XIV had small pieces as tables, mirror frames, etc., wholly made of silver, exquisitely wrought in the Baroque manner. When the treasury was depleted most of it was melted down for bullion, disregarding the artistic value. Charles II brought the vogue to England; much woodwork was covered with thin sheets of silver. It was extensively used for handles and mounts through the Early Georgian period.

SILVERWOOD.   18th century name for English Harewood or stained Sycamore.

SINGERIES.   Rococo decoration of monkeys at play. 998.

SINGLE ARCH MOULDING.   Small astragal or half round moulding around the drawers of chests of the William and Mary Period.

SINGLE CHAIR.   Old name for side chair.

SINGLE GATE TABLE.   Tuckaway table; one with gate on only one side and one leaf.

SINKAGE.   Dropped or set-back surface; set-in panel in post or pilaster or other flat member.

SIRENS.   Mythological figures, half woman, half bird, used as a carving motive in Renaissance furniture. 1045.

SIX-BACK.   American ladderback chair with six slats, usually slightly arched. Infrequent, but chiefly from the Delaware Valley. 21.

SIX-LEGGED HIGHBOY.   The William and Mary type of England and America. See *Highboy.* 668 et seq.

SKIRT. Apron: part of a piece of furniture.

SLANT FRONT. Desk or secretary with writing section enclosed by a fall lid which when closed slants back; probably originally to rest a book or writing material upon. 43, 439 et seq. See *Desks, Secretaries.*

SLAT BACK CHAIR. Back having horizontal rails or crossbars similar to ladder-backs; in Early American work, the slats are characteristically thin and finely shaped. 228 et seq.

SLATS. Cross pieces supported on side rails of bed to carry the spring; horizontal cross-bars in chair back to brace uprights and to support back of sitter.

SLEEPY HOLLOW CHAIR. Comfortable upholstered chair with deeply curved back and hollowed seat and low arms. American type, middle 19th century.

SLEIGH-BED. American version of the Empire bed, the scrolled ends slightly reminiscent of sleigh fronts. They are usually used lengthwise to a wall.

SLIDE, SLIDER. Sliding panel or pull out shelf, flush framed and fitted between the top drawer and top of a chest of drawers. Also the pull-out leaves in secretaries, designed to hold candlesticks.

SLIPPER CHAIR. Small side or arm chair with low legs, designed for bedroom use. Generally upholstered.

SLIPPER FOOT. Elongated club foot (similar to snake foot) Queen Anne.

SLIP SEAT. Same as Loose Seat—separate upholstered wood frame, let into the framework of the chair seat.

SMITH, GEORGE. English cabinetmaker and designer. In 1808 his book, "Household Furniture," appeared with comment on the current revolution in taste. This was the Regency taste, with archeological correctness after the Greek, Roman and Egyptian models. A later book (1826), goes much further toward formulating the 19th century styles as we know them now. Smith was employed by Thomas Hope and patronized by George IV. The initials G.S. are occasionally found on important pieces of furniture of the period.

SNAKE FOOT. Foot of a tripod table, 18th century English or American, which suggests a snake shape by its slender, swelling curve.

SOCKETING. Joining by fitting one piece of wood into a cavity in another, as chair legs into solid seats.

SOCLE. Plain block used as a plinth or base for a case piece, or as a pedestal of a statue.

SOFA. Long upholstered seat for two or more persons. The name "Sopha" is of Eastern origin and was first used about 1680 to designate a divan-like seat in France; the same type had also been called *canape.* It had a back and arms at each end, but was distinct from the settee

by its greater comfort. Sofas followed the usual evolution of the succeeding styles, varying in ornament, bulk and comfort through the styles of the 18th and 19th centuries. Also *Rest beds, Couch*
46, 70, 78, 608, 615, 623, 632, 675, 805, 824, 850, et seq., 960.

SOFA TABLE. Long narrow table with drop leaves at the ends and drawers. Occurs chiefly in late Georgian work, in designs by Sheraton and others, but prototypes appear in the early 18th century work. 568.

SOFFIT. Under side, as of any projecting or ceiling member, or the underside of a projecting cornice or wide moulding which forms a shelf-like projection.

SOMNOE. Night table, or bedside table.

SOUPIÈRE. Antique vase form often used in Louis XVI and Empire furniture as the central motive in pedimented tops of beds, chairs, cabinets, etc., and at the intersection of stretchers. 1001.

SPADE FOOT. A rectangular tapered foot suggesting the outline of a spade; common in Hepplewhite designs. 895.

SPAIN. The history of Spain after the decline of Rome falls into three major periods.

(1) Mohammedan Spain, 700-1400.
(2) The Rise of Christian Spain to World Dominion, 1400-1600.
(3) Decline of Spanish World Power, 1600-1900.
Spanish culture following these divisions is definable into periods:
(1) Mudejar; the art of Christianized Moors, 1250-1500.
(2) Plateresque: 1500-1556. The Early Renaissance.
(3) Herrera, or Desornamentado, 1556-1600. Reaction toward severity.
(4) Baroque-Rococo, 1600-1700, including the Churrigueresque.
(5) Cycle of Foreign forms, 1700-1900.

Thruout these periods runs one fact: furniture always appears in foreign form, but always rendered in native style. The Spanish interpretation is without exception more vigorous, more masculine, even barbarous, than its foreign prototype.

MUDEJAR

Moorish inspiration. The Moors were superlative woodworkers, but required little furniture. Seats were merely cushions; tables only low platforms. The Christianizing of Spain culminating in the expulsion of the Moors in 1492, brought European trends. A magnificent Gothic expression in architecture showed Moorish traces; in furniture the basic forms were handled with Moorish construction technique and ornamentation. Walnut was the best wood; pine, cedar, olive, were used. Moorish inlaying with ivory, bone, mother-of-pearl, metals, and woods remained; star patterns and minute abstract interlacing geometrical forms are typical. The term **arabesque** springs from these ornamental bands. Color was brilliant. Leather for seats, chests, etc., was tooled, stamped, embossed, gilded and painted. 198.

PLATERESQUE

Spain and Italy were in close touch, particularly thru the Pope. The Renaissance came from Italy about 1500. Charles V ruled a vast empire, including Germany, Austria and the Netherlands; inevitably Flemish and other Northern trends were exchanged. The term Plateresque is from "platero"—silversmith, suggesting the pre-eminence of the metal work of the period.

Even the earliest Renaissance work shows no direct copying; the Italian influence only suggested. Craftsmanship was inferior; heavier proportions resulted from uncertainty, and obvious joinery, even by nails, is visible. Polychrome painting helped cover inferior workmanship. Turned profiles are repetitious or flat without suave modelling. Structure is supported with metal members. Walnut, pine, oak, chestnut, cedar, pearwood are commonly used, with metal ornaments, nail heads, inlays, chip or gouge carving used for ornament.

Table forms are distinct; splayed trestles, either of turned, squared or curved cut-out members, are connected by iron stretchers beautifully wrought. Thick plank tops are braced only with cleats; edges are square-cut.

Chairs are of simple rectangular form (220); the upholstery is often stretched across (214); nail heads are universally ornamental. The X-type chair was common, a rather top-heavy version of Italian form, or a light, Moorish type of repeated slats with inlay.

A ladderback type (229) appeared early, richly painted, rush seated, the top slat enlarged to accommodate carving.

Beds often had iron posts, or head panels of decorative iron; the Portuguese influence showed in rows of turned spindles, arches, etc.

Cabinets were important; the outstanding achievement of the period is the *Vargueno,* a desk box with fall front, mounted on a table support. The base often has a pair of double or triple turned posts with an arched colonnade between (456); the upper part contained many small drawers, inlaid or moulded, with some architectural features; the flap had pierced iron mounts with decorative hinges and hasp.

Leather covered chests and cabinets were studded with nails in outline designs.

HERRERA

Was architect to Philip II, who succeeded Charles V in 1556. Reactionary to the prevailing richness of the High Renaissance, his style produced harsh, colorless and bare rooms; furniture was sparse and austere and is known as Desornamentado—lacking ornament.

CHURRIGUERA

Another architect, gave his name to the Churrigueresque style: a robust explosion of Baroque extravagance, under the auspices of the Jesuit Counter-Reformation. From about 1600 to 1650 the Italian Baroque style was handled in bizarre Spanish fashion. After that the French influence dominates. The furnishings of great palaces followed in general form the current styles in Europe: there are Spanish Louis XIV, Spanish Louis XV, Rococo, etc. No clear schools evolved after the 17th century; details were borrowed and assembled. Moorish traits persisted through the 18th century, in inlaying and carving; even the manner of Chippendale and Hepplewhite was so treated. Descending the social scale, the provincial types adhered even longer to the old clichés.

Even in the period of *Rococo* delicacy the interpretation was vigorous and exaggerated, instead of daintily feminine. Walnut always was favored, but painting was popular, and some mahogany was imported with foreign influences.

The late 18th century classicism, the Empire and 19th century eclecticism followed the European trend. Palace furniture had an imported elegance which only the grandees could afford; provincial styles maintained directness and honesty of manner. 99, 109, 198, 214, 220, 229, 364, 455-8, 849, 909 et seq., 966.

SPANISH CHAIR. English term for a carved high-back chair with upholstered seat and back, introduced into England late in the 16th century.

SPANISH FOOT. Rectangular ribbed foot larger at the base, usually with a weak scroll. 27, 265.

SPAN-RAIL. Crosspiece between two uprights, as on a chair, bedframe, etc.

SPARVER. Tester or canopy.

SPHINX. Mythical winged monster, half woman and half lion. Of Egyptian origin, it occurs in all classical schools of furniture. 126, 434.

SPHINX

SPICE CUPBOARD. A small cupboard to hold spices, etc., usually hanging. Often miniatures of floor cabinets in the 18th century. 694.

SPINDLE. A thin turned member, often tapered or moulded, used in chair backs, etc.

SPINET. Early stringed instrument with keyboard similar to but smaller than a harpsichord; ancestor of the piano. Spinet cases of the early 19th century were often converted into shallow writing desks, giving form to the type so named. See *Desks.*

SPINET Ca 1660

SPINNING JENNY. Small spinning wheel used for flax.

SPINNING WHEELS. Spinning was a genteel occupation for women until the early 19th century; as the spinning wheels often stood in handsomely decorated rooms, they too, were decoratively treated. Late 17th century wheels in England have ornamental turnings and are made of beech, yew, box and oak; mahogany examples survive from the 18th century, embellished with inlay and ivory finials. The simple medieval types persisted in country districts and in America.

SPIRAL EVOLUTE. Continuous wave-like scrolls in a band ornament.

SPIRAL TURNING. Twisted turned work, typical of chair and table legs of the 17th century. They were often exercises in technique and were favored in Germany and Flanders. In less robust forms they are found in late 17th century English work. 110, 169, 218, 265, 591, 658.

SPLAD, SPLAT. Flat central vertical member in a chair back. Typical developments of splats are important indices of style, as the Queen Anne scrolled splat, or the pierced splats of Chippendale. 269.

SPLAY. Pitch; rake; cant; outward spread or slant, as of a surface or leg. 152.

SPLINT. Thin splits of hickory or oak woven into chair seats. Early American; persists in rustic types. 232.

SPLIT BALUSTER, SPLIT SPINDLE. Turned members cut in half and applied to flat surfaces as decoration, or used in chair backs as spindles where the projecting turnings might be uncomfortable. The former use is a very common decoration in Jacobean and derivative work. 227.

SPOOL BEDS. Most common type of turned work in America, early and middle 19th centuries.

SPOOL TURNING. Continuously repeated bulbous turning suggesting rows of spools. They appear early in North European work and were much used in Cromwellian and similar chairs. In America in the 19th century it was a favorite turning after the introduction of the power lathe, and appears in all forms, both free standing and split. Table legs, bed frames, mirrors, etc., were so decorated through the entire middle 19th century. 505.

SPOON BACK. Queen Anne chair backs were often curved like a spoon to fit the shape of the body.

SPOON CASES. Boxes similar to knife boxes, but arranged for spoons.

SPOON RACK. Hanging case for spoons, found principally in country furniture in England and France.

SPOONED-OUT, SPOONING. Hollowed out surface as wooden chair seats of Windsor chairs, etc.

SPRING EDGE. Upholstered edge which is supported by springs rather than the hardwood frame. Now universally used in good lounge chairs.

SPRINGS. Upholstering with coil springs originated in France during the reign of Louis XV, replacing the method of stuffing hair, feathers, etc., over webbed frame covers. They are now also used in cased form to fill cushions and mattresses.

SPRUNG MOULDING. Moulding applied to a curved surface by springing it into place.

SQUAB. Removable stuffed cushion of chairs; 17th and 18th centuries, originating in France. 322.

SQUARE BACK CHAIR. The typical Sheraton chair back is square, with variations in the center ornamentation and the crestings.

SQUARE LEG. The Chinese influence gave Chippendale the square leg, which he ornamented with either vertical mouldings or panels of delicate sunken fretwork. The inner surface was usually bevelled. Simpler versions, chiefly American, have only a quarter round bead on the outer edge.

SQUIRREL CAGE. Revolving framework on top of the pedestal of a tilt-top table, upon which the top is pivoted. 51.

S-SCROLL. Decorative form, carved or applied, in the shape of letter S, either continuous or broken. Used as corner and apron ornament in Baroque and Rococo styles. 815.

STALL. Ecclesiastical chair for dignitary or choir member. Early chairs were founded on these types. 197 et seq.

STAND. Any small table, used for holding or displaying objects; as shaving-stands, music-stands, candle stands, etc. See *Tables*.

STANDARD. Adjustable or swinging mirrors are carried on uprights called standards.

STANDING SHELVES. Small bookcase.

STEPPED CURVE. Broken curve, the parts being interrupted by right angles. 659.

STICK-BACK. Chair made up of spindles or small members, as in a Windsor chair. 236 et seq.

STILE. Outside vertical member of a cabinet or door, which frames a panel.

STIPO (Italian). Drop lid cabinet desk, usually tall and highly ornamented. 464.

STOCK. Bed stock, or the framework of a bed which is detached from the canopy structure in the great beds of the English and French styles.

STOOLS. Most ancient form of seating, having neither back nor arms. Egyptian stools were X-shaped, usually folding, and having skin or fabric seat; or solid-framed with rush or wood seats. The Greeks

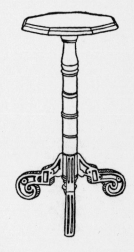

STANDS

and Romans used stools extensively except for ceremonial purposes, the forms resembling the ancient Egyptian ones. The curule chair is a developed stool. Throughout the Middle Ages and through the 17th Century stool or form types were proper seating for all but the most important persons; etiquette prescribed who sat on chairs, who on stools of one type and who on another and who stood. The side chair developed from the stool by the addition of the back. Italian sgabelli show the stuck-on appearance of early efforts and little improvement appears in northern work for another century. Stools and forms were thus slowly pushed down the social scale until they were either completely rustic or, in more elegant surroundings, only for ornamental or lounging purposes. The handsome cabriole-leg types of the Queen Anne period were footstools primarily. Ornamental types were used for dressing tables, window seats, etc., and this use is now most prevalent. 919 et seq.

STOPPED-CHANNEL FLUTING. Interrupted or filled fluting. 121, 149.

STRAIGHT FRONT. In chests, secretaries, etc., a flat front, however decorated; differing from the convex, concave, or serpentine front.

STRAIGHT PEDIMENT. Triangular or gable pediment of a cabinet or secretary, unbroken and uninterrupted. 471.

STRAP HINGE. Hinge with long straplike leaves, usually of iron and common in Gothic work in England and on the continent. 165.

STRAPWORK. Carved surface ornament in bands or panels, based on interlacing straplike bands. It is typical of Elizabethan and Jacobean work, and was probably imported with French Renaissance and Italian and Flemish models. It also appears in much German work of the 16th and 17th centuries. 152.

STRAPWORK

STRAW CHAIRS. French chairs seated with plaited or woven straw or rush. The framework is generally turned. They originated as rustic types in Europe at an early date, and were designed with a decorative purpose after the 17th century in France. In the 18th century straw chairs were used even in the palaces, and were designed in a charming and decorative manner. 642.

STRETCHER. Cross pieces or rungs connecting legs of chairs, tables, etc. Simple turned stretchers occur in Windsor, ladderback and similar chairs, usually arranged like an H; other types have diagonal or X stretchers; box stretchers connect the legs in a continuous line. Greater variety on tables include Y stretchers, double-H stretchers, serpentine, arched and other types, distinct in the various styles.

STRINGING. Narrow inlay band.

STUART. The Stuart kings, James I, Charles I, Charles II and James II, ruled England from 1603-1688, excepting the period of the Commonwealth, 1649-1660. The epoch is better divided into Early Jacobean, Cromwellian and Restoration. It covers the transition from oak to walnut, and the subordination of old English structural forms to the incoming Baroque influence. See *England*.

STUDS. Large or fancy upholstery nails used as decoration.

STUMP. The lowest part of the tree, in which the grain produces odd figures, curls, shakes, mineral streaks, etc., which may be utilized in cross sections of veneers to make beautiful symmetrical patterns.

STUMP BEDSTEAD. Beds with neither canopy nor posts. 97.

STYLE. Style signifies the distinctive manner of designing typical of any given time, place, person or group. In its narrower sense it means fashion, usually a short lived aspect of taste. Style in reference to art is always given the broader interpretation, synonymous with "school," "period"; as the Gothic style or Elizabethan, Louis XIV, Sheraton, Empire styles. It is more inclusive than the actual name; the style of Sheraton may refer to the work of contemporaries, copyists, or successors who work in a similar manner, Sheraton's designs being sufficiently well known to provide a standard or criterion of the general type. Thus the style may readily be accredited to the compiler of a book formulating its characteristics. In the case of a period name, as Régence or Queen Anne, it is a loose characterization of the style-spirit of the era, but it is by no means able to be confined to the exact years of the political designation. Again, a style may be a major movement, as Renaissance or Rococo, which is in turn treated with individual variation in different countries and times.

SUMMER BED. Two single beds placed together and joined by a cornice. An uncommon Sheraton design.

SUNBURST. Figured grain in wood in which cross fire or divergent rays radiate out from a center.

SUITE. The suite of furniture is a modern invention, although sets or groups of similar or related chairs were made and sold in England during the late 18th century. The notion of a single motive in all the furniture of the dining room or bedroom is a pure commercial product. It is unwholesome in that it is seldom possible to stretch the same theme over several distinctive shapes and retain the original quality of the idea.

SUNKEN PANEL. Sinkage or set-in panel in posts or other flat parts of furniture. 96.

SWAG. Festoon; swinging or suspended decoration, representing drapery, ribbons, garlands of fruit and flowers, etc. Greek and Roman examples were copied in stone from the practice of decorating altars and temples with such garlands; Renaissance reproductions were both freer and more conventionalized. All styles of classic inspiration use swags, painted, carved or inlaid in every form on all manner of pieces. Textile 111, Inlaid 420. Carved 738.

SWAG

SWAN. Typical motive of Directoire style, especially in Italy. Chair backs (878), bed and chair posts, and uprights. 790, 1061.

SWAN, ABRAHAM.   English cabinetmaker, 18th century.

SWAN-NECK.   Curved broken pediment of two S-curves, usually ending in paterae; a definitely Baroque concept beautifully treated in 18th century work. 477.

SWEDEN.   See *Scandinavian*.

SWEDISH MODERN.   Currently popular style of simple modern furniture, reminiscent of simplified Swedish rendition of the Empire style. Its straightforward outlines and lack of applied ornament make it acceptable in unstylized rooms, but it is basically decorative in concept. It uses light, plain woods in simple curves and roundings, with tapered feet and flat turnings. 955 et seq.

SWELL FRONT.   Convex curved front, as in a chest or commode or any case piece. 407 et seq.

SWING GLASS.   Mirror carried by two uprights or standards on pivots, so as to swing freely; cheval glass. 788 et seq.

SWING-LEG.   Hinged leg to support a drop leaf; similar to gate-leg, but lacking the lower stretcher. 542.

SWISS furniture is predominantly Alpine German, a well-to-do peasant style with positive Italian qualities. Native woods alone are used —pine, walnut, birch and oak. Much carving of good quality, and even more painted decoration are typical. Renaissance German influences are most persistent in chests, cabinets and tables; chairs of three-legged sgabelle type are common.

SWIVEL CHAIR.   Revolving seat on a fixed frame, used for desk chairs, dressing chairs, music stools, etc.

SYCAMORE.   Hard, light, dense wood with maple grain, but distinguishing flakes closely and regularly placed. The American sycamore is prone to warp and check; hence its limitation to interior parts. The English sycamore grain resembles maple; where curly it has more regularly parallel markings. Dyed gray, the English sycamore is known as Harewood. It is properly the Maple-leaved or London Plane Tree.

SYNTHETIC MATERIALS.   Manufactured materials as celluloid and other plastics derived from cotton, casein, etc., the product of the laboratory. These are coming into increased use in the decorative field, substituting surface materials as Bakelite, Micarta, Formica, etc., for wood, metal or glass. Synthetic textile yarns, such as rayon are familiar in all fabric uses.

TABERNACLE.   Niche or recess in a piece of furniture, as a cabinet, for a statue or a vase.

TABLE CHAIR.   Armchair or settle with hinged table-top as the back. 2.

TABLES. Tables have changed since ancient times according to the evolution of social customs, yet the few table forms remaining from Egypt are astonishingly similar to ours. These were four-legged types; the use of which we can only surmise. In Greece and early Rome, tables suggest altars in shape and probably that was their original use. Later Rome had bronze pedestal tables and tables with carved slab sides. Both shapes were prototypes for Renaissance styles. Prior to that Gothic tables were cruder, based on trestle forms; they were really not essential in the Gothic scheme, as dining was done off boards temporarily set on trestles. Other tables of ceremonial or ecclesiastical significance were adapted to general purposes as the need arose. Italian tables of the 15th century are trestle types, elaborated by means of turning. Long narrow types used in the monasteries have remained to be known as refectory tables. Other specialized types appeared from this time on, as the amenities of living increased.

DINING TABLES. Expanding types appeared in Italy, France and England early in the 16th century, the draw-top being commonest. Drop leaf and center-opening tables are known from the 16th century. The ultimate development came in 18th century England when social usage in general changed so rapidly. Continental Europe took its table forms from England after that. (962 et seq.)

SIDE TABLES. Tables with fixed tops were used along the walls of dining rooms to assist in the service after 1700. Earlier types, developed from simple frames, had carried chests with linens, silver, liquor, utensils, etc. From these evolved the serving tables, buffets, lowboys, etc., not identical with tables in form. 1029-1047.

CONSOLE TABLES are more decorative side tables probably designed originally as architectural compositions. At first symmetrical, they ceased to be decorated on the side against the wall; finally the emphasis was permitted to be entirely on the front. In some cases this necessitated their being fastened to the wall. 992 et seq.

WRITING TABLES OR FLAT-TOP DESKS developed from ordinary tables by the addition of drawers under the top. They are also known as library tables. 1005 et seq., 1024 et seq.

DRESSING TABLES appeared commonly about the end of the 17th century. The luxury of the period in England and France encouraged their development in many varieties. Men made much of dressing tables in England and France, and for over a century much ingenuity was expended on arrangements of mirrors, lighting, etc. The "Beau Brummels" of England and the "poudreuses" of France are outstanding types. 1014 et seq.

WORK AND GAME TABLES in various forms appeared with the rise of fads for needlework, painting, etc., late in the 17th century. Whole families of small tables for sewing, tea service, drawing, reading, games, etc., came under this heading. The types are not necessarily distinct, so that few forms have special characteristics and all types today are adapted, scaled up or down, or revised for any purpose desired. 1053 et seq.

TABLET CHAIR. Armchair with one flat arm wide enough to use as a writing table. Frequent in American Windsor types, 18th century. 238, 249.

TABLE DORMANT. First type of table to assume permanent stationary form in the Middle Ages, in place of the usual boards set on trestles. 676.

TABOURET. Low upholstered footstool, French, 18th century.

TAILPIECE. A tongue on the back of some Windsor chair seats, designed to receive two spindles which act as a brace for the bow.

TALLBOY. Highboy or chest-on-chest, a wide low chest carrying a slightly narrower taller chest. The top tier of drawers is often divided into two or three. English and American. 61, 687 et seq.

TAMBOUR. Flexible shutter or door, operating either vertically or horizontally, made of thin strips of wood glued to linen or duck. It runs in a groove and may follow any shape. Favored in Louis XVI work, English work of the Sheraton period and contemporary American work, as in roll top desks. 68, 487.

TAMO. Japanese ash; light yellowish wood with strong oak-like figure.

TANGUILE. Red-brown Philippine wood with striped figure and soft texture, sometimes called Philippine mahogany. It is not accepted as mahogany.

TAPER. Diminishing toward a point, characteristic of furniture legs, round or square, of the eighteenth century. The taper produces the effect of lightness and grace.

TAPESTRY. Fabric of wool with silk or linen, usually poctorial in design. An ancient method of weaving, it came to be used to upholster chairs, etc., in the 17th century. It is therefore an appropriate type of covering for all styles of this time, as French styles through Louis XV, English work through Queen Anne. William Morris revived tapestry weaving with his neo-Gothic style about 1880.

TARSIA. Same as Intarsia.

TASTE. In the narrow sense as applied to furniture, an affectation of historical influence, as, "in the Gothic taste," "in the Chinese taste."

TAVERN TABLE. Low oblong table on simple framework of turned or square members; chiefly American and English, 18th and early 19th centuries.

TEA. TEA TABLES. The introduction of tea into Europe created a fad which was responsible for changes in manners. Tea and its service was so important that it required a ritual with many appurtenances, among them a series of small tables for the service. These are also known as *tea-caddies, tea-kettle stands,* and *teapoys,* a family of graceful, well designed small stands.

TEAK. Large family of Oriental woods best known for resistance to moisture and decay. They are very heavy, light to medium brown in color, with a straight, open grain. Extensively used for furniture in the East. Its appearance in Occidental furniture is chiefly decorative.

TELAMONES. Atlantes; human figures on a supporting member.

TENON. Tongue or projecting part of wood which is fitted into a corresponding hole or mortise.

TENT BED. Field bed; smaller four-poster resembling a tent, with rather low canopy.

TERM. Pedestal, plinth or pillar, often carrying a bust or decorative figure, used as accents in decorative compositions. 567.

TERMINAL FIGURES. Ornamental use as a finish motive of the conventionalized human figure, all or part. They are often found mounted in full relief on the pillars of cabinets, etc., particularly in Late Renaissance work of Italy, France and England.

TERN FEET. Three-scrolled feet, sometimes merely grooved with three lines.

TESTER. Canopy of a four-post or draped bed, either of wood or fabric. 99-105.

TETE-A-TETE. Small two-seat sofa or love seat of the 19th century in which the two seats face in opposite directions, the backs forming an S-curve. Also *Siamoise.*

TEXTILES. Woven materials were essential to the earliest furniture for upholstery and decoration value. Egyptian stools had seats of stretched fabric, linen, cotton, wool and silk, and Roman couches were made comfortable with silk cushions. European textiles of the Middle Ages were largely influenced by the Orient. China and Japan sent silks; Persian, Mohammedan and Byzantine textiles added color, vivid pattern and texture to the harsh medieval halls. In the 12th century weaving began in Italy, and silks and damasks and velvets came into European use in the form of hangings for beds and walls, cushions, etc. Lucca, Venice, Florence and Genoa produced velvets and silks in rich patterns current to this day. Renaissance furniture is usually upholstered in these materials, as well as in the tapestries which were woven in France and the Lowlands, after the 16th century. Tapestry covered chairs of most English periods through the early Georgian. Needlework and embroidery were universally used through the 17th century. Crewel embroidery is typical of all Late Jacobean work. Beds were draped in costliest velvets and silks of Italian, French, and Spanish workmanship. There were many simple weaves of linen, wool, mohair, and cotton, as rep and moquette.

TERM

Rococo styles everywhere used the most elegant materials: silks, satins, damasks, brocade, brocatelle, taffeta and velvet of European and Oriental make. Colors were light pastel tones; textures were refined and smooth, and remained so in fine work for almost two centuries. Rococo patterns while small in scale were widely spaced or rambling.

The Classic Revivals—Louis XVI, Adam, etc., returned to small overall patterns in silks, velvets, and all other fine materials. Smooth surfaces were favored. The printing of material, usually cotton, silk or linen, like the Toiles-de-Jouy made in France by Oberkampf, spread over Europe, and by 1800 was in general favor for upholstery and hangings. The Empire style re-established smooth, plain materials in hard colors and finishes. Victorian England and America used haircloth and durable fabrics. Later the Paris styles brought back the elegancies of the 18th century.

Modern fabrics are less dependent on pattern than on the textural interest of weaves and specialties in yarns. Rayon has added to the list of original fibers, and a new catalogue of textiles includes rayon, cellophane and other synthetics—even glass—woven in both historical and new patterns.

THERM LEG.   Four sided or square tapered leg.

THERM FOOT.   Tapered foot of rectangular plan; spade foot.

THIMBLE TOE.   Spade foot, more often turned than square.

THIRTEEN-STATE TRACERY.   Geometric tracery pattern found in 18th century English and American secretaries, based on a Chinese motive. The coincidence of its dividing the space into thirteen divisions has led to the belief that it symbolizes the thirteen original states.

THREE-PLY.   Plywood or veneered work of three layers, the grain of the two outside layers being across the grain of the center. Not practical in panels over 3/8 inch thick.

THROWNE WORK.   Turning, from the old name for turning, or throwing.

THROWNE CHAIR.   Turned chair: old English. 221 et seq.

THUMB MOULDING.   Convex moulding shaped in a flattened curve, like the profile of the thumb.

THUYA (Thuja).   Wood of the North African arbor-vitae, used entirely as veneers. Burly grain and a rich brown red in color. It is one of the most decorative veneers, and has been so recognized since Roman times.

TILL.   Drawer or compartment in desks, chests, etc., for money, jewels, etc. They are often made with secret locks or springs.

TILT-TOP TABLE.   Table top hinged to the base or pedestal so that it may be tipped to a vertical position to save space or to display the decorative features of the top. The type is largely an 18th century development of English usage, when the customs of tea service, etc., inspired the design of many small tables. 28.

TIP-UP, TIP-TOP TABLE. Table whose top either folds down like a book over the base, or tips over the unfolded base. 28, 545.

TODDY-TABLE. Small Georgian drinking stand.

TOE. The end or tip of a foot.

TOILET-GLASS, TOILET-TABLE. Accessories to dressing or the toilet. The use of these articles seeped down from royalty to the nobles and gentry in the 17th century, and became very common in the 18th century when luxury was the keynote of furnishing. See *Dressing table.*

TOILES de JOUY. See *Jouy, Oberkampf.*

TOLE. Painted tin, particularly for small articles and accessories.

TONGUE-AND-GROOVE. Wood joint, in which a continuous projecting member fits into a corresponding rabbet or groove.

TOOTH ORNAMENT. Carved ornamental repeat moulding, like dentils. Also called Dog-tooth. It occurs in Romanesque, Gothic and very early Renaissance work, chiefly in England and Northern Europe.

TOPRAIL. Top cross member of the back of a chair, settee, etc.

TORCH. The torch or flambeau occurs as an ornamental motive in Roman architecture; it reappears in Renaissance furniture and again in the Classic Revivals of the late 18th century. The flaming torch is typical of Louis XVI ornament; Directoire decoration includes a formal torch while the burning torch is common in Empire ornament, usually in bronze appliqué.

TORCHERE. Stand for holding lights; developed from the Gothic flambeau, the Early Renaissance types were chiefly iron, delicately wrought. Sixteenth Century Italian torchères were either column forms or after the Roman candelabra or lampadaires. Baroque types were ornately classical or twisted columns. France had great torchères through Louis XIV's reign, highly ornamented with carving, gilding, Boulle work, etc. Rococo forms were light and graceful, finally coming to be hung entirely on the walls. In England the torchère was important during the early 18th century, borrowing from French sources. Chippendale and the Adams used torchères of large classical types as decorative features, the Adams copying the Roman forms literally. French Empire torchères were likewise large and ornate, closely following antique designs. 717, 729.

TORTOISE SHELL. Small pieces of the shell of the sea turtle used in inlays on furniture in combination with brass strips and wood. Originated by Boulle during the reign of Louis XIV and extensively copied in Germany and elsewhere.

TORUS. Bold convex round moulding, usually half circle or more, sometimes flattened. See *Mouldings.*

TORCHERE
ENGLISH·G. 1785

TRACERY. Delicate lattice-like forms of bars and lines with spaces for glass or openings. These derive from the Gothic windows in which a framework within the large opening was necessary to sustain the glass, which at first was in small sections. The shapes evolved were beautifully designed within the whole opening. The principle was applied to windows, bookcase doors, etc., where large areas of glass appeared impracticable or too bare, and in the 18th and 19th centuries produced interesting variations. Chippendale developed Gothic, Chinese, Rococo and simple geometric themes for tracery, which like his fretwork is the epitome of 18th century types. Sheraton used metal latticework similarly, and the Biedermeier and other 19th century styles developed characteristic designs.

Tracery, when it encloses glass should, properly, actually separate pieces of glass, but modern commercial work merely uses a cut out pattern or filigree *over* a pane of glass. 132, 150.

TRAY. Shallow drawer, usually with a low front, or the front cut out for hand hold; also an additional box placed in the top drawer of a chest for jewelry and small articles.

TRAY TABLE. Folding stand used to support a serving tray.

TREFOIL. Three-cusped or three-arc ornament characteristic of Gothic work. Usually inscribed within a circle.

TRESTLE TABLE. Originally all tables were merely loose boards placed upon trestles or horses. In the Middle Ages the "dormant table" was a permanent structure of table with trestles attached; this became the fixed-table type. The trestle form survived, as distinguished from the four legged or pedestal table, in various arrangements of posts and feet, more or less ornate, in all styles to the present. 964.

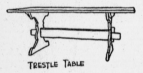

TRESTLE TABLE

TRIANGLE SEAT, CHAIR. Corner chair. One of the early types of chairs of Northern Europe, made of turned posts and rungs on a triangular plan. Alpine countries after the 14th century; England after the 16th. 221, 226.

TRIGLYPH. Ornament for a frieze, spaced at regular intervals and consisting of a flat raised surface with three grooves, or two whole and two half V-shaped depressions. Derived from Greek temple architecture and used in classical interpretations in furniture.

TRIPTYCH. Three-panelled altar piece later used decoratively; any mirror frame or decorative unit of a center panel with two hinged leaves. Byzantine and Gothic religious triptyches on wood and ivory were among the finest artistic productions of the Middle Ages.

TRIPOD

TRIPOD TABLE. Pedestal table with three outswinging legs. A favorite shape for small incidental tables in Georgian work, particularly of the Adam and Chippendale schools.

TRIVET. Three-legged metal table or stand used near a fireplace for warming dishes. England, 18th-19th centuries.

919.   **920.**   **921.**

EGYPTIAN STOOLS—1600-1500 B.C.
Metropolitan Museum of Art

STOOLS AND BENCHES

ENGLISH, CROMWELLIAN OAK. *Cavallo*   **923.**   ENGLISH, TUDOR OAK BOX STOOL. *Cavallo*   **924.**   ENGLISH, CAROLEAN (Oak).
Anderson Galleries

927.   FRENCH, HENRI II. Oak.
Anderson Galleries

6.   (Center)   ITALIAN, HIGH RENAISSANCE,
th Century.   *Metropolitan Museum*

5.   ITALIAN (TUSCAN), 17th Century.

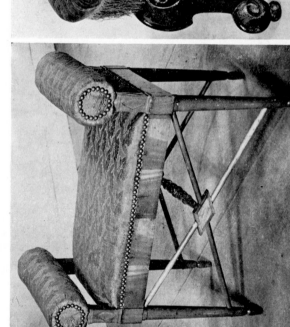

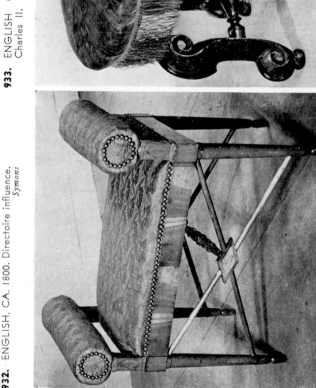

928. FLEMISH TURNED STOOL, 17th Century. Walnut. *Metropolitan Museum of Art*

929. ENGLISH, 18th Century. Mahogany. *Vernay*

930. ENGLISH, early 18th Century. Walnut. Style of Queen Anne. *Vernay*

931. FRENCH, EMPIRE BANQUETTE. *Anderson Galleries*

932. ENGLISH, CA. 1800. Directoire influence. *Symons*

933. ENGLISH OR FLEMISH, period of Charles II. Ebonized.

934. AMERICAN, CA. 1800. Mahogany. *Weil*

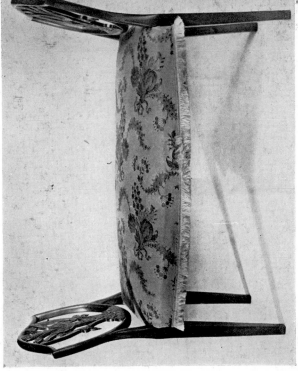

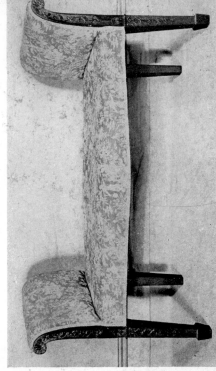

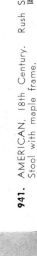

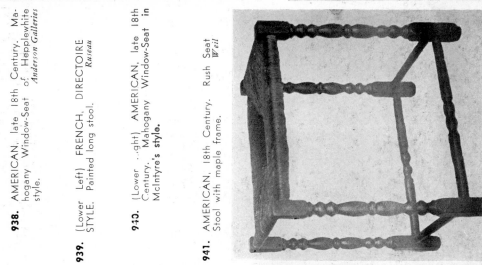

935. ENGLISH, Mid-18th Century, Mahogany, needlepoint cover, French influence. *Vernay*

936. (Right) FRENCH, DIRECTOIRE STYLE. X-Stools of classic form. *Cassard Romano*

937. ENGLISH, 18th Century, Mahogany Window-Seat of French inspiration. *Vernay*

938. AMERICAN, late 18th Century, Mahogany Window-Seat of Hepplewhite style. *Anderson Galleries*

939. (Lower Left) FRENCH, DIRECTOIRE STYLE. Painted long stool. *Ruseau*

940. (Lower Right) AMERICAN, late 18th Century, Mahogany Window-Seat in McIntyre's **style.**

941. AMERICAN, 18th Century, Rush Seat Stool with maple frame. *Weil*

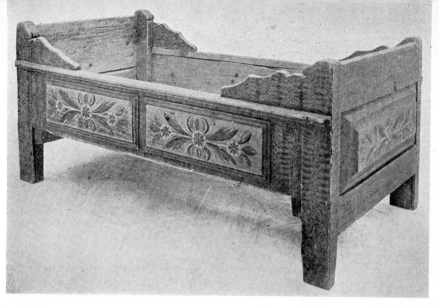

SCANDINAVIAN FURNITURE

Top Row:
942. SWEDEN, DECORATED CHAIR, probably 17th Century.

943. SWEDEN, PROVINCIAL BED, 17th Century. Painted.

944. SWEDEN, CHAIR, dated 1667. Renaissance influence.

945. (Center, Left) SWEDEN, CA. 1600. Cupboard with suggestion of Elizabethan English influence.

946. (Center, Right) SWEDEN, late 18th Century. Painted Cupboard with panel construction. Rococo influence.

947. SWEDEN, OR NORWAY, 14th-15th Century. Gothic Oak Chest with typical carving.

948. SWEDEN, late 18th Century. Chest of pine with painted decorations.

BAROQUE AND ROCOCO STYLE

949. BOMBÉ COMMODE made in Stockholm by Christian Linning, 1744-1779.

950. PAINTED CHAIR in Rococo style, carved back.

951. (Left) SWEDEN, CA. 1700. Cabinet in the English and Dutch style, lacquered and decorated with silver and gold. Period of Frederick I.

952. (Right) NORWEGIAN CORNER CUPBOARD of individualized Baroque style, probably late 17th Century.

SWEDEN ADOPTED THE EMPIRE STYLE ENTHUSIASTICALLY. IT IS REFERRED TO AS "KARL-JOHANS" STYLE.

953. PAINTED BED with applied composition ornaments.

954. MAHOGANY TABLE with bronze ornaments, in Greco-Roman style.

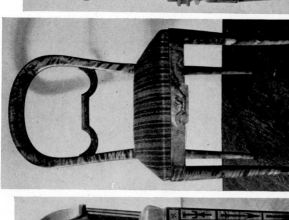

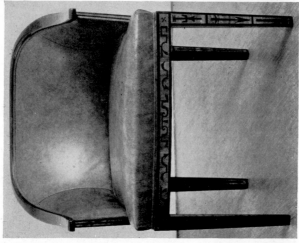

SWEDISH FURNITURE OF THE TWENTIETH CENTURY

THIS STYLE IS BASED ALMOST WHOLLY ON PURE CLASSIC FORMS, WITH HIGHLY INDIVIDUAL INTERPRETATIONS IN PROPORTION AND DETAIL.

955. BOOKCASE IN SWEDISH BIRCH.

956. ARMCHAIR FOR DESK, with inlaid detail, leather cover.

957. SIDE CHAIR OF BIRCH, with carved ornaments.

958. (Right) ARMCHAIR OF CLASSIC FORM.

959. CHEST OF SWEDISH BIRCH, inlaid.

960. SOFA WITH TOOLED LEATHER COVER, inlaid frame.
Designs by Carl Malmsten, Courtesy Swedish State Railways.

961. ROMAN, CARVED MARBLE TABLE BASE.
Metropolitan Museum of Art

962. (Upper Left) ITALIAN, LATE RENAISSANCE WALNUT TABLE. *Cavallo*
End of 16th Century.

963. (Left) FRENCH, HIGH RENAISSANCE, WALNUT DRAW TOP *French & Co.*
TABLE. Late 16th Century.

TABLES

THE TABLE FORM LAPSED IN
IMPORTANCE IN THE MIDDLE
AGES. ANCIENT ROMAN TYPES
WERE REVIVED IN THE RENAISSANCE.

964. TUSCAN WALNUT REFECTORY TABLE WITH PLANK TOP. Early 16th Century.

TABLES OF THE MIDDLE AGES WERE TRESTLE-TYPE
THE TRESTLE IDEA PERSISTED IN THE EARLY RENAISSANCE

965. ITALIAN (BOLOGNESE) REFECTORY TABLE, 16th Century. Thick walnut top in one piece.
French & Co.

66. SPANISH WALNUT TABLE, 17th Century.   *French & Co.*

967. SWEDISH. 18th Century. Pine, survival of Gothic f
with stretcher step foot rest.

968 FRENCH HIGH RENAISSANCE TABLES. 1570-1640. **969**
French & Co.

THE DRAW-TOP EXTENDING DINING TABLE APPEARED IN THE FIFTEENTH CENTURY

0. ELIZABETHAN TABLE, CA. 1600. Oak, inlaid aprons; bulbous supports with Ionic caps and claw feet.

French & Co.

ENGLISH (TUDOR) OAK DRAW TABLE with plain bulb-turned legs,
C. 1600.
Starr & Co.

972. EARLY 17th CENTURY ENGLISH OAK TABLE with fine melon bulb turning with Acanthus carving, gadrooning and Ionic caps.
Charles of London

973. (Above) DINING TABLE
center extension, walnut. Ita
late 17th Century.   *Lav*

974. (Center) ITALIAN, 17th Cen
Walnut Table in two parts, fo
ing a circular table together.
                              French &

EXTENSION TABLES

975. ENGLISH, late 18th Cen
Round Table with center extens
leaves.   *Ver*

6. ENGLISH, JACOBEAN GATELEG TABLE. CA. 1620.
Baluster shaped end cut-out.　　*Stair & Co.*

977. AMERICAN, BUTTERFLY TABLE. Maple. 1650-1700.
Metropolitan Museum of Art

978. AMERICAN: SWING LEG TABLE OF CHIPPENDALE STYLE, New York, CA. 1770.　　*Metropolitan Museum*

ENGLISH GATE LEG, CA. 1670.　　*Charles of London*

980. ITALIAN (TUSCAN), drop leaf with vase shaped standards.
Walnut. CA. 1600.　　*Anderson Galleries*

931. ENGLISH, CA. 1790. Extension Table of 3 parts, center being a detachable drop leaf table.

Vern

982. ENGLISH, CA. 1795. Mahogany with inlaid band on top edge. Sheraton style.

Vernay

983. ENGLISH, mahogany oval extension. *Vernay*

984. AMERICAN, early 19th Century, style of Duncan Phyfe. Extension Table with drop legs. *Metropolitan Museum of*

5. ROMAN, 2nd Century A.D. Bronze and Marble Pedestal Table.
Metropolitan Museum of Art

986. ENGLISH, OAK PEDESTAL TABLE, Jacobean style.

987. (Upper Center) ENGLISH, TURNED STAND, 17th Century. Oak. *Vernay*

PEDESTAL TABLES

NCIENT FORM ADAPTED
O EVERY TYPE OF TABLE.
NING TABLES ON TWO
EDESTALS WERE A LATE
IGHTEENTH CENTURY
EVELOPMENT, CHIEFLY
HROUGH SHERATON.

989. AMERICAN, CA. 1800.
Weil

988. ENGLISH, SHERATON STYLE. Mahogany with leather top. *Vernay*

990. FRENCH, CA. 1840. Development of Empire. *Bruce Buttfield*

991. ITALIAN EMPIRE, CA. 1815.
Lavezzo

992. (Above.) ENGLISH OAK, Ca. 1620. *Charles of Lo*

993. (Left.) EAGLE CONSOLE TABLE. Carved wood with m top. English, Ca. 1730. *Sy*

SIDE TABLES DESIGNED TO STAND AGAINST A WALL ARE CALLED "CONSOLES"

994. ENGLISH, painted Satinwood. Ca. 1785. *Vernay*

995. FRENCH, LOUIS XVI. Attributed to Saunier. Kingwood and Ormolu, marble top. *Symons*

996. ENGLISH, Satinwood and Mahogany. Ca. 1780. *V*

997. ITALIAN, Late 18th Century, painted. *Sy*

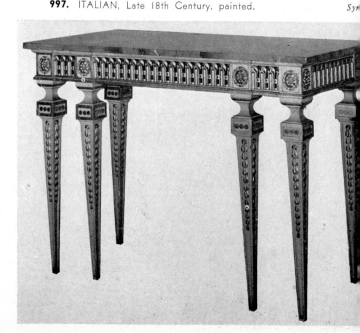

998. FRENCH, height of Louis XV Rococo style. Carved oak console.

French & Co.

SOME CONSOLE TABLES ARE FASTENED TO THE WALL

ENGLISH, SHERATON STYLE.
Vernay

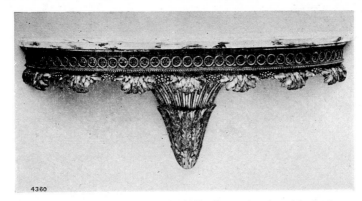

1000. FRENCH, HANGING CONSOLE, gilt wood and marble. Louis XVI Period.
Metropolitan Museum of Art
1001. FRENCH, LOUIS XVI CONSOLE.
Anderson Galleries

1003. ITALIAN, ROCOCO, GILT.
Lavezzo

1004. FRENCH, OAK, LOUIS XVI.
Metropolitan Museum

ITALIAN ROCOCO, late 18th Century. *Ruseau*

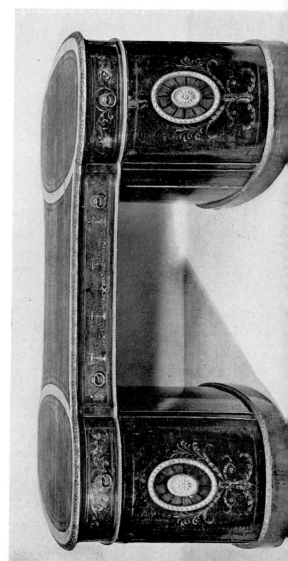

LIBRARY AND DESK TABLES

THE HIGHEST DEVELOPMENT OF THIS TYPE WAS ATTAINED IN ENGLAND IN THE EIGHTEENTH CENTURY.

1005. (Right) FOUR-SIDED PEDESTAL DESK of mahogany, middle 18th Century. *Vernay*

1006. (Lower Right) MAHOGANY PEDESTAL DESK. CA. 1750. *Vernay*

1007. LIBRARY TABLE DESK with oval pedestals; sycamore with painting in the classic manner. *Anderson Galleries*

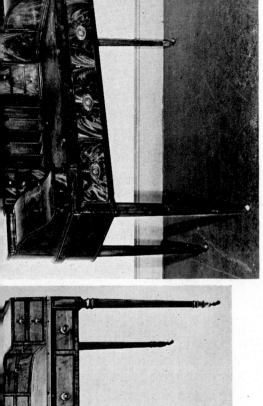

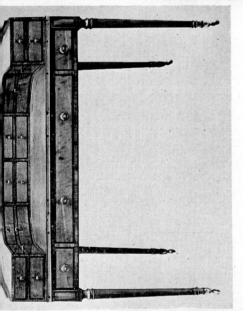

1008. FOLDING TOP WRITING TABLE, with gate legs and side drawers. Inlaid Walnut, Ca. 1690.

Symons

1011. WRITING TABLE in the style of Chippendale, Ca. 1760.

Brady Collection, Anderson Galleries

1009. "CARLTON-HOUSE" TABLE-DESK of Satinwood. Reeded legs, Ca. 1795.

Vernay

1010. "CARLTON-HOUSE" TABLE-DESK of figured Mahogany. Ca. 1780. Curved back.

Colchester

1013. ARCHITECT'S DESK of inlaid Mahogany. Ca. 1780. Swing legs support folding top.

Brady Collection, Anderson Galleries

1012. READING TABLE, with candle brackets. Provision for writing and drawing materials.

Saint James Galleries

1014. (Above.) "BEAU BRUMMEL," in the French taste. Ca. 1770.
Brady Collection, Courtesy Anderson Gallerie.

1015. (Upper Left.) SMALL KNEEHOLE TABLE for writing or dressing. Walnut Burl
Ca. 1720.
Vernay

1016. (Left.) AMERICAN KNEEHOLE TYPE OF MAHOGANY. Rhode Island blockfront
Metropolitan Museum of Ar...

DRESSING TABLES

ENGLISH DRESSING TABLES, FREQUENTLY DE-
SIGNED FOR MEN, WERE MORE MASCULINE IN
FORM. THEY ARE OFTEN IDENTICAL WITH
DESK FORMS.

1017. GEORGIAN "BEAU BRUMMEL"
MAHOGANY CHEST with compli-
cated mirror arrangements. Type
known as "Multum in Parvo," after
Rudd.
Brady Collection, Courtesy Anderson Galleries

1018. DRESSING TABLE. Ca. 1780. Yew-
tree-wood.
Vernay

19. DRESSING TABLE of Rosewood and Tulipwood. Style of Louis XV. *Don Ruseau*

20. (Upper Right.) ENGLISH TABLE in the Louis XVI style. *Vernay*

21. (Right.) MECHANICAL TABLE made by Riesener for Marie Antoinette, about 1778. *Metropolitan Museum of Art*

FRENCH POUDREUSES

WERE INVARIABLY LIGHTER THAN THE ENGLISH STYLES, ALTHOUGH EQUIPPED WITH SIMILAR MECHANICAL CONTRIVANCES.

1022. POUDREUSE of Cherry and Lemon woods. Late style of. Louis XVI. *Anderson Galleries*

1023. SMALL POWDER TABLE of Mahogany and Ormolu. *Symons* Louis XV style.

1024. ENGLISH, C. 1760. Mahogany Table in Chinese taste. *Symons*

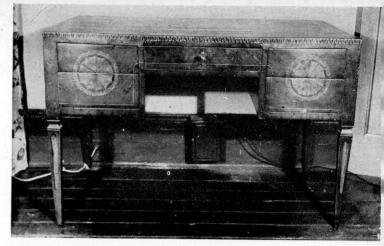

1025. ITALIAN, late 18th Century Classicism showing English influence in inlays. *Lavezzo*

1026. FRENCH, ROCOCO STYLE OF LOUIS XV in rosewood and Ormolu. *Olivotti*

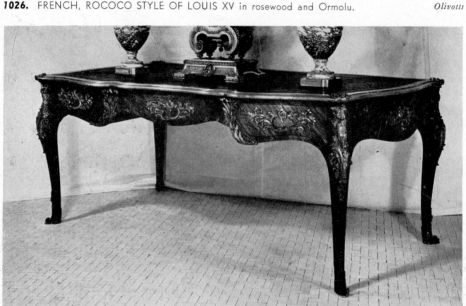

TABLES OF GENERAL KNEEHOLE TYPE ARE USED
BOTH AS DRESSING AND WRITING TABLES

1027. FRENCH, LOUIS XVI PERIOD TABLE with pull-out leaves. *Ruseau*

1028. FRENCH, LOUIS XVI TABLE of mahogany with Ormolu mounts. Attributed to Riesener. *Symons*

SIDE TABLES

SIMPLE FOUR-LEGGED TABLES ARE AMONG THE EARLIEST ARTICLES OF FURNITURE. FOR GENERAL UTILITY THEY ARE COMMONLY PLACED ALONG WALLS AND ARE THUS CALLED SIDE TABLES.

1029. (Top) EGYPTIAN, 1600-1500 B.C.
Metropolitan Museum of Art

1030. (Right) ENGLISH, early 17th Century.
Charles of London

ITALIAN, 16th Century, walnut, tilt top.
Metropolitan Museum

1032. ENGLISH, JACOBEAN, oak.
Vernay

1033. FRENCH, early 17th Century, walnut.
Ruseau

4. ITALIAN, 16th Century, walnut extension top.
Metropolitan Museum

1035. FLEMISH, 17th Century, walnut.
Metropolitan Museum of Art

1036. AMERICAN, early 18th Century, slate top.
Metropolitan Museum

1037. AMERICAN, Mid-18th Century, Chippendale style. Mahogany, marble top. *Weil*

1038. ENGLISH, EARLY GEORGIAN, marble top.

1039. ITALIAN, late 18th Century Classicism. *Lavezzo*

1040. ENGLISH, LATE JACOBEAN. *Charles of L*

SIDE TABLES

1041. ENGLISH, late 18th Century. *Vernay*

1042. AMERICAN, early 19th Century. Probably by Duncan Phyfe. *Metropolitan Museum*

3. AMERICAN, 18th Century. Maple, pine top.   *Weil*

1044. ENGLISH, C. 1790. Harewood Pembroke Table, inlaid border.   *Colchester*

5. FRENCH, 17th Century.   *Symons*

1046. ENGLISH, WILLIAM AND MARY, Marquetry.   *Anderson*

SIDE TABLES

1047. AMERICAN, 18th Century. Mahogany.   *Anderson Galleries*

1048. AMERICAN, 18th Century.   *Weil*

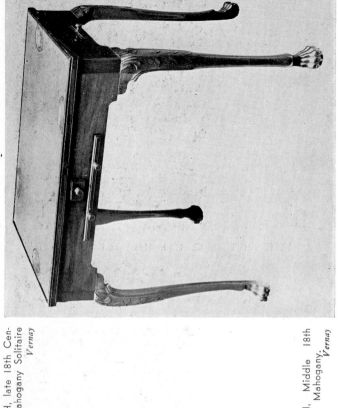

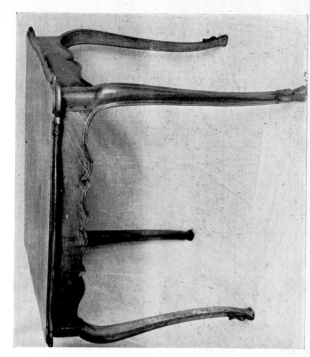

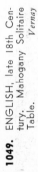

1049. ENGLISH, late 18th Century. Mahogany Solitaire Table. *Vernay*

1050. ENGLISH, Middle 18th Century. Mahogany. *Vernay*

1051. ENGLISH, Mid-18th Century. Style of Chippendale. Mahogany. *Vernay*

1052. FRENCH, PROVINCIAL STYLE OF LOUIS XV. *Ruseau*

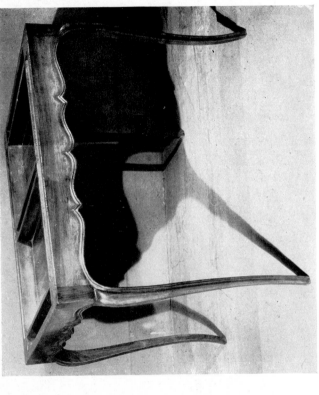

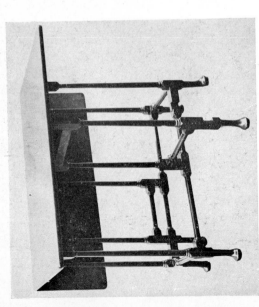

1054. (Left) GAME TABLE with removable top. French, Provincial Louis XV.

1055. (Above) DETAIL OF SAME, showing Backgammon Board.

Courtesy Don Ruseau

1053. ENGLISH, Mid-18th Century. Mahogany Gateleg Table used for games. *Vernay*

GAME TABLES

1060. ENGLISH, LATE JACOBEAN. Needle work playing surface. *Colchester*

1059. ENGLISH REGENCY, 1810. Satinwood, inlaid. *Colchester*

1058. FOLDING TOP CARD TABLE. Italian, Directoire style. *Lavezzo*

1057. SHERATON STYLE, CA. 1790. Mahogany. *Vernay*

1056. FOLDING TOP CARD TABLE. English, Early Georgian. *Vernay*

1061   **1062**   **1063**   **1064**   **1065**

WORK TABLES

TOP ROW, LEFT TO RIGHT

1061. FRENCH WORK TABLE, C. 1815.
Swan neck, revolving top.

1062. AMERICAN SEWING STAND, C. 1770.
Hepplewhite style.   *Weil*

1063. ENGLISH BAG TABLE, C. 1790.
Painted Satinwood.   *Metropolitan Museum of Art*

1064. ENGLISH, C. 1750.   *Vernay*

1065. ENGLISH BASIN STAND, C. 1750.
LEFT
1066. FRENCH LYRE TABLE, C. 1800.

RIGHT
1067. GERMAN BIEDERMEIER, C. 1810.

LOWER ROW, LEFT TO RIGHT
1068. FRENCH GUERIDON, Louis XV.

1069. FRENCH WORK TABLES, end of 18th
century.   *Anderson Galleries*

1070. AMERICAN, manner of Phyfe, C. 1810.
Weil

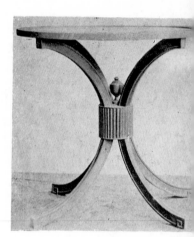

1067

1068   **1066**   **1069**   **1070**

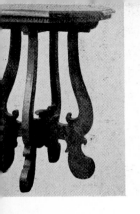

1071 **1072** **1073** **1074**

SMALL TABLES

TOP ROW, LEFT TO RIGHT

1071. ITALIAN, 17th Century Walnut.

1072. ENGLISH, C. 1790. REVOLVING BOOK STAND. Painted.

1073. ENGLISH, late 18th century.

1074. ITALIAN, C. 1805.   *Cavallo*

LEFT

1075. AMERICAN, EARLY 19th CENTURY PIVOT TOP TABLE.   *Weil*

RIGHT

1076. ENGLISH GEORGIAN TILT-TOP TABLE. Mahogany.   *Vernay*

LOWER ROW, LEFT TO RIGHT

1077. ENGLISH, LATE 18th CENTURY NEST OF TABLES AND PLANT STAND.
                    Vernay

1078. URN STAND, English, 1760.
        Metropolitan Museum of Art

1079. CHIPPENDALE FRETWORK TABLE.
                Symons

1080. ENGLISH WALNUT TEA-TABLE.

1075

1076

1077 **1078** **1079** **1080**

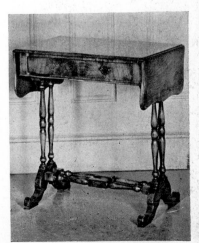

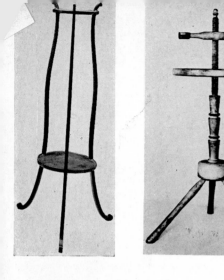

STANDS FOR VARIOUS PURPOSES WHILE NOT PRECISELY TABLES, EVOLVED FROM THE ANCIENT TRIPOD TYPE AS WELL AS FROM THE TABLE FORM.

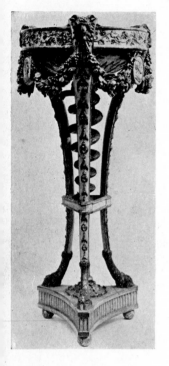

Top Row: Left to Right:

1081. ENGLISH, CANDLESTAND.   *Vernay*

1082. AMERICAN, 17th Century CANDLESTAND.   *Weil*

1083. FRENCH, EMPIRE PEDESTAL STAND.

1084. ITALIAN, EMPIRE STAND.   *Cavallo*

1085. ENGLISH PEDESTAL, C. 1690.   *Symons*

1086. ENGLISH, C. 1780. CANDLESTAND.

1087. (Left) ATHENIENNE, FRENCH, late 18th Century.
Metropolitan Museum of Art

1088. (Right) ENGLISH BASIN STAND, C. 1780.   *Vernay*

Lower Row, Left to Right:

1089. ENGLISH BOOKSTAND, C. 1780.

1090. ENGLISH, SATINWOOD WORK TABLE, C. 1790.

1091. ENGLISH, REVOLVING BOOK STAND, C. 1810.

1092. ENGLISH REGENCY BOOK TABLE.

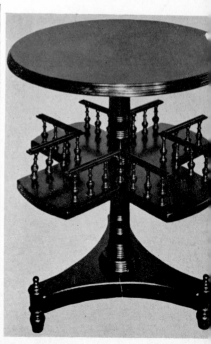

TRUCKLE BED. Trundle Bed.

TRUMEAU. Overmantel treatment of Louis XV and Louis XVI style, consisting of mirror and painting. Subsequently detached and used as a decorative mirror in composition with a commode or chest, console tables, etc. 618.

TRUMPET TURNING, LEG. Turned leg with flaring profile of a trumpet turned upward. Typical of English work, Restoration period and later, and similar American furniture. 692.

TRUNDLE BED. Low rolling frame fitted as a bed, designed to roll under a larger bed. American and English 18th and early 19th centuries. Also called truckle bed.

TRUSS. In furniture a brace or understructure for tables and chest-stands, or a bracket. Usually ornamentally treated.

TUB-CHAIR. Round large easy chair with wide wings. English, time of Sheraton and later.

TUCK-AWAY TABLE. Compact folding table with cross-legs which fold together to permit the top leaves to drop close together. Early American modification of a narrow English gate-leg table.

TUDOR. English Rulers, comprising

> Henry VII —1485-1509
> Henry VIII—1509-1547
> Edward VI —1547-1553
> Mary   —1553-1558
> Elizabeth   —1558-1603

Their reigns cover the last phases of the Gothic style and the introduction of Renaissance ideas. Furniture is heavy, richly carved oak. 154, 157, 159, 368, 970. See *England*.

TUDOR ARCH. Elliptical arch pointed in the center, representative of the English Tudor style.

TUDOR ROSE. Conventionalized rose used as a symbol of the Tudors; frequently a decorative motive in English carved oak furniture of the 16th and 17th centuries. 157.

TUDOR ROSE

TUFFT, THOMAS. Died 1793. Philadelphia cabinet- and chairmaker; his label is known on a lowboy of simple but good style.

TUFTING. In upholstery, the tying down of an upholstered surface by means of a button sewed through the upholstery. The arrangement of buttons and the resulting folds produces patterns in the upholstering.

TULIP. A conventionalized flower pattern suggesting the tulip leaf and flower. It occurs both carved and painted on chests of the Netherlands, South Germany, England and America between the 15th and early 18th centuries. 25.

TULIPWOOD. Heavy tan wood with red markings, from Central America. Extensively used in Louis XV furniture.

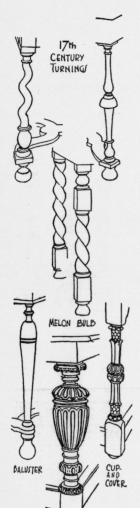

17th CENTURY TURNINGS

MELON BULB

BALUSTER

CUP AND COVER

TUPELO. Gumwood, greyish white in color, medium hard and strong, subject to warping unless carefully cut and dried. Used chiefly in lower priced furniture as posts and face veneer, generally stained to imitate walnut or mahogany.

TURKEYWORK. Embroidery work, popular in the 17th century for upholstery. Many early American inventories list pieces so covered.

TURKISH. Furniture of Turkey is based on a different domestic organization and has little parallel in Western work. Beds are chiefly piles of rugs in divan form, whence the interpretation of Turkish divans, Turkish beds, etc., in various periods. Turkish chairs are softly overstuffed and other so-called Turkish features are simply allusions to the softly cushioned effect associated with Turkish rooms. Turkish woodwork is primitive in outline depending for decorative effect on complex inlays.

TURKISH ROCKER. Overstuffed easy chair mounted on a spring platform. Late 19th century, American.

TURNING. Turning, one of the most ancient woodworking processes, is done by the application of cutting tools to the rotating surface. The device for rotating or turning the wood is called the lathe. This is the oldest idea in woodworking machinery. Egyptian lathes were operated by a bowstring; later lathes were worked by treadles. In the Middle Ages, a form of spring lathe depended on the elasticity of a wood lever alternately winding and unwinding a winch. Probably the earliest application of water power and later steam power was to the lathe, so that in all ages turning has been a convenient and direct method of treating wood decoratively. Legs, posts, feet, spindles and rungs, stretchers, etc., are most often turned. Turnings are also cut through (split turnings) and applied to flat surfaces as decoration, as in Jacobean work. (379).

Almost every style has distinctive profiles in its turnings, so that the outline and character of a turning may be a key to the style. Early Italian Renaissance turnings are mostly of the baluster type (965), with well proportioned fillets, etc., in the classical manner. Spanish turnings, influenced by the characteristic Moorish style, consist of closely repeated disks and ball forms, deeply and sharply incised. (109, 996) They also used a straight turning with collars and fillets suggesting the column form. Early Spanish and Portuguese legs were also spiral-turned, probably brought from India. Spiral turnings are a feature of Flemish work (1035), whence it came to England as a prime detail of late 17th century furniture. French 17th Century work shows tremendous variety of turnings, particularly combinations of profiles of twisted, column, and baluster forms (591), deeply cut disks and ball types. The most characteristic turning of Northern Europe through the 17th century was the ball or sausage type (222), a much repeated simple profile which is familiar in Cromwellian and American work of the 17th century. (505).

In England the large melon-bulb turning is an outstanding key to furniture of the Tudor and Stuart periods. (907) Later, the William and Mary turnings were of unique trumpet (1036), inverted cup and bell turnings (688), besides the much-varied spiral (690) and composite types. The practice of carving on turned surfaces, prevalent in Early Jacobean work, reappeared in Early Georgian times, richly ornamented and fluted turned shafts forming the pedestals of tables, etc. Clustered turnings (288) suggested bamboo in the Chinese taste, and a definite imitation called *bamboo turning* appeared in English and American furniture. (348).

Turning, almost absent in Rococo work, reappeared in the Louis XVI style. Legs were invariably a sharply tapered turning with severe fillets and bands and usually fluted. (321) These were favored by the Adams, Hepplewhite and Sheraton. (335) There was a typically flared-out turning, (342) one of several eccentric turnings; another was the country turned leg with the spoon or pad foot suggesting a cabriole leg. This appears in American work, along with the simple balusters and the vase turning typical of the Windsor chair. With the advent of power machinery came the spool turning, a monotonous repetition of a simple profile which overflowed America in the 19th century. Machine turnings are now made on the automatic lathe in which the cutting edge has the whole profile of the finished turning.

TURTLE BACK. Oval or elliptical boss or half-turned decoration. Common in Jacobean and similar American cabinetwork as applied decoration; also found on some Renaissance work on the Continent.

TUSCAN. Simplest order of Roman architecture. See *Orders*.

TWIST. Spiral or screw-turning.

UNDERBRACING. The arrangement of stretchers on chairs, tables, and stands with legs, etc., distinctive to various styles.

UPHOLSTERY. Upholstering consists of stretching of textiles or leather across a wooden framework. Elementary upholstering used nothing more; in Egypt and other ancient cultures, as well as in the earliest Renaissance, skins or leather were merely nailed across such a framework. Later, cushions were placed over this; finally the padding or cushion was sewed together with the covering material. Padding was made still more comfortable by increasing the depth of cushions, filled with down, horsehair, soft feathers, wool, etc.; in the sixteenth century the upholstering, now thick, was further softened by the use of additional loose cushions or *carreaux*. Springs came into use in the 18th century, and with this improvement modern upholstery begins.

Upholstery today is classified as (a) simple padding, (b) overstuffed upholstering over springs. Simple padding may use nothing more than

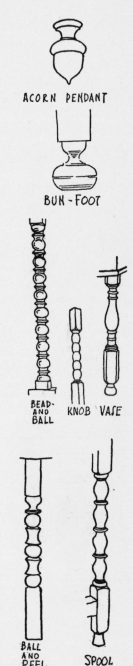

ACORN PENDANT

BUN-FOOT

BEAD-AND-BALL KNOB VASE

BALL AND REEL SPOOL

a layer of cotton felt, wadding, hair, moss, etc., over a wooden panel, with the finish material stretched over; or it may be a true webbed construction. The latter employs an open wood framework, over which is stretched crossed webbing, stitched together; to this is applied a layer of hair framed in with roll stitching to form a firm edge; the whole covered with muslin and finally covered with the finish material. This method is used chiefly in the better "tight seats" of light chairs as the English and French types shown in 296, 297.

Spring upholstery requires a deeper wooden frame. Frames are best made of hard non-splitting woods as ash, or birch, securely joined with glued dowels and braced with corner blocks to resist the tension of tied springs. On the bottom the webbing is crisscrossed and stitched together. The springs are arranged over this in rows; they are stitched down and tied together in such a way as to brace them against tension from any direction. Burlap covers the top of the springs; over this hair or felt, then a layer of wadding, then muslin, and finally the finish material. In much modern work loose cushions are placed over the spring seat or platform; these cushions may be filled with down, floss, hair, cotton felt, springs, etc. With loose cushions a special roll or stitched edge is sewed on the platform.

The variations in quality of material, labor and design are infinite and too complex for any but the expert to judge. The practice of advertising one or more features as indicative of quality is often misleading, and a dangerous guide to the amateur judge of values. Legislation has established certain minimums of quality and cleanliness in manufacture, but in the medium and better qualities the purchaser has no better guide than the guarantee of a sufficient price and a reputable manufacturer.

URN. Vase-shaped vessel used as decorative motive in Greco-Roman carving, and borrowed in the Renaissance and subsequent styles based on classic styles. In French work it is sometimes referred to as "soupïere." It is used free standing as finials, at the intersection of crossed stretchers, etc., particularly in the Adam and Louis XVI styles. 747, 1001.

URN STAND, URN TABLE. Small table accessory to the tea service, Chippendale school.

VALANCE. The drapery of the tester or canopy of a bed; later the top or horizontal section of any drapery arrangement.

VANBRUGH, SIR JOHN, 1664-1726. English architect and designer, influential in the development of the early Georgian style.

VANITY, VANITY TABLE. Modern name for a dressing table.

VARGUEÑO. Spanish cabinet-desk with fall front, most distinguished furniture type of Spain, 16th, 17th and early 18th centuries. 455 et seq., 910.

VARNISH.   Wood-finishing material of gum dissolved in linseed oil, applied in films or skins, by brush or spray, to protect and beautify wood surfaces. It appears to have been known to the ancients, but the secret was lost to medieval workers who used only oil and wax which was absorbed into the wood. True brushing varnishes, using damar or copal in oil, were probably the basis of the "Vernis Martin" but no reliable records indicate that varnish was made before 1848. Spirit varnishes or gums like shellac in alcohol, chiefly padded on the wood, had been known in Europe since the 17th century. At first varnishes presented a sticky, over-glossy look, but rubbing and improved quality today produces a fine satiny gloss. Varnishes for special purposes are made with tung-oil or synthetic bases like cellulose derivatives.

VASE.   Ornamental vase or urn shapes after the classic sources are used extensively in Adam, Louis XVI and similar work. Carved or painted it is often the source of freely scrolled foliage designs. Free standing it is used as finials, or decorative accents. 280.

VASE SPLAT.   Chair back suggesting vase form common in most Renaissance types; most highly developed in Queen Anne chairs. 269.

VASE TURNING.   Profile in turnery which suggests a vase with bulbous base and tapering neck. Commonly found in the leg turning of Windsor chairs.

VEILLEUSE.   French type of chaise longue, period of Louis XV.

VELVET.   Fabric with soft close pile usually of silk or rayon: velveteen is of cotton.

VELOUR.   Velvet or plush, often of wool or mohair.

VENEERS.   The art of utilizing fine woods decoratively for their color and markings appears in earliest history. Simultaneously it was realized that such use is not always consistent with the best structural advantages. The device of glueing a thin layer of decorative wood to a thicker backing for substance—the essence of veneering—goes back to ancient Egypt and Rome. It virtually disappears until the Renaissance, reappearing as inlaying—intarsia, etc., in the sixteenth century wherever the Renaissance influence touched. Not until the 17th century was veneering of whole surfaces practised extensively, when the invention of a finer saw permitted slicing the wood into thin sections.

When large enough sections of the wood could be successfully cut and glued, the style of veneering changed from excessive marquetry to plain surface designs. In England this transition is noted at the end of the 17th century. The William and Mary style had favored Seaweed Marquetry and Oystering. The Queen Anne style displayed the actual pattern of the wood grain in its own beauty.

In the 19th century the technique of wood veneering was improved by new methods of cutting and applying veneers and later by the study of better adhesives, but not enough to avoid giving veneers a bad name. Until recent years there was an unfortunate literary allusion to "thin veneers" and "cheap veneers" which left a prejudice in many minds. Actually, the advantages of veneering are manifold:

(1) It is the only way to utilize the beauty of the wood in repeated surfaces, or to make patterns by matching the lines of the grain.

(2) It permits the use of fragile woods, or of cuts which sacrifice strength to beauty, as burls and crotches by backing them with a sturdy wood of no special beauty or value.

(3) It reduces the cost of rare woods by yielding many surfaces per inch of thickness.

(4) It provides a method of increasing the strength of wood many times, since the process of laminating veneers in successive layers at right angles offsets the cross-grain weakness of wood.

(5) Shaped work such as curved sections when cut out of the solid are apt to split due to uneven internal stresses; when built up of veneers these inequalities are avoided.

Modern veneering, utilizing specific glues, with equipment for proper drying and testing of wood, applying great and equal pressure, precise preparation of surfaces and joints, yields a fabricated product superior in strength and beauty to the solid wood.

Veneers are sawn, sliced, or shaved, or peeled by rotary cutting on a sort of lathe. Each method produces a different grain.

The whole log, cut into veneers, is called a flitch. The sheets are applied in a variety of ways to produce different wood patterns,— book-matched, diamond, butted, side- or end-matched, etc.

VENICE, VENETIAN. Control of sea trade in the Middle Ages brought great wealth and cosmopolitanism to Venice; prior to the Renaissance her art was of mixed origins and secular splendor. Early Renaissance Venetian work shows mixture of Eastern and European forms. Her cultivated social life created furniture styles of rich individuality; with the decline of commerce came social decadence and extravagant living. 18th Century Venetian furniture is highly ornamental, fancifully painted and theatrical in outline. The whole school of Italian Rococo is sometimes called Venetian. 729, 733, 736, 739, 761. See *Italy*.

VERNIS MARTIN. Varnish process invented by the Martin brothers in France during the period of Louis XIV. It had great brilliancy and depth, and the process was widely used. It proved to be less durable than the Oriental lacquering which inspired it.

VICTORIAN. General term for period of Victoria's reign, 1837-1901, in England and America. See *England*. 1093 et seq.

EARLY VICTORIAN

ENGLISH, 1837-1860

1093. BREAKFRONT BOOKCASE. Ca. 1840. Figured Mahogany. Later Sheraton influence with classic Regency characteristics. *Cavallo*

1094. FOLDING CARD TABLE. Ca. 1835. Mahogany. Coarser Empire detail on Sheraton outline. *Cavallo*

1095. MAHOGANY SIDE CHAIR. *Metropolitan Museum of Art*

1096. MAHOGANY ARMCHAIR. *Metropolitan Museum of Art*

1097. CABINET BY WILLIAM MORRIS; Reaction toward medievalism. *Metropolitan Museum of Art*

1098. TILT TABLES AND WORK-TABLE OF PAPIER-MACHE; black with gold decoration; CHAIR and BLACKAMOOR of same style; American, 1845-1870.

1099. (Right) OAK CHAIR BY BELTER, New York, CA. 1850. *Bruce Buttfield*

LATER NINETEENTH CENTURY

MIDDLE VICTORIAN WORK IN ENGLAND AND AMERICA WAS ECLECTIC. TYPICAL ARE INTRICATE CURVES BASED ON LOUIS XV LINES, WITH EXCESSIVE DETAIL.

1100. AMERICAN, 1860-1880. Overstuffed Armchair and Walnut What-Not. *Metropolitan Museum of Art*

1101. PIANO AND CHAIRS with Antimacassar. French influence, 1865-1885. *Metropolitan Museum of Art*

VIGNOLA, GIACOMA, 1507-1573. Italian architect who classified the orders of architecture after the standardized proportions of Vitruvius.

VINE MOTIVE. Decorative banding of leaves and tendrils, a conventional rhythmic band ornament. Occurs as carved decoration in Gothic style. Painted bands appear in classic English and French work of the 18th century, in imitation of its use on Greek and Roman vases. 381.

VIOLETWOOD. Amaranth or purpleheart.

VIS-A-VIS. Tete-a-tete or *Siamoise* sofa, in which two sitters face in opposite directions.

VITRINE. Cabinet with clear glass door, sometimes glass sides and top, for the storage and display of china, curios, etc. 666, 905.

VITRUVIAN SCROLL. Wave-like series of scrolls in band ornament, carved, inlaid or painted. Also called Running Dog.

VITRUVIUS. Roman writer on architecture, used as source by Renaissance designers.

VOLUTE. Spiral scroll. Its earliest form is in the capital of the Greek Ionic order, after which it is found extensively in Roman work and all later classic styles. A Gothic form is based on plant life, naturalistic leaves curling inward.

VINE
MOTIVE
(GOTHIC)

WAGON SEAT. Crude early American double seat on a frame, used both in a wagon or in the house. Some had splint or rush seats, but most were merely wood. 875.

WAINSCOT. Panel work not covering the wall all the way to the ceiling.

WAINSCOT CHAIR. Panelled chairs of French and English type, 16th and 17th centuries. American types follow the English examples. They were probably developed from the detachment of a piece of wall panelling with a seat-board attached. 198 et seq.

WALL FURNITURE. The classification of all pieces of furniture intended for use against the wall: cabinets, buffets, chests, cupboards, bookcases, hanging cabinets, etc.

WALNUT. Since ancient times walnut, the JUGLANS family, has been the leading furniture wood, due to its prevalence wherever civilizations have flourished, as well as its excellence and wide adaptability. Walnut has great strength without excessive weight, is hard enough to withstand much shock, yet cuts well, carves handily, and takes a fine polish. It is durable and able to resist much internal stress from moisture changes, as well as the ravages of many insects. As solid lumber and veneer it has the greatest variety of colors, textures, and figures; there are stripes, burls, crotches, mottles, curls and wavy figures, butts, etc., as well as a variety of freaks and cuts that produce interesting patterns. Like mahogany and maple, walnut has been injudiciously finished in the past; the unfortunate connotation of black walnut grows from the malpractice of dark staining in Victorian America.

The characteristic American walnut is the black walnut, one of the best in the world; moderately dark, gray-brown with a simple figure. American Butternut or white walnut, lighter in color, is not quite the equal of black walnut, but a beautiful and serviceable wood. English, French, Italian and Spanish walnuts are lighter in color, finer in texture, but otherwise the equal of American black walnut. The Circassian or Caucasian walnut is a gnarly tree whose wood shows contorted grain markings in vividly contrasting light and dark browns. Other walnuts— Persian, Russian, Turkish, Bolivian, Brazilian (Imbuya) and Japanese —have varying characteristics.

African and Australian, Oriental or Queensland walnuts are not true walnuts, the latter being of the laurel family.

In historic times walnut occurs in furniture of the entire Italian and Spanish Renaissance. In France it displaced oak as soon as Renaissance forces came in; similarly it was accepted in Flanders and the Low Countries and South Germany with the earliest Renaissance influences. In England walnut had only slight acceptance until the Restoration. Then all manner of craftsmen were imported and these brought with them the preference for the wood in which they had been trained. The reign of Queen Anne is the Age of Walnut, and walnut held sway until fashion turned to Mahogany about 1730. In America walnut was used wherever found, particularly in Pennsylvania.

WARDROBE. Large cabinet or cupboard for hanging clothes. In Europe where clothes closets are not commonly provided in the plan of the room, such wardrobes are extensively used. They are often planned in the proportions of the old armoire.

WARP. Twisting or bulging of wood boards resulting from changes of moisture content within the fibers. All wood absorbs and throws off moisture, but if unevenly restrained or improperly protected it may curve or twist as the moisture causes the uneven swelling or drying of the fibers. Also the lengthwise threads in fabric.

WASHSTAND. Small table or cabinet holding a basin and the accessories for washing, developed during the 18th century in many forms by all designers in England, America and the Continent.

WATER LEAF. Ornamental detail based on the elongated laurel leaf. Its simple delicate form is typical of Hepplewhite, Sheraton, Adam, Louis XVI and late 18th century American work.

WAVE SCROLL. Continuous spiral band decoration also called Vitruvian scroll. 149.

WAX INLAYING. Wax filled into cut-out patterns in wood.

WEBBING. Linen or jute bands from 2½ to 4 inches wide, used in upholstery as a base for springs or stuffing like hair. The bands are tacked at the ends to the wood frame and woven across, and then stitched together.

WEB-FOOT. Grooved or carved foot of a cabriole leg suggesting the webbed feet of animals.

WEDGWOOD. English pottery ware of fine hard texture. The Wedgwoods were interested in the classic revival in the 18th century and duplicated many of the antique vase forms under the direction of Robert Adam. They also made plaques which were used as inserts in the same manner as Sèvres plaques were applied in France.

WEISSWEILLER, ADAM. Cabinetmaker, latter part 18th century, of German origin, who worked in France during the Louis XVI period and early stages of the Empire.

WELSH DRESSER. Cabinet with drawers and door-compartments below, the receding upper part having open shelves for the display of china.

WHAT-NOT. French Etagère. Tier of shelves supported by turned posts, used for the display of curios, etc. English 18th century and later. 146, 1096.

WHEAT EAR. Carved ornament of several ears of wheat used in chair backs, mirror frames, etc., by Hepplewhite and in America by McIntire and others.

WHEEL BACK. Round or oval chair back with radiating spindles or bars resembling the spokes of a wheel, found mostly in later 18th century English chairs. 328.

WHITEWOOD. Woodworkers' name for yellow poplar, although the name sometimes includes basswood and magnolia. Light yellowish color with satiny sheen; sometimes called canary wood in England. It holds paint well, and is moderately firm in structural use. Has a faint grain and does not polish well.

WICKER. General term for furniture which is woven of various natural or synthetic materials, as willow, reed, rattan, or spirally-twisted paper. Particularly used in summer and outdoor furniture.

WILLARD. Massachusetts family of clockmakers active 1743-1848. Benjamin established a factory in Grafton, Mass. about 1765; Simon working in Roxbury invented the banjo clock about 1800. Aaron worked in Boston after 1790.

WILLIAM AND MARY. Ruled England 1688-1702. Of Dutch origin, William brought a complete style to replace the deteriorating late Jacobean. This period is marked as the Age of Walnut. Its furniture is more domestic in scale, more elegantly designed and finished than the preceding Restoration style and is characterized by innovations like the cabriole leg, seaweed marquetry, the highboy, and flat serpentine stretchers. 514, 518 et seq., 688, 754, 1046. See *England*.

WINDOW SEAT

WINE COOLER

WINE TABLE

WINDOW-SEAT. Bench with two ends, as arms, or a small backless settee used in the embrasure of a window. Best types in 18th century English work; also found in French and Italian styles after 1750 as well as in American Federal work. 935 et seq.

WINDSOR. Style of chair using bentwood back frame and wood or rush seat with the legs pegged directly into the seat instead of being framed with aprons. The type seems to have originated around Windsor Castle in England between 1700 and 1725, and appears always to have been made by wheelwrights or turners rather than by cabinetmakers. It is likely that they attempted to imitate the finer Queen Anne chairs with rustic attempts at round backs and splats; the English Windsor usually has a pierced slat flanked by turned spindles suggesting wheel spokes. The legs were invariably splayed, as often cabriole as turned. The American colonists carried the Windsor to its ultimate development, producing a chair of the utmost strength, comfort, lightness and ease of manufacture. The first Windsors appeared around Philadelphia after 1725; by 1760 they were the predominant chairs for common use. They appeared in infinite variations of comb-back, fan, hoop, and bow-backs, made in combinations of woods. The saddle-shaped seat was generally of thick pine, sometimes of soft birch. The bent members were beech, hickory, ash, or birch, and the turned parts were maple, ash, birch, oak, or beech. They were often painted or left in the raw wood. 22, 37, 39, 236 et seq. The type was later extended to settees (18, 880), beds, tables, etc.

WINE COOLER. Metal lined tub for wine service, decoratively treated in the 18th century English styles. 567.

WINE TABLE. Horseshoe shaped table for the serving of wine, etc.

WING BOOKCASE. Breakfront, the receding side portions, suggesting the wing form.

WING CHAIR. Comfortable large chair with side pieces, usually overstuffed. The general type existed in France as the "Confessional" but the usual implication is the type evolved in England and America after 1750. 40, 44, 526.

WINGED-CLAW. Heavy couch foot used in Empire Sofas and other heavy pieces. 78.

WOODS. Wood has always been the basic material for furniture; it has in fact never had a serious rival. Its preeminence is the result of many virtues:

1. Various woods are readily available wherever conditions have favored human living.

2. It is among the strongest of organic materials and stronger for its weight than other materials. It offers a variety of strengths and weights for different structural and decorative uses.

WOODS

Top Row:

1102. (Left) BRAZILIAN ROSEWOOD, flat cut.

1103. (Center) ZEBRAWOOD, quartered.

1104. (Right) MAHOGANY, flat cut.

Center:

1105. (Right) MAPLE, BIRD'S EYE FIGURE.

Below:

1106. (Left) MAHOGANY, BROKEN STRIPE, quartered.

1107. (Center) MAHOGANY, ROPE FIGURE.

1103. (Right) MAHOGANY, MOTTLE FIGURE.

Courtesy American Forestry Association

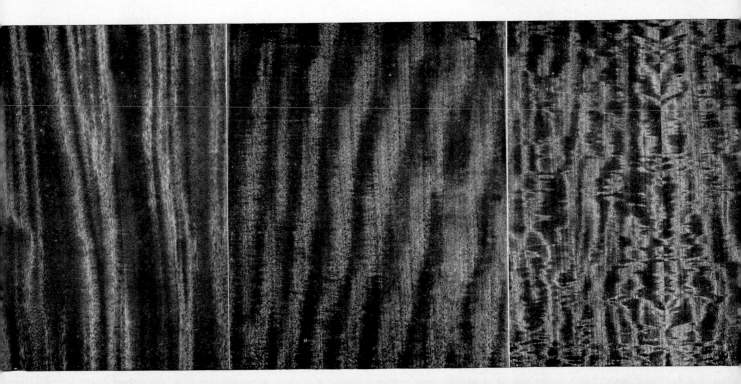

WOODS

1109. (Left) CURLY FIGURE IN CHERRY.

1110. (Right) KNOTTY FIGURE IN CEDAR.

1111. (Center) FOUR-PIECE MATCH IN WAL-
NUT STUMPWOOD. (BUTT)

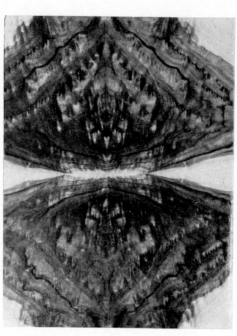

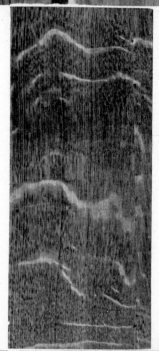

1112. (Center left) FIDDLEBACK FIGURE IN
MAHOGANY.

1113. (Lower left) PLUM PUDDING FIGURE IN
CUBAN MAHOGANY.

1114. (Center right) WHITE OAK, FLAKE
FIGURE.

1115. (Lower right) LACEWOOD. FIGURE DUE
TO PROMINENT PITH RAYS OR FLAKES,
AS IN OAK.

3. It is easily worked: it grows in convenient sizes, it cuts easily with simple tools, it can be agreeably surfaced with no great labor.

4. It can be joined together in many ways:—nailed, glued, joined, etc. (See *Joinery*).

5. It is agreeable to the touch; it "feels" good. Being a poor conductor of heat, its temperature is less startling than that of other materials.

6. It produces less noise under impact than other materials of equivalent strength.

7. It is relatively light in weight.

8. It may be easily repaired when broken or injured.

9. It possesses intrinsic beauty in infinite variety of color, texture and pattern; it can be worked in many ways to exploit and enhance this beauty. Selection of woods and grains; matchings of veneers and other methods of accentuating the grain; various methods of finishing, polishing, etc., to bring out and preserve these qualities, offer a range of beautiful effects unique to wood and to wood alone.

The disadvantages of wood are largely the result of its organic nature.

1. The fibers of wood are capable of absorbing and losing moisture according to the humidity of the surrounding air. This causes cracking, swelling and shrinking, warping or twisting, checking or surface cracking. The remedy lies in (a) the careful growth and selection of grains for various uses (b) proper drying, both by air and applied heat in kilns (c) the protection of the wood from too sudden changes of temperature and humidity, by coating with a resistant film like varnish, lacquer, etc. (See *Finish*); (d) fabrication of wood in plywood. (See *Plywood*).

2. It is inflammable. Wood can be chemically treated to resist fire, but the process is costly and used only rarely.

3. It is subject to attack by worms and insects. Various treatments and finishes afford more or less protection.

The grain of wood is produced by cutting cross sections of various types through the fibers, the arrangement of which is different and distinctive in every wood, as well as in different logs of the same wood, and different parts of the same tree. Thus, woods present different appearances according to (a) botanical variety (b) method of cutting the log (c) part of the tree from which it is cut.

The typical structure of wood consists of long fibers, differently placed in different woods, but always in concentric rings out from the center of the tree. These rings are the results of alternate growth and dormant periods in the seasons; they are called annual rings and indicate the age of the tree. There are also radial lines—*medullary* or *pith rays*—which cross the annual rings. The combinations of these rings, the size and arrangement of the fibers, is infinitely complex and variable, but assume definite character in the different woods, by which the woods are identified. Oak, for example, has a coarse, open grained texture, the pores are large and the pith rays so distinct as to be known as flakes. In maple, on the other hand, the fibers are so fine and close that the surface of the wood is silky smooth. Straight-grains or comb-grains are common to some varieties while other figures are known as curly grain, mottled, fiddleback, blister, birdseye, etc.; more specialized are bees-wings, rope figures, quilted, roe, rain-drop, plum-pudding, broken stripes, swirls, etc. Color is likewise a distinguishing factor of the species. The pigment may be evenly distributed as in mahogany or may be strikingly contrasting between the heartwood and the sapwood as in birch; it may also be arranged contrastingly in the annual rings, causing a strong stripe figure, as in zebrawood. Pigment may also be deposited irregularly by stains from decay or injury which produce an erratic interesting pattern when cut through.

There are several ways of cutting the log which produce various figures. A board cut through the middle of the whole log will show straight comb stripes on the outer sides while the midsection will appear as a more irregular figure. Such a board is called plain-sawed. When the log is first cut into quarters, then sawed into boards at approximately right angles to the concentric rings, it is called quarter-sawed. Each method produces its distinct grain, with separate properties and uses.

In cutting veneers there are many processes which produce highly varied figures. The oldest method of *slicing* veneers yields a grain similar to the long grain; it can be cut at any angle between the flat grain and the quarter. *Sawed* veneers show the same tendencies. *Peeled* or *rotary cut* veneers are literally unrolled from the log by rotating the log against a long knife. The grain appears very actively figured. Cross sections of small limbs used whole in veneering are known as OYSTERING; these odd designs of concentric circles were favored in late 17th century English work. KNOTS are utilized as a decorative feature, particularly in cedar and pine.

The part of the tree from which the wood is cut is readily classified. The *long grain* is the best and commonest all-purpose wood; the fibers being straightest, the wood is strongest. Decorative grains are cut from other parts. The *crotch* where the tree forks into two limbs produces a vivid irregular V-shaped grain, sometimes with markings described as plumes or feathers, cross-fire, etc. The SWIRL, or the outside of the crotch-block is very irregular, but lacks the V-shape of the crotch figure. The BUTT or STUMP figure, cut from the base of the log where it spreads horizontally toward the roots is also a slightly V-shaped figure, often with smaller cross rays, curls, etc. The BURL is a tumor or wart, an erratic wild growth anywhere on the tree, which shows a finely pitted or gnarly figure in cross-section of most woods. BIRDS' EYE, an erratic spotty figure occurring chiefly in Maple, is formed by the growth of buds too deep to break through the bark. CURLY or WAVY figures are an unexplained phenomena in which more or less fine cross stripes appear at right angles to the long grain; they may be partially the result of the swaying of the tree. Differing in fineness of the curl are the fiddleback, roll figure and blister figures.

The selection of woods best suited to structural or decorative uses is a matter of expert knowledge as well as choice. The distinction between soft and hardwood is not always correctly used; many properly called soft woods are physically harder than some hardwoods. Actually the terms soft-wood may be applied only to evergreen or non-deciduous trees, as pine, hemlock, fir, spruce, etc. All deciduous or leaf shedding trees are hardwood whether the wood is as soft as basswood and poplar or hard as maple or oak. The leading American woods of general structural value in furniture are oak, maple, birch, walnut, cherry, gumwood, pine; less used except for specialized purposes are beech, chestnut, poplar, basswood, ash, fir, elm, magnolia, butternut, cottonwood, redwood, spruce, cedar, sycamore, cypress. These are used both as veneers and solid lumber. Of the imported woods mahogany is by far the best and most commonly used, its vast range of hardness and strength, color and figure lending it to almost every purpose. Others frequently used both as lumber and veneers are rosewood, prima vera, avodire, European and tropical walnuts, holly, ebony, sycamore, satinwood, eucalyptus, pear, teak, tulip, zebra, amaranth, koa, vermillion. Almost exclusively used as veneers are amboyna, snakewood, yew, thuya, olive, kingwood, myrtle, acacia, laurel, cocobolo, box, sandalwood, laburnum, and a vast list of more or less similar varieties. There is considerable confusion and obscurantism in the nomenclature of these woods, resulting from confusion of identification, local or foreign names, the ambiguity of trade promotions, and the effort to disguise a familiar wood with its botanical or literary name, etc.

WORK TABLES. Various small tables designed to hold needlework and equipment, chiefly sewing. Their development historically follows the custom of sewing, embroidery, knitting, etc., as practised by noble ladies originally. 1061 et seq.

WREATH. A classical motive, chiefly Roman, which recurs in the Renaissance and all later revivals of the classical style. Early Renaissance wreaths were severely round and firm in outline; later they grew richer and ornate. These were painted, carved or appliqued, often in conjunction with coats-of-arms or monograms. In the Empire style they were commonly bronze appliques, using laurel leaves or other austere shapes. 129, 193.

WREN, SIR CHRISTOPHER, 1632-1723. English architect largely responsible for the Restoration style, following the classic manner of Palladio. He directed the reconstruction of much of London after the great fire. While he is known to have designed little mobile furniture his general direction influenced the school of woodcarving of which Grinling Gibbons was preeminent.

WRITING ARM.   Tablet arm; wide board arm suitable for a writing tablet, as in Windsor Chairs, 238, 249.

WRITING-DESK, WRITING-TABLE.   Flat-top desk or any table type of proper size for writing, usually fitted with drawers or desk compartments. Original desk or "Bureau" was merely a table with cloth called "Bure." See *Tables; Library Table; Desks.* 602 616, 1005 et seq., 1024 et seq.

WRITING ARM
AMERICAN WINDSOR

X-CHAIR.   Ancient type of chair based on the folding chair. It was known in Egypt and Rome, and appears in the Middle Ages. 253 et seq. 707, 711.

X-STOOL.   The simplest form of folding stool, found in ancient Egyptian remains and most subsequent types. Earliest forms had leather or skin seats. Renaissance stools were solid, often having the crossed members curved. This was the curule chair of the Romans, and is particularly characteristic of the Empire style. 936.

X-STRETCHER.   Crossed stretchers on chairs or tables, etc. 39.

YEW.   Hard, close grained red-brown wood, resistant to wear and decay. Takes a high polish; used on furniture chiefly for decorative veneered effects and inlaying since 17th century, although it was also so used by the ancients.

YORKSHIRE CHAIR.   English carved side chair of the 17th century, peculiar to Yorkshire. It stems from the panel or wainscot chair and is invariably of oak with turned front legs and stretchers. 208.

YORKSHIRE DRESSER.   Dresser or dish cupboard with a low back. It originates in Yorkshire and is usually of oak or deal.

YUBA.   Tasmanian oak; has dense texture and regular curly figure.

ZEBRAWOOD.   Hard decorative wood from British Guiana; named for its vigorous stripings of dark reddish-brown on creamy ground. Used chiefly for inlays and bandings, but more extensively on large surfaces in modern work.

ZUCCHI, ANTONIO.   1726-1795. Italian decorative painter who worked in England, often under the direction of Robert Adam, painting medallions and wall designs and probably furniture decorations. Husband of Angelica Kauffmann.

BIBLIOGRAPHY

AMERICAN

Andrews, E. A. and F.—Shaker Furniture. (1937)

Cornelius, C. O.—Furniture Masterpieces of Duncan Phyfe. (1922)

———— Early American Furniture. (1926)

Dow, G. F.—The Arts and Crafts in New England, 1704-1775. (1927)

Dyer, W.—Early American Craftsman.

Elwell.—Colonial Furniture and Interiors. (Boston, 1896)

Halsey and Cornelius.—Handbook of the American Wing of the Metropolitan Museum. (New York, 1928)

Holloway, E. S.—American Furniture and Decoration, Colonial and Federal. (1928)

Hornor, W. M.—The Blue Book of Philadelphia Furniture, William Penn to George Washington. (Philadelphia, 1935)

Lockwood, L. V.—Colonial Furniture in America. (1902)

Lyon, J. W.—Colonial Furniture of New England. (Boston, 1891)

Millar, Donald—Colonial Furniture. (1925)

Miller, E. G.—American Antique Furniture. (Baltimore, 1937)

†Nutting, Wallace—Furniture Treasury, 3 vols.

———— Furniture of the Pilgrim Century. (1921)

Nye, Alvan—Colonial Furniture. (1895)

Singleton, E.—Furniture of our Forefathers. (1901)

ANCIENT

Richter, G. M. A.—Ancient Furniture. (1926) (Greek, Etruscan and Roman)

ANTIQUES AND COLLECTING

Cescinsky, H.—Gentle Art of Faking Furniture, Fakes in General. (1931)

Guild, L. van A.—The Geography of American Antiques. 1927)

Litchfield, F.—Antiques, Genuine and Spurious. (1921)

Lockwood, Sarah M.—Antiques. (1926)

Lucas, A.—Antiques. Their Restoration and Preservation. (1932)

ASIATIC

Cescinsky, H.—Chinese Furniture. (1922)

Roche, O.—Les Meubles de la Chine. (Paris, 1926)

Yoshida, Tetsuro—Das Japanische Wohnhaus. (Berlin, 1935)

ENGLISH

*Adam, R. and J.—The Works in Architecture of Robert and James Adam. (1773)

Batsford, B. T.—The Decorative Work of Robert and James Adam. (1900)

Bell and Hayden—The Furniture of George Hepplewhite. (1910)

Binstead, H. E.—English Chairs. (1923)

Blake and Reveirs-Hopkins—Little Books About Old Furniture. (4 vols.) (1911-13)

Brackett, O.—An Encyclopedia of English Furniture. (1927)

———— Georgian Art, 1760-1820.

Cescinsky, H.—English Furniture from Gothic to Sheraton. (1929)

────────────

*Source Books
†Important

Cescinsky, Herbert—English Furniture of the 18th Century. (1911)

Cescinsky, Herbert and Gribble, Ernest R.—Early English Furniture and Woodwork. (1922)

*Chippendale, Thomas—Gentleman and Cabinet Maker's Director. (1754)

*———— Household Furniture in Genteel Taste. (1760)

*———— Designs of Interior Decorations in the Old French and Antique Styles. (1800)

*Eastlake, C. L., Jr.—Hints on Household Taste in Furniture. (1872)

Ellwood, G. M.—English Furniture and Decoration, 1680-1800. (1899, London)

Heaton, J. A.—Furniture and Decoration in England During the 18th Century. (1889-92)

*Hepplewhite, A.—Cabinet Maker and Upholsterer's Guide. (1794)

*Hope, T.—Household Furniture and Interior Decoration. (1807)

Hurrell, J. W.—Measured Drawings of Old Oak English Furniture. (1902)

*Ince and Mayhew—Universal System of Household Furniture. (1762)

Jourdain, Margaret—English Decoration and Furniture of the Early Renaissance. (1924)

———— English Decoration and Furniture of the Later 18th Century. (1922)

———— Regency Furniture, 1795-1820. (1934)

Lenygon, Francis—Furniture in England from 1660-1760. (1914)

MacQuoid, P.—A History of English Furniture. (4 vols.) (1904-08)

†MacQuoid, P. and Edwards, H.—The Dictionary of English Furniture. (1924)

*Manwaring, R.—The Cabinet and Chair Maker's Real Friend and Companion. (1765)

———— Chair Maker's Guide. (1766)

Marx and Taylor—Measured Drawings of English Furniture (Oak Period). (1931)

*Shearer, T.—The Cabinet Maker's London Book of Prices, 1788.

*———— Designs for Household Furniture. (1788)

*Sheraton, Thomas—The Cabinet Maker and Upholsterer's Drawing Book. (London, 1791-3)

*———— The Cabinet Dictionary. (1803)

Singleton, E.—French and English Furniture. (1904)

*Smith, G.—A Collection of Designs for Household Furniture and Interior Decoration. (London, 1808) (Regency)

Strange, T. A.—English Furniture, Woodwork, and Decoration. (1903) (Detail Drawings)

Symonds, R. W.—Old English Walnut and Lacquer Furniture. (1923)

———— English Furniture from Charles II to George II. (1929)

FRENCH

Adams, L.—Decorations Interieures et Meubles des Epoques Louis XIII et XIV.

Bayard, E.—Les Meubles Rustiques Regionaux de la France.

*Berain.—Son Ouvre Complete. (The Style of Louis XIV)

Clouzot, H.—L'Ameublement Français Sous Louis XV.

Collection de l'Art Regional en France. (Survey of French Provincial Furniture in 12 volumes)

Dilke, E. F. S.—French Furniture and Decoration in the XVIIIth Century. (1901)

Dreyfus, C.—Le Mobilier Francais. (Paris) (Vol. 1—Epoques de Louis XIV and XV. Vol. 2—Epoque de Louis XVI)

Dumonthier, E.—Le Mobilier Louis XVI. (Paris)
—— Les Sieges de Jacob Freres. (Directoire and Consulate) (Paris, 1921)
Felice, R. de.—Little Books on Old French Furniture. (4 vols.) (1922)
Gauthier, J.—Le Mobilier des Vielles Provinces Francaises. (Paris, 1933)
Hessling, E.—Empire-Moebel. Meisterstuecke Franzoesischer Kunsttischlerei aus der Zeit Napoleons I. (Leipzig, 1914)
Hessling, E. and W.—Moebel im Directoirestil. (Berlin, 1914)
Janneau, G.—Les Beaux Meubles Français Anciens. (5 vols.) (Paris)
Longnon, H. and Huard, F. W.—French Provincial Furniture. (Philadelphia, 1927)
*Percier and Fontaine—Recueil de Decorations Interieures, Meubles, Bronzes, Etc. (Paris, 1801)
Ricci, C.—French Furniture and Decoration of the Louis XIV and Regency Styles.
Ricci, Seymour de—Louis XVI Furniture. (1913)
Salverte, C. de—Les Ebenistes du XVIII° Siecle. (Paris, 1937)
Strange, Arthur—French Interiors, Furniture, Woodwork. (London, 1900)

GENERAL

Aronson, J.—Book of Furniture and Decoration: Period and Modern. (1936)
Bajot, E.—Encyclopedie Du Meuble. (1900)
Clifford, C. R.—Period Finishing. (1927)
Eberlein, H. D. and McClure, E. Abbott—Practical Book of Period Furniture. (Philadelphia, 1914)
Foley, Edwin—The Book of Decorative Furniture, Its Form, Colour and History. (1912)
Hunter, George Leland—Decorative Furniture. (1923)
Litchfield, F.—Illustrated History of Furniture. (1889)
Salomonsky, V. C.—Masterpieces of Furniture Design. (Grand Rapids, 1931)
Schmitz, H.—The Encyclopedia of Furniture. (1926)
Storey, Walter Rendell—Period Influence in Interior Decoration. (New York, 1937)
—— Beauty in Home Furnishings. (New York, 1928)
Whiton, Sherrill—Elements of Interior Decoration. (New York, 1937)

GERMAN, SCANDINAVIAN, FLEMISH, ETC.

Baer, C. H.—Deutsche Wohn and Festrame aus 6 Jahrhundert.
Folnesics, J.—Innenraume und Hausrat der Empire und Biedermeierzeit, in Osterreich-Ungarn. (Vienna, 1922)
Loukomski, G.—Mobilier et Decoration des Anciens Palais Imperiaux Russes. (Paris)
Luthmer and Schmidt—Empire und Biedermeier-mobel. (1922)
Lux, J. A.—Empire und Biedermeier. (Stuttgart, 1930)
Sauerlandt, M.—Norddeutsche Barockmoebel. (1922)
Schmitz, H.—Vor Hundert Jahren. (Festraeume und Wohnzimmer des Deutschen Klassizismus und Biedermeier. (Berlin, 1920)
—— Deutsche Moebel. Vol. 2, Barock and Rokoko. (Stuttgart, 1923)
—— Deutsche Moebel. Vol. 3, Klassizismus. (Louis XVI, Empire, Biedermeier) (Stuttgart, 1923)
Singleton, E.—Dutch and Flemish Furniture of the Middle Ages and Renaissance. (1908)
Wettergren, Erik—Modern Decorative Arts of Sweden.
Wollin, N.—Modern and Swedish Decorative Art. (1931)
Zweig, M.—Weiner Buergermoebel. Viennese Furniture of 1740-1790. (Vienna, 1922)

ITALIAN AND SPANISH

Arte y Decoracion en Espana—(1920-1928)
Bode, W. von—Italian Renaissance Furniture. (1921)

Byne and Stapley—Spanish Interiors and Furniture. (1928)
Eberlein, H. D.—Spanish Interiors, Furniture and Details. (New York, 1925)
Eberlein, H.—Interiors, Fireplaces and Furniture of the Italian Renaissance. (1927, Reprint)
Eberlein, H. D. and Ramsdell, R. W.—The Practical Book of Italian, Spanish and Portuguese Furniture. (1915)
Ferrari, G.—Il Legno E La Mobilia Nell'Arte Italiana. (1925)
Helburn, Wm. Inc. (Publisher)—Italian Renaissance Interiors and Furniture.
Holme, C.—Peasant Art in Italy. (1913)
Hunter, George Leland—Italian Furniture and Interiors. (1918)
Lessing, J.—Italienische Moebel, XVI Jahrhundert. (Berlin, 1893)
—— Italienische Truhen, XV-XVI Jahrhundert. (Berlin, 1891)
Marangoni, G.—Enciclopedia Delle Moderne Art Decorative Italiane. (Milano, 1925)
Pedrini, A.—L'Ambiente, il Mobilio e le Decorazioni del Rinascimento in Italia. (Turin, 1925)
Schottmuller, F.—Furniture and Interior Decoraiton of the Italian Renaissance. (Stuttgart, 1928)
Schubring, P.—Cassoni, Truhen und Truhenbilder der Italienischen Fruehrenaissance. (Leipzig, 1923)

MEDIEVAL

Lessing, J.—Gothische Moebel. (Berlin, 1889)
Pugin.—Designs for Gothic Furniture. (Neo-Gothic) (London, 1835)

MODERN

Aloi, R.—L'Arredamento Moderno. (Italy, 1934)
Chareau, Pierre—Meubles. (Paris, 1928)
Dieckmann, Erich—Mobelbau in Holz, Rohr und Stahl. (Stuttgart, 1931)
Dorp, E. van—Moderne Eenvoudige Meubels. (Dutch-Amsterdam)
Frankl, P. T.—Form and Re-Form. (New York, 1930)
Griesser, P.—Das Neue Mobel. (Stuttgart, 1932)
Havelaar, J.—Het Moderne Meubel. (Modern Dutch) (Rotterdam, 1924)
Hoffman, Herbert—Modern Interiors. (1930)
Holme, G.—Industrial Design and the Future. (1934)
Olmer, P.—Le Mobilier Français D'Aujourdhui (1910-1925, Paris)
Retera, W.—Het Moderne Interieur. (Amsterdam, 1937)
Schneck—Das Mobel Als Gebrauchsgegenstand Series: 4 vols.
Schuster, F.—Ein Mobelbuch. (Modern Simple Furniture) (Stuttgart, 1933)
Todd, D. and Mortimer, R.—The New Interior Decoration.

FURNITURE CRAFTS, WOODS AND WOODWORKING

Howard, Alexander L.—Timbers of the World.
Johnson and Sironen—Manual of the Furniture Arts and Crafts. (1928)
Pattou, A. B. and Vaughn, C. L.—Furniture Finishing, Decoration and Patching. (Chicago, 1927)
Rowe, E.—Practical Woodcarving. (1930)
Rudd, J. H.—Practical Cabinet Making and Drafting. (1912)
U. S. Forest Products Laboratory—The Identification of Furniture Woods. (Madison, Wis.)
Wheeler, C. G.—A Manual of Woodworking. (New York)

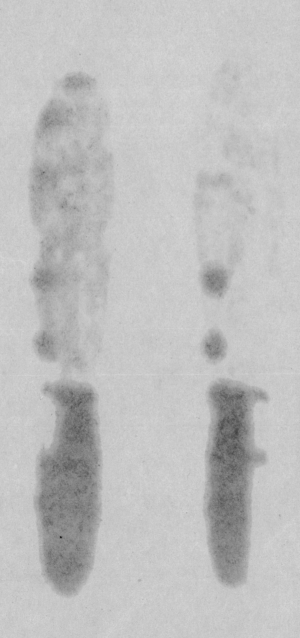